Open Source Web Site Construction Kit

Thomas Schenk

201 West 103rd St., Indianapolis, Indiana, 46290 USA

Open Source Web Site Construction Kit

International Standard Book Number: 0-672-32087-8

Library of Congress Catalog Card Number: 2001093493

Printed in the United States of America

First Printing: September 2001

04 03 02 01 4 3 2 1

Trademarks

All terms mentioned in this book that are known to be trademarks or service marks have been appropriately capitalized. Sams Publishing cannot attest to the accuracy of this information. Use of a term in this book should not be regarded as affecting the validity of any trademark or service mark.

Warning and Disclaimer

Every effort has been made to make this book as complete and as accurate as possible, but no warranty or fitness is implied. The information provided is on an "as is" basis. The author and the publisher shall have neither liability nor responsibility to any person or entity with respect to any loss or damages arising from the information contained in this book.

Associate Publisher
Jeff Koch

Acquisitions Editor
William Brown

Development Editor
Mark Renfrow

Managing Editor
Matt Purcell

Project Editor
Natalie Harris

Copy Editor
Barbara Hacha

Indexer
Cheryl Landes

Proofreader
Plan-It Publishing

Technical Editor
Bill McEachran

Team Coordinator
Chris Feather

Interior Designer
Dan Armstrong

Cover Designer
Aren Howell

Page Layout
Rebecca Harmon
Lizbeth Patterson

Contents at a Glance

Introduction **9**

Part I **Introduction to Linux and Open Source**

1 Why Should Your Company Leverage Linux? **13**

2 What Makes Open Source So Compelling? **29**

3 So You Want to Build an Internet Site **43**

Part II **Building Different Kinds of Internet Sites**

4 Content and Media Sites **57**

5 The Telecommuter's Journal **71**

6 Community Sites **103**

7 The Del Valle Junior High Parent/Teacher/Student Organization **115**

8 E-commerce Sites **161**

9 E-commerce Sites: Two Case Studies **175**

Part III **Growing Your Site and Keeping It Running**

10 Keeping the Site Running **201**

11 High Availability and Scalability **243**

12 Architecture for High Availability and Scalability **255**

13 Hardware Reliability **271**

14 Selecting Software Components **289**

15 Site Management Issues **299**

16 Open Source High Availability and Scalability **315**

17 Commercial Load-Balancing Alternatives **359**

Part IV **Appendixes**

A Sources of Further Interest **369**

B Installation and Configuration of Linux **377**

C Getting the Tools Covered in the Book **401**

Index **415**

Table of Contents

Introduction 9

Part I Introduction to Linux and Open Source

1 Why Should Your Company Leverage Linux? 13

What Is Linux? 14
An Open Source Operating System Kernel 14
Distributions—A Kernel Plus Supporting Software 16
Features of Linux Distributions 18
Linux Versus Other Internet Server Platforms 19
Linux Versus Windows 19
Linux Versus Commercial Unix 20
Linux Versus Other Freely Available Operating Systems 22
A Look at the Total Cost of Ownership for Linux 23
Software Licensing Costs 24
Hardware Requirements 25
Maintenance Costs 26
Training Requirements 26
Summary 27

2 What Makes Open Source So Compelling? 29

Open Source Software Versus Proprietary Software 30
A Different Development Model 30
The Keys to the Kingdom 31
The Pros and Cons of Open Source Software 33
Increased Flexibility 34
Access to Developers 36
Project Abandonment 37
Lack of Support 38
Examples of Open Source Software 38
Apache 38
MySQL 39
PHP 40
The Support Issue 40
Community Support 40
Commercial Support for OSS 42
Summary 42

3 So You Want to Build an Internet Site 43

Reasons for Building an Internet Site....44
Marketing 44

Customer Convenience 45
Expanding Beyond Local Boundaries 45
Maintaining Internet Sites....................46
Using a Hosting Service 46
Hosting It Yourself 48
Developing In-house Solutions Versus Outsourcing 50
Rolling Your Own Solution 50
Outsourcing Internet Site Development 51
Summary 53

PART II Building Different Kinds of Internet Sites

4 Content and Media Sites 57

Characteristics of a Content and Media Site 58
Static Content 58
Frequent Updates 58
Archived Content 59
Desirable Features 59
A Document Management System 59
User-Feedback Mechanisms 61
Search Capabilities 62
Some Tools to Consider 63
Document Management Tools....................63
User-Feedback Tools 65
Search Tools 68
Summary 69

5 The Telecommuter's Journal 71

Site Charter and Design 72
Creating an Online Magazine 72
The Site Design 73
Web Site Features 73
The Supporting Platform 74
Implementing a Document Management System 74
Creating the Site Framework 76
Issue Management Tools 87
The User Feedback Features 94
The Search Engine 99
Challenges Going Forward....................100
Attracting Readers to the Site 101
Providing Interesting Content 101
Summary 101

6 Community Sites 103
Characteristics of a Community Site 104
Collaboration Features 104
Relatively Few Static Pages 104
User-Driven Content 105
Desirable Features 105
Community Calendar 105
Notice Board 106
Chat System 107
Some Tools to Consider 109
Calendar Systems 109
Notice Boards 110
Chat Software 111
Summary 113

7 The Del Valle Junior High Parent/Teacher/ Student Organization 115
Site Charter and Design 116
Publicizing the Purpose of the Group 116
Communicating Events to the Group 117
Providing Communication Channels 117
Publishing the Newsletter Online 117
Web Site Features 117
Designing the PTSO Web Site 118
Installation and Configuration of the Support Tools 131
Installing the Applications 135
Challenges 158
Publicizing the PTSO Web Site 158
Preventing Stagnation 159
Dealing with Unruly Visitors 160
Summary 160

8 E-commerce Sites 161
Characteristics of E-commerce Sites 162
Database-Derived Content 162
Dynamic Pages 163
Need to Maintain State 163
Desirable Features 163
Online Catalog 164
Shopping Cart 165
Credit Card Processing 167
Customer Feedback Mechanism 168

Some Tools to Consider 168
Symphero 168
Interchange 172
Summary 173

9 E-commerce Sites: Two Case Studies 175

Introduction 176
A Brief History of E-commerce 176
Open Source E-commerce Systems 179
What Is an E-Commerce System? 180
The Database: Heart of an E-commerce System 180
What Is a Web Server? 180
What Is Apache-SSL? 180
What Is PERL? 181
Perl Features 181
Perl Is Open Source 181
Perl and the Web 181
CP Commerce 182
The Case of Mia Casa 183
The Mia Casa Product Line 184
The Mia Casa Customer Base 185
The Mia Casa Business Model 186
Business Challenges/Objectives 186
Firebreath.com 190
How Firebreath.com Got Started 190
Preparing Your Business for E-commerce 196
Notes on Hosting an E-Commerce Site 196
Summary 197

PART III Growing Your Site and Keeping it Running

10 Keeping the Site Running 201

After Completion 202
The Care and Feeding of Internet Sites 202
Business Requirements 203
Monitoring Tools 205
Server Monitors 205
Security Monitors 205
Other Security Resources 207
Other Server Monitors 209
Web Site Log Analysis 217
Business Requirements 217
Interpreting Web Server Logs 219

Issue Tracking Software 227
Business Requirements 227
Mail/Web-Form Issue Tracking 229
Live Operator Issue Tracking 229
Content Management 231
All Content Is Not Equal 232
Managing Updates to the Site 232
The Dangers of the Live Hack 234
Which Root Is Root? 235
Content Management Tools 235
Business Requirements 236
Summary 242

11 High Availability and Scalability 243

High Availability 244
Aspects of High Availability 244
Defining High Availability 245
Weighing the Costs 246
Scalability 247
Vertical Scalability 248
Horizontal Scalability 249
Vertical Versus Horizontal Scalability Solutions 252
Summary 253

12 Architecture for High Availability and Scalability 255

Approaches for Achieving High Availability 256
Hot-Swap Systems 256
Failover Systems 260
Combining Approaches 261
Scaling Your Internet Site 264
Benchmarking to Determine Limitations 265
Performance Tuning to Reduce Limitations 266
Planning Is Key 268
Summary 269

13 Hardware Reliability 271

Mean Time Between Failures (MTBF) 272
Maintaining Spare Systems and Components 274
Spare Storage 274
Spare Systems 275
Cost Considerations 275
Sales Pitches—Separating the Wheat from the Chaff 275
Hardware Technologies Used to Achieve Reliability 277
Redundant Arrays of Inexpensive Disks (RAID) 277

Hot-Swappable Components 279
Infrastructure Requirements 280
Routers, Switches, and Hubs 280
Uninterruptible Power Supplies 282
Choosing Hardware Vendors 283
Questions to Ask 284
The Importance of FCC and UL Ratings 286
Summary 287

14 Selecting Software Components 289

Determining Software Reliability 290
Stress Testing 291
Benchmarks 292
Factors That Affect Software Reliability 293
Dealing with Software Vendors 295
OSS Vendors (aka Project Leaders) 295
Individual Leaders 297
Questions to Ask Vendors During the Planning Phase 297
Summary 298

15 Site Management Issues 299

Self-Hosting Versus Colocation Facilities 300
Drawbacks of Self-Hosting 301
Pros and Cons of Colocation 304
Colocation Options 307
Selecting a Colocation Provider 309
Business Requirements 309
Narrowing the Field 310
Customer Referrals 313
Summary 313

16 Open Source High Availability and Scalability 315

Two Sample Network Designs 316
Linux Virtual Server Project 318
What It Does 318
The Tool Suite 325
Completing the Example 330
Ultramonkey 332
What It Does 332
The Tool Suite 332
Piranha 341
What It Does 341
The Tool Suite 342

Super Sparrow 353
What It Does 353
The Tool Suite 356
Summary 357

17 Commercial Load-Balancing Alternatives 359

BigIP 360
BigIP Product Description 360
Features of the BigIP Product Line 360
Advantages and Disadvantages of BigIP 362
Cisco LocalDirector 362
Overview 362
The Cisco LocalDirector Feature Set 362
Advantages and Disadvantages 364
Other Products 364
Software Load Balancers 364
Load-Balancing Switches 366
Load-Balancing Appliances 366
Summary 366

Part IV Appendixes

A Sources of Further Interest 369

Linux-Related Sites 370
Kernel.org 370
The Linux Documentation Project 370
Linuxcare 371
Red Hat Linux 371
Caldera Systems 371
The Debian Project 371
Open Source Software Sites 371
Freshmeat 372
SourceForge.net 372
General News and Information Sites 372
Slashdot 372
Linux Today 373
Linux Weekly News 373
NewsForge 373
Other Sites 373
Perl Resources 373
The Apache Web Server 374
PHP Resources 374
MySQL and PostgreSQL 374
Usenet and Mailing Lists 375

B Installation and Configuration of Linux 377

Obtaining a Linux Distribution 378
Purchasing a CD 378
Downloading from the Internet 378
Installing Your Linux Distribution 379
Conducting a Hardware Inventory 379
Selecting an Installation Method....380
Selecting a Partitioning Scheme 381
Selecting Packages for Installation 381
Basic Network Setup 381
Assigning IP Addresses....382
Network Hardware Issues 382
Protecting Your Linux System 383
Managing Services Running on the System 384
A Practical Example 386
Further Steps to Take 386
Monitoring Systems and Services 389
Packet Filtering with the ipchains Utility 390
Other Sources of Information 400

C Getting the Tools Covered in the Book 401

Web and FTP Sites 402
Freshmeat 402
SourceForge 402
RPMfind.net 403
Building Software from Source Code 403
Why Build from Source Code? 403
Setting Up a Build Environment 404
Building from Raw Source Code 406
Building Using Source RPMs 412
Summary 413

Index 415

About the Author

Thomas Schenk is a Professional Services Engineer with Penguin Computing, where he provides consulting services to Penguin Computing customers, designing solutions using Linux and open source software. His primary areas of expertise are Linux system administration, automation, and networking. He has been involved with Linux and open source software since 1992 and is the author of two books on Linux System Administration. In addition to working with Linux, Tom has been a developer and administrator for most flavors of commercial Unix as well as many of the other freely available ones.

When not working as a consultant for Penguin Computing customers and writing, his interests include volunteering at his children's schools, listening to all kinds of music, and cooking. To round out his busy schedule, he runs the Del Valle Junior High School PTSO Web site, which is described in Chapter 7 of this book, and is a volunteer coach with Players in Progress (PIPs), an organization that helps promote positive life traits while teaching players basketball-handling skills.

About the Technical Editor

Bill McEachran (`wj_mceachran@yahoo.com`) introduced himself to computers by tinkering around with a Commodore 64. Soon after, he dropped all computer science courses in University upon discovering line-ups at the (even then antiquated) punch card machines. As his family's business grew, he found himself nominated "the computer guy" and learned Unix system administration in the stress-filled environment of "learning by doing." Bill is now a computer consultant specializing in helping small-to-medium-sized businesses. When not working, he enjoys woodworking and goofing off with his children, Leigh and Brennan, and his lovely wife Vikki.

Dedication

To my wife, Eun Joung, who provides the inspiration, and my children, Nicholas and Nia, who keep me motivated.

Acknowledgments

This book would not have been possible without the patience of my family, who allowed me the time to work on it and the encouragement to keep at it, and my editor, William Brown, who had the patience to see this project to completion. It has been a learning experience for me and I would like to thank everyone involved in bring it to fruition. I would also like to thank the Linux and open source communities for providing the raw materials that allowed me to write this book.

Tell Us What You Think!

As the reader of this book, *you* are our most important critic and commentator. We value your opinion and want to know what we're doing right, what we could do better, what areas you'd like to see us publish in, and any other words of wisdom you're willing to pass our way.

As an Associate Publisher for Sams, I welcome your comments. You can fax, e-mail, or write me directly to let me know what you did or didn't like about this book—as well as what we can do to make our books stronger.

Please note that I cannot help you with technical problems related to the topic of this book, and that because of the high volume of mail I receive, I might not be able to reply to every message.

When you write, please be sure to include this book's title and author as well as your name and phone or fax number. I will carefully review your comments and share them with the author and editors who worked on the book.

Fax: 317-581-4770
E-mail: `feedback@samspublishing.com`
Mail: Jeff Koch
Sams Publishing
201 West 103rd Street
Indianapolis, IN 46290 USA

Preface

Many people think that the most compelling reason for leveraging open source technologies is that they are low cost. Indeed, using open source technologies to construct and maintain your Web site is quite economical. However, there are other valuable reasons to consider using open source to support your Web site and other types of business applications.

First, many open source "projects" have led to commercial "products" that come with full support. Examples of these include the Red Hat Linux operating system distribution and the Lutris Enhydra Web application server platform. Other open source projects have not been "productized" but have been widely adopted because of the quality of their implementation. Examples of these include the Apache Web server and databases such as MySQL and PostgreSQL.

Whether the result is a product or a project, open source technologies have achieved success because of the formation of global software developer communities. Connected via the Internet, these communities can work very quickly to create a project or product or to address changes that are needed. Taking a dynamic, virtualized approach to software development rather than following more traditional development strategies lets open source software better match the types of business cycles present in today's marketplace. People and companies that leverage open source gain by being able to obtain updates and changes quickly without having to wait for a traditional vendor's product cycle to conclude.

In addition—and perhaps more importantly—those who use open source technologies can directly impact future directions for the project or product. Unlike commercial software vendors who may or may not listen to your feedback, the open source community directly leverages feedback from you—the user or customer—to shape the way the project or product will change and the functionality it will support in the future. Getting involved in the community that supports an open source project or product that you use on your Web site will benefit you directly.

Getting Visible

Being smart enough to recognize the value of leveraging open source technologies to construct Web sites is one thing, but after the sites are built, do you know what the next smart move is? You can have the coolest Web site on the planet, but if no one knows about it, you might as well not even have a Web site. Making your Web site visible is of paramount importance.

Many companies and individuals mistakenly think that they need to spend thousands of dollars so the world will know that they have a Web site. This does not have to be the case. Obviously, if a company or person does have deep financial pockets and wants to invest in a huge marketing splash, they certainly can do so.

Widely marketing your Web site can be achieved with a few hundred dollars, a bit of time, and by adopting a mindset similar to that of the open source community (more on this in a minute).

You'll likely spend most of your money on Web hosting (unless you're doing it yourself) and a domain name that directly relates to your business. Obviously, you'll want to be certain that whoever hosts your site (even if it's you) gets your site into the major search engines.

Beyond that, your next important objective should be to make sure your Web site is designed with the user in mind. Open source technologies can be used to build very poorly designed Web sites or ones that users will find compelling. In the latter case, users will likely return to your site again and again. Invest some money in design talent that specifically focuses on human/computer interaction.

We've passed the first generation of Web site design, and most of the first generation sites were designed with static information presentation in mind. Today the emphasis is shifting away from broadcasting or publishing information to sites that support user interaction and dynamic content.

However, implementing a Web site that uses open source technologies combined with a highly user-centric design does not have to break the bank either. Many academic institutions are focusing on the field of human/computer interaction and are providing student instruction on how to design (in both the online and offline worlds) with the user in mind. Seek out academic institutions that offer this material and contact them to find out how you might connect with either an existing student or one who recently graduated. For a minimal investment, students infused with the latest design techniques can help you view your Web site in terms of usability and interaction.

So, now you've found economical ways to design, construct, and run your Web site, and the funds you've designated to support your low-cost approach to implementing your Web site might be running a bit thin. But you still haven't yet told the world about your site. What can you do? Here is where you adopt the mindset similar to the open source community that was mentioned previously.

What is it that helps the open source community be successful? In a word, connectivity! The Internet provides the infrastructure that supports the globally connected Web. Open source software developers use this infrastructure and the tools available to maximize their efforts and to avoid costs.

You can use the same approach to market your Web site. Use the low-cost and, more likely, no-cost tools available on the Web to make your Web site visible without spending huge sums of money. There are hundreds of options to consider when leveraging, but the ten options that follow are some of the most commonly used. As the owner of a Web site, you should always seek out new tools that will widen the reach of your site.

Now, let's examine the ten most commonly used techniques to market your Web site economically.

Send Out Newsletters

You need to reach out to others and let them know about your Web site. Write a brief newsletter that outlines what is available at your site or what interesting or compelling benefits one might find at your site. In general, newsletters contain a brief summary list at the top that tells the recipient what is contained in the newsletter. The summary is usually followed by a brief paragraph for each item contained in the summary. At the end of each paragraph is a link that takes the reader directly to the part of your site that pertains to the material described in the newsletter. Newsletter templates are available for word processing programs, such as Star Office.

After you've written a wonderful newsletter, you'll want to distribute it to the world. To do this, take advantage of one of several free distribution tools available on the Web. Some of these include Listbot (`www.listbot.com`), Yahoo! Groups—formerly known as eGroups (`groups.yahoo.com`), and Topica (`www.topica.com`). After you set up your initial newsletter with one of these services, you'll want to provide a link to your newsletter distribution service on your Web site to enable visitors to subscribe to it. Then, as updates to your site occur or you have interesting news to share, you can send out information easily and get additional visitors to your site.

Get Your Discussion Going

The Web is all about one-to-one communication. If you doubt this, just read the Cluetrain Manifesto (`www.cluetrain.org`). Get people talking by creating a discussion group where people can talk about topics that relate to the content at your Web site. You can set up a discussion group by using an outside service or implementing one of the many fine free or low-cost discussion solutions.

For example, one Web site I recently set up using open source technologies was designed to help me connect with others to obtain more information on genealogical-related research I was doing. I used the free discussion service available at EzBoard (`www.ezboard.com`) to set up several discussion groups related to the various facets of my research. I then linked the discussion groups to my Web site.

It should be noted that many Web-based discussion services have recently implemented ad-based additions to their services. That is, your discussion group will be free, but visitors will see one or more advertisements. You can pay a small fee (usually between $30-$60 annually) to remove the advertisements.

If you want to avoid advertisements and fees and you have a bit of time (an afternoon), you might also implement free discussion software directly on your Web site. Two of my favorites solutions are UBB (`www.infopop.com`) and Coolboard (`www.coolboard.com`). You can go so far as to set up a Community section within your Web site or even use a community-centered design for your entire Web site by using an open source community solution, such as SlashCode (`slashcode.com`), which powers Slashdot, or Scoop, (`scoop.kuro5hin.org`) which powers the K5 community.

Whether you choose to leverage discussion-group technology or a community-based approach, be sure to integrate it tightly with your Web site so that people can easily visit and interact with you and others.

Even More Discussion

It's one thing to get your own discussion or community going, but quite another to let the rest of the world know about it. You can certainly mention your discussion group or community in a newsletter, but you should take additional action, too.

Spend some time on the Web locating other discussion groups, forums, and communities where the topics that are addressed relate directly to the content of your Web site. For example, perhaps your site helps people book vacation getaways to exotic destinations. You'd want to attract local business and perhaps support bookings over the Web to attract a wider clientele. Therefore, you'd want to locate two kinds of discussion groups or communities.

First, in this example, you'd locate any online groups that might be discussing your local community and travel (or that have a travel section). And you might look for groups on the Web—regardless of location—where travel is being discussed.

When you locate groups where the subject matter matches your Web site, don't interact with the group by placing a marketing message into the discussion. This is considered spamming. Instead, "talk" directly with the people in the discussion. Get to know what they like and don't like about similar sites, and then mention your site as a part of the conversation (but minus the marketing messages).

Writing for Marketing

Nobody knows the purpose of your Web site better than you. What better way to spread the word about your site and to establish your credibility in the marketplace than to write one or more articles that directly pertain to your site objectives.

Whether you want to sell plumbing parts, pizza, or help other researchers in a particular topic area, by distributing your expertise via written works, you stand a good chance of increasing the number of visitors. Write one or more papers—they can be fairly short—and locate sites that are related to your Web site objective. Submit one or more papers for online publication, and publish the same papers on your own site. Be sure to reference your Web site address and present your credentials whenever you write something.

Linking Online and Off

You need to find ways to make your Web site address visible to the widest audience possible. One way to do this is via free online listing services. These services are typically based on industry type or regional sector. They can be considered portal-type Web sites that provide related links on a given topic or region.

For example, if you manufacture textile goods, you might go to the Google directory (`directory.google.com/Top/Business/Industries/Manufacturing/Textiles_and_Nonwovens/Services/Marketing/`) and obtain free links from any of the services offering this feature. Likewise, if your Web site represents your winery in Monterey, California and you want visitors to the area to find your site and, subsequently, your winery, you might obtain a link on a travel site such as Monterey travel planning portal GoMonterey (`www.gomonterey.com`).

However, don't confine your thoughts of expanding the visibility of your Web site address to the online world. Think about your voice mail greeting. Could you include your Web site address there? What about your stationery, logo, or personal letterhead? Put your Web address in as many places as possible, including your company letterhead, business cards, invoices, print advertisements, and the like.

Can We Be Pals?

Do you do business with other companies? Does your Web site subject matter warrant mention by one or more organizations? Be willing to write some short testimonials that can be posted on the Web sites of business partners or related organizations. These testimonials should also present your credentials and, of course, your Web site address.

For example, if you own and operate Pete's Surf Shop, and your Web site is designed to help surfing enthusiasts find the best boards, you might write something about how your major supplier (for example, Joe's Surf Board Parts and Accessories) provides you with the highest quality parts in the shortest time. Then, get your write-up posted on your supplier's site (and your site, too). This is called crosslinking.

Marketing by Association

Are there associations that represent the type of business you have or the content on your Web site? Contact these organizations and see how joining them might help increase traffic on your Web site. You might agree to be interviewed or write one or more articles that would appear on the association's Web site. Here again, you could obtain cross-linking to your site and the opportunity to reach a wider audience.

For example, if the purpose of your Web site is to expand research of your family history and your family has roots in the Utah area, you might want to join the Utah Genealogical Association (`www.infouga.org/`) and write material that might appear on their Web site.

If you are a small mortgage company or a mortgage broker in the U.S., for example, you might consider joining the Mortgage Bankers Association of America (`www.mbaa.org`). This association is nationally recognized, so the audience you could potentially reach by joining and participating is enormous.

Getting Press

You might just be launching your new open source-based Web site or have major news you want to get out to the world. Leveraging online press release services is a great way to make your site highly visible. These services can target your materials to a wide audience at a low cost—in some cases, no cost.

You can locate some of these services via Google's directory (`directory.google.com/Top/Computers/Internet/Web_Design_and_Development/Promotion/Press_Release_Services/`. Several hundred of these services exist and their reach and costs differ. Carefully investigate choosing a press release service.

Published Information

It is difficult and tricky to obtain press attention these days. However, many offline and online publications are looking for freelance-written subject matter, or they might seek out subject matter experts to interview. Query print and online publications that relate to your business or the content on your Web site. Ask if they are looking for articles or experts to interview. Offer to write, be interviewed, or to participate in a Web cast.

For example, the owner of Pete's Surf Shop might send e-mail to the editor at *Extreme Surfing* magazine and offer to write an article on the best way to handle maneuvering a long board. He also might ask if the magazine would like to interview him on the topic.

Of course, any content that results from your query should include links to your Web site.

Rings

Finally, think rings—Web rings! You might think of a Web ring as a loosely coupled group of Web sites that pertain to the same subject matter. Yahoo offers Web ring facilities (see `dir.webring.yahoo.com/rw`) as do several other portal-type sites.

Let's say your company (and your Web site) supports the creation of peer-to-peer service components that are written in Java. You certainly would want to join an existing Java Web ring and link your site to it. You might also start a new Web ring that pertains to peer-to-peer computing.

It's All About Connectedness

The 10 techniques previously listed are common ones used to market Web sites. Some require a small monetary investment, some are free, and some require that you invest your time to write materials or contact people. There are many other techniques you might use to increase the visibility of your Web site.

As you market your open source-based Web site, the best advice is to remain cost conscious and leverage connectivity and Web-based tools to get your message out. Then, your marketing efforts will equal your smart decision to implement an open source-based Web site.

--Maggie Biggs

Introduction

Building Internet Sites

If you are looking at this book, you have probably made or are at least in the process of making the decision to build an Internet site. This is a big decision and one that can have important implications for your organization, whether or not it is a commercial entity. An Internet site is your representative to the continually growing number of people on the Internet who will potentially access it. As such, you should strive to make your site a positive reflection on your organization. This book is designed to help you accomplish this task.

This site is intended primarily for developers of Internet sites. The reader should be familiar with the basic techniques and tools used to create Web pages, including HTML, JavaScript, CGI programs and scripts, and Web servers. This book is not for beginners and does not attempt to teach these topics.

The Organization of This Book

This book is divided into three sections, each with a different focus.

The first section includes a discussion of how you can leverage Linux as a platform for creating an Internet site; it explains what open source is and what makes it so compelling, and finally, it describes some of the reasons for creating an Internet site for your organization.

The next section discusses some of the different types of Internet sites. It looks at content/media sites, whose primary purpose is to disseminate information; community sites, where groups can come together and interact; and electronic commerce sites, whose purpose is to sell a product or service via the Internet. The characteristics of each of these types of sites are discussed along with some examples of open source tools that can be used to build them. To round out this section, three case studies are included that present a site of each type built using open source software.

The final section is a collection of topics related to making your site a success. It starts with a discussion of maintaining your Internet site, including the importance of monitoring to keeping your site healthy. It also includes a discussion of how to select appropriate hardware and software components and the importance of proper planning and design. Finally, the topics of high availability and scalability are discussed, including how to incorporate these ideas into your network design and some of the open source tools that can be used to implement load balancing and failover so that your site can grow as your needs grow.

How to Use This Book

This book is not like many other books that discuss building Internet sites. It does not include cookie-cutter recipes for building sites using a limited set of tools. It is intended as a reference for the site designer. It describes an approach to building Internet sites by integrating tools created by the open source community. It shows how by combining these tools and customizing them, you can create sites that are not only functional, but that are also effective. It also demonstrates techniques for building sites that can serve a small audience or a large one, depending on the needs of the organization for which the site is built. It provides alternatives to expensive, proprietary solutions and demonstrates techniques that can be used to make maintenance and growth easier while not costing a fortune. Finally, it provides examples of these techniques so that you can understand not only the theory of operation, but also the implementation of these theories. I hope you enjoy this book.

PART I

Introduction to Linux and Open Source Software

IN THIS PART

1 Why Should Your Company Leverage Linux? 13

2 What Makes Open Source So Compelling? 29

3 So You Want to Build an Internet Site 43

Why Should Your Company Leverage Linux?

CHAPTER

1

IN THIS CHAPTER

- What Is Linux? 14
- Linux Versus Other Internet Server Platforms 19
- A Look at the Total Cost of Ownership for Linux 23

After you have made the decision to create an Internet presence, you need to select the hardware and operating system platform on which to build it. In this chapter, we discuss Linux as this platform, beginning with a description of the Linux kernel and what makes a Linux distribution. We then look at Linux as an Internet server platform, comparing and contrasting it with Windows NT and then with Unix. Finally, we look at the total cost of ownership for Linux, covering software costs, hardware requirements, the cost of maintaining your Linux systems, and training requirements. So let's get started with a look at what Linux is.

What Is Linux?

If you are involved with computer or Web industries, you have no doubt heard something about Linux, but you may not be familiar with what Linux is and why you should consider it for your network servers. In this section, we take a look at the Linux operating system kernel and Linux distributions. We start with a couple of definitions as to what Linux is, what a distribution is, and then look at the features of both that make Linux a good choice for running Internet sites. Along the way, we cover a bit of Linux history, such as how it started and how it grew to the point where it is today. So, let's get started.

An Open Source Operating System Kernel

Every operating system consists of many parts. At the heart of each is a piece of software known as a kernel. This kernel is responsible for managing hardware, scheduling tasks to run, dealing with memory management, and providing other services to the software that will run on it. Linux is a Unix-like operating system kernel, which implements the POSIX specification. What this means is that Linux looks like Unix and implements services normally found on Unix systems, but it is not Unix. The reason is that Linux has never been certified by The Open Group, which holds the Unix trademark. For an operating system to be called Unix, a set of certifications must be passed and a license must be granted by The Open Group. Because Linux is not owned by a corporate entity willing to pay the licensing fees for this to happen and because doing so would make it unprofitable to continue distributing Linux at no cost, this has never been done. Therefore, Linux is not Unix.

What differentiates Linux from most other operating system kernels is the way in which it was developed and the fact that you can obtain the source code for the kernel without having to pay a license fee. This development model, called open source development, is discussed further in Chapter 2, "What Makes Open Source So Compelling?" Most operating systems are developed by a corporate or research entity and by a limited group of developers who maintain tight control over the source code to it. An example of this is Windows. Windows was developed by Microsoft Corporation, and the only way to obtain the source code to it is by signing nondisclosure agreements and paying a substantial licensing fee. Now let's take a look at how Linux developed.

Linux is the brainchild of Linus Torvalds, who started working to build an operating system to run on his Intel 386-based personal computer while he attended university. He started this project because he wanted to run an environment similar to the Unix systems at school, and because he was not satisfied with the operating systems that he could afford to run on his PC. The closest thing that he found to what he was looking for was Minix. Minix is an operating system used in many colleges and universities to teach operating system theory, and it resembles Unix in many ways. A number of limitations exist, however, which is part of what prompted Linus to do what he did. He started working and soon had a rudimentary kernel. He realized that the work would go much faster if he could get some help, and he made an important decision. He decided to share his fledgling operating system with others via the Internet. It should be noted that at the time, the early 1990s, Internet usage was not nearly as widespread as it is today, and a large proportion of the Internet usage was by the government and academic communities in which sharing data and technology is a time-honored tradition. To this end, he announced his project to people on Usenet in the Minix newsgroups because he was using Minix to bootstrap his kernel. What followed was rather amazing.

Other people became interested in his project and began to contribute code and fix bugs they found in each other's code. Some of these contributors were other college students, but some were people who were interested in operating system research; others were simply computer enthusiasts. As more people joined the effort, more functionality was added to the kernel until it began to be reliable enough to use for real work. With the explosion of the Internet that occurred in the years that followed, the audience for Linux grew. Coupled with this growth, considerable growth also occurred in other areas, such as the GNU project, which contributes a substantial portion of the software that supports the Linux kernel to make up distributions such as Red Hat, Debian, and others. Today, hundreds of people are credited with contributing code to the Linux kernel, and thousands more assisted by reporting bugs and testing. In addition, corporations such as IBM, SGI, and others are making technology from their commercial Unix flavors available to the Linux community to make it more compatible with their products and to make it more robust and full featured. What are some of these features?

As noted earlier, Linux is a Unix-like operating system that implements the POSIX specification. It is a multiuser, multitasking operating system that runs on common PC hardware that includes support for many features, including the following:

- Virtual memory
- Multiple processors
- Multiple native and foreign filesystems
- TCP/IP networking

The kernel is designed in such a way as to allow you to select only those features that you need. The user has two options for building support for these features. One approach is to build support directly into the kernel, using what is referred to as the monolithic approach. An alternative and more popular approach is to build in a minimal set of features and to take advantage of the kernel's modular design that allows for the loading and unloading of features on an as-needed basis. The approach that you decide to take is up to you. If you are running special-purpose servers that do one thing and one thing only, such as Web serving, you may find that it is easier to use the monolithic approach. On the other hand, if you are using Linux-based systems for general purpose servers or workstations, the modular approach may be better suited to your needs. The features that are available are selected by using configuration tools that come with the kernel source code. This is an important feature because it allows you to customize the kernel to support only those features that you require, making the Linux kernel small and fast.

The features that make the Linux kernel suitable for use on Internet servers are the TCP/IP networking support and the fact that it runs on common PC hardware. Because the source code is freely available, many people can examine the system for problems. This peer review has made the Linux kernel very stable. It is not uncommon for Linux systems to run for many months or even years without requiring intervention or a reboot. It is this stability that attracts many Internet service providers to Linux.

Now that you have a little background on the Linux kernel, we can move on to our discussion of Linux distributions.

Distributions—A Kernel Plus Supporting Software

The Linux kernel is an interesting piece of software, but by itself, it is not very useful. For any operating system to be useful, it must have utilities and applications that run on it. This is the reason for the birth of the Linux distribution. In the early days of Linux, you were provided with a boot disk and a root disk that contained the Linux kernel and a very basic set of utilities, and it was up to you to download a compiler and build the rest of the system yourself. Linux was a true do-it-yourself operating system. Although this might sound like a grand adventure to hardcore Linux enthusiasts, to most people it was a stumbling block. To make things a little easier for new Linux users, a few enterprising people decided to package the kernel with a bunch of utilities and applications. They also created installation scripts to transfer them from the download media to the system hard drive. Thus, the Linux distribution was created.

Early distributions were created by different groups, which included the MCC distribution from the Manchester Computing Center, the TAMU distribution from Texas A&M University, and SLS from Softlanding Systems. These distributions made it much easier to get Linux installed and running and included plenty of software to get you started. A large portion of this software was created as part of the GNU project, but other portions came from the BSD Unix source code and other sources. The common thread of all these sources is that the software was freely available in source code form and distributed by groups that not only allowed but encouraged this use. This is especially true of the contributions of the GNU project. The GNU project and the Free Software Foundation, which was started to further it, promote the idea that software should be distributed freely with source code. It also promotes the idea that the rights of the software user should include the right to modify the software to suit the user's needs and to distribute those modifications to others, but that they should not be allowed to restrict these rights for others. This philosophy is embodied in the GNU General Public License, which is used on the software developed by the GNU project and which also is used for the Linux kernel. For more information on the GNU project and their ideals, visit the GNU Web site at `http://www.gnu.org`.

Today, literally dozens of Linux distributions are available, from general purpose distributions, such as Red Hat, Caldera, SuSE, Debian, and Mandrake, to specialized distributions that are used in network appliances. Each of these distributions has strengths and weaknesses, and the one that you choose should be based on your needs and your answers to questions such as

- Do I need a general purpose distribution?
- Do I want or need technical support?
- Do I want or need to run commercial software?

There are, of course, other questions, but let's take a look at these three, starting with whether you need a general purpose distribution. A general purpose distribution is one that you can adapt to many purposes, depending on your needs. Examples of general purpose distributions include

- Red Hat
- Debian
- Mandrake
- Caldera
- SuSE
- Slackware

Each of these distributions allows you to use them for workstations, servers, or any other purpose you can imagine. For example, you can do a minimal installation of Debian and configure it to serve as a router for your local network. Likewise, you could take Slackware and install only those components required to serve as a firewall. You also could take any of these distributions and set up a departmental server, running Samba to provide file and print services to Windows clients, run an intranet Web server, and provide electronic mail services. The choice is up to you. On the other hand, if you are interested only in running a Linux-based firewall, you could select one of the specialized distributions designed for that purpose.

The next question is whether you want, or need, technical support. If you are building an Internet site for a commercial entity that will derive income from the site, you would probably answer yes. In this case, you should look for a distribution that provides technical support as an option. Most of the major distributions do this, as do a number of independent companies. On the other hand, if you are just setting up a Web site for a local club, you may not care whether support is available. In this case, the support available on the Internet from Linux newsgroups, Web sites, and mailing lists may be sufficient. Your answer to this question determines how flexible your choice of distributions can be.

Another question to ask is whether you want, or need, to run commercial software on your Linux systems. For example, if you require an Oracle database server, you would probably want to select a distribution that is supported by Oracle, such as Red Hat. If not, you again have more flexibility in which distribution to choose. The important thing to remember when considering this question is not only whether you want or need commercial software now, but whether it is likely that you will want or need it in the future. It should be noted that although this is very true of commercial software, it is also true in some cases for free software, and if a particular software package that you require is best suited for a particular distribution, you should weigh this fact when making your decision.

Having answered these questions, you can select the distribution that best suits your needs. Now let's take a look at some of the features that are common to most distributions.

Features of Linux Distributions

As a Unix-like operating system, Linux comes with a wealth of software and utilities that make it a good platform for Internet sites. To begin with, Linux comes with most of the servers required to support the most common Internet protocols. Some of the services supported out of the box by the general-purpose Linux distributions include

- Electronic mail (SMTP)
- Usenet news (NNTP)
- File transfers (FTP and scp)
- Remote login (telnet, SSH and rlogin)
- Remote command execution (rexec and rsh)
- World Wide Web (HTTP and HTTPS)

In addition to these services, packages also are available that support file sharing, print services, and others. This means that you do not have to purchase these products separately from the operating system as you do for many of these services on other platforms.

You also can use Linux as your development platform for your Internet sites. The majority of Linux distributions come with a wealth of development tools that can be used for creating compelling sites that will keep your visitors coming back for more. These tools include compilers, interpreters for scripting languages, HTML editing tools, debuggers, database software, and supporting tools. Some of the languages supported include C, C++, Perl, Python, Tcl/Tk, PHP, Fortran, and Pascal. Database software is available in the form of MySQL or PostgreSQL. Also available are multiple implementations of Java. All these either come standard with Linux or are additions available at no cost over the Internet.

As you can see, Linux distributions offer all the features you need to serve as an efficient and full-featured Internet server platform. Next, let's take a look at how Linux compares with other platforms.

Linux Versus Other Internet Server Platforms

In this section, we take a look at some other Internet server platforms to see how Linux compares to them. We compare the relative strengths and weaknesses of Linux to Windows, commercial Unix products, and other freely available operating systems such as FreeBSD.

Linux Versus Windows

If you consider Linux as a flavor of Unix, current surveys indicate that Unix systems power more than seventy percent of the Web, news, and FTP servers on the Internet. These same surveys indicate that Linux is number one in all three of these categories. Windows has a significant share in each of these as well, ranking second or third in each category of server. So let's take a look at the features of Windows and how it compares with Linux. In this discussion, Windows generally refers to Windows NT or Windows 2000, although some of the comments also extend to include Windows 95, Windows 98, or Windows Me.

Windows, like Linux, is a network operating system that provides the TCP/IP networking support required to serve as an Internet server platform. If you purchase the server editions, Windows NT and 2000 both ship with the Internet Information Server, which provides Web and FTP services. Also available for the Windows 95 and 98 platforms is the Personal Web Server software. This is a lightweight Web-serving platform that is designed for running personal home pages. If you are interested in providing other services, such as Usenet news and electronic mail, these must be obtained as add-ons to the operating system, either from Microsoft or third-party vendors.

One area in which a remarkable difference exists between Linux-based distributions and Windows is in the area of security. Linux distributions vary in the security measures that they provide out of the box; however, the Linux kernel has a number of built-in security features, and patches are available that make Linux even more secure. It is relatively easy to secure a Linux system against unwanted intrusion, and because of the open source nature of the Linux kernel and most of the software that comes with it, security flaws that are detected tend to be corrected very quickly. An example of this can be seen in the response to the Pentium F00F bug that was discovered in the original Pentium chips. This particular bug was a design flaw in many Pentium chips that caused a system to lock up if a byte sequence of F0 0F was received. As you might suspect, this meant that a denial-of-service attack could be launched against any Pentium-based system relatively easily. The Linux response to this problem took approximately four hours. Within four hours, the first patch to the Linux kernel was made available to work around this problem. This is in stark contrast to the Windows response, which took significantly longer. Although some people fear that having the source code to the operating system would mean that it would be easier to add back doors or other security-compromising measures to the Linux kernel, the exact opposite is true. Having access to the source code means that many more people can see defects or deliberate attempts to compromise the security of a system. This peer review actually prevents a large number of security flaws before they can occur. In contrast, Windows security flaws, when found, must be fixed by the operating system vendors on their timetable, provided that they even acknowledge the problem in the first place.

On the development side, Windows comes with nothing out of the box. There are plenty of development tools for Windows, both commercial and freely available; however, you must purchase or download them separately. The same is true of HTML editors, debuggers, and other products that come standard with Linux distributions. The advantages of using these tools is that they are often more polished than their counterparts on Linux. However, as with many products that concentrate on ease of use, you give up some flexibility. Also missing from Windows as shipped are any database management tools.

The biggest difference between Windows and Linux is the hardware requirements. Whereas Linux is capable of running as a Web server on a 486 system with as little as 16MB of RAM, current versions of Windows require at least a Pentium 133MHz system with 128MB of RAM to even run. Recommended configuration for a Windows server is a Pentium II or III running at 500MHz or faster, with 256MB of RAM.

Linux Versus Commercial Unix

When comparing Linux to commercial Unix, it is more of an apples to apples comparison than comparing Linux to Windows. This is because Linux implements many of the same features as commercial Unix variants, such as Solaris or AIX. Because Solaris is one of the most popular Unix varieties used for Internet servers, I will use it as my basis of comparison.

Solaris is a System V-based Unix variant, with features also taken from the BSD releases. Users of Linux will find many similarities when looking at Solaris. Like Linux, Solaris comes with most of the software you need to run an Internet site, including software to support electronic mail, FTP, `telnet` and `rlogin`, and other services. It does include a Web server; however, it is for evaluation only, and if you want to put it into production, you must purchase a separate license. If you choose not to purchase it, you easily can obtain a number of Web servers, including the popular Apache Web server, from the Internet for no cost because Apache, like Linux, is available under an open source license. Also, the Sun-supported compilers for Solaris are available separately, or you can choose to use the GNU compiler suite that is included on the Solaris companion CD.

On the topic of security, Solaris has a number of advantages over Windows because the security of Solaris and other Unix variants is much greater. In contrast with Linux-based systems, however, Linux still has a slight advantage, again owing to the open source nature of the system. Just as with Windows, commercial Unix security flaws must be fixed by the operating system vendor and you, as a user, must wait for the fixes.

Again, the biggest difference between Solaris and Linux is the hardware requirements for running it. Solaris is available for Intel-based personal computers; however, like Windows, the minimum hardware requirements are higher than those for Linux. Solaris requires a minimum of a Pentium processor and 64MB of RAM. In addition, the list of supported hardware, by Windows standards, is rather limited. On the other hand, most Solaris implementations are run on the Sparc platform, which is Sun's proprietary hardware. Sparc systems are more expensive than personal computers based on Intel processors; however, the advantage of choosing Sparc systems is that they scale much better, and you can purchase systems that support up to 64 processors and 64GB of RAM. Of course, this would be overkill for a Web server, but it serves to illustrate the level of computing that is available with the Sparc platform. Even on the lower end, however, the hardware required to run Solaris is more costly than most Intel-based servers.

You can select several other variants of commercial Unix, including AIX, True-64, HP/UX, Irix, and Unixware, for an Internet site; however, with the exception of Unixware, which runs on the Intel platform, these variants run on specialized servers based on specialized processors. Like the Sparc platform, these hardware platforms are typically more expensive than Intel-based servers.

One of the reasons for the popularity of Linux-based servers is that Linux has relatively modest hardware requirements. Because the developers of Linux and other software that make up Linux distributions are often poor students and part-time hackers, Linux has been optimized to run on systems that many would consider obsolete or outdated. This makes it possible for computers that are not capable of running the latest version of many of the commercial operating systems out there to run Linux. You therefore can extend the life of your PC hardware, making Linux a very economical choice for servers. This is one of the reasons that you often find Linux sneaking in the back door of IT departments and providing services such as DNS, Web serving, and other functions.

Linux Versus Other Freely Available Operating Systems

Linux is not the only freely available network operating system that can be used to run your Internet servers. Another choice, or rather three choices, are the BSD-based operating systems: FreeBSD, OpenBSD, and NetBSD. All three are offshoots of a project called 386BSD that started about the same time as Linux. Because of differences between the project leaders and the community, the three independent groups formed. Each had slightly different goals; however, they share code among the three groups and they are all very similar from a user and administrator perspective. These three operating systems are implementations of the BSD 4.4 specification and are unencumbered by the licensing issues of earlier BSD releases.

The development model of the BSD projects is slightly different from that of Linux in that much tighter control is exercised by the kernel developers over what goes into the system. This may be one of the reasons why more developers flocked to the Linux project; however, this is just speculation on my part. There are some advantages to the model adopted by the BSD projects. One of these is that the somewhat slower pace of kernel development and more stringent control by the project organizers has resulted in a tighter security model. In fact, the OpenBSD project, in particular, is noted for its emphasis on security.

A major area in which the BSD projects differ from Linux distributions is that the projects include not only the kernel, but all the basic utilities required to run a system. When you download one of the BSD distributions, you get the kernel and much of the supporting software required to make a complete system. This means that, unlike Linux-based systems, there are not a large number of distributions to decide among and more consistency exists from system to system. Because there are not a lot of different groups packaging distributions, the filesystem layout, standard libraries, and file locations are the same. This is in contrast to Linux, where each distribution maintainer puts files in different locations, includes different versions of key libraries, and makes other decisions that can cause incompatibilities. This also means that unlike the Linux community, which tries to address these problems by creating standards after the fact, such as the Linux Standard Base (LSB) and the Filesystem Hierarchy Standard (FHS), no such standards are required in the BSD communities.

In the following discussion, I will refer to FreeBSD, the BSD implementation with which I am most familiar. However, the points discussed also can be applied to OpenBSD and NetBSD in most cases.

FreeBSD, like Linux, is a Unix clone for personal computers. It runs on multiple hardware platforms, including Sparc and Alpha, in addition to the Intel platform. Unlike Linux, FreeBSD can trace its lineage directly to the original Unix implementation. Like Linux, it supports all the networking services you would expect from a Unix system, and very little software is available for Linux that is not available for FreeBSD as well. This includes the development tools and other software used to create Internet sites.

Some differences between FreeBSD and Linux are in the so-called enterprise features. Two of these features are multiprocessor support and journaling filesystem support. Although FreeBSD does have support for multiple processors just as Linux does, that support is not as mature. This is rapidly changing because of the open source nature of both systems and the fact that the two projects can learn from the mistakes of the other. The other feature, journaling filesystem support, is lacking in FreeBSD. A journaling filesystem is important because they are more crash resistant. A journal file allows for disk transactions to be played back in the event of a crash, which allows for much quicker recovery after a crash. Without a journaling filesystem, checking a disk for consistency following a crash is much more difficult, and on large filesystems it can cause very long downtimes. At least four different journaling filesystem implementations are being developed for Linux. One of these, the Reiserfs, is the most mature and is a standard feature of the SuSE distribution. In addition, IBM and SGI are both actively porting their journaling filesystems, known as JFS and XFS respectively, to Linux. The Ext3 project also is available, which provides a forward migration path from the current Linux standard filesystem, Ext2.

Several interesting features of FreeBSD include its Linux binary support and the ports collection. If you choose to install the Linux binary support packages, you will have the capability to run many applications designed for Linux. This is most useful for commercial software that has not been ported to FreeBSD. The ports collection is another very interesting method employed by the BSD groups to make building third-party software easier on your system. If you install the ports package, you can build many common packages simply by changing directory to the directory in the source tree for that package and typing **make**. This retrieves the source code from the Internet, applies any patches required to build under FreeBSD, and then builds it. In addition, if you use the CVSup software on your system, you can keep your FreeBSD system up-to-date with the latest bug fixes to the kernel and the rest of the software on your system.

The choice between FreeBSD and Linux is much more difficult than the choice between Linux and Windows. For one thing, FreeBSD, like Linux, is freely available, and they both run on the Intel platform. In most cases, the choice comes down to which system you are most comfortable with. If your background is with BSD style systems, FreeBSD might be the more natural choice. On the other hand, if you are most familiar with System V-type systems, Linux might be for you.

A Look at the Total Cost of Ownership for Linux

If the cost of the operating system were the only consideration, Linux would be a pretty easy choice. When selecting a computing platform, however, it is important to remember that there are other factors to consider. You should look at the big picture of all costs associated with your choice, or the total cost of ownership. Following is a list of some of the factors that you should consider when making your choice of platforms for Internet servers:

- Software licensing costs
- Hardware requirements
- Maintenance costs
- Training requirements

In this section, we take a look at each of these factors and show how Linux stacks up with the competition, starting with software licensing costs.

Software Licensing Costs

One of the reasons for the rise in popularity of Linux is that you are not required to pay a licensing fee to use it. You can download it from the Internet, or if you prefer, you can purchase copies on CD for as little as one or two dollars. Other options, including borrowing a CD from a friend, also are available. This is because of the GNU Public License and other similar licenses used by most software you find in Linux distributions. Table 1.1 shows a comparison of Linux to Windows that lists some features and whether they are included in the cost of the operating system or are add-ons.

TABLE 1.1 A Feature/Cost Comparison Between Windows and Linux

Feature	*Linux ($180)*	*Windows 2000 ($1200)*
Electronic mail server	Included	Add-on ($1,000 and up)
Remote server access tools	Included	Add-on ($1,000 and up)
Web server	Included	Included
FTP server	Included	Included
C/C++ Compiler	Included	Add-on (about $500)
Java development tools	Free Download	Add-on (about $500)
Database management system	Included	Add-on ($1,500 and up)

NOTE

The base price shown for Linux is for a Red Hat Professional Server boxed set. The prices shown for Windows 2000 and other Microsoft products were obtained from the Microsoft Web site at `http://www.microsoft.com/`. The C/C++ compiler quoted was Visual C++ 6.0, and the Java development tool was Visual J++ 6.0. The electronic mail server quoted was Exchange Server 5.5. The database management system quoted was SQL Server 2000, Standard Edition with 10 client licenses. Remote server access tools include tools such as telnet/rsh/ssh for Linux and Citrix/PC Anywhere for Windows.

As you can see from the information in Table 1.1, the cost for Windows 2000 and the add-ons required to make it comparable in functionality to the standard software shipped with a common Linux distribution, is significantly more than the Linux solution. When you consider that you are permitted by the license to install your copy of Linux on as many systems as you like, the cost difference is even greater.

The comparison with commercial Unix systems is even more dramatic. However, most of the free software tools available on Linux are available on commercial Unix systems, such as the GNU compilers and other software. On the other hand, if you choose to go with the compiler tools and other software from the OS vendor, you are looking at a substantial cost difference between Linux and the commercial Unix systems.

The comparison between Linux and the other freely available operating systems is dead even because the tools available for one also are available for the others.

Hardware Requirements

As shown in the preceding discussion comparing Linux and Windows, although both run on Intel-based personal computers, Linux is capable of running on less-powerful systems. Assuming, however, that you were running on equivalent hardware, this efficiency of the Linux system means that Linux can support more capacity per server than Windows running on the same hardware. This means that to obtain a specific level of performance, you can run fewer systems under Linux than under Windows, thus reducing cost. Part of this is because you can tune the Linux kernel by removing unneeded features and because the Linux kernel does not include the graphical user interface, or GUI. Therefore, the Linux kernel can run much more efficiently.

Another factor to consider is that new releases of Linux normally do not precipitate a hardware upgrade as do new releases of Windows. Systems that were capable of running Linux version 1.2.0 are just as capable of running Linux version 2.4.0. The same cannot be said of Windows NT. The hardware requirements for each subsequent release of Windows NT have gone up. For example, the minimum hardware requirements for running Windows NT 3.1 were a 486, 33MHz system with 16MB of RAM. According to Microsoft's Web site, the requirements for running Windows 2000 are now a Pentium 133MHz system with 128MB of RAM. Users of Windows 2000 tell a different story, however, and recommend at least a Pentium II or Pentium III system running at 500MHz or better with 256MB of RAM. Linux, on the other hand, runs on 386 or 486 systems with as little as 8MB of RAM; however, for server systems, you will naturally want something more modern. The point is that you get more bang for your buck out of the same hardware under Linux than you would out of Windows.

When comparing the cost of hardware required to run commercial variants of Unix to Linux, the cost differential can be even greater because most of the commercial variants of Unix run on hardware platforms other than Intel, and these systems tend to be very expensive. Part of the reason for this may be because a significant part of the revenue stream for the commercial Unix vendors comes from the sale of this hardware, in contrast to the operating system. This is changing, however, as Intel server systems are starting to compete with these other hardware platforms. This new competition is forcing the price of the lower-end systems from vendors such as HP and Sun to come down. At the top end, however, the systems remain extremely expensive.

Maintenance Costs

Maintenance costs are a factor that often is overlooked, but you should keep them in mind when selecting the hardware on which to run your Internet site. Every computer system requires maintenance, and this usually does not come cheap. Let's consider a few of the costs associated with maintenance of your Internet site.

The first category of costs to consider is the cost of administrators for your systems. If you start looking at the differences in salary between a Windows system administrator and a Linux system administrator, you will see that the Linux administrator usually commands a larger salary. Part of the reason for this is related to supply and demand. Microsoft has done a remarkable job of developing training programs for its system administrators. As a result, Microsoft Certified Systems Engineers (MCSE) are fairly easy to find. On the other hand, people qualified to administer Linux systems are more difficult to come by, and if you want to find someone certified on Linux systems, these people are even more rare. This is partly because the certification programs for Linux to some extent are still in the organizational phases or are vendor specific, and many Linux administrators disdain any type of certification. Two factors make this lack of certified people unimportant. The first is that because Linux is so like Unix, most administrators of Unix systems can come up to speed on Linux in short order. The second is that because Linux is growing so rapidly, the number of Linux-experienced people also is growing. Another factor to consider is that because Linux allows system maintenance remotely without the requirement of a lot of special equipment or software, you can usually get by with fewer Linux administrators than you could if you use Windows.

Another maintenance cost to consider is the cost of support personnel. In this case, the situation is a little better, especially if you live near a college or university with a computer science program. Because of the cost, Linux is very popular among college students, and you usually can find plenty of people familiar with Linux to fill support positions.

Training Requirements

Two aspects of the cost of training relate to running a Internet site on Linux. The first is the training required for system administrators and support personnel. Training for these people can be satisfied in a number of ways, such as through training programs from the Linux vendor. For example, Red Hat offers training and certification on its Linux distribution through its Web site at `http://www.redhat.com/`. Other vendors, such as Caldera, have created training programs in conjunction with local universities. Another option is the purchase of video training materials. As Linux grows, more and more videos are becoming available, and they cover the basics as well as the more advanced topics of system administration and support. In addition, many of the Linux vendors have computer-based training programs in development.

Yet another option is to seek basic Unix training and to augment it with books on Linux. Unlike the situation just a few years ago when Linux books were very rare, there are now a number of excellent books covering Linux. Topics range from getting started with Linux, to advanced system administration, to programming in the Linux environment. Specialized books also are available, such as this one, that cover a wide range of topics, from writing device drivers to Web development. In addition, many of the Linux distributors, such as Red Hat, Caldera, and others are implementing, or supporting, independent training initiatives. For more information on Linux training sources, visit `http://lintraining.com or http://www.lpi.org`.

The other training you might have to consider is end-user training. If you are using Linux as a Web development platform, this will not be a major concern, because Linux can easily coexist with other operating systems in a networked environment. However, if you are considering using Linux for more than just servers, you will be faced with training nontechnical people to use Linux. In this case, having a good system administration staff and a help desk will be essential. This can mean substantial cost to train your staff on using Linux. The biggest hurdle is usually getting people used to using Linux office suites and teaching them not to arbitrarily reboot their desktop systems. Again, books and video tapes can be helpful in this regard. Other options include on-site training by the system administration staff or training consultants.

Again, the path of least resistance may be to use Linux for servers and to leave the desktop users on systems that they are more familiar with, such as Windows. Many companies have a delineation between administrative users and developers, with the former using Windows or Macintosh systems and the latter using Linux. The key training issue then becomes educating the Windows users on how to successfully exchange documents with the Linux users.

Summary

In this chapter, we have taken a look at Linux and distributions and some of the factors to consider when making the choice of Internet server platforms. Some of these factors include lower total cost of ownership, better price/performance ratio, more flexibility, and generally better security. Overall, I think that most readers will agree that the available features combined with the excellent price/performance you get from Linux make a compelling argument for using Linux as your platform for Internet servers.

What Makes Open Source So Compelling?

CHAPTER

2

IN THIS CHAPTER

- Open Source Software Versus Proprietary Software 30
- The Pros and Cons of Open Source Software 33
- Examples of Open Source Software 38
- The Support Issue 40

As we discussed in Chapter 1, "Why Should Your Company Leverage Linux?," Linux and most of the software available for it are freely available in both binary and source code form. If you are most familiar with the PC world of Windows, this might seem rather strange because much of the software written for Windows is available only in binary form and at substantial cost. In this chapter, we discuss the differences between open source software and proprietary software. We also take a look at some popular open source software projects and then look at the biggest concern many people have about open source software—support.

Open Source Software Versus Proprietary Software

To begin our discussion, let's study the difference between open source software and proprietary software by looking at the development models of open source projects and what having the source code to the software can mean. Although free software purists will claim a difference, for purpose of this chapter, I will use both the terms open source software and free software interchangeably to refer to software that is available in source code form under a license that allows for modification and redistribution. If you are interested in why these purists disagree with this usage, you can refer to the GNU Web site at `http://www.gnu.org/`.

A Different Development Model

Most of the software people use on personal computers, unless you are a user of a freely available operating system such as Linux or FreeBSD, was developed by a software company, which grants you a license to use it. You are not normally given the source code to the software; you are not permitted to modify it, and giving it away is called piracy. It is illegal under the terms of the license. This is in contrast to open source software, which by definition comes with source code, allows you to modify that source as you see fit, and not only allows—but encourages—you to share it with others. Although this is the primary difference between proprietary software and open source software, another key difference is the way in which this software is developed.

Let's take a look at a popular piece of software that was developed using the proprietary model. For this discussion, we will consider Microsoft Word. Microsoft Word is a product of the Microsoft Corporation and represents many years of development by programmers employed there. These employees, under the direction of their managers and with the input of marketing and salespeople, worked to create a software program to meet a specific need that the company perceived in the software market. The source code that they created is the intellectual property of Microsoft and is a closely guarded secret. You might be able, as a third-party developer, to gain access to this source code, but only if you sign a nondisclosure agreement and pay a hefty licensing fee. These characteristics are common to much of the software developed today.

The software development model just described is the cathedral model that Eric Raymond describes in his essay on open source development, "The Cathedral and the Bazaar." This essay, which is available online at `http://www.tuxedo.org/~esr/writings/cathedral-bazaar/cathedral-bazaar/`, compares and contrasts the proprietary development model, which he likens to building a cathedral, with the open source development model. In this essay, Eric describes the development of fetchmail, an open source tool for retrieving mail from mail servers and delivering it locally. He also looks at the development of Linux and describes how it has been developed out of seeming chaos, the bazaar, to become a robust and viable system. This essay is credited with influencing Netscape to release the source code that would eventually become the Mozilla project.

By contrast, in the free software community, the model employed to develop software is quite different. In our discussion of Linux in Chapter 1, you will recall that Linus Torvalds began his project to create a new operating system to satisfy a personal need. To further his project, he released the source code to his kernel and invited others to assist him in its development. New features were added to meet the needs of the users, primarily programmers, and other personal needs. Release schedules were nonexistent. There were no marketing people to rush the product to market, and the source code added by each contributor was shared with everyone else in the community. If you look at other open source projects, you will see that this is a common trait. This might sound like a pretty inefficient way to develop software, but it has proven in many cases to be quite successful. The main reason is the availability of the source code, which we discuss next.

The Keys to the Kingdom

If you suggested to most large software companies that they give away the source code to their products, they would think that you were crazy, but this is exactly what open source software developers do all the time—in effect, they give you the keys to the kingdom. You are free to study the source code, reuse it in other software products, add features, fix bugs, or customize it to suit your needs. This freedom to do with the source code whatever you like is the cornerstone of the open source software movement. There are, however, different degrees of freedom when it comes to software. The amount of freedom depends on the terms of the license under which the software is published, and any number of licenses can be used to make a software product open source. The following are a few of the licenses that apply to a software product:

- The GNU General Public License
- The GNU Library General Public License
- The Artistic License
- The BSD License

Each of these has slightly different provisions. It is not my intention to discuss the relative merits of them, but to present them and describe their key features. Of course, you also could create your own license or simply release your software into the public domain. Which license you choose is up to you. Let's take a look at the freedoms that these licenses grant you.

The GNU General Public License

The GNU General Public License, or GPL, was originally developed by Richard Stallman and is considered by many to be the ultimate license for free software. The protection of the GPL is ensured by the author retaining the copyright on all source code that makes up the software project and granting a license without cost to users of the software. This idea of using the copyright to ensure freedom, rather than restrict it, has led to the coining of the term *copyleft*, which is commonly used in the Open Source software community when referring to software covered by the GPL. Richard Stallman developed this license to promote his ideas for free software, which he describes in one of the early guiding documents of the GNU project—"The GNU Manifesto." This manifesto outlines the goals of the GNU project and is a call to action. It has been revised and updated over the years and is available online at `http://www.gnu.org/gnu/manifesto.html`. The GPL has provisions that are designed to ensure that not only are you granted an unrestricted license to use the software and the source code, but you may not create derivative software that restricts these rights for others. In other words, if you take a piece of software covered by the GPL and modify it to create a new piece of software, that software also must be released under the GPL. The complete text of the GPL can be found on the Web at `http://www.gnu.org/copyleft/gpl.html`. In the case of libraries, if you use a library covered by the GPL, your software also must be covered by the GPL, which means that you cannot create proprietary software using GPL libraries. This restriction is one of the reasons why the next license was created.

The GNU Lesser General Public License

The GNU Lesser General Public License, or LGPL, is in many respects very similar to the GPL in that you are granted the right to use the software covered by it, and you are not permitted to create derivative works that are restricted. This license is the successor to the GNU Library General Public License, although it is still possible to use that license if you so desire. The big difference between the LGPL and the GPL is in the definition of what constitutes a derivative work. The LGPL is designed primarily for libraries of software functions. Under the terms of the GPL, if a software program was linked with a covered library, the software program also must be covered by the GPL. This restriction was found to discourage some people from creating software using free libraries. To ease this restriction, the LGPL was created with a provision that explicitly states that the mere act of linking a program with a LGPL-covered library does not create a derivative work. This means that you can create software that uses a library covered by the LGPL, and you do not have to make your software freely available. Free software purists tend to disdain this license because it does not result in the software created being covered by the GPL. However, if you are a pragmatist, and your goal in creating a library is to allow it to be used by the Open Source community, as well as commercial software companies, the LGPL might be a good choice. The full text of the LGPL can be found at the GNU Web site at `http://www.gnu.org/copyleft/lesser.html`.

The Artistic License

The Artistic License is one of the licenses used by Perl, the scripting language, and by NcFTP, a popular ftp client. The intent of this license is to allow the free use and distribution of the program in binary and source code form, but also to allow the author to maintain some level of artistic control over the standard package. To this end, users are granted a license to make modifications to the software, provided that the user doesn't distribute them. However, if you do distribute modifications to the package, you must clearly label your modifications and provide them along with the unmodified package. This license differs from the GPL in that a major facet of it is to let the software creator maintain creative control over the package to which it is applied. The GPL permits anyone to create custom versions of the software covered by it and release them under the same name as the original. The Artistic License does not. A copy of this license is included with the NcFTP software and can be viewed at `http://www.appwatch.com/license/ncftp-3.0.2.txt`.

The BSD License

BSD advocates will tell you that this license is the most open of the open source licenses because it allows for free distribution of the software and source code, provided that you leave copyright notices intact. It also allows you to make proprietary versions of the software. GPL advocates tend to not like the BSD license because of this capability to take a BSD-licensed software package, modify it, and create a software package that is less free than the original. This, in fact, has occurred many times—for example, in each of the commercial Unix variants based on the BSD distribution, such as Ultrix, SunOS, and early versions of AIX. Other software that uses the BSD license includes many of the networking utilities used by Linux distributions. A sample of the BSD license, from the source distribution of PostgreSQL, can be viewed online at `http://www.postgresql.org/idocs/index.php?ln8.html`.

Now that we have seen how open source and proprietary software differ, let's take a look at some of the pros and cons of open source software.

The Pros and Cons of Open Source Software

Although many advantages exist to using open source software, there are also some disadvantages. In this section, we cover both. Two advantages that we will consider are the following:

- Increased flexibility
- Access to developers

We also will look at two disadvantages, specifically the following:

- Project abandonment
- Lack of support

Other advantages and disadvantages exist that we could consider; however, these are the ones most often cited. So let's get started by taking a look at how open source increases your flexibility.

Increased Flexibility

When contrasted with closed source software, open source software projects are much more flexible. By this I mean that access to the source gives you some advantages that are not available in closed source software products. Let's take a look at a few of these areas of increased flexibility, such as:

- The capability to add missing features
- The capability to fix bugs in the software
- The capability to customize the software

The Capability to Add Missing Features

Imagine for a moment that you are working on a project developing a Web site. You are using an HTML editor that does just about everything you want but is missing one feature that would make your job much easier—a syntax checker. You have such a syntax checker, but because you cannot call it from your HTML editor, you must develop your HTML document, save it, exit from the editor, and then run the syntax checker on the resulting document. If the editor you are using is a closed source project, this is the end of the story. You must either live with this inconvenience or switch to another HTML editor that includes the feature you want. You could request that the software vendor add this feature for you, but unless this is a commonly requested feature, they can choose not to add it. In addition, they might want to use a syntax checker other than the one you prefer, making the feature, even if added, of less utility to you.

Now let's look at the situation if your editor was an open source software product. Because you have the source code and are permitted to modify it as you choose, you could solve your problem, assuming that you know how to program, by writing the code required to call your HTML syntax checker from within the HTML editor. Even if you can't program, you could hire a programmer to add this feature for you, or if you have programmers in your organization, they could add it. Yet another option would be to contact the software developer or development group responsible for this product and request that this feature be added. As you can see, having the source code gives you more options for solving this problem.

The Capability to Fix Software Bugs

All software is susceptible to defects—or as they are commonly referred to, bugs. There are many causes, and the more complex the software, the more bugs it is likely to have. This is true both of proprietary and open source software. The difference is that with closed source software, you are at the mercy of the software vendor to fix them. This assumes, of course, that they even acknowledge that the bug exists. Nothing is more frustrating than discovering a software bug in a program and finding that it is not acknowledged by the vendor. The only thing worse is having to wait for a fix that is promised in the next release.

Open source software is a totally different story. One of the tenets of open source development is to release early and often. This usually means that there will be multiple alpha and beta releases that are designed to shake out a lot of the bugs before a project is declared ready for regular use. To this end, mailing lists are established and bug-reporting mechanisms are defined to allow user feedback during the alpha and beta periods. Because the source code is open to all users, more opportunities exist to discover software defects. In addition, if you have programming experience, or someone in your organization does, you often can discover the source of the bug and correct it instead of having to wait for the software developers to find and correct it. Even if you are unable to fix the problem yourself, if you can locate the source of the problem and report it to the software developers, you might receive a fix or workaround more quickly than with proprietary software. An example of this can be seen with the Linux kernel. Some of the early Pentium processors contained a defect that would cause them to freeze when they received a certain byte sequence. This was the so-called f00f bug, named for the byte sequence that triggered the problem. Within a few hours of the discovery of this problem, the Linux developers had developed a fix for the problem, which was immediately distributed to the rest of the community. There are many more examples of this process, as well. One side effect of the open source model is that because it relies heavily on the ability of developers to collaborate with each other, mailing lists and newsgroups are usually formed to discuss the development of projects. These mailing lists and newsgroups are excellent resources for information on bugs that creep into the development process and fixes that become available. Even if you are not a developer, most of these lists allow you to subscribe and just *lurk* (follow the discussion without participating). You also can participate by providing detailed descriptions of bugs, or missing features, directly to the developers, and if you are a developer yourself, you can contribute code to the project.

The Capability to Customize the Software

Another advantage of having the source code is the capability to customize the software to meet a special need. Suppose that you are using a commercial product, such as a Web search tool designed for intranets. The software consists of some HTML pages along with some CGI programs that generate HTML containing the results of the search. Unless the programmers included the capability to modify the generated HTML, you will get results formatted in whatever fashion they wanted. This format might not fit well with the rest of your site design, but because you don't have the source code, you are stuck. Unless this was an application developed specifically for you, the developers are unlikely to modify the HTML generated by the CGI programs to match the particular style of your site. On the other hand, if your search engine was an open source project, you could modify the source code and make the generated HTML look however you prefer. This capability to customize software to meet your specific needs gives you a flexibility that is simply not available in closed source software products.

Access to Developers

Unlike most closed source software, open source software projects are created by individuals, or groups, to meet a personal need. Another motivating factor for most of these developers is to allow others the opportunity to use their software and to get feedback so that they can make the software better. To achieve this, the developers usually provide a way to communicate directly with them. This is very different from most software companies, who go to great lengths to shield their programmers from users. This direct access to developers means that if you have a problem or a feature request to make regarding an open source software package, you can send it directly to the person or persons who are responsible for adding such features or fixing bugs. The following is an example of how this access to developers can be an important advantage.

At a company where I once worked, we were using Linux as a platform for providing Web services. We discovered a problem with file transfers between Linux systems that was causing data corruption. Specifically, four null characters were injected into the data stream when large amounts of data were passed from one machine to another. Because the company I worked for had significant programming talent, we first attempted to solve this problem ourselves, but after six months of trying, we were getting nowhere. Most of the attempts up until I started looking at the problem were centered around the commands used to transfer the data; namely, the `rcp` command. I decided to try a different tack. I suspected that the problem might not be with the command being used, but with the TCP/IP stack itself. This hypothesis was confirmed when I found that not only did the `rcp` command suffer from this data corruption problem, but other file transfer methods did as well. I decided to see if I could isolate the problem, so I started building kernels with combinations of options different from the normal options we used when building kernels. After a few days of testing, I found that the problem went away if a single kernel option was turned off.

At this point, I decided to ask for help. I sent an electronic mail message to the kernel developers' mailing list describing the problem in detail. I received a reply in a matter of hours from one of the key Linux developers, Alan Cox, who sent me some diagnostic tools he had created, along with a request for additional data. Using the tools that Alan provided, we were able to further isolate the problem, and with this additional data, Alan was able to develop a fix that was incorporated into the next kernel release. If this same problem had occurred on a closed source operating system, I would have had to contact the technical support organization of the software vendor, demonstrate the problem to the satisfaction of the support person, and wait for it to be escalated to the development group, who may or may not have been able to provide me with a fix. Because I had direct access to the Linux developers through the mailing list, I was able to get a much quicker resolution to my problem.

Project Abandonment

One of the disadvantages of open source software is that because the projects are often initiated to meet some personal goal of the developer, the project stands the risk of being abandoned. Some of the common reasons for project abandonment are

- Competition from other projects.
- The developer's need for the software goes away.
- The developer loses interest in maintaining the project.

There might be other reasons, but let's take a look at these three.

Competition from Other Projects

One of the main reasons for project abandonment is that some other project comes along that does the same thing. This is not always the case. For example, there are many e-mail clients, several competing mail transport agents, and any number of FTP clients. However, if you look at personal finance software, you will find a very different story. One of the applications that has long been desired on Linux and other free OS platforms is an application for managing personal finances that can read files created by Quicken. At one time, several groups were working on creating such a piece of software. It turned out that the number of developers working on each of these competing projects was not sufficient to sustain development of all of them. As a result, the projects began merging until only a couple of them were left. Today, the primary project of this type is the GNUCash project. As a result of the mergers, it is the most fully featured of the projects that remain in the genre.

The Developer's Need Goes Away

As we have noted previously, many software projects in the Open Source world develop to satisfy a need for the developer. For example, Andrew Tridgell, the primary developer of Samba, had a need to share files between his Windows computer and a Unix system. As a result, he created a utility. When his need went away, he set the utility aside, but his need returned and this utility was revived as the Samba project.

The Developer Loses Interest

Another reason why software projects are started is to satisfy the intellectual curiosity of the developer. This is often the case with projects started by college students. They work feverishly on the project as long as there is something more to learn from it, but when the newness of the project wears off, they lose interest and move on to the next challenge. If the project is their work alone, and no one else has an interest in continuing it, the project can languish.

There are other reasons why projects are abandoned, but these are the most common. The risk that you, as an end user of the software, take is that a project on which you depend will be abandoned. In this case, you must either find a new piece of software to take the place of the one that was abandoned or take control of the project yourself and assume the maintenance.

Lack of Support

Another disadvantage of some open source projects is the lack of a formal support structure. This is not to say that you cannot get support for open source projects, but rather that the support channels are less formal. Open source projects often are supported only by the developers via personal e-mail. This might sound like a serious drawback; however, you will often find that developers are eager to talk to you and get your feedback, even if it is not entirely positive. For larger projects, a mailing list or newsgroup might be the primary support channel. In still other cases, such as the Apache Web server, the Linux operating system, and other widely used open source software projects, companies are formed that provide support for a fee. This is the exception rather than the rule, however, and this has been a common reason for not selecting open source projects over proprietary alternatives. This is changing as open source continues to make inroads into IT departments, and the number of support options increases.

Having taken a look at some of the advantages and disadvantages of open source software, let's now take a look at a few of the open source projects that will be used in Part II of this book to build our sample Internet sites.

Examples of Open Source Software

Many open source software packages are available that can be used to build your Internet site. In this section, we take a look at three sample OSS projects. We look at how they began, how they are supported by the developers, and where you can look to find out more details.

Apache

One of the best-known open source software projects, other than Linux, is the Apache Web server. The Apache Web server is a descendent of another open source software project created by researchers at the National Center for Supercomputer Applications (NCSA), the NCSA httpd software. The NCSA HTTP daemon was one of two popular HTTP servers in the early days of the Web. Because it was easier to configure and build from the source code than the other server, the CERN HTTP server, it quickly gained popularity and a community of users and developers formed. Among this group of developers, a patch set was created and the name of the Apache project is said to be a pun of sorts in that the original version was "a patchy" version of the NCSA server. Over time, the NCSA project that had created the original version was discontinued, and a group of developers of the patch set formed the Apache project. This group has continued to enhance the software and add features, and over time Apache has become the leading Web server in use on the Internet today. It has become so popular, in fact, that IBM has adopted it as one of its supported products and made it part of its Web offering. In addition, numerous companies, including some of the major Linux vendors such as Red Hat and VA Linux, offer support for the Apache Web server.

The premier Web site for Apache information, including information about the latest development releases, plans for future releases, and bug fixes is `http://www.apache.org/`. This is the official home page of the Apache project. If you are interested in the latest breaking news related to the Apache Web server, including support from third-party software vendors, press releases, and Apache-related security announcements, you can visit the ApacheToday Web site at `http://www.apachetoday.com/`.

MySQL

Another project that has only recently achieved full open source status is the MySQL database management system. MySQL is a relational database that implements a significant subset of the SQL language. The MySQL database system is similar to the Apache project in that it owes its existence to another software project, the mSQL database management system. The MySQL developers looked at the mSQL database and decided that although it was close to what they wanted, it did not quite meet their needs. They decided to reimplement the mSQL application programming interface (API), and the MySQL project was born. This database management system had the primary design goals of speed, robustness, and ease of use, and the reason for deciding to reimplement the mSQL API was to make it easier for third-party application developers to port their applications to both databases. MySQL, like the Apache project, has become one of the most popular open source projects on the Internet, and it is widely used as a database back end to Web sites, including many high-traffic sites, such as Slashdot and Freshmeat. Also like the Apache project, several companies have sprung up to offer support for the MySQL database, including TCX DataKonsult AB, the company that originally created the software. Because of its widespread popularity among Linux users, there also is support available from some of the larger Linux vendors, just as with Apache.

The home page for the MySQL database, where you can obtain source code and binaries for the current version of the software, is located at `http://www.mysql.com/`. In addition, pointers are there to third-party products that use the MySQL database engine or that provide a language binding not supported by the MySQL developers, such as Perl and Python interfaces. In addition, a mirror of the source code repository is maintained at the SourceForge Web site at `http://www.sourceforge.net/`.

PHP

One of the most popular modules for the Apache Web server is the PHP server-side scripting module. This module implements the PHP language, which at the time this book was written, is at version 4. PHP is rapidly replacing Perl as the language of choice for creating Web sites with dynamic content or that require a database back end. It includes support for accessing a number of different databases, including MySQL and PostgreSQL, two of the most popular database back ends in use for Web sites. PHP is used to create many of the most popular Web applications available on open source software sites such as Freshmeat and SourceForge, and the number and quality of these applications is growing daily. Part of the reason why PHP is so popular is that it is fairly easy to learn. It is similar to several other popular programming languages, including C, Java, and Perl. Some examples of popular Web sites that use PHP include Slashdot, SourceForge, Freshmeat, and many others. As the popularity of PHP has grown, more and more Web development companies are adding support for PHP to their offerings. As far as the language itself, PHP has gained support from Zend Technologies, which created the Zend engine—the core of the PHP language, and they offer commercial support for PHP.

If you are interested in learning more about PHP, an excellent resource is the PHPBuilder Web site located at `http://www.phpbuilder.com/`. This site includes source code and binaries for PHP, tutorials, and an online language reference. Other information is available from the Zend Technology Web site at `http://www.zend.com/`.

The Support Issue

To conclude our discussion, I would like to readdress the issue of support for open source software, specifically two aspects. The first is the idea of community support and its value. The second is a look at where you can obtain commercial support for open source software. So let's get started with a look at community support.

Community Support

A long tradition exists in the Open Source community of users helping users. To this end, mailing lists are created, newsgroups are formed, and user groups spring up. As an example, consider the Linux operating system. Within the first few months following the release of the first version of Linux, several mailing lists and newsgroups were devoted to users and developers. If you had a problem with the Linux operating system, you could send a description to these public forums and usually within a few hours, you could have a solution—or at least a response indicating that the problem was being looked at by developers. Examples of how quickly the developers can respond to a problem can be seen in the Linux response to a bug found in the Pentium processor. A byte sequence was found that resulted in the processor locking up. This is the so-called f00f bug, named after the byte sequence that triggered it. This defect meant that it was possible to mount a denial of service attack against any server that was based on the Pentium processor. Each of the operating system vendors responded, but none so quickly as Linux, which had a kernel patch available within approximately four hours of the announcement of the bug. This turnaround time is unheard of in the commercial software world, where it took days, weeks, or even months to release an official fix for this defect. Part of the reason why this response by the Linux developers was possible was that anyone could look at the Linux source code. Various people who were involved in Linux kernel development submitted fixes to the problem. The developers discussed the merits of each of the fixes and eventually came up with an official fix, which was incorporated into the next kernel release. In the meantime, the original fix was still available. This is an extreme example; however, it serves to illustrate how effective community support can be.

Another aspect of community support by the Open Source community is direct access to the developers. Unlike commercial software vendors, which often go to great lengths to insulate their developers from direct contact with customers, open source developers usually are directly accessible to the end users of their software. Part of the reason for this is that one form of payment that open source developers receive is status among their peers. Open source developers want people to use their software, and therefore are willing to directly interact with them to gain a reputation as a good programmer. This applies to projects of all sizes. It is not uncommon for end users to send an e-mail directly to Linus Torvalds or any of the other kernel developers and get a response. In fact, this is one of the purposes of maintaining the Linux kernel mailing list. Contrast this to the developers of the Windows 2000 kernel, most of whom are unknown to the user community. If you have an issue with Windows 2000, you must go through the Microsoft support organization, and whether the developers ever see it is a mystery.

Yet another source of community support can be seen in user groups. Users of software have often found that having the capability to talk to other users is a valuable asset. To that end, they self-organize into user groups. In the case of Linux, these are known as LUGs, and they exist all over the world. If you are a Linux user, you can attend these meetings, and through discussions with other users, receive help with problems. In addition to these types of user groups, you often can find special interest groups, or SIGs, that are part of other groups, such as an application SIG within a PC user group.

You might be wondering how useful this type of support is. The problem, according to some people, is that because no company is behind these support channels, there is no guarantee that you will get the help you need. This can be true of commercial software vendors, as well, if your problem cannot be reproduced by a software vendor's support organization. It is important to note that even without a company backing support for Linux, the Linux community was given an award for the best customer support by one of the popular trade magazines.

To get a better feel for how to go about getting support for open source software from the community of users and developers, take a look at an example. Suppose that you are using the editor Emacs and discover that it is corrupting your files. One of the first things you should do is to determine whether this problem is reproducible. Assuming that you can reproduce the problem, what do you do next? The first thing that you might do is a Web search to determine if anyone else is having the same problem. One of the places you can conduct your search is at Google.com, which maintains an archive of Usenet newsgroups and allows you to search them. You also might see if you can locate a mailing list related to Emacs and see if you can browse old messages on it. If a mailing list exists, you also could subscribe to it and post a description of the problem you are having. If you do so, be sure to include as much information relevant to the reproduction of the error as possible. A final option is to find out who the current maintainer of the software is and e-mail them directly. This is generally a good tactic for smaller software projects, but for large packages, such as Perl or Emacs, this might not work. Finally, see if you can locate a FAQ, or frequently asked questions, list. Chances are that if you are having a problem, others are, too, and enough of them might have asked for a fix to make it a FAQ.

If you are still not comfortable with support from an informal group of users, there are other options. Let's discuss the opposite end of the spectrum—support from commercial sources.

Commercial Support for OSS

If you are familiar with the tenets of the free software movement, you are aware that one of the ways in which people are encouraged to make a living from software, in contrast to selling licenses, is to provide support. To this end, numerous companies exist that do just that. Some of these companies include the Linux vendors. Each Linux vendor, including Red Hat, Caldera, VA Linux, TurboLinux, SuSE, and Corel, offers support for the operating system and the software packages that are included in their Linux distributions. In addition, many independent contractors can be found that specialize in particular software packages, such as MySQL, Apache, and others. Information on these sources of support normally can be found at the home page of the software project. This is certainly true of projects such as Apache, Squid, and MySQL.

Summary

In this chapter, we have taken a look at some of the differences between open source software and proprietary software. We have looked at these differences by studying the development model, some of the different licenses used, and the advantages and disadvantages of open source. We also have taken a look at a few open source projects that show the effectiveness of the open source model. Finally, we have taken a look at how effective community support of software can be, and we reemphasized that if you take the time to look, commercial support is indeed available from a number of sources.

So You Want to Build an Internet Site

CHAPTER

3

IN THIS CHAPTER

- Reasons for Building an Internet Site 44
- Maintaining Internet Sites 46
- Developing In-house Solutions Versus Outsourcing 50

ιding this book, you are probably at least considering creating an online presence nization. In this chapter, we examine some of the reasons for building an Internet ıt options for maintaining your site after it is built, and then we look at the d disadvantages of developing the site yourself versus outsourcing. So let's get started with a look at some of the reasons for building an Internet site.

Reasons for Building an Internet Site

There are any number of reasons for building an Internet site. Individuals build sites to show off their pets, their kids, or their cars. They build sites about their likes, their dislikes, and their favorite cartoon characters. For organizations, however, the reasons usually fall into one of three major categories. These categories are

- Marketing
- Customer convenience
- Expanding beyond local boundaries

In this section, we take a look at each of these reasons and discuss how an Internet site can be used to achieve them.

Marketing

One of the primary reasons for an organization to create an Internet site is to promote or market something. This something might be anything, from tangible products, such as books or software, that you might find at an online store. It could also be an idea or political agenda, such as those you might find at the site for a political party or community group. It could even be to market yourself, such as a home page on which you outline your interests and experience. Regardless of the item, person, or ideas being showcased, the objective is the same—to make people aware of its merits. This is the heart of marketing, and there are a number of advantages to using the Internet as a marketing vehicle. Some of these advantages of creating an effective Internet site, which is not guaranteed, are

- Lower cost than other traditional media
- Greater availability to potential customers
- Availability to a wider audience

One of the key advantages is that creating an Internet site can be significantly less expensive than traditional media. If you are able to create your own Web pages and have low space requirements, a Web site can cost as little as a couple of hundred dollars per year. Of course, if you are building a major site for an international corporation to promote your products or ideas, the cost can be significantly higher. Another advantage is that unlike traditional media, which is usually available for a limited time, a Web site is available twenty-four hours a day, seven days a week. If part of your marketing plan is to run an advertisement in a magazine, for example, the life of the ad is the length of time that the issue of the magazine containing your advertisement is current. The Internet has no such time limits. The final advantage is the capability to make your message available to people all over the globe. Unlike other forms of marketing, the Internet enables you to easily get your message out to people who are not geographically nearby, even if your marketing budget is limited. As the number of people with access to the Internet continues to grow, this becomes an even greater advantage.

As you can see, the Internet can be quite effective as a marketing tool. This assumes, of course, that people are able to find your site and are receptive to the message that you present to them. This is not as easy as it sounds, but with some careful planning, some research into how to make sure that people looking for what you are marketing, and a little luck, you can ensure that your site appeals to the desired audience. Now let's take a look at another reason why people create Internet sites—customer convenience.

Customer Convenience

People today demand instant gratification. They want the convenience of pharmacies open twenty-four hours a day, news on demand, and even hardware and home improvement stores open all night. The Internet is an easy way to facilitate this desire for instant gratification. For example, if you want to order the latest novel from your favorite author on the day that it becomes available, you can choose from any number of online book stores and order it at 12:01 a.m. on the day it is released. This is an important reason for creating an Internet site. If you are selling products in an international market, the Internet provides you with a virtual storefront that is open twenty-four hours a day, seven days a week. Customers no longer have to wait for your store hours or for operators to be standing by to take their order. They can log on and access your site when the mood strikes them. When you compare the cost of having people available around the clock to the cost of running a Web site, you will see that the Internet option can be much more economical. By making your products, services, or message available via the Internet, you are giving your audience the ultimate convenience.

Expanding Beyond Local Boundaries

Yet another reason, which we have already touched on, is the capability to expand your reach beyond local boundaries. Consider the case of a small retail business. Without an Internet presence, this small retailer might—if hugely successful—become known in the city in which the retailer is located and in nearby cities. Based on this success, if the business expands to include catalog-based mail order, it might be able to reach a much wider audience, but the cost might be a prohibiting factor. Consider the alternative case. This small retailer creates a Web site and begins to accept orders online. He or she registers the site with the major search engines so that people searching for the company's products can find the site. By this act, the retailer has expanded the potential market beyond the local boundaries at a relatively low cost. And as the number of people with Internet access continues to grow, this argument for maintaining an Internet presence becomes more compelling. This is not to imply that simply creating a web site will make your small business a success in markets outside your local area, but the potential is there.

Maintaining Internet Sites

One of the primary considerations when you're deciding to create an Internet site is what it is going to take to maintain it after you have built it. In this section, we consider your two basic options: to use a hosting service, which maintains the servers on your behalf and you worry only about the content, or hosting your servers yourself, where you are concerned not only with the content on the Internet servers, but with the Internet servers themselves. We will take a look at the trade-offs involved with each option. Let's start with a look at using a hosting service.

Using a Hosting Service

These days, outsourcing is usually considered the way to go on many things, including hosting Internet services. As a result, you have many options if you do not want to host your own Internet servers. Most ISPs, especially those that cater to business customers, offer hosting services. What this means is that to run your Internet servers, the ISP provides space on a system that they own. It is possible to run a Web server, an FTP server, an electronic mail server, or even an application server without having to purchase a single system—and there are advantages to doing this. The primary advantages are reduced cost and reduced staffing requirements. Because the hosting service provider can host multiple clients on a single system, it can do so cost effectively. It is not unheard of for a single-server system to host thousands of domains, providing Web services to each of them. If you are a small organization with limited requirements, this might be a good option for you. In addition, because you don't own the servers, you don't have to hire the system administrators who are required to maintain them. However, the following are some drawbacks that exist to hosting services:

- Hosting services typically have limits on the amount of space you can use on their systems.
- Servers are typically shared with other customers.
- You are limited by the hosting service's choice of operating system and tools.
- You might be restricted from adding features to your site until the software is approved by the hosting service.

Let's examine each of these drawbacks in a little more detail and then you can decide if using a hosting service is the right choice for your organization.

Space Limitations

Many Internet service providers offer hosting services as part of the package when you select their service. For example, a local ISP in the town where I live offers Web-hosting services that include 10 e-mail accounts, 100MB of disk space, and 4GB of bandwidth for about $50 a month. Additional bandwidth costs extra, as does additional disk space. This might seem like a lot of space, but when you start to add up the amount of space required to run a site containing dynamic content, such as user forums, files for download, and so on, you can quickly exceed this. Of course, if you are just running a site to campaign for a local political candidate or you sell a limited number of products, these space limitations might work fine for you. In addition, due to the highly competitive nature of the web hosting business, these costs vary and have come down substantially in the past few years.

Shared Servers

Another potential drawback is that at most hosting services, you will not be given your own system but will share it with other customers of the service. You might be thinking that this is not a problem, but consider the impact on your Web site if a CGI script run by another customer on your server runs amok, if they become the target of a denial-of-service attack, or crackers get into their system. All these scenarios can mean downtime for your site. Also consider that software upgrades required to make your site more useful can conflict with another customer's requirements.

Limited OS and Tools Choice

The final drawback is that you might be limited by the hosting service's choice of operating system and tools. Most hosting services offer a limited choice of operating systems and tools to their customers. For example, your hosting service might host all Web pages on Windows NT or Windows 2000. If you develop your Web site using Linux and open source tools, you might have a hard time dealing with this limitation. The hosting service might offer other operating systems as an option; however, you might still find that the OS chosen by them lacks features that you believe are necessary. Finally, you might find that the choice of tools provided by the hosting service does not match your needs. For example, if you developed a prototype for your site using the latest version of PHP and MySQL, taking advantage of some recent features such as replication or transaction support in MySQL, you must ensure that the version of these tools provided by the hosting service supports these same features, or you could be forced to remove desired features to make it work on their systems.

Limits on Adding Desired Features

In addition to the limits just described, you might find that your hosting service also limits the addition of features until they have approved them. For example, if you wanted to implement a CGI script written in Perl to allow your users to send you feedback by electronic mail, many hosting services would require a security audit of the code prior to implementing it or simply would not allow it to be implemented at all. The same is true of features, such as search engines, forums, and features that you might want to make your site more compelling.

These limitations may not affect you, and a hosting service might be the way for you to go; however, you should consider the trade-offs carefully and possibly consider the other option—hosting it yourself.

Hosting It Yourself

For small organizations, hosting your own Internet services can be more trouble than it is worth, but if you want absolute control, it might be the way to go. You will have to consider many things if you choose to host your own Internet servers. Some of the factors that you should consider before making the decision to self host are

- Self hosting is more expensive than a hosting service.
- You must maintain and upgrade all equipment that powers your Internet site.

Let's take a look at the factors individually and then look at an option that helps to minimize the impact of these factors.

Self Hosting Is Expensive

The cost of hosting your own Internet servers includes many costs that are simply not present if you use a hosting service. These costs can be broken down into three basic categories:

- Hardware costs
- Maintenance costs
- Communication costs

Under the category of hardware costs are the costs of computer systems, network hardware—including routers, switches, and hubs—power management equipment such as uninterruptible power supplies, and other miscellaneous equipment, such as racks, power strips, monitors, keyboards, and the like. Depending on your needs, this cost can run into the millions of dollars.

Another category of costs is maintenance costs. These costs include the cost of repairing hardware that fails, upgrades to hardware, and also the cost of the people required to do this maintenance. The people cost tends to be less with Linux/Unix systems; however, they can still be quite substantial. If you remember our discussion in Chapter 1, "Why Should Your Company Leverage Linux?," you might recall that a Linux/Unix administrator commands a higher salary than administrators for Windows systems. How then can the people costs be less? They can be less because it usually takes fewer people to administer a Linux/Unix-based site than it does to administer an equivalent Windows-based site. Some estimates are that it takes up to four times as many people to manage a Windows site as it does a Linux/Unix-site with an equivalent number of systems. You will require system administrators to maintain the infrastructure and operators to ensure that the applications running on that infrastructure keeps running as designed by the development staff.

A final category of costs to consider when making the decision whether to self host is communications costs. These costs include the recurring costs of the communications services provided by your ISP and the local phone company. Costs such as the cost of a T1 line—or more likely, multiple T1 lines—can be significant. In the case of a small site, you could probably get away with using a much cheaper DSL or cable modem connection; however, this cost can still be substantial. This is because you could be forced to pay a premium based on the number of machines you are connecting to the Internet or to have static IP addresses assigned to your site. In addition, you will require equipment to connect these communication lines to your router, adding to your hardware costs.

Equipment Maintenance Issues

As mentioned in the discussion on costs associated with hosting your own site, you must consider maintenance costs. In addition to those costs, you also must consider the other aspect of maintenance—namely, the time you will spend. As mentioned previously, you will need system administrators to maintain your Web site. Depending on the nature of your Internet servers, these administrators might need to be on call 24 hours a day. One important consideration is that you hire sufficient staff to allow for a rotation of these types of duties. Failure to staff to appropriate levels leads to employee discontent and high turnover in the positions. Given the difficulty of finding qualified staff in today's job market, this can be an expensive proposition. In addition, you should plan on staffing operators to maintain the applications that run on your Internet servers. These operators would be responsible for staffing the network operation center where your site is monitored. They would also serve as a first line of response so that the more experienced system administrators are not constantly having to deal with interruptions. If your system administrators are constantly called on to deal with interruptions, you will find that they have lower job satisfaction and that projects that require their experience and skills will be pushed back constantly.

Having examined these factors, you might think that self hosting is not for you. However, an option is available that can help overcome some of these factors. This option is using a colocation provider. A colocation provider is a company that takes care of most of the infrastructure requirements for hosting Internet servers. Common services provided include

- A secured facility
- Power redundancy options
- Communications infrastructure
- Network monitoring services

For example, a local colocation provider where I live offers clients rack space in its facility. As part of its service, guards are on duty twenty-four hours a day, and the company provides badge and biometric access control methods, as well. The company has multiple high-bandwidth connections to several Internet backbone providers, providing redundant communication channels. The entire facility is monitored from the network operation center by a staff of network professionals. In addition, in the event of an extended power event, all the power provided to clients is backed by an industrial grade UPS with back-up generators. By hosting your Internet servers at a colocation facility, you can reduce your costs because you don't have to foot the entire cost for the communications line and the power management equipment. Most good colocation providers provide some level of network monitoring as part of their service. In addition, you don't have to pay the cost of building out a machine room to house your servers.

There are, of course, trade-offs. Because you own the servers, you are responsible for their maintenance and upgrades. Self hosting is also more expensive than using a hosting service. However, if you are a large organization with high-availability needs and a significant part of your business depends on your Internet presence, self hosting is almost always the way to go.

Now that we have taken a look at the issue of using a hosting service or self hosting, we can move on to the next topic—the decision whether to develop your own Internet services or to outsource their development to a external contractor or Web development company.

Developing In-house Solutions Versus Outsourcing

If you are reading this book, you have most likely already decided to build your own Internet servers instead of outsourcing their development. However, it can still be useful to look at outsourcing part of the development effort, such as the development of high-availability or load-balancing capabilities. In this section we take a look at developing in-house versus outsourcing.

Rolling Your Own Solution

If you have decided to build your own Internet server, especially if you are going to build it using open source software, there are several factors to consider. These factors include finding developers to help develop your site using open source software and finding support for parts of your solution, such as Apache or MySQL.

When selecting developers to assist you in development of your Internet servers, you might want to start by looking to the open source community. You might find that the developers who created the software you are using to build your site are available for hire. This is true because many developers in the open source community are college students. Even if you cannot hire the developers of open source projects you select as part of your Internet service, it is still a good idea to select developers who are familiar with open source. In doing so, you will find it easier to interact with the open source developers if your own developers come from the same community.

If you are building your Internet site in support of a commercial entity, you will probably be concerned with support for the products you select. For some of the major pieces of technology selected, such as Apache or MySQL, this is no problem; numerous commercial support options are available, as you saw in Chapter 2, "What Makes Open Source So Compelling?" On the other hand, as we discussed in Chapter 2, you should be prepared for a lack of formal support for some of the software you select if you use an open source software solution.

Outsourcing Internet Site Development

Your other alternative for building your Internet site is to outsource it. You might be saying to yourself, "If I am going to outsource the development of my Internet site, why am I reading this book?" Fortunately, outsourcing is not an all-or-nothing proposition. You could, for example, choose to use existing applications to construct your site and use your in-house staff to make customizations to meet your particular needs. To meet your scalability or high-availability needs, you could choose to rely on the expertise of one of the large Linux vendors, such as VA Linux, Penguin Computing, or Red Hat. In this way, you gain the advantage of having people with extensive experience in these areas while not having to outsource the entire project. In addition, even if you decide to develop your solution in-house, you could use these companies to review your design and make recommendations.

The following are some of the factors to consider when selecting a company to outsource your Internet site development, especially when you are using primarily open source software:

- What level of experience does the company have with open source software?
- Do the developers at the company have specific experience with the open source software products that will be used to build your site?
- Is there an existing relationship between the developers at the company and the open source community?

We will examine each of these questions and see why it is important to consider these factors if you decide to outsource part or all of your Internet site development.

Experience with Open Source Software

One of the problems with consultants is that often they are also value-added resellers, or VARs, for software. As a result, they have a vested interest in getting you to purchase this software along with their services as a consultant. You will often find that these VARs are resistant to open source software solutions because it means less profit for them. In selecting a consultant to assist you in the development of your Internet site built using open source software, you should check to see if they have a history of using open source solutions. You might do this by searching of USENET archives or mailing lists to see if they participate in the discussions of the open source packages you plan to use. You should also ask whether they can provide examples of their work with the types of products that you are considering.

Experience with Specific Open Source Software

Suppose you select Apache as your Web-serving platform and decide to seek outside assistance in configuring and optimizing your installation to get the best performance possible. In this case, it makes sense to seek out a company with experience using Apache on your chosen operating system platform. The problem is that it has become too common for people to claim that as a general consultant, they have the requisite experience. A good way to avoid this problem is to ensure that you request and check references from previous clients of this consultant. Another way is to look at the Apache Web site, where a number of companies are listed that provide support and consulting for the Apache Web server. In addition, most of the large Linux vendors offer consulting and support services as well, in large part because of the popularity of Linux as a Web-serving platform. This is just one example. However, the same principle applies to other software products.

Relationship Between a Company and the Open Source Community

Another good indicator of whether a consulting company will be a good choice for helping to build your Internet site is when a good relationship exists between the company and the open source community. If a consulting firm works with open source software, it is often the case that they will have worked to establish a relationship with the developers of the open source products that they typically use. For example, if a consulting firm claims experience with the Linux Virtual Server patches, it would probably be known on the mailing list maintained by that community of developers. It is also a good sign if one or more of the consultants had contributed patches or bug reports back to the developers of the software. This usually can be verified by checking mailing-list archives or by querying the open source developers directly. Companies that use open source software but that do not have this type of relationship with the development community are often those who are either not very experienced with open source or who have in some way antagonized the community. In these cases, your selection of them to assist you can actually hinder your efforts at obtaining support from the community if the need arises.

Again, if you are reading this book, you might have already decided to do all the development of your Internet site yourself. However, keep in mind that if your site is likely to grow and you are concerned about scalability and high availability, it might be worthwhile to consider the services of a consultant—if not to actually do the work, to provide design help to get you started.

Summary

In this chapter, we have taken a brief look at why you might want to create an Internet site. Some of the reasons we discussed include the fact that the Internet can be an effective marketing tool, it can allow you to expand your business beyond local boundaries, and it offers convenience for your customers. We then considered the issue of maintaining that site, looking at the comparative advantages of using a hosting service versus self hosting. Finally, we took a look at the issue of developing your Internet site in-house versus using consultants and outsourcing that development. Hopefully, you now have the information you need to make the decisions on whether you really want to create an Internet site and whether to host it yourself, or to let someone else host it for you.

Building Different Kinds of Internet Sites

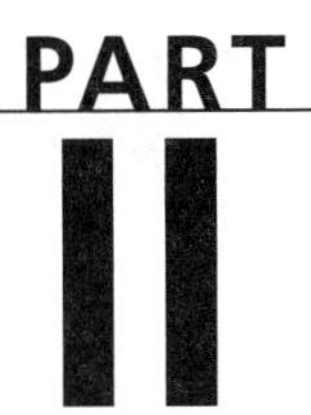

IN THIS PART

4 Content and Media Sites 57

5 The Telecommuter's Journal 71

6 Community Sites 103

7 The Del Valle Junior High Parent/Teacher/Student Organization 115

8 E-commerce Sites 161

9 E-commerce Sites: Two Case Studies 175

Content and Media Sites

CHAPTER

4

IN THIS CHAPTER

- Characteristics of a Content and Media Site 58
- Desirable Features 59
- Some Tools to Consider 63

One of the common types of Internet sites you will find these days is what I refer to as a content and media site. Sites that fall into this category are sites that have as their primary goal the promulgation of information, such as online magazines. In this chapter, we discuss the characteristics of sites of this type and then take a look at some of the open source software tools that are available to help build sites of this type. This chapter is a lead in to Chapter 5, "The Telecommuter's Journal," in which we use some of the tools discussed here to build a sample online magazine.

Characteristics of a Content and Media Site

As stated, the content and media site is primarily focused on the dissemination of information. Some examples include online sites for newspapers, such as the *New York Times* at `http://www.nytimes.com/`, or sites such as the one at `http://www.cnn.com/`, the site for the Cable News Network. These sites all share some common characteristics, and in this section, we take a look at them to determine the types of tools we will need to build a content and media site. Some of these characteristics are

- Content that is largely static
- A need for frequent updates
- A need to archive historical content

Now let's take a look at each of the characteristics in more detail to see how they apply to the creation of a content and media site.

Static Content

Most content and media sites share the characteristic of content that is largely static. By this I mean that the content is not generated on-the-fly by a script or other mechanism. What you find is content, such as that in a newspaper or a magazine article, which, once prepared, is not changed substantially at a later time. For these types of sites, the pages can be stored in a database or as flat files, depending on your preference. There are advantages to both approaches. One of the advantages of storing the pages in a database is that it can make searches easier. On the other hand, depending on the database, these searches can be quite expensive, and storage in flat files might be a better option because this allows the use of text search engines.

Frequent Updates

Another characteristic of content and media sites is the need for frequent updates. For a site of this type to be successful, the content must change periodically. Who would want to revisit an online magazine that never came out with a new issue? Likewise, who would visit a news media site that never published new articles? Obviously, the answer to both of these questions is no one. It is, therefore, critical to the successful creation of a content and media site that you provide for updates to the pages. As we consider tools for the creation of a content and media site later in this chapter, we will be looking for this capability as a feature.

Archived Content

Another characteristic of content and media sites that most successful sites share is that they archive their content for some period to allow users to go back to old content. For online magazines, this can be done by providing the previous two or three back issues. Alternatively, sites could use a database to store a much larger set of content that is searchable. Examples of sites that do this include Deja.com at `http://www.deja.com/usenet/`. This site indexes Usenet newsgroups in a searchable database. In this case, the content is the text of the newsgroup messages. What gives this site value is the archiving of old content and the capability to search this content. If this site did not archive the content, little audience interest would exist.

Desirable Features

Having taken a look at some of the common characteristics of content and media sites, let's now take a look at the features that are desirable for these types of sites. You might wonder what the distinction is between characteristics and features. For purposes of this discussion, features are implemented and they result in a site having specific characteristics. A few of the features that are desirable for content and media sites include

- A document management system
- One or more user-feedback mechanisms
- The capability to search content

We will take a look at each of these features and see how they help to ensure that your content and media site exhibits all the characteristics appropriate to a site of this type. In this section, we will not be looking at tools that implement these features, but we'll focus on why these features are desirable.

A Document Management System

One of the characteristics we mentioned for content and media sites is frequent updates. To facilitate this, one of the desirable features of any content and media site is a document management system. Such a system should allow document authors to submit new documents. It also should allow for updates to these documents by editorial or content approval staff and have an archive feature to keep track of changes over time. In addition, it should have the capability to prevent multiple users from stepping on each other, either through the use of a locking mechanism or through a method of identifying and merging changes from multiple people working on the same document. This capability is especially important if you have a lot of people working on the content for your site.

Having described the desired features of a document management system, let's examine a couple of reasons why a document management system is desirable.

- It provides content authors and editors with a consistent mechanism for handling documents.
- It maintains a history of revisions to documents.
- It provides a centralized repository independent of the site where documents can be retrieved in the event of a system failure and that can be backed up instead of backing up the Web servers.

Each of these reasons assumes that you have selected an appropriate document management system. If the document management system you select does not fit these reasons, you probably should consider selecting a different one. To see why these reasons are important, let's consider an example.

A Consistent Mechanism for Document Handling

As an author, I have had occasion to contribute articles to Web sites for publication. In the most recent case, I created a document that I had to submit to a technical editor, who then had to pass it on to a development editor, who then passed it back to me for review and correction. After my corrections were made, I passed it back to the development editor who, assuming no more corrections were to be made, passed it to a content manager, who approved it for publication. This whole process was accomplished using e-mail, and I had no way of knowing where in the process the document was without bugging the coordinating editor, whose function it was to track this document through the cycle. This process was further complicated because each of us used a different mail client with different capabilities. In more than one case, passing the document through the mail system resulted in minor document corruption. If a document management system had been employed instead, each of us could have used a common method to access the document and avoid the corruption problem.

A History of Revisions

Another problem I was faced with was determining where in the editing cycle my article was at any given time. The coordinating editor, who would poll each of the people in the chain whenever I asked him where the document was, also experienced this problem. A good document management system keeps track of this information as part of the revision history functionality. It also keeps track of who is currently working on a document. If the site where I submitted the article had used a document management system, I could have simply queried the system to determine who had the document checked out, and when they were done with it, I could have read comments on any changes made. Given the document flow I described previously, I could have used this information to see what the technical editor thought of my article when he handed it off to the development editor, and I could have prepared for any changes that I might have to make. This would have saved time because while the development editor was checking for grammar and structure problems, I could have been gathering the information required to correct deficiencies found by the technical editor.

A Central Repository for Documents

In addition to writing, I am a system administrator for Unix and Linux systems. As such, one of my responsibilities is backing up important data so that it can be recovered in the event of a hard-drive failure or other catastrophe. For this reason, I think that the document management system should be independent of the site accessed by visitors. If you keep all your documents in a central repository independent of the site, you only have to back up this repository. Then all your documents are protected, along with the revision history, and you don't have to back up your Web servers. This is not such a big deal if you have only a single Web server. However, if you have multiple Web servers, each of which serves a different part of your site content, this can be a big win.

User-Feedback Mechanisms

Another characteristic of successful content and media sites is a mechanism for your visitors to provide you with feedback. For example, sites such as ZDNet (`http://www.zdnet.com/`), Linux Today (`http://linuxtoday.com/`), and other news sites and online magazines include ways for visitors to the site to comment on articles and talk back to the authors of articles. This capability to talk back to authors and express their agreement or disagreement is very attractive to readers of online magazines and news sites and is one way to draw users to your site. In fact, these features are so popular that sites exist where user debate and discussion is the key attraction of the site, such as Slashdot (`http://www.slashdot.org/`).

Different types of feedback mechanisms include mail forms, such as a CGI script, that send private messages to authors or editors, forums where visitors can discuss the content at your site, or mailing lists where people can use their preferred e-mail software to have discussions with each other and where you can announce new features of your site.

As we stated earlier, allowing users to express their opinions through some feedback mechanism is very attractive to readers of online magazines and news sites. There are many reasons for this, but two that come to mind immediately are

- People are opinionated and love to share their opinions with others.
- Allowing people to express themselves makes them feel like part of a community.

Everyone Has an Opinion

People are opinionated—some more so than others. They call in to radio and television programs, write letters to the editor of their favorite magazines and newspapers, and even stand on street corners and rant and rave at passersby. User-feedback mechanisms allow people to express these opinions and get up on a virtual soapbox to be heard.

To see just how popular public forums are, consider the explosion of Usenet. Before the creation of the Web, one of the ways in which users of the Internet expressed themselves was through Usenet. Usenet is a system of public forums, called newsgroups, on just about any subject you can imagine. When it started, relatively few newsgroups existed, partly because relatively few people had access to the Internet; but as the number of people with access to the Internet grew, so did Usenet. Currently, more than 50,000 forums make up Usenet, with more being added all the time. Some of these newsgroups have thousands of people participating in them. User-feedback features of Web sites serve the same purpose and are an easy way to improve the dynamics of your site.

Feeling Like Part of a Community

User-feedback mechanisms are also popular because they let people feel that they are part of a community and that their opinions matter. You, as a site developer, may not care at all what your site visitors think. However, by allowing them an opportunity to feel that you do, you build loyalty to your site and people will come back again and again. You might even find that people are more interested in the responses to your articles than the articles themselves. By interacting with your visitors through forums or mailing lists, you can learn what they like and dislike about your site and get valuable information that will make your site more successful.

Search Capabilities

A final capability that your content and media site should have is the capability to search the site for content. This feature should, at a minimum, enable users to search the current content of the site. However, to be most compelling, the search capabilities also should allow users to search for old articles. This implies that you would keep old issues of your magazine online or that articles at your news site are archived in some manner. As we stated earlier in this chapter, this is a desirable feature to have and one that your visitors will greatly appreciate. One thing to consider, however, is that you might not want to keep your old article archive on the front-line Web servers because the search functionality can be costly from a performance standpoint. When we discuss a sample content and media site in Chapter 5, we take this fact into account in the site design. The other decision that must be made is whether to archive feedback from your users and to make that searchable. If you plan on doing so, you should clearly state this fact on your site and possibly incorporate a mechanism for users to indicate whether they agree with this policy and if not, to reject their feedback.

Have you ever read an article at a site and wanted to read it again later, only to find that it is no longer available? If so, you are not alone. On sites that lack them, search capabilities are usually the most requested feature.

Some Tools to Consider

Now that we have covered the features that our content and media site should have, we'll consider some specific tools that can be used to implement these features. We will look at each of the feature categories and cover a couple of available open source tools that we could use to build our content and media site. Commercial alternatives also exist that could be used to implement these features; however, we will not be covering them here.

Document Management Tools

As we have already discussed, a document management tool is a desirable feature to have for a content and media site because it provides the people working on the documents with a consistent method to exchange documents. It also provides a mechanism for tracking where in the edit/publish cycle the document currently is, and it makes it easier to manage backups and other administrative tasks if all your documents are maintained in a document repository. Now let's take a look at a couple of tools that could be used to implement this feature:

- The Concurrent Versioning System (CVS)
- The Document Manager

CVS as a Document Management System

One software package you could use to manage documents on your Web site is the Concurrent Versioning System (CVS). This might sound odd because CVS is normally thought of as a source-code revision-control system. However, if you think about it, the documents for your Web site are actually source code written in the HTML (or PHP or Perl) language, so using CVS is not such a stretch. The advantage of using CVS as a document management system is that it comes with just about every Linux distribution, and clients are available for most popular client operating systems, including Windows, Macintosh, and just about every Unix variant in existence. The disadvantage of using CVS is that your contributors to the Web site are probably unfamiliar with it unless they are programmers, and they might find that it is difficult to learn. Another disadvantage is that if you are using a binary format for documents, such as Microsoft Word or StarOffice, you must make sure that everyone accessing the documents in the repository knows how to make CVS deal with binary files. If you fail to do this, you might inadvertently corrupt the documents.

When considering CVS as a document management tool, you should keep the following items in mind. First, CVS may seem unnatural to your authors and editorial staff because it is project oriented. This is not a serious problem. However, it does mean that you must be prepared to properly train people to use CVS. One suggestion is to make each issue of your content and media site a project, so that people are encouraged to deal with all the files for an "issue" as a unit. Another feature of CVS that can be a problem is that CVS allows multiple people to check out the same documents simultaneously. This might sound like a problem, but CVS has the capability to merge changes from multiple sources and to flag conflicts that it cannot automatically resolve, so that a person can make the decision as to which change takes precedence. This capability to allow multiple people to work on the document simultaneously can be a big win, especially if you have to have multiple editors looking at different facets of the documents. For example, if documents are required to be reviewed for technical content, grammar and spelling, and legal issues, a person from each area could check out the documents simultaneously and when done could merge their comments. Because they are addressing different areas, this would allow the document flow to be streamlined with little possibility of conflict.

One final thing to remember about CVS is that people must be encouraged to make sure that their local copies of documents are periodically synchronized with the central repository so that backups are effective in preventing the loss of work by the writing and editorial staff.

Document Manager

Another option that you might consider for your online magazine is called Document Manager. Document Manager is a system written in PHP that permits you to share files via a Web interface that allows for checking out, checking in, and updating documents using a Web interface. If you choose, you can use Document Manager in conjunction with an SSL-enabled Apache server, and it uses standard Apache authentication to control access to the documents under the control of the software.

To use Document Manager, you need to install an Apache Web server and PHP version 4 (it doesn't work with PHP version 3). Installation is very straightforward and basically involves unpackaging the tar file, creating a couple of symbolic links, and running a script to add users to the system. The system allows you to create new documents, update documents, attach notes to a document, and create new directories to hold documents. To ensure that multiple people don't check out the same document at the same time, locks are used, and to prevent people from checking out a file and holding a lock forever, an option is provided to allow for locks to be broken. Figure 4.1 shows a screen shot of the directory interface presented when you log in to Document Manager. For more information regarding Document Manager, you can visit the product home page at `http://www.rot13.org/~dpavlin/docman.html`.

One of the advantages of using Document Manager rather than CVS is that it is much easier to learn. In addition, because it is Web based, you do not need to install a special client software utility to interact with the repository. A disadvantage is that it does require you to use PHP version 4, which might conflict with other PHP applications at your site if any of them require PHP version 3 or earlier.

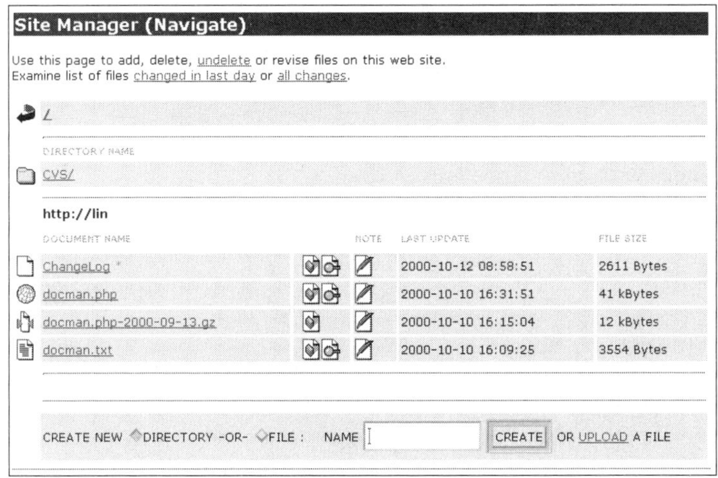

FIGURE 4.1
Document Manager directory interface.

User-Feedback Tools

When selecting user-feedback tools, you must first decide on how you want to interact with your site visitors. Some of your options include mailing lists, forums, or bulletin board services. We will cover each of these categories and let you decide. Remember that you are not limited to a single category and that it might be desirable to have more than one, depending on how much interaction you want to have on your site.

Mailing-List Management Software

One of the easiest ways to interact with your users is through a mailing list. The beauty of a mailing list is the flexibility it allows you. For example, depending on the nature of your site, you could use the mailing list to keep visitors up-to-date on when new issues or features are added to your site. You also could also use it to allow users to communicate with each other. Some of the things to consider when you're deciding whether to run a mailing list include the following:

- Mailing lists are low maintenance; however, they are not no maintenance.
- You should never automatically subscribe visitors to your Web site to a mailing list. Give them the option to subscribe, with the default being no.
- If you use your mailing list to make announcements about the site, make sure that you give people the option to receive text-only mail. HTML mail is prettier, but many people still use mail clients that are unable to process it.

- If you decide to allow people to subscribe and unsubscribe from your mailing list via a form, make sure that you use some form of authentication so that people cannot subscribe e-mail addresses of others.

If you do decide to have a mailing list, the following are a few mailing-list management packages for you to consider:

- MailMan
- Majordomo
- Ezmlm

MailMan

One of the most popular mailing-list management systems available today is MailMan. This software is written in the Python scripting language, which means that you must have Python installed to use it. It has a Web interface available that allows users to subscribe and unsubscribe from the mailing lists it manages. One of the nice features of this software is that although it was originally written to work with Postfix as the mail transport agent (MTA), it also is capable of working with Sendmail, Exim, and Qmail. The authors of this software use Postfix as the development platform and it is the recommended MTA to use with it. You can obtain MailMan from `http://www.list.org/`, where you will find extensive documentation regarding how to set up and use it.

Majordomo

One of the older mailing-list management packages—but one that still does a pretty good job—is Majordomo. Majordomo is in the middle of an extensive rewrite, however, and unless you like living on the bleeding edge, I recommend that you stick with the latest stable version. Majordomo is written in Perl and works best with Sendmail as the MTA. In fact, if you use another MTA instead of Sendmail, you might find that you have to apply some patches just to get it to work. Various packages can be used to put a Web interface on Majordomo, the most popular being Majorcool. In addition, you also can use a tool called Hypermail to create a Web archive of all mailing list messages. Information on how to obtain, install, and configure Majordomo can be found at the Majordomo home page at `http://www.greatcircle.com/majordomo`. This site also contains information regarding Majorcool.

Ezmlm

If you are using Qmail as your MTA, an excellent mailing-list management package called Ezmlm is available. This mailing-list manager was designed specifically to work with Qmail and features the capability to allow users to create their own mailing lists without requiring root access. Although this is not a consideration for servers, if you have need of a mailing-list manager elsewhere in your organization, it might be something to consider.

Web-Based Forums Software

Another user-feedback mechanism that is available for you to implement is the Web-based forum or bulletin board. Forums and bulletin boards allow users to interact with each other and with the site through a Web interface. These packages are quite popular at many sites and many options are available in this genre in the open source world. A few that you might consider are

- Phorum
- Netzbrett
- Blaze Board

Each of these products is slightly different, but they all provide the basic functionality required for a Web-based forum package.

Phorum

This package is a forum system written in PHP that uses a database to store and manage messages. Although it has been criticized by some because of the coding style of the author, it works well and is used by many sites. If you would like to take a look at Phorum in action, you can visit `http://talk.thewb.com/`, the discussion site for the WB network. This software is very customizable and because you get the complete source code, you can modify it to fit your needs. Phorum supports multiple databases for the back end, including MySQL, PostgreSQL, Sybase, and even MS SQL 6.x. The Phorum home page can be found at `http://www.phorum.org/`.

Netzbrett

Another package written in PHP, Netzbrett, like Phorum, uses a database to store messages. However, it also can work with flat files. The list of supported databases is larger in that in addition to the databases supported by Phorum, Netzbrett also can support Oracle 8, MySQL, Interbase, Storage, and ODBC. One nice thing about this package is that it supports not only English, but other languages as well, including German, Chinese, Italian, and others. The home page for Netzbrett can be found at `http://www.subjective.de/en/netzbrett/`.

Blaze Board

The most fully featured of the forums software described here is Blaze Board, which is written in PHP and uses a database back end. This product is interesting because it not only implements user forums, but also includes instant messaging in the features list. This software assumes that your online site will have members, and it allows you to rank members based on how often they post, the quality of their posts, and other factors. If you plan on forums being a major part of your content and media site, this software, which you can get at the company's home page at `http://www.bbhacks.com/`, is well worth a look.

Search Tools

Now that we have covered the document management and user-feedback features, we can take a look at implementing search functionality on your site. Although search capabilities for a Web site are not essential, if you decide to archive content on your site and allow users to access it, you will find that it quickly becomes one of the most-used features. This is especially true if your site becomes very popular. If you are not self-hosting, you might find that getting your hosting service to allow you to implement these can be difficult. In that case, you might find that a simple site map can be used to help people navigate your site. In addition, services are available, both free and paid, that implement search capabilities for hosted pages, such as `www.whatuseek.com`. Fortunately, if you are self-hosting, a number of tools are available that allow you to implement this feature. Here are a few:

- mnoGoSearch
- ht://Dig
- MiniSearch

mnoGoSearch

Formerly known as UDMSearch, this product is very capable as a Web site search engine, and it has a couple of unique features that make it very attractive. One of these features is that it includes both a Perl and a PHP interface with the software, which you can download at the mnoGoSearch Web site at `http://search.mnogo.ru/`. Unlike other search engines, mnoGoSearch can index not only text and HTML files, but also can access FTP servers, NNTP servers, and other types of documents such as Postscript, PDF, and DOC files through the use of external parsers. In addition, you have the choice of multiple back ends to store the results of indexing your site. These choices include several database types, from the built-in database to MySQL, PostgreSQL, Oracle, and many other databases. This flexibility makes mnoGoSearch an excellent choice for a search engine.

ht://Dig

Another excellent search engine that is available with source code is the ht://Dig search engine. This search engine is designed for searching any type of text document, including HTML files. However, unlike mnoGoSearch, it cannot store the search indices in a database back end other than the database format created by the ht://Dig creators. This search engine is comparable in features to the once popular Excite for Web Servers search engine of a few years ago. It can be obtained from the ht://Dig Web site at `http://www.htdig.org/`. Some of the nice features of this search engine are that it supports the inclusion of keywords in HTML documents to better refine the search results. In addition, it can be configured to index Web servers that are protected by authentication mechanisms, such as the Apache basic authentication method.

MiniSearch

If both of these search engines sound like overkill for your site, you might want to try out MiniSearch. This tool consists of two Perl scripts: one to search a site and the other to create the index that the search CGI script searches. Although not as full featured as ht://Dig or mnoGoSearch, it might be just the ticket if you are looking for a search engine to support a small site. This script uses template files so that the results of the search can be formatted to match the rest of your site to a great extent. In addition, because it is written in Perl, it is easily modifiable by any competent Perl scripter. MiniSearch is downloadable from the author's Web site at `http://www.dansteinman.com/minisearch/`.

Summary

In this chapter, we have looked at one of the popular types of Web sites—the content and media site. We have looked at some of the characteristics of this type of site and at some of the open source tools that can be used to create a site of this type. In Chapter 5, we actually will be creating a sample site of this type called the Telecommuter's Journal, an imaginary online magazine. We will use some of the tools discussed in this chapter to implement the desired features of a content and media site.

The Telecommuter's Journal

CHAPTER

5

IN THIS CHAPTER

- Site Charter and Design 72
- Web Site Features 73
- Challenges Going Forward 100

One of the interesting facets of the Internet explosion is the fact that anyone with an idea and time on their hands can now become a content provider. This chapter discusses the creation of a content/media site, The Telecommuter's Journal, which is an online magazine that I created to cater to the interests of people who, like me, have moved out of the office setting and work from their homes a significant amount of time. We will cover the site charter and design, the features of the Web site and the tools used to implement them, and the challenges that must be met to make this site work.

Site Charter and Design

In the past few years, the Internet explosion has enabled many people to change the way in which they work. This is especially true of people whose job, to a large degree, consists of working on computers or doing other tasks that do not require extensive interaction with other people in the office. This has led to an increasing number of people working from home and telecommuting. No longer do people have to drive to work and sit in an office or cubicle all day. Instead, they use their computers to interact with the office over the Internet. The Telecommuter's Journal was conceived as a forum for such people. In this section, we look at why the site was created and some of the design decisions that were made along the way.

Creating an Online Magazine

A few years ago, I was working as a system administrator for a software development firm. My primary job function was to make sure that the computer systems used by the rest of the company stayed up and running all the time. To help me accomplish this task, the company provided me with access to the company network from home, via a dial-up connection. In this way, if a computer problem arose in the evening or on the weekends, and the problem could be fixed without requiring physical access to the machines, I could simply connect from my home system, do the required work, and then go about my business instead of having to drive in to the office. Over the next couple of years, this method of working increased, not only on weekends and in the evenings, but during the regular work week as well. Because of improved connectivity and the nature of the work, it became not only possible, but more convenient to work from a home office. Along the way, I learned some interesting lessons about telecommuting and began looking for online resources for people like myself that have made the transition from the traditional work environment to the home office setting. This was the impetus for creating "The Telecommuter's Journal." I envisioned this as a collaborative site at which issues relating to this way of working could be discussed, and people could contribute and possibly make the transition easier for others who were considering this move. After the decision had been made to create such a resource, it was time to move on to working out a site design.

The Site Design

One of the first design decisions made for this online site was to include a system whereby others could contribute articles and columns for each issue. Because this site was not to be a money-making proposition, making this as nonintrusive on my schedule as possible was a goal. This led to the decision to include a Web-based document-management system, where people could download a template for the articles and upload them again when they were done. In this way, I would not have to spend too much time coordinating the efforts of the contributors and e-mailing documents back and forth during their development. In addition, a method would be needed that would take content out of the document-management system and turn it into an issue of the online magazine. Again, the desired goal was to make this as simple as possible. To accomplish this, I decided that the templates should include a set of tags that could be parsed by a script to turn them into the pages that readers would actually see. Finally, as a way to attract readers to the site, I included user-feedback mechanisms so that the readers could discuss the content of the articles. I provided two such mechanisms: a Web-based forum and a mailing list. In this way, the site would cater to people who like the public interaction of a Web-based discussion area, as well as those who prefer the subscription-based and less-public method offered by the mailing list. The final design decision was to keep old issues of the magazine online and to provide a search mechanism so that people could come back to an article later, even if a new issue came out. So now that I had a site design in mind, it was time to start selecting tools and putting it all together.

Web Site Features

Because I had control of the server on which the magazine was to be hosted, I had a great deal of flexibility in what software I could use to construct it. In this section, we cover the choices I made, including my selection of supporting software and the applications that were used to achieve the design goals. As discussed earlier in this chapter, these design goals included the following:

- Enabling contributions through a document-management system
- Automating the issue-publication process
- Providing user-feedback mechanisms
- Making the site searchable

We begin with a description of the platform on which the site was built, and then discuss each of the preceding goals. The discussion covers installation and configuration, as well as the customizations that were made to integrate the individual packages into a cohesive whole.

The Supporting Platform

Before we get into the details of the applications used to implement our design, let's take a look at the supporting platform. The host system used for this site was an Intel server running a Linux-based operating system, although it could just as easily have been hosted on FreeBSD or some other Unix-based system. For the Web server, Apache was used because it was already installed. To support the automation goal, Bash, the Bourne Again shell, and Perl were used. Again, these were selected primarily because they were included with the distribution and didn't require any extra effort. Finally, to support the applications, I installed PHP as a server-side scripting language. In addition to the Web-serving software, a mail server was required for the hosting of the mailing list. This server was another Linux system, running Sendmail as the mail-transport agent. Implementing this site required very little customization of this supporting software; basically, it ran out-of-the-box. Any changes I made are covered when I discuss the individual applications later in this chapter.

Implementing a Document Management System

As previously discussed in Chapter 4, "Content and Media Sites," much of the site was going to be static content in the form of articles and columns. This being the case, a document-management system was needed. The features desirable in this document-management system included a Web interface, revision control, and some means of authenticating users before granting them access to the documents. To implement this feature, I selected a package called Document Manager. This package is a PHP application that is available at the Document Manager home page at `http://www.rot13.org/~dpavlin/docman.html`. One of the reasons for selecting this package was that it did not require a database-management system on the back end, although it does support one if you choose. Installation was a snap and consisted of the following steps:

1. Choose a directory in which to install Document Manager and extract the application files into this directory.
2. Edit the docman.conf file and set some configuration variables.
3. Create a couple of symbolic links from the directory you want to have managed to the docman install directory.
4. Update the Apache httpd.conf file.

Let's examine each of these steps in a bit more detail, starting with unpackaging the application.

Installing the Application Files

After you have downloaded Document Manager, you must decide where to install it. You can install it anywhere on your system that you choose, and I chose to install it at /opt/docman. Installation consisted of running the following commands as root:

```
# cd /opt
# gzip -dc docman-1.6.tar.gz | tar -xvf -
# ln -sf docman-1.6 docman
```

I used the `ln` command so that if I decided to upgrade the version of Document Manager at some later date, I could unpackage the files and simply change the symbolic link to point at the new version.

Editing the docman.conf File

Because I did not choose to install Document Manager in the default location of `/home/httpd/docman`, I was required to change the docman.conf file. This consisted of changing the definition of `$gblIncDir` from the default of `"/home/httpd/docman"` to `"/opt/docman"`. The only other change was to comment out the line that read `$gblUsers = "htusers_sql";`. This line tells Document Manager that you want to use a SQL database instead of the default .htusers file to store user information. The place where this change takes place is indicated by comments in the docman.conf file. I was now ready to move on to the next step.

Creating Symbolic Links to the Document-Manager Software

My directory structure for The Telecommuter's Journal site included a directory called development. This directory was the one that I wanted Document Manager to handle. To accomplish this, I issued the following commands as root:

```
# cd /home/httpd/html/tj
# mkdir development
# cd development
# ln -sf /opt/docman/docman.php .index.php
# ln -sf /opt/docman/docman.conf .docman.conf
# chown -R apache.apache /home/httpd/html/tj/development
```

These commands created a directory that I wanted to have Document Manager handle, created symbolic links to the docman.php and docman.conf files in the Document Manager install directory, and made the directory writable by the user of which Apache runs. This last step was required to allow users to upload and modify the files under control of Document Manager.

Apache Configuration Changes

The final step to get this to work was to update the Apache Web-server configuration file `/etc/httpd/conf/httpd.conf` and to restart Apache. Because Apache was already configured to use PHP, no changes were required for that; however, to get Apache to automatically load the Document Manager software for the development directory, the DirectoryIndex directive needed to be modified to include `.index.php`. This meant changing the line that read

```
DirectoryIndex index.html index.htm index.php
```

to read

```
DirectoryIndex index.html index.htm index.php .index.php
```

The reason for the period at the beginning of the last entry was so that the index file would be hidden from the users of the Document Manager interface. After the change was made and Apache restarted, I was ready to add myself as a user and start using Document Manager. To add myself as a user, I used the supplied adduser.pl script in the development directory, which prompted me for the information it needed and created a `.htusers` file. After all these steps were completed, I pointed my browser at the directory, and after entering my username and password, was presented with the Document Manager interface. I used the form to create a working directory for the first issue of "The Telecommuter's Journal," and the result is shown in Figure 5.1.

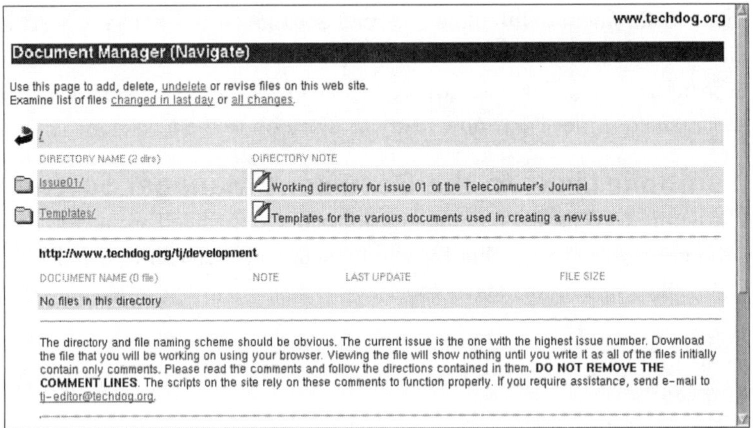

FIGURE 5.1
Document Manager interface.

Having my document-management system in place and ready for use, I was ready to start creating the framework for the site.

Creating the Site Framework

For my online magazine, the site documents fall into two basic groups. These groups are what I refer to as the framework documents, which are those pages that provide the menus, the site logo, and other parts of the site that are unlikely to change. For this framework, I decided on a four-frame layout with a logo frame at the top of the screen, a button menu along the right side of the page, a footer with text links and a copyright notice, and a large main frame that would be used to display the articles and other parts of the content that would change from issue to issue. The result appears in Figure 5.2 with listings of the HTML used to create this look in Listings 5.1–5.5.

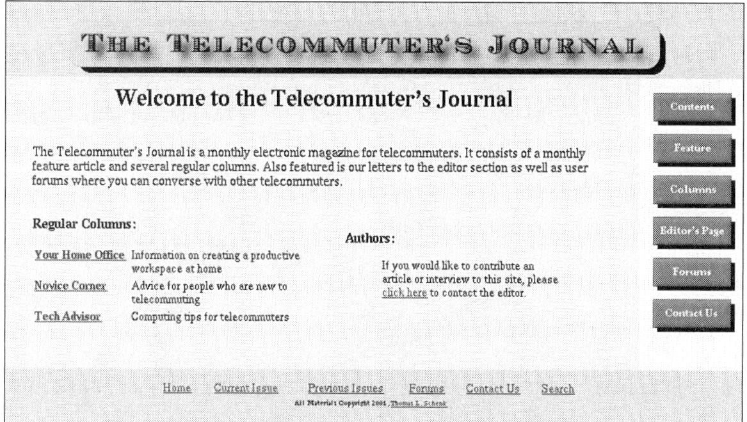

FIGURE 5.2
Site home page.

Listing 5.1 shows the frameset creation source. To create the four-frame layout, I needed to create three nested framesets, and with the exception of the main frame, each of these was set to not scroll, and none of the frames were permitted to be resized.

LISTING 5.1 Frameset Creation Source (index.html)

```
<html>
<head>
<title>The Telecommuter's Journal</title>
</head>
<frameset rows="80,*" border=0>
 <frame name="title" src="/tj/title.html" marginwidth="10"
  marginheight="10" scrolling="No" frameborder="No" noresize>
 <frameset rows="*,60" border=0>
  <frameset cols="*,120" border=0>
   <frame name="main" src="/tj/main.html" marginwidth="10"
    marginheight="10" scrolling="Auto" frameborder="No" noresize>
   <frame name="right" src="/tj/navigation.html" marginwidth="10"
    marginheight="10" scrolling="No" frameborder="No" noresize>
  </frameset>
  <frame name="bottom" src="/tj/footer.html" marginwidth="10"
   marginheight="10" scrolling="No" frameborder="No" noresize>
 </frameset>
</frameset>
</html>
```

For the top of the page, I created a logo image with The Gimp, a graphics package for Linux. I opted to make this logo a link that would take the user back to the home page, to complement the home link that would appear in the footer navigation frame. To avoid having a border drawn around the image, I set the link and visited link colors to match the background color. The source for this title frame is shown in Listing 5.2.

LISTING 5.2 Title Frame Source (title.html)

```
<HTML>
<HEAD>
<TITLE>The Telecommuter's Journal</TITLE>
</HEAD>
<BODY BGCOLOR="#E0E0E0" TEXT="black" LINK="#E0E0E0" VLINK="#E0E0E0">
<CENTER>
<A HREF="/tj/index.html" TARGET="_top">
<IMG SRC="/tj/images/title_logo.gif"></A>
</CENTER>
</BODY>
</HTML>
```

As shown in Figure 5.1, the right side of the screen has a set of buttons that allows you to navigate to various parts of the site. I opted to use a little JavaScript to give visual feedback that the mouse was over a particular button. In addition, I made sure that each image include alternative text for those people who like to surf with images turned off. The code for this navigation frame is shown in Listing 5.3.

LISTING 5.3 Button Menu Frame Source (navigation.html)

```
<HTML>
<HEAD>
 <SCRIPT LANGUAGE=javascript>
 <!-- // hide script from old browsers
 // define the button images

 if(document.images) {

  image1a = new Image;
  image1b = new Image;
  image2a = new Image;
  image2b = new Image;
  image3a = new Image;
  image3b = new Image;
  image4a = new Image;
  image4b = new Image;
  image5a = new Image;
```

LISTING 5.3 Continued

```
  image5b = new Image;
  image6a = new Image;
  image6b = new Image;

 // source images

  image1a.src = "/tj/images/buttona.gif";
  image1b.src = "/tj/images/buttonb.gif";
  image2a.src = "/tj/images/buttonc.gif";
  image2b.src = "/tj/images/buttond.gif";
  image3a.src = "/tj/images/buttone.gif";
  image3b.src = "/tj/images/buttonf.gif";
  image4a.src = "/tj/images/buttong.gif";
  image4b.src = "/tj/images/buttonh.gif";
  image5a.src = "/tj/images/buttoni.gif";
  image5b.src = "/tj/images/buttonj.gif";
  image6a.src = "/tj/images/buttonk.gif";
  image6b.src = "/tj/images/buttonl.gif";

 }

 // onMouseOver Function

 function swapOn(imgLocation) {
  if(document.images) {
   document.images[imgLocation].src = eval(imgLocation + "b.src");
  }
 }

 // onMouseOut Function

 function swapOff(imgLocation) {
  if(document.images) {
   document.images[imgLocation].src = eval(imgLocation + "a.src");
  }
 }

 // end hiding script -->
 </script>

 <TITLE>The Telecommuter's Journal</TITLE>
</HEAD>

<BODY BGCOLOR="#FFFFFF" TEXT="black" LINK="blue" VLINK="blue">
 <CENTER>
```

LISTING 5.3 Continued

```
<TABLE>
 <TR>
  <TD>
   <a href="/tj/current/index.html" target=main
       onMouseOver="swapOn('image1');"
       onMouseOut="swapOff('image1');" >
       <img src="/tj/images/buttona.gif" name="image1"
       border="0" alt="Table of Contents"></a>
  </TD>
 </TR>
 <TR>
  <TD>
   <a href="/tj/current/feature.html" target=main
       onMouseOver="swapOn('image2');"
       onMouseOut="swapOff('image2');" >
       <img src="/tj/images/buttonc.gif" name="image2"
       border="0" alt="This Month's Feature Article"></a>
  </TD>
 </TR>
 <TR>
  <TD>
   <a href="/tj/current/columns.html" target=main
       onMouseOver="swapOn('image3');"
       onMouseOut="swapOff('image3');" >
       <img src="/tj/images/buttone.gif" name="image3"
       border="0" alt="Columns"></a>
  </TD>
 </TR>
 <TR>
  <TD>
   <a href="/tj/current/editor.html" target=main
       onMouseOver="swapOn('image4');"
       onMouseOut="swapOff('image4');" >
       <img src="/tj/images/buttong.gif" name="image4"
       border="0" alt="Letters To The Editor"></a>
  </TD>
 </TR>
 <TR>
  <TD>
   <a href="/tj/forums/" target=main
       onMouseOver="swapOn('image5');"
       onMouseOut="swapOff('image5');" >
       <img src="/tj/images/buttoni.gif" name="image5"
       border="0" alt="Forums"></a>
  </TD>
 </TR>
```

LISTING 5.3 Continued

```
    <TR>
     <TD>
      <a href="/tj/contact.html" target=main
          onMouseOver="swapOn('image6');"
          onMouseOut="swapOff('image6');" >
          <img src="/tj/images/buttonk.gif" name="image6"
          border="0" alt="Contact Us"></a>
     </TD>
    </TR>
    <TR>
    </TR>
   </TABLE>

  </CENTER>
</BODY>

</HTML>
```

To complement the menu on the right side of the screen, I also created a footer navigation frame. Some of the links there were redundant; however, I find that by providing this option, it makes it easier for people to move around on the site. In addition, some of the site pages were made accessible only through this text menu, such as the Previous Issues section of the site and the Search menu. The source code is shown in Listing 5.4.

LISTING 5.4 Page Footer Frame Source (footer.html)

```
<HTML>
<HEAD>
<TITLE>The Telecommuter's Journal</TITLE>
</HEAD>
<BODY BGCOLOR="#E0E0E0" TEXT="black" LINK="blue" VLINK="blue">
<CENTER>
<TABLE WIDTH="60%" BORDER=0>
 <TR>
  <TD ALIGN="CENTER" VALIGN="CENTER">
   <FONT SIZE="-1">
   <A HREF="/tj/index.html" TARGET="_top">Home</A>
   </FONT>
  </TD>
  <TD ALIGN="CENTER" VALIGN="CENTER">
   <FONT SIZE="-1">
   <A HREF="/tj/current/index.html" TARGET="main">Current Issue</A>
   </FONT>
  </TD>
```

LISTING 5.4 Continued

```
  <TD ALIGN="CENTER" VALIGN="CENTER">
   <FONT SIZE="-1">
   <A HREF="/tj/previous/index.html" TARGET="main">Previous Issues</A>
   </FONT>
  </TD>
  <TD ALIGN="CENTER" VALIGN="CENTER">
   <FONT SIZE="-1">
   <A HREF="/tj/forums/" TARGET="main">Forums</A>
   </FONT>
  </TD>
  <TD ALIGN="CENTER" VALIGN="CENTER">
   <FONT SIZE="-1">
   <A HREF="/tj/contact.html" TARGET="main">Contact Us</A>
   </FONT>
  </TD>
  <TD ALIGN="CENTER" VALIGN="CENTER">
   <FONT SIZE="-1">
   <A HREF="/tj/search/search.cgi" TARGET="main">Search</A>
   </FONT>
  </TD>
 </TR>
 <TR>
  <TD COLSPAN="6" ALIGN="CENTER" VALIGN="TOP">
   <FONT SIZE="-2">All Materials Copyright 2001,
   <A HREF="mailto:tj-webmaster@techdog.org">Thomas L. Schenk</A>
   </FONT>
  </TD>
 </TR>
</TABLE>
</CENTER>
</BODY>
</HTML>
```

Finally, to complete the home page look, I created a file that is displayed by default when the site URL is loaded. This document gives a brief description of the site and a short blurb about contributing articles. The source code for this document is shown in Listing 5.5.

LISTING 5.5 Main Frame Source (main.html)

```
<HTML>
<HEAD>
<TITLE>The Telecommuter's Journal</TITLE>
</HEAD>
<BODY BGCOLOR="#f0f0f0" TEXT="black" LINK="blue" VLINK="blue">
```

LISTING 5.5 Continued

```
<CENTER>
<H1>Welcome to the Telecommuter's Journal</H1>
</CENTER>
<TABLE width="100%" BORDER=0 CELLSPACING=10 CELLPADDING=10>
 <TR>
  <TD COLSPAN=2>
   The Telecommuter's Journal is a monthly electronic magazine for
   telecommuters. It consists of a monthly feature article and
   several regular columns. Also featured is our letters to the
   editor section as well as user forums where you can converse with
   other telecommuters.
  </TD>
 <TR>
  <TD>
   <B>Regular Columns:</B>
   <BR>
   <BR>
   <TABLE WIDTH="100%" BORDER=0>
    <TR>
     <TD ALIGN="LEFT" VALIGN="TOP" NOWRAP>
         <FONT SIZE="-1">
          <B>
      <A HREF="/tj/current/homeoffice.html">Your Home Office</A>
      </B>
          </FONT>
         </TD>
     <TD ALIGN="LEFT">
          <FONT SIZE="-1">
          Information on creating a productive workspace at home
          </FONT>
         </TD>
    </TR>
    <TR>
     <TD ALIGN="LEFT" VALIGN="TOP" NOWRAP>
          <FONT SIZE="-1">
          <B>
      <A HREF="/tj/current/newbies.html">Novice Corner</A>
      </B>
          </FONT>
         </TD>
     <TD ALIGN="LEFT">
          <FONT SIZE="-1">
          Advice for people who are new to telecommuting
          </FONT>
         </TD>
```

LISTING 5.5 Continued

```
    </TR>
    <TR>
     <TD ALIGN="LEFT" VALIGN="TOP" NOWRAP>
          <FONT SIZE="-1">
          <B>
      <A HREF="/tj/current/techcorner.html">Tech Advisor</A>
      </B>
          </FONT>
        </TD>
     <TD ALIGN="LEFT">
          <FONT SIZE="-1">
          Computing tips for telecommuters
          </FONT>
        </TD>
    </TR>
   </TABLE>
  </TD>
  <TD>
  <B>Authors:</B>
  <FONT SIZE="-1">
  <BLOCKQUOTE>
  If you would like to contribute an article or interview to this
  site, please <A HREF="mailto:tj-editor@techdog.org">click here</A>
  to contact the editor.
  </BLOCKQUOTE>
  </FONT>
  </TD>
 </TR>
</TABLE>
</BODY>
</HTML>
```

With these basic framework documents in place, I had one additional static document to create. This was the Contact page. This Contact page would include e-mail links for contacting me in my various roles as editor, Webmaster, and other functions, and also would let readers know that there was a mailing list that complemented this site. The source code for this Contact page is shown in Listing 5.6.

LISTING 5.6 Contact Page Source (contact.html)

```
<HTML>
<HEAD>
<TITLE>The Telecommuter's Journal</TITLE>
</HEAD>
<BODY BGCOLOR="#f0f0f0" TEXT="black" LINK="blue" VLINK="blue">
```

LISTING 5.6 Continued

```
<CENTER>
 <H1>Contacting Us</H1>

 <TABLE BORDER=0 CELLSPACING=2 CELLPADDING=2 COLS=2 WIDTH="75%">
  <TR>
   <TD ALIGN="LEFT">
    <B>
     <FONT SIZE=-1>
      Letters to the editor:
     </FONT>
    </B>
   </TD>

   <TD ALIGN="RIGHT">
    <FONT SIZE=-1>
     <A HREF="mailto:tj-editor@techdog.org">
      tj-editor@techdog.org
     </A>
    </FONT>
   </TD>
  </TR>

  <TR>
   <TD ALIGN="LEFT">
    <B>
     <FONT SIZE=-1>
      Information regarding reprints:
     </FONT>
    </B>
   </TD>

   <TD ALIGN="RIGHT">
    <FONT SIZE=-1>
     <A HREF="mailto:tj-reprints@techdog.org">
      tj-reprints@techdog.org
     </A>
    </FONT>
   </TD>
  </TR>

  <TR>
   <TD ALIGN="LEFT">
    <B>
     <FONT SIZE=-1>
      How to contribute articles:
     </FONT>
```

LISTING 5.6 Continued

```
    </B>
   </TD>

   <TD ALIGN="RIGHT">
    <FONT SIZE=-1>
     <A HREF="mailto:tj-contribute@techdog.org">
      tj-contribute@techdog.org
     </A>
    </FONT>
   </TD>
  </TR>

  <TR>
   <TD ALIGN="LEFT">
    <B>
     <FONT SIZE=-1>
      Questions or Problems with the Web site:
     </FONT>
    </B>
   </TD>

   <TD ALIGN="RIGHT">
    <FONT SIZE=-1>
     <A HREF="mailto:tj-webmaster@techdog.org">
      tj-webmaster@techdog.org
     </A>
    </FONT>
   </TD>
  </TR>

  <TR>
   <TD COLSPAN=2>
    <BR> 
    <BR> 
    <FONT SIZE=-1>
         <BLOCKQUOTE>
          <B>
      If you would like to receive e-mail notification when the
          site is updated and converse with other readers, subscribe
          to the tj-readers mailing list by sending an e-mail to
      <A HREF="mailto:tj-readers-request@techdog.org">
      tj-readers-request@techdog.org</A> with the word "subscribe"
          in the body.
          </B>
         </BLOCKQUOTE>
        </FONT>
```

LISTING 5.6 Continued

```
      </TD>
    </TR>
  </TABLE>
 </CENTER>

</BODY>
</HTML>
```

I was then ready to start work on the support tools I would need to take the articles and generate each issue.

Issue Management Tools

Because I desired a consistent look for the various articles and columns that would compose each issue of "The Telecommuter's Journal," I decided that I would create a basic template for each section of the site. This would allow contributing authors to concentrate on the text of their articles. I started with the feature article and created a template with instructions to the authors. This template is shown in Listing 5.7.

LISTING 5.7 Feature Article Template

```
<!--

   This is the template file for the monthly feature article for the
   Telecommuter's Journal. It is processed by a script that generates
   the headers up to the <body></body> tags. This means that you
   should not include any tags that are not appropriate in that
   context. If your HTML editor inserts any such tags, please remove
   them before uploading your article to the document manager.

   Please edit the following variables. They are parsed by various
   scripts used on the site to create a table of contents, author
   attribution, etc. E-mail addresses are not displayed to the
   readers unless the publish value is changed to "TRUE". Addresses
   are displayed to readers as "yourid at domain dot tld". For
   example, tschenk@techdog.org would show up on the site as "tschenk
   at techdog dot org" to help prevent address harvesting. If you do
   not publish your e-mail address, an alias will be created for you
   to collect mail from users. If you would like to retrieve this
   mail, contact the site administrator at tj-editor@techdog.org and
   it will be forwarded to you. Sample values are shown below. If
   these values are not changed, your article will be rejected.
   Please also write a short (1 - 3 sentence) abstract of your article
   between ABSTRACT_BEGIN and ABSTRACT_END below.
```

LISTING 5.7 Continued

```
### Author = "Joe Author"
### Title = "Telecommuting 101"
### E-mail = "jauthor@authorsforhire.com"
### Publish = "FALSE"

ABSTRACT_BEGIN
This is a where the abstract about your article should be included. Just
replace this text with yours.
ABSTRACT_END

-->
```

As you can see, this template file contains instructions to the author contained in a large comment block. It also includes some tags that the scripts will parse to create the actual `feature.html` file, which will have the comment block removed. The templates for the columns are very similar, except that they do not include the abstract section. To convert this template into an article, I created a Perl script that would add a standard header and footer, and would honor the author's request either to publish the e-mail address or not. This script is shown in Listing 5.8.

LISTING 5.8 build_current_feature.pl

```
#!/usr/bin/perl

# First subroutines that we will be using later on.
sub munge_email {
  my $value = shift;

  $value =~ s/@/ at /;
  $value =~ s/\./ dot /;

  return $value;
}

# Define a few variables to save some typing.
$tjhome = "/home/httpd/html/tj";

# Read the current issue number from the .issuenum file.
open(ISSUENUM, "<$tjhome/scripts/.issuenum");
$issuenum = <ISSUENUM>;
chomp $issuenum;
close(ISSUENUM);
```

LISTING 5.8 Continued

```
# Construct the name of the feature article file based on the issuenum
# and make sure that this file exists in the appropriate location.
$featurename = $tjhome . "/development/Issue" . $issuenum
       . "/" . "feature.html";

$outputfile = $tjhome . "/issues/" . $issuenum . "/"
      . "feature.html";

if (! -f $featurename ) {
  print "Error. Unable to locate $featurename.\n";
} else {
  open(COLUMN, "<$featurename");
  @text = <COLUMN>;
  close(COLUMN);

  # Parse the values from the header comments and spit them out in
  # our standard format.
  @author = grep /^#.* Author/, @text;
  if (scalar @author == 1) {
    chomp $author[0];
    $author[0] =~ s/^#.* Author = "//;
    $author[0] =~ s/"$//;
    $author = $author[0];
  } else {
    $author = "Anonymous";
  }

  @title = grep /^#.* Title/, @text;
  if (scalar @title == 1) {
    chomp $title[0];
    $title[0] =~ s/^#.* Title = "//;
    $title[0] =~ s/"$//;
    $title = $title[0];
  } else {
    $title = "Random Musings";
  }

  @email = grep /^#.* E-mail/, @text;
  if (scalar @email == 1) {
    chomp $email[0];
    $email[0] =~ s/^#.* E-mail = "//;
    $email[0] =~ s/"$//;
    $email = munge_email($email[0]);
  } else {
    $email = "tj-editor at techdog dot org";
  }
```

LISTING 5.8 Continued

```
  @publish = grep /^#.* Publish/, @text;
  if (scalar @publish == 1) {
    chomp $publish[0];
    $publish[0] =~ s/^#.* Publish = "//;
    $publish[0] =~ s/"$//;
    $publish = $publish[0];
  } else {
    $publish = "TRUE";
  }

  foreach (@text) {
    chomp $_;
    $alltext .= $_ . "TlSjR";
  }

  $alltext =~ s/<!--.*-->//;
  $alltext =~ s/TlSjR/\n/g;

  open(OUTFILE, ">$outputfile");

  print OUTFILE "<HTML>\n<HEAD>\n";
  print OUTFILE "<TITLE>This Month's Feature</TITLE>\n";
  print OUTFILE "</HEAD>\n<BODY BGCOLOR=\"#F0F0F0\" ";
  print OUTFILE "TEXT=black LINK=blue VLINK=blue>\n";
  print OUTFILE "<H1>$title</H1>\n";
  print OUTFILE "<B><I>$author</I></B><BR>\n";
  if ($publish ne "FALSE") {
    print OUTFILE "<I>$email</I><BR>\n";
  }
  print OUTFILE "<P>\n<FONT SIZE=-1>\n$alltext</FONT>\n</P>\n";
  print OUTFILE "<HR WIDTH=80%>\n<CENTER>\n<BLOCKQUOTE>\n<B>\n";
  print OUTFILE "Have something to say about this article? If so,\n";
  print OUTFILE "join us in the <A HREF=\"/tj/forums/\">forums</A>\n";
  print OUTFILE "and sound off.\n";
  print OUTFILE "</B>\n</BLOCKQUOTE>\n</CENTER>\n</BODY>\n</HTML>\n";

  close(OUTFILE);

}

exit;
```

The idea is that after the author has uploaded the `feature.html` file to the Document Manager, this script would be run to create the final output file that would be placed in the document tree for the magazine. The same technique was applied to the column templates, as well as the

Letters to the Editor page. A sample of a processed column template is shown in Listing 5.9 and a screenshot of this column in the site framework is shown in Figure 5.3.

LISTING 5.9 Processed Column Template File

```
<HTML>
<HEAD>
<TITLE>Your Home Office</TITLE>
</HEAD>
<BODY BGCOLOR="#F0F0F0" TEXT=black LINK=blue VLINK=blue>
<H1>Your Home Office</H1>
<H2>Furnishing Your Home Office</H2>
<B><I>Tom Schenk</I></B><BR>
<I>tschenk at techdog dot org</I><BR>
<P>
<FONT SIZE=-1>

<P>
When I first started telecommuting, my computer sat on a desk in the
corner of my bedroom. Since I was just working from home occasionally,
this was okay. When I made the move to telecommuting full time, however,
the situation changed, and I found that having the bed so close
to my workspace was just too much of a temptation. I therefore decided
that I needed a home office. Fortunately, my house has what the builder
called a formal dining room. Since my kids keep us busy most nights
and we are not big on entertaining, my wife and I decided that I could
use this room for my home office, and I was now faced with the task of
how I would furnish this room.I was fortunate that the room already had
a phone jack in it, and when I started, I just had an extra phone line
installed, moved my existing computer desk and chair from the bedroom
and<B>Presto!</B>instant office. Now, I would get up in the morning, walk
from the bedroom to the office and sit in this sparsely furnished room
until I called it quits for the day. The problem was that I soon started
dreading the &quot;daily commute&quot; just as much as I used to dread
driving in to work. I needed to do something to make my surroundings more
pleasant. To get started, I sat down and thought about the features of
offices I have worked in that I have liked. The things that I focused on
were in three major areas:
<UL>
<LI>Furniture</LI>
<LI>Lighting</LI>
<LI>Decorating</LI>
</UL>
The remainder of this column will cover these three areas
and after you are finished reading it, hopefully you might come away
with some ideas that will help you make the most of your home office.
</P>
```

LISTING 5.9 Continued

```
<H3>Furniture</H3>
<P>
The first thing that I decided to change in my home office was the
furniture. As I mentioned, to start out, I had simply moved my
existing computer desk and chair from their old place in the bedroom.
I decided that I needed a new desk and chair to go with my new
surroundings. When I started looking at desks, I discovered a plethora
of options that my old space had not permitted. I first considered a
modular desk that would wrap around the room similar to ones I have
used at work in the past. The problem with this turned out to be space
and the fact that my office wasn't square. When I made some measurements,
I found that I could fit in a modular desk but would have very little
room for anything else. In addition, because the room wasn't square, I
would end up wasting a lot of usable space. I then considered a fancy
wooden desk like many of the executives I know like to put in their
offices. This idea was rejected because I spend most of my time on
the computer and cabling would have been a mess and the cost. Fancy
wooden desks are (as least to my mind) outrageously expensive. I
finally found what I considered the perfect desk. This desk was a
wall unit that surrounded the central work space with bookshelves, a
shallow drawer for desktop supplies like pens and stuff, a hanging
file drawer, and a few shelves with a locking door on the front. It
also included space designed to hold CD jewel cases as well as a few
general-purpose spaces where I could put things like boxes of floppies.
The central area was designed to hold a computer and had slots for cables
to pass through. It also included a nice sliding tray for my keyboard and
mouse. The kicker though was that it not only held my computer nicely, but
since I needed bookshelves, too, the integration saved me both space
and money.
Once I had my desk and didn't need to look for bookshelves, I moved on
to the next item, a desk chair. When I first moved into my home office,
I moved my ergonomic kneeling chair with me. This chair was comfortable
for short periods, but I soon came to think of the thing as a medieval
torture device. I decided that I needed to find a chair similar to the
ones that I had used at work. What I ended up with was a chair which,
like most good office chairs, would allow me to lean back, adjust the
height, and that had a sturdy set of wheels to allow me to move around
easily. One thing to consider when selecting your chair is whether or
not your home office is carpeted. If it is and you choose a chair with
wheelsas I did, you may also want to consider getting a good plastic
chair pad. This will help your chair roll easier as well as provide
some protection for your carpeting.
The final piece of furniture that I needed for my office was some shelves.
As a computer consultant, I have a lot of computer equipment in my home
office. Every few months, I seem to acquire a new piece of hardware and
```

LISTING 5.9 Continued

```
I soon realized that I needed a work space for all of it. I ended up
with a bread rack that provided me with ample space to not only store
but also to use the various pieces of equipment that I was accumulating.
</P>
<H3>Lighting</H3>
<P>
Having finished with the required furniture in my office, I decided
next to do something about the lighting. My home office was situated
in the front of my house, and I found that the afternoon sun shining
through the windows was creating unwanted glare on my computer screen.
In addition, the builder in his infinite wisdom had installed a light
fixture that, although well suited to lighting a dining room, was not
well suited to an office environment. Since I had plans on someday moving
to a better house, I didn't want to change the light fixture, but I still
needed to change the lighting in the room. My answer to this dilemma was a
torchèr with a dimmer switch and a smaller desk lamp for those times
when I needed more light on my desk. With this combination, I could create
the perfect amount of light to allow me to work without being too bright.
The problem of the afternoon sun was solved with adjustable blinds that
allowed me to let in some sunlight without blinding me or creating too
much glare on my screen.
</P>
<H3>Decorating</H3>
<P>
The final area I tackled to make my home office complete was decorating.
Unlike the offices I had worked in, where I had little control over
what went on the walls, in my home office, I could indulge myself.
This meant having a space for awards and plaques that I had collected
over the years, a nice wall clock, and a few selected pictures. My
favorite is a beautiful Oriental piece depicting a lake and mountains
that was a gift from my brother-in-law.
I hope that you have found this discussion useful. The thing I most
want you to remember as you go about furnishing your home office is
that you should try to make your workspace as pleasant as possible.
You will be spending a lot of time there, and unlike cubicles or
offices in an office building, you can do a lot to make your home
office not only functional, but also a pleasant place to work.
</P>
</FONT>
</P>
<HR WIDTH=80%>
<CENTER>
<BLOCKQUOTE>
<B>
```

LISTING 5.9 Continued

```
Have something to say about this column? If so, join us in the
 <A HREF="/tj/forums/">forums</A> and sound off.
</B>
</BLOCKQUOTE>
</CENTER>
</BODY>
</HTML>
```

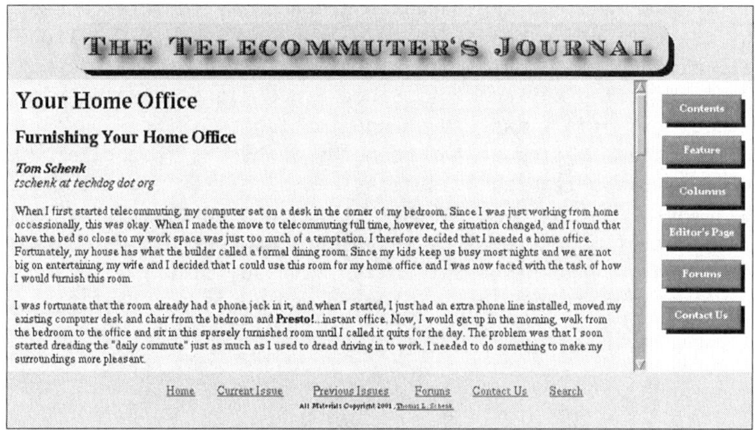

FIGURE 5.3
Sample column.

In addition to the processing of columns and feature articles, I also created scripts that would create a Table of Contents page for each issue, which included the name of the feature article and an abstract, along with the topics of each of the regular columns. If you are interested in seeing the results of these scripts, you can visit the sample issue of the Telecommuter's Journal at `http://www.techdog.org/tj/` and you can download the scripts by pointing your browser at my home page at `http://www.techdog.org/tj-scripts.tgz`.

The User Feedback Features

The next design features that needed to be implemented were the user feedback mechanisms. These were the forums software and the mailing list management packages. For these features, I started by doing a search at Freshmeat at `http://freshmeat.net/`. The packages I selected were Netzbrett for the Web-based forums and Majordomo for the mailing list. So let's take a look at what was required to get these packages installed and configured.

Netzbrett

Netzbrett is a forums software package written in PHP. It is capable of using either a SQL database, such as MySQL, as the message store, or using its own built-in flat file database. To keep things simple, I opted to go with the built-in database support. This meant that because I already had PHP installed as part of the Linux distribution, I didn't need to install any support tools to use this software. The installation procedure was well outlined in the readme.txt file that came with the software, which I downloaded from the Netzbrett home page at `http://www.subjective.de/en/netzbrett/`. Installation consisted of unzipping the downloaded software in a directory under the Apache document root, creating a directory writable by the user account running Apache, and then modifying the conf.php file included with Netzbrett. This modification consisted of changing the value of the `$adminpass` variable, which determines the administrative password. Other than this, I made no modifications to the files at all; pointing my browser at the directory where I had installed the Netzbrett software, I was presented with a form that allowed me to create a new message. A picture of the forums interface that Netzbrett creates can be seen in Figure 5.4.

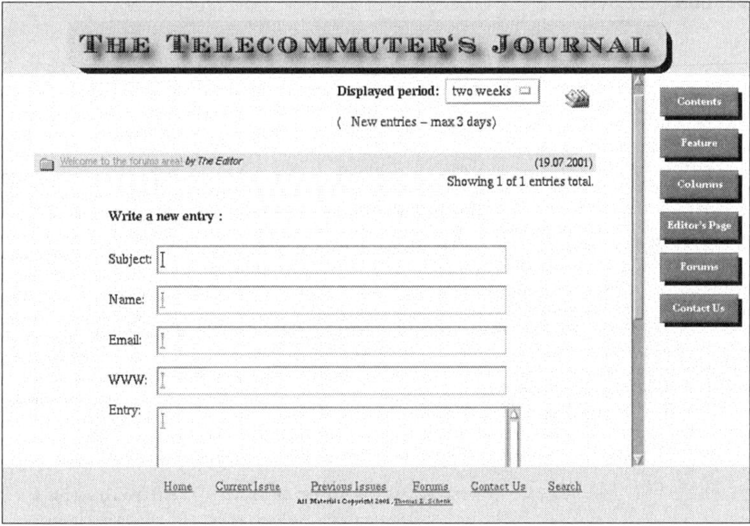

FIGURE 5.4
Netzbrett forums interface.

This software was chosen for its simple design. Unlike other forums software, which typically segregate discussions into individual discussion areas, the Netzbrett enables you to create a single large forum with discussion threads. If your forum needs are more complex than that, you might want to look at a different package.

Majordomo

Now that forums were working, I moved on to the mailing list management software, Majordomo. Majordomo is written in Perl and is available from `http://www.greatcircle.com/majordomo`. I chose to use the RPM package that Red Hat built for its Powertools collection. Installing this package creates a majordomo user and group as part of the installation. After the software was installed, I modified my Sendmail configuration. This involved making the majordomo account a trusted user and creating a file for the aliases required by adding the following lines to my /etc/sendmail.cf file:

```
Tmajordomo
O AliasFile=/etc/aliases,/usr/lib/majordomo/majordomo.aliases
```

After these lines were added, I created the /usr/lib/majordomo.aliases file, which is shown in Listing 5.9.

LISTING 5.9 Majordomo Aliases File

```
#
# Basic majordomo aliases
#
majordomo:              "|/usr/lib/majordomo/wrapper majordomo"
owner-majordomo:        postmaster
majordomo-owner:        postmaster

# mailing list for the Telecommuter's Journal
tj-readers:             "|/usr/lib/majordomo/wrapper resend -l tj-readers
             tj-readers-list"
tj-readers-list:        :include:/var/lib/majordomo/lists/tj-readers
owner-tj-readers:       tj-editor
tj-readers-request:     "|/usr/lib/majordomo/wrapper majordomo -l
             tj-readers"
tj-readers-approval:    tj-editor
```

This is a relatively simple Majordomo setup, and it doesn't support archival or digest subscriptions to the mailing list. However, these features can be added by following the directions that come with Majordomo. After this file was created, I ran the following commands as root:

```
# touch /usr/lib/majordomo/majordomo.aliases.db
# ln -sf /usr/lib/majordomo/wrapper /etc/smrsh/wrapper
# /etc/rc.d/init.d/sendmail restart
```

The `touch` command creates an empty file and prevents Sendmail from complaining about an unsafe map file when it tries to create the hash map from the `majordomo.aliases` file. The `ln` command is required if you use `smrsh`, the Sendmail restricted shell for executing commands found in aliases (which is the default on Red Hat), and the final command restarts the Sendmail daemon. After I completed these steps, I had to finish my configuration of Majordomo. The first step was to check the `/etc/majordomo.cf` file. The file that comes with the Red Hat packaged version of Majordomo was preconfigured; however, I checked it to make sure that it was set up correctly. This file is heavily commented, and after reading the comments and the settings, I was satisfied that no changes were required. The next step was to create my mailing list. The instructions for creating a new list are found in the NEWLIST file that comes with Majordomo. These instructions told me that I must create a file to hold the list of subscribers for my mailing list, create a list information file, and then send a command to Majordomo to create the list configuration file. This was accomplished by running the following commands:

```
# touch /var/lib/majordomo/lists/tj-readers
# echo "Welcome to the Telecommuter's Journal Mailing List" >> \
  /var/lib/majordomo/lists/tj-readers.info
# echo "config tj-readers tj-readers.admin" | \
  mail -s "" majordomo
```

The last of these commands, which sent a mail message to majordomo, created a configuration file called `tj-readers.config` in `/var/lib/majordomo/lists`. To complete my list configuration, I edited this file to reset the list password and set a few other options. This file, minus the comments, is shown in Listing 5.10 (naturally, the password shown is not the one I really use on my system) and those items that I changed are preceded by a comment line that says `Changed by me`.

LISTING 5.10 Config File for tj-readers Mailing List

```
# The configuration file for a majordomo mailing list.

# Changed by me
admin_passwd     =  It$A$ecret

administrivia     =  yes
advertise       << END

END
announcements     =  yes

# Changed by me
approve_passwd    =  It$A$ecret

archive_dir      =
comments        << END

END
date_info        =  yes
date_intro       =  yes
```

LISTING 5.10 Continued

```
debug           =  no
description      =
digest_archive    =
digest_issue     =  1
digest_maxdays    =
digest_maxlines    =

# Changed by me
digest_name      =  tj-readers

digest_rm_footer  =
digest_rm_fronter  =
digest_volume     =  1
digest_work_dir    =
get_access      =  list
index_access     =  open
info_access      =  open
intro_access     =  list
maxlength       =  40000

# Changed by me
message_footer   << END
-
-
=======================================================
To unsubscribe from this list, send an e-mail with the
word "unsubscribe" in the body (not in the subject) to
$LIST-request@techdog.org.
END

message_fronter   << END

END
message_headers   << END

END
moderate       =  no
moderator       =
mungedomain      =  no
noadvertise      << END

END
precedence      =  bulk
purge_received    =  no
reply_to       =
```

LISTING 5.10 Continued

```
resend_host      =
restrict_post     =

# Changed by me
sender        =  owner-tj-readers

strip         =  yes

# Changed by me
subject_prefix    = [tj-readers]

subscribe_policy  =  open+confirm
taboo_body      << END

END
taboo_headers     << END

END
unsubscribe_policy =  open
welcome        =  yes
which_access     =  open

# Changed by me
who_access      =  list
```

When all these steps were completed, I tested the list subscribing and unsubscribing myself from the tj-readers mailing list. This is done by sending mail to the tj-readers-request alias with the word "subscribe" or "unsubscribe" in the body of the message. After I was satisfied that this worked, I was ready to move on to setting up the search functionality on my site.

The Search Engine

To implement the capability to search the issues of the magazine, I opted to use a package called mnoGoSearch. This search engine is available under the GNU General Public License and can be downloaded from the home page at `http://www.mnogosearch.org/`. After downloading and building the software, I installed it on my system under the directory `/opt/mnogo`. To configure this software, you are required to create three configuration files, and you might optionally modify the search page template. Fortunately, sample configuration files come with the package. To create the configuration files, I issued the following commands:

```
# cd /opt/mnogo/etc
# for f in *-dist; do cp $f `basename $f -dist`; done
```

I then edited the indexer.conf file and set the Server variable to point to the directory I wanted indexed. When this was completed, running the command

```
# /opt/mnogo/sbin/indexer
```

was all that was required to create the search index. I then chose to modify the search page template slightly. By default, when a hit list is generated by the `search.cgi` program, the links cause a new browser window to pop up with the document being referenced in the hit list. This is caused by the `TARGET="_blank"` modifier found in the `search.htm` template file. I wanted the page to show up in the main frame instead, so I used a text editor to change all instances of `TARGET="_blank"` in `/opt/mnogo/etc/search.htm` to `read TARGET="main"`. The final step was to copy the `search.cgi` executable from `/opt/mnogo/bin` to the cgi-bin directory of Apache. The resulting Search page for my site is shown in Figure 5.5.

FIGURE 5.5
The site search form.

With this installation of the search engine completed, my site was complete and I was ready to start creating content for the first issue. If you would like to see the result, you can visit "The Telecommuter's Journal" on the Web at `http://www.techdog.org/tj/`.

Challenges Going Forward

Now that my site was complete, I started to think about the challenges I would face in making it a success. The main two challenges were to the following:

- Attracting readers to the site
- Providing interesting content so that people would return each month

In this section, I discuss these two challenges and consider some ways that I might overcome them, starting with the difficult task of attracting readers to the site.

Attracting Readers to the Site

If you run a content/media site, attracting visitors to it can be something of a challenge. To overcome this challenge, you must know your target audience and how to get the word out to them. One suggestion is to look for existing mailing lists, Web sites, or newsgroups that also are targeted at your audience. Announcing your new site in these areas is a first step to getting people to visit you. After you start getting a few readers, you then can encourage them to spread the word to others. This will happen, however, only if you make a favorable impression on them, and this is where providing meaningful content comes in. You should try to ensure that the content at your site is compelling enough to make them want to return. This is also why it is important to provide user feedback mechanisms at your site. If you get e-mail from your readers saying that your site is no good, you should try to find out from them why they feel this way. Although it might hurt your feelings to find out that they don't like your site, if you can engage them in conversation and seek their input on how to make your site better, you might be able to change their opinion and after you do this, they might become advocates of your site. This brings us to the next challenge, providing interesting content.

Providing Interesting Content

Even if you are an excellent writer and create good content for your site, you might eventually run out of ideas for new articles or columns for your site. This is where contributing authors become key. Even if you are very well-known among your target audience, you are unlikely to appeal to everyone. By seeking contributions from other people in the group, you bring variety to your content and make your site more compelling. In addition to keeping your content interesting, seeking out contributors from your audience is one way to keep them engaged and to increase traffic to your site.

Summary

In this chapter, we have discussed the creation of a content/media site from tools that are commonly available on the Internet. By far the most difficult part of creating this site was the creation of the automation tools for turning the content provided by the authors into an issue of the online magazine. This step was not strictly required. However, the fact that the development tools were available at no cost and were already installed provided the incentive to invest the time required to do this. We discussed the reasons why the site was created, took a look at a few design goals that the site maintainers wanted to achieve, and discussed how these design goals were actually implemented. Finally, we considered some of the challenges that the site maintainer would face in attempting to make this site a success. In the next chapter, we will discuss another type of Internet site, the community site, and see how it differs from the content/media site.

Community Sites

CHAPTER

6

IN THIS CHAPTER

- Characteristics of a Community Site 104
- Desirable Features 105
- Some Tools to Consider 109

One type of Web site that is very common is the community site. This type of site is designed to bring together people of like interests. Although not common among businesses, these sites are very popular for organizations, such as political groups, clubs, nonprofit organizations, and other groups in which the membership wants a place where they can come together. In this chapter, we take a look at the characteristics of a community site, the types of features that a good community site will have, and some of the available tools that can be used to create such a site. So let's get started with a description of the characteristics of a community site.

Characteristics of a Community Site

The community site is designed for the express purpose of providing information to members of that community. Examples of groups that might want to build a community site include non-profit organizations, political action groups, homeowner associations, and user groups. For example, if a Linux user group is in your area, chances are that they have a community site built where they can disseminate information relevant to the group, such as membership guide-lines, information about meetings, a calendar of events, and so on. Some of the things that are typical of the community site are

- Collaboration features
- Relatively few static pages
- User-driven content

Let's take a look at these three characteristics to understand their importance to the community site.

Collaboration Features

Communities are formed to allow people to interact, or collaborate, with other members of the community. The group members come together to share ideas, discuss events in the commu-nity, and interact with each other in various ways. One way that the community site can facili-tate this is by providing features such as shared calendars, bulletin boards or forums, a community mailing list, and possibly chat or instant-messaging features. These features are a must because a community that doesn't communicate is not a community at all.

Relatively Few Static Pages

As you will see in Chapter 7, "The Del Valle Junior High Parent/Teacher/Student Organization," when we build the sample community site, most community sites have relatively few static pages. This is in contrast to the content/media site, which is composed largely of static pages that change periodically. Community sites, on the other hand, might have a few static pages where members post a newsletter, a contact page, and a mission statement or similar page.

Other than these few pages, most of the pages will be devoted to collaboration between the community members and user-generated content. This makes the job of the site administrator easier in one sense because the site probably doesn't need a document-management system, and it can have a site map instead of a search tool. On the other hand, it also means that the site administrator will have more applications to deal with to support the collaboration features.

User-Driven Content

Another characteristic of community sites is that the content is very much user driven. By this, I mean that unlike the content/media site discussed in Chapters 4 and 5, in which the content is driven by the site owner, the content at a community site will be generated mostly by the members of the community in the form of bulletin board postings, messages to the mailing lists, and other transient content. This is not to say that content won't be created by the site managers; however, this content will make up only a small portion of the site.

Desirable Features

Now that we have covered the characteristics of the community site, let's consider the features that you can implement to give your community site these characteristics. Some of the features are

- A community calendar
- A notice board application
- A chat system
- Mailing-list management software
- A bulletin board system

In the sections that follow, we briefly describe these features and discuss why they are desirable for your community site.

Community Calendar

One feature that many community sites include is a community calendar. This feature enables the members of the community to keep up with events. The community calendar might be a simple shared calendar that allows any member to post an event. Alternatively, the calendar system could be more complex and allow each user to maintain an individual calendar with private and public events; the system can include the capability to merge the individual calendar view with other calendars. Which one you choose largely depends on the type of group that your community site supports. This community calendar is important to the site in that it provides a simple mechanism to keep the membership up-to-date on planned events. In addition, if the calendar feature of your site permits it, you can export the data to a format that might be useful for generating a paper newsletter. Again, whether your calendar needs to support this feature depends on the nature of the group being served.

Having seen some of the features you might look for in a calendar system, let's discuss why the calendar is a desirable feature of the community site. Two reasons that come to mind are

- It provides a central location for events to be posted, lessening the need for phone trees, paper calendars, and flyers.
- It makes the job of the group's leadership easier by enabling the work of maintaining the calendar to be decentralized.

Centralized Posting of Community Events

Even if your group does not have a Web site, it still needs to schedule events and notify users when these events will occur. To accomplish this, many groups establish phone trees to notify people of upcoming events, publish a newsletter with a calendar page, or post a calendar on a bulletin board in a location frequented by the members of the group. Utilizing a Web-based calendar system, in this instance, can help to eliminate the need for these solutions because people can access the calendar via a Web browser whenever they like, and changes can be made quickly without having to reprint the calendar and redistribute it.

Maintaining the Community Calendar Made Easier

The maintenance of a calendar for a group usually falls to the group secretary or a small group of people. If your group relies on paper calendars or a phone tree to notify members of upcoming events, a number of problems can arise. The phone tree method of notifying people can be very labor intensive, especially if your membership is very large or widely dispersed. This is true because not only do you have to maintain the calendar of events, but you also have to maintain the phone tree. Paper calendars published in newsletters or posted in public locations suffer from a different problem—updating them can be a problem in the event of a last-minute change. These problems are mitigated if you have a Web-based calendar system; updates can be made easily in near real-time, and the members can be allowed to update the calendar themselves instead of having to rely on a group secretary or other person. It then becomes the responsibility of the membership to check the calendar regularly.

Notice Board

One feature that many community sites include is a notice board, which is a feature that allows people to post short notices and is analogous to the old cork bulletin boards placed where people could tack up flyers and notes. Computer-based analogs to this come in a variety of flavors. Some create a virtual cork board and allow people to create notes on them. Other systems allow people to post messages to a special forum or group on a bulletin board system. It doesn't really matter how they are implemented. What matters is that the members of a group are given a place to post unofficial news, information, or requests that are short lived. Examples of the kind of things that you might use a notice board application for include

- Notice of unofficial functions such as birthdays, parties, and so on
- Items offered for sale or trade (if this is not the purpose of the group)
- Requests or offers for services among the members, or any number of other things that are not related to the regular business of the group

By using a notice board system instead of the official forums or the group mailing list, these areas are kept on topic and the signal-to-noise ratio remains high. Consider the following example. You are creating a Web site for the local Linux user group. You set up two mailing lists for the group: one for announcements of meetings and topics related to the management of the group, and one intended to be a help forum for Linux questions. In addition, you use forums software to create special interest groups for gaming, system administration, and programming. What you failed to set up is a general forum that is open to all topics. You will find that over time, the forums you have created will be used to buy, sell, or trade computer equipment, solicit consulting services, coordinate rides to meetings, and include other topics that are not related to the topics of your mailing lists and forums. This creates what is called a low signal-to-noise ratio. This means that the amount of off-topic messages being generated in the forums and mailing lists you created is high in relation to the number of on-topic messages.

This is why creating a notice board of some type is desirable; it allows you to keep this type of noise to a minimum on the focused discussion areas. Failure to address this problem usually means that the people who are interested in the topics presented in your forums and mailing lists end up not using them, thus diminishing the value of these features of your site.

Chat System

People form groups so that they might interact socially, and chatting is a key component to that interaction. Chat is like e-mail in that it allows people to carry on discussion, but differs in that chat is more immediate. You only have to look at the immense popularity of instant messaging services such as IRC, ICQ, or AOL Instant Messaging to see that people love to chat online. You can do several things with chat that are either impossible, or very difficult via e-mail. Two of these things are

- Carry on a group discussion
- Get immediate help with a problem or answers to questions

Carrying on a Group Discussion

Although it is possible to carry on a group discussion via e-mail, it can, at times, be very difficult. This is especially true because you must send a message, wait for a reply, respond to each reply that you get, and make sure that all members of the group see all replies. This makes coming to a consensus via e-mail a time-consuming process, and unless you poll every person in the group, you can never be sure that everyone has read all the messages.

Chat, on the other hand, is well suited to group conversations. When you organize a group chat, you can immediately tell if everyone is present whom you want to communicate with, and feedback from the group members is much more immediate. This makes chat well suited for doing things such as conducting virtual meetings or allowing several people to interact with each other. For example, suppose that you need to get the members of your group to vote on a particular issue. You could call a real meeting and hope that everyone shows up; you could send out an e-mail and hope that everyone responds promptly; or you could organize a virtual meeting in a chat room. The chat room option allows people to attend meetings that they might not otherwise be able to attend and has the immediacy that you need to take a vote without having to wait for everyone to respond to e-mail.

Getting Immediate Help or Answers

Sometimes you need help quickly, or you need an answer to a question that cannot wait for e-mail. You have three options: You can meet with the person whom you think will be best able to provide you with the help or the answer that you need. This is fine if he or she is nearby. Another option is to use the telephone to contact the person, but if that person is not located nearby, this can be expensive, and if he or she is not near a phone, you are out of luck. The third option is to use a chat system, which has a couple of advantages over both of these methods. Most modern chat systems include a mechanism for one-on-one conversations in addition to group chats. These mechanisms give you the immediacy of a phone conversation without the long distance. Just as with a phone call, however, it assumes that the person you need to reach is near a computer.

Mailing List Management Software and Bulletin Board Systems

Like the content/media site discussed in Chapter 4, community sites also benefit from having bulletin board systems and mailing lists. The primary difference is what these features are intended to facilitate. On the content/media site, the primary focus of mailing lists is for announcements or advertisements to flow from the site owners to the people who register with the site. This is primarily a one-way communication. Likewise, the forums are intended primarily as a way for people to talk back to the content providers, which again is mostly one-way communication in which users of the site sound off about content on the system. On the other hand, mailing lists at a community site are used so that community members can collaborate with each other in two-way conversation. Forums, or bulletin boards, are used not as a feedback mechanism, but as a way to organize the group into subgroups that share a common goal or interest; again, they are intended as a means for group members to engage in two-way conversation.

Some Tools to Consider

Now that we have covered the desirable features of a community site, let's consider some of the open source tools that you can use to implement these features, starting with the calendar systems. One thing to remember when considering tools is that if you are not self hosting, you will need to get the site administrator of your site to approve the installation and usage of these tools. Naturally, if you host your own Web site, this is not an issue.

Calendar Systems

One of the most common uses for computers seems to be maintaining a calendar, as evidenced by the number of calendar applications available. This is as true of Web-based calendar solutions as any other, and when you set out to select one for your Web site, you will find a wealth of options. Before you start your search, it is a good idea to have an idea of the features that you require in a calendar system. The following is a list of the features that I would look for in the calendar system for a community site:

- Individual calendars with private and public events
- Shared calendars with private and public events
- A security model that allows groups to be established
- The capability to combine multiple calendar views
- The capability to customize the look of the calendar

Meeting these features narrows the field somewhat, and as we examine a couple of calendar solutions, we will focus on how the product meets these criteria.

Using the listed criteria, we will look at two calendar solutions. These products were found on Freshmeat, which maintains a database of software, most of which is open source or free software. The two calendar solutions selected for comparison to our desired feature list are

- CyberCalendar
- WebCalendar

Let's take a look at each of these, in turn, and see how well they meet our needs, starting with CyberCalendar from CyberWeavers.

CyberCalendar

CyberCalendar is a calendar system written in Perl that can be run as a CGI script or using the Apache mod_perl module. It uses MySQL as a database to keep track of events that are entered by the calendar users. Some of the more interesting features of this calendar solution are that it can be displayed on your Web site either in a full-screen mode, or if you prefer, as a small calendar in a corner of your Web page. It includes some useful features, such as e-mail notification of events and compatibility with other calendar applications that adhere to the vCalendar standard used by many personal information managers, including those on some PDAs, such as the Palm Pilot. As for the remainder of our desired feature list, CyberCalendar allows multiple calendars to be created and public events to be entered, but it does not allow for stacking of calendars. Calendar stacking is the capability to view multiple calendars at the same time. Although this feature is missing, the TODO file that comes with the source indicates that a feature to allow inheritance between calendars is planned for a future release. You can download CyberCalendar from the CyberWeavers Web site at `http://www.cyberweavers.com/download/`.

WebCalendar

If you prefer a PHP solution, one option is WebCalendar. This software works with both PHP version 3 and version 4 and supports multiple database back ends, including open source databases MySQL and PostgresSQL, as well as commercial databases including Oracle. This calendar supports the majority of the features we are looking for, including support for multiple users, calendar stacking, and interface customization. It does not directly support shared calendars; however, the stacking feature allows each user to include other calendars, and you easily could create a community calendar which all users could include for common events. Other features that are of interest include e-mail reminders, multiple language support, and daily, weekly, monthly, and yearly views of events stored in the database. This calendar solution is a better fit to our desired feature list; however, it does lack the capability to display in a corner of your Web page, like CyberCalendar. WebCalendar is available for download from its homepage at SourceForge at `http://webcalendar.sourceforge.net/`.

Notice Boards

The next feature that we wanted for our community site is the notice board. The notice board is intended as a way for users to post notices to each other in a manner similar to how they would use a cork board. The idea is to allow your Web site visitors a way to put up unofficial notices, or items of interest to the community that are not necessarily appropriate to a forum system or a news feature. Two products that could be used to implement this feature that are radically different in implementation are

- phpMyBoard
- My Classifieds

We will take a look at each of these systems to see how they might meet the needs of a community site, starting with phpMyBoard.

phpMyBoard

One item common to most community centers or meeting halls is a bulletin board where people can tack up notices. phpMyBoard is a script that enables you to create a visual representation of this on your Web site. You load a page that looks like a bulletin board, and using your mouse, you open a note on it into which you can type. Just like the real bulletin board, your notes can overlap each other, and what you see on the screen ends up looking just like a real bulletin board. If your site is a relatively small one, this product might be very appealing to you because it is simple to set up and requires no maintenance; notices are automatically deleted when a user-definable maximum number of notes is reached, and the oldest notes are deleted first. This package uses MySQL as the database back end, and if you are already using MySQL as the back end to your calendar solution, this might be appealing to you. If you are using some other database already, you will either have to install MySQL or take on the task of porting phpMyBoard to another database system. This software is available for download at `http://phpmyboard.sourceforge.net/`.

My Classifieds

If you prefer a less cluttered-looking approach to implementing a notice board system, you might prefer My Classifieds. Written as a CGI script in Perl, this system allows site administrators to define categories and users to add and delete entries. It is available in two versions, one of which requires a MySQL database back end and one which does not. One advantage of this package is that it is customizable simply by editing a file that defines variables such as how long before an ad expires, whether an ad can contain a URL, and which icons to use for each category of ad. In the SQL version, much of this data is stored in the database, making it even easier to configure. To download this software and look at a working demo, you can visit the author's Web site at `http://www.fuzzymonkey.org/perl/`.

Chat Software

The final category of software that we will look at, is some simple chat software that you can use on your site to allow your visitors to talk to each other. We will look at three simple chat programs:

- ARSC Really Simple Chat
- Clatter
- phpMyChat

These programs were selected primarily based on their ease of installation. When it comes to chat, many options exist, some of which are very complicated to set up. For example, you could use IRC, Internet Relay Chat, to let your users chat with each other. However, most IRC servers are more complicated to set up than the selected products and require much more maintenance. Of course, by using the simple chat software described here, you lose many of the features of a more complex chat system, but I think that for the small- to mid-sized community site, these packages are more appropriate. One word of warning, however, is in order. The potential for abuse of the chat system at your Web site is pretty high. You might find that after you implement chat on your site, people will make no effort to stay on topic and your chat rooms might become infested with trolls. A troll is a person who likes to hang out on mailing lists or in chat rooms, and stir up trouble by making inappropriate or downright offensive comments about the topic or about other people in the discussion. If this turns out to be the case, you might find that having chat is more trouble than it is worth. Fortunately, with a little effort, you can still use chat for special events even if you do not want to deal with chat regularly. That being said, let's take a look at the selected chat packages.

ARSC Really Simple Chat

This software is a PHP package that uses a MySQL database. To use this software, you select a login name, sometimes called a handle or screen name, select a room, and start chatting. This software does not support private messaging and is intended for group chats only. One nice feature is that it works with just about any browser that supports frames, and although it works best with browsers that also support JavaScript, it does not require it. The software can be customized to suit your needs and it supports multiple chat rooms. The basic screen layout shows users in the chat room to the right, has a text entry box at the bottom of the screen, and the remainder of the screen is used for displaying the chat messages flowing back and forth. The software home page includes a working demo of this software that you can try out before deciding if this package is what you want. You can download the software and try the demo by visiting `http://www.kiessling.net/home/manuel/projects/software/arsc/`.

Clatter

If you don't want to have to deal with yet another database-backed application, but still want chat as part of your site, you might consider Clatter. This software also is written in PHP, but unlike ARSC, it does not use Java, JavaScript, or anything else that your users might not have available. Clatter is the most basic of chat clients, and the onscreen display is divided into two parts. The top of the screen is used to display the messages as they are entered by the chat participants. The lower half of the screen is where you log in and enter your chat messages. This package is extremely easy to set up, and because it does not require a database back end, it is very low maintenance. A demo of this software is available at the product Web site at `http://kimihia.org.nz/projects/clatter/`, and the author has included several links to sites that use the software so that you can see the types of customizations that are possible.

phpMyChat

Another chat package that you might want to consider is phpMyChat. This package is written in PHP version 4 and requires a database back end. It supports MySQL, PostgresSQL, as well as ODBC, which means that you could use it with a number of commercial databases. This package looks much like the ARSC package. One difference is that the frame used to display the users in the chat room also includes the list of available chat rooms, so that you easily can jump from room to room. Some other features that your users might enjoy include the option to have a bell sounded when users enter and leave a chat area. This package is available for download at `http://www.phpheaven.net/chat/`. Like the other chat packages, you can try a demo. One item of interest about this package is that it allows users to register so that they can use the same handle each time they visit.

Summary

In this chapter, we have examined the characteristics of the community site. These sites are most popular for small groups, although this is not always the case. The key to creating a popular community site is to enable the users to interact with each other. This is why features such as mailing lists, chat rooms, notice boards, and forums are among the desired features of the community site. By implementing these features, you can keep your community communicating and well informed, which is important if you want it to grow. In the next chapter, we will be implementing such a community site for a junior high school's parent/teacher organization; that site will incorporate most of the features we have described here.

The Del Valle Junior High Parent/Teacher/Student Organization

CHAPTER

7

IN THIS CHAPTER

- Site Charter and Design 116
- Web Site Features 117
- Challenges 158

Although some companies might have a desire to create a community site, most community sites are built in support of clubs, community service organizations, or nonprofit groups. This chapter describes a site built to support a parent/teacher volunteer organization at a junior high school. Please note that the site described in this chapter is not a demo. It is a real site supporting a real community.

Site Charter and Design

Del Valle Junior High School is a junior high school with an enrollment of about 1,000 students in Austin, Texas. Like most public schools, this school has a parent involvement group, which at Del Valle is called the Parent/Teacher/Student Organization, or PTSO, whose primary function is to provide a way for parents and students, in cooperation with the teachers and staff, to make their school better. The group does this by coordinating the activities of volunteers, fund raising for items such as an ID card system for the school, and by publishing a newsletter. This newsletter for parents passes on information about the school that is obtained from meetings of the group executive board, which is made up of parents, teachers, a staff liaison, and the school principal. The PTSO recently decided that it wanted to create a Web site. Some of the things it wanted to accomplish with its Web site included the following:

- Publicize the purpose of the group
- Communicate events in a more timely fashion
- Provide a way for group members to communicate with each other and with the executive board
- Provide the newsletter in electronic form

In this section, we look at each of these purposes and discuss how these goals can be accomplished in a way that is easy to maintain. We also look at some suggestions for making the Web site a dynamic one that will make the effort worthwhile, so that the site doesn't become stagnant.

Publicizing the Purpose of the Group

Unfortunately, many parents in Del Valle have come to think of the PTSO and similar groups in a rather negative way. They believe that all the PTSO does is have fund raisers and that the things they give back to the school are not worth the hassle. People also believe that if they sign up as a volunteer, the PTSO will be calling them constantly to ask them to do things that they don't want to participate in. The PTSO thinks that this is largely because people don't understand what the purpose of the PTSO is and what the goals of the group are. To combat this, the PTSO wants the home page of the PTSO site to clearly state the goals of the group. The home page, which is the first thing that people see, should state the mission of the group, tell people who the officers are, and include information about volunteering and what volunteering involves, because volunteers are the key to the group being able to do anything. Other than that, the home page will do little else except provide a mechanism to link to other parts of the site.

Communicating Events to the Group

Communicating events to the parents in the PTSO is a difficult task. Most of the parents work, and getting information about meetings and other events typically has been done via memos sent home with the students and a phone tree. The problem with the memos is that many of the children lose them. With so many working parents, contacting everyone by phone is next to impossible; it is difficult to contact people in a timely manner, and as the membership grows, this problem is compounded. When discussing the features that the PTSO would like to have on its Web site, the most frequently mentioned feature was an online calendar that could list not only PTSO events, but also information from the community liaison and the staff. The online calendar would be controlled by members of the executive committee and should be read-only for other people visiting the Web site.

Providing Communication Channels

Because Del Valle is a geographically large school district, it faces some challenges when it comes to communication. Some students live as much as 40 minutes away from the school; therefore, the PTSO wanted to provide as many means of communication as it could. On the other hand, the PTSO did not want to create too much of a burden on the maintainer of the Web site. Some of the ideas that people had for the Web site included having a chat function, forums, and a place where people could place temporary notices, such as on an online bulletin board.

Publishing the Newsletter Online

One final item that the PTSO wanted to provide was an online version of the newsletter that they publish. Because getting children to remember to bring home the newsletter to their parents was a problem, the PTSO wanted to be able to provide the same information in an electronic format that people could pull up and view at their leisure. They also expressed an interest in keeping previous issues of the newsletter online so that people could go back to them if they so desired. With this in mind, along with the other design goals described, the next step is to start implementing the features that will be used to meet these goals.

Web Site Features

In this section, we cover the design of the PTSO Web site, including the tools selected, how they were configured and installed, and any modifications made to make them fit in with the rest of the site. We also cover the supporting packages required to make this site work, how they were installed, and how they were configured.

Designing the PTSO Web Site

The task of designing the PTSO Web site was made easier because it has relatively little static content. This means that little need exists for a complicated document-management system or other mechanism for tracking changes to the static documents on the site. I opted to go with a frames layout with a title frame at the top of the page and a navigation frame on the left side of the screen. Although some browsers cannot handle frames, I did not code a nonframes version of the site for two reasons. First, the vast majority of parents in my target audience have frames-capable browsers. I know this because I did a survey of my target audience before I started coding the site. Second, one of the applications I planned on using in the creation of this site would not work with a browser incapable of frames. In addition, because this school district is in a rural area where broadband access to the Internet is limited, I chose to make the site light on graphics so that people using dial-up service wouldn't have to wait for a lot of complicated images to download. The only feature that might be considered flashy on this site is a small amount of JavaScript to make the buttons in the navigation frame change color when the mouse moves over them. The end result, including the content for the main frame, can be seen in Figure 7.1.

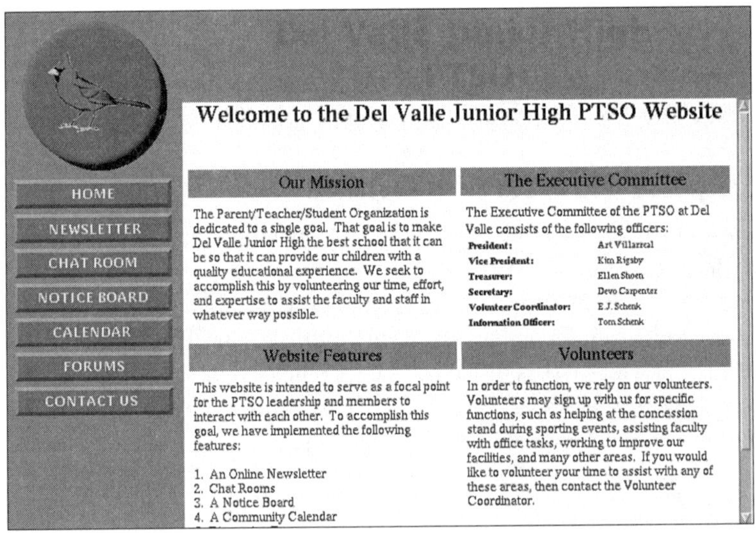

FIGURE 7.1
PTSO home page.

As you can see from an examination of the home page, I opted for no frame borders and I also turned off the option to resize the frames. Scrolling was disabled for the title and navigation frames and set to automatic for the main frame. The index.html file for the site is shown in Listing 7.1.

LISTING 7.1 PTSO Web Site (index.html)

```
<HTML>

<HEAD>
<TITLE>DVJH PTSO</TITLE>
</HEAD>

<frameset cols="200,*" border=0>
  <frame name="side" src="side.html" marginwidth="0"
   marginheight="0" scrolling="No" frameborder="no" noresize>
  <frameset rows="100,*" border=0>
    <frame name="top" src="top.html" marginwidth="0"
     marginheight="0" scrolling="No" frameborder="no" noresize>
    <frame name="main" src="main.html" marginwidth="0"
     marginheight="0" scrolling="Auto" frameborder="no" noresize>
  </frameset>
</frameset>
<noframes>
<body>
<p>
This site is not accessible unless your browser supports frames.  If
you are seeing this text, this is the case for your browser.  You may
obtain a frames capable browser by downloading a current version of
Netscape Communicator or Internet Explorer.  Netscape Communicator is
available at <A HREF="http://www.netscape.com/">the Netscape home page
</A> and Internet Explorer from <A HREF="http://www.microsoft.com/">
the Microsoft home page</A>.
</p>
</body>

</HTML>
```

Having established the framesets, I then created the title frame, which always is visible. The source code for the title frame is shown in Listing 7.2.

LISTING 7.2 Title Frame Source (top.html)

```
<HTML>

<HEAD>
```

LISTING 7.2 Continued

```
<TITLE>DVJH PTSO</TITLE>
</HEAD>

<BODY BGCOLOR=FF0000 TEXT=FFFFFF LINK=FFFF00 VLINK=0000FF>
 <CENTER>
  <IMG SRC="/ptso/images/title.gif"
   ALT="Del Valle Junior High PTSO">
 </CENTER>
</BODY>

</HTML>
```

The navigation frame came next. Like the title frame, this frame is visible all the time. I could have opted to create a bottom frame with text links; however, I thought at the time that this would simply create more clutter. Listing 7.3 shows the source code for the navigation frame. Note that I specified alt tags for the button images for people who like to browse with images turned off, and for the benefit of any search engines that might try to index the site.

LISTING 7.3 Navigation Frame Source (side.html)

```
<HTML>

<HEAD>
 <script language=javascript>
 <!-- // hide script from old browsers

 // define the button images

 if(document.images) {

  image0a = new Image;
  image0b = new Image;
  image1a = new Image;
  image1b = new Image;
  image2a = new Image;
  image2b = new Image;
  image3a = new Image;
  image3b = new Image;
  image4a = new Image;
  image4b = new Image;
  image5a = new Image;
  image5b = new Image;
  image6a = new Image;
  image6b = new Image;
```

LISTING 7.3 Continued

```
// source images

 image0a.src = "/ptso/images/buttona.jpg";
 image0b.src = "/ptso/images/buttonb.jpg";
 image1a.src = "/ptso/images/buttonc.jpg";
 image1b.src = "/ptso/images/buttond.jpg";
 image2a.src = "/ptso/images/buttone.jpg";
 image2b.src = "/ptso/images/buttonf.jpg";
 image3a.src = "/ptso/images/buttong.jpg";
 image3b.src = "/ptso/images/buttonh.jpg";
 image4a.src = "/ptso/images/buttoni.jpg";
 image4b.src = "/ptso/images/buttonj.jpg";
 image5a.src = "/ptso/images/buttonk.jpg";
 image5b.src = "/ptso/images/buttonl.jpg";
 image6a.src = "/ptso/images/buttonm.jpg";
 image6b.src = "/ptso/images/buttonn.jpg";

}

// onMouseOver Function

function swapOn(imgLocation) {
 if(document.images) {
  document.images[imgLocation].src = eval(imgLocation + "b.src");
 }
}

// onMouseOut Function

function swapOff(imgLocation) {
 if(document.images) {
  document.images[imgLocation].src = eval(imgLocation + "a.src");
 }
}

// end hiding script -->
</script>

<TITLE>Del Valle Junior High - PTSO</TITLE>
</HEAD>

<BODY BGCOLOR=FF0000 TEXT=FFFFFF LINK=FFFF00 VLINK=0000FF>
 <CENTER>
  <IMG SRC="/ptso/images/logo.gif" border=0 alt="logo">
 </CENTER>
```

LISTING 7.3 Continued

```
<CENTER>

 <TABLE>
  <TR>
   <TD>
    <a href="/ptso/main.html" target=main
     onMouseOver="swapOn('image0');"
     onMouseOut="swapOff('image0');" >
     <img src="/ptso/images/buttona.jpg" name="image0"
      border="0" alt="Home">
    </a>
   </TD>
  </TR>
  <TR>
   <TD>
    <a href="/ptso/newsletter/index.shtml" target=main
     onMouseOver="swapOn('image1');"
     onMouseOut="swapOff('image1');" >
     <img src="/ptso/images/buttonc.jpg" name="image1"
      border="0" alt="Newsletter">
    </a>
   </TD>
  </TR>
  <TR>
   <TD>
    <a href="/ptso/chat/index.php" target=main
     onMouseOver="swapOn('image2');"
     onMouseOut="swapOff('image2');" >
     <img src="/ptso/images/buttone.jpg" name="image2"
      border="0" alt="Chat Rooms">
    </a>
   </TD>
  </TR>
  <TR>
   <TD>
    <a href="/cgi-bin/notices/classifieds.cgi" target=main
     onMouseOver="swapOn('image3');"
     onMouseOut="swapOff('image3');" >
     <img src="/ptso/images/buttong.jpg" name="image3"
      border="0" alt="Notice Board">
    </a>
   </TD>
  </TR>
  <TR>
   <TD>
    <a href="/ptso/calendar/index.php" target=main
```

LISTING 7.3 Continued

```
      onMouseOver="swapOn('image4');"
      onMouseOut="swapOff('image4');" >
      <img src="/ptso/images/buttoni.jpg" name="image4"
       border="0" alt="Calendar">
     </a>
    </TD>
   </TR>
   <TR>
    <TD>
     <a href="/ptso/forums/" target=main
      onMouseOver="swapOn('image5');"
      onMouseOut="swapOff('image5');" >
      <img src="/ptso/images/buttonk.jpg" name="image5"
       border="0" alt="Forums">
     </a>
    </TD>
   </TR>
   <TR>
    <TD>
     <a href="/ptso/contact.html" target=main
      onMouseOver="swapOn('image6');"
      onMouseOut="swapOff('image6');" >
      <img src="/ptso/images/buttonm.jpg" name="image6"
       border="0" alt="Contact Us">
     </a>
    </TD>
   </TR>
  </TABLE>

 </CENTER>
</BODY>

</HTML>
```

Finally, I created the main content frame, which is the one that changes when a button in the navigation frame is pushed. The file that is displayed when you first open the site is main.html, which is shown in Listing 7.4. This file is the one that displays the mission statement of the PTSO, the list of officers, and information about the features of the Web site.

LISTING 7.4 Main Content Frame Source (main.html)

```
<html>

<head>
```

LISTING 7.4 Continued

```
  <title>Welcome to the PTSO Website</title>
</head>

<body text="#000000" bgcolor="#FFFFFF" link="#0000FF"
 vlink="#800080">

 <center>
  <h1>Welcome to the Del Valle Junior High PTSO Website</h1>
 </center>

 <center>
  <table BORDER=0 CELLSPACING=5 CELLPADDING=5 COLS=2
   WIDTH="100%" NOSAVE >
   <tr ALIGN=CENTER VALIGN=CENTER BGCOLOR="#FF0000" NOSAVE>
    <td NOSAVE>
     Our Mission
    </td>
    <td>
     The Executive Committee
    </td>
   </tr>

   <tr ALIGN=LEFT VALIGN=TOP NOSAVE>
    <td>
     <font size=-1>
      The Parent/Teacher/Student Organization is dedicated
         to a single goal. That goal is to make Del Valle Junior
         High the best school that it can be so that it can
         provide our children with a quality educational
         experience. We seek to accomplish this by volunteering
         our time, effort, and expertise to assist the faculty
         and staff in whatever way possible.
        </font>
       </td>

    <td VALIGN=TOP NOSAVE>
        <font size=-1>
         The Executive Committee of the PTSO at Del Valle
     consists of the following officers:
        </font>
     <table BORDER=0 COLS=2 WIDTH="100%" NOSAVE >
      <tr>
       <td>
           <b><font size=-2>President:</font></b>
       </td>
       <td>
```

LISTING 7.4 Continued

```
        <font size=-2>Art Villarreal</font>
    </td>
   </tr>

   <tr>
    <td>
        <b><font size=-2>Vice President:</font></b>
    </td>
    <td>
        <font size=-2>Kim Rigsby</font>
    </td>
   </tr>

   <tr>
    <td>
        <b><font size=-2>Treasurer:</font></b>
    </td>
    <td>
        <font size=-2>Ellen Shoen</font>
    </td>
   </tr>

   <tr>
    <td>
        <b><font size=-2>Secretary:</font></b>
    </td>
    <td>
        <font size=-2>Devo Carpenter</font>
    </td>
   </tr>

   <tr>
    <td>
        <b><font size=-2>Volunteer Coordinator:</font></b>
    </td>
    <td>
        <font size=-2>E.J. Schenk</font>
    </td>
   </tr>

   <tr>
    <td>
        <b><font size=-2>Information Officer:</font></b>
    </td>
    <td>
        <font size=-2>Tom Schenk</font>
```

LISTING 7.4 Continued

```
        </td>
       </tr>
      </table>
     </td>
    </tr>

    <tr ALIGN=CENTER VALIGN=CENTER BGCOLOR="#FF0000" NOSAVE>
     <td NOSAVE>
         Website Features
        </td>
     <td>
         Volunteers
        </td>
    </tr>

    <tr ALIGN=LEFT VALIGN=TOP NOSAVE>
     <td NOSAVE>
         <font size=-1>
          This website is intended to serve as a focal point for
          the PTSO leadership and members to interact with each
          other. To accomplish this goal, we have implemented the
          following features:
       <p>
           1. An Online Newsletter<br>
           2. Chat Rooms<br>
           3. A Notice Board<br>
           4. A Community Calendar<br>
           5. Discussion Forums
          </p>
       <p>
           It is our intention to make this a dynamic site with
           frequent updates and we hope that you will visit us
           often and participate.
          </p>
         </font>
        </td>
     <td>
         <font size=-1>
          In order to function, we rely on our volunteers.
          Volunteers may sign up with us for specific functions,
          such as helping at the concession stand during sporting
          events, assisting faculty with office tasks, working to
          improve our facilities, and many other areas. If you
          would like to volunteer your time to assist with any of
          these areas, then contact the Volunteer Coordinator.
```

LISTING 7.4 Continued

```
      <br> 
      <br> 
      <p>
          We love our volunteers! Please join us in making Del
          Valle Junior High a better place.
      </p>
        </font>
       </td>
   </tr>
  </table>
 </center>

</body>

</html>
```

Now that I had the home page frameset completed, I was ready to build the remainder of the site. Two more sections of the site, that would be relatively easy to build, were the contacts page and the newsletter page. Again, these sections of the Web site were parts that would be relatively static, with the contacts page changing roughly once per year (when the new officers are elected) and the newsletter page changing about once per month. Figure 7.2 shows the contacts page, and a listing of the HTML for it is found in Listing 7.5.

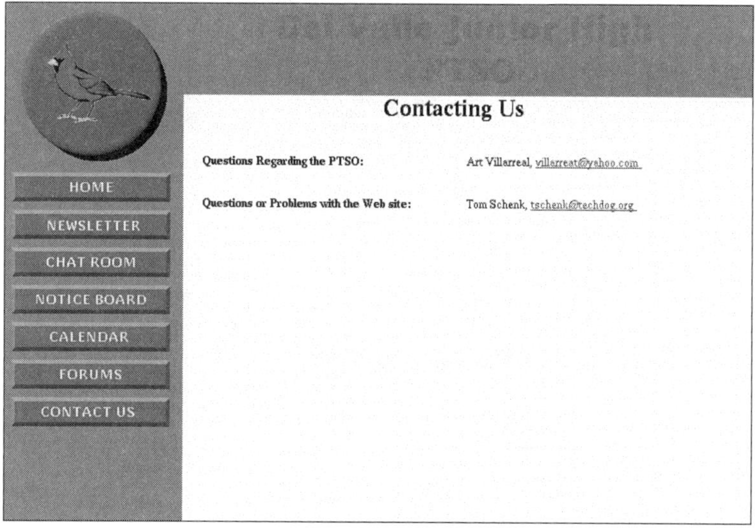

FIGURE 7.2
The contacts page.

LISTING 7.5 Contacts Page Source (contact.html)

```
<html>

<head>
  <title>Contacts</title>
</head>
<body text="#000000" bgcolor="#FFFFFF" link="#0000EF"
 vlink="#51188E" alink="#FF0000">

 <center>
  <h1>Contacting Us</h1>
 </center>

 <table BORDER=0 CELLSPACING=10 CELLPADDING=10
  COLS=2 WIDTH="100%" NOSAVE >
  <tr NOSAVE>
   <td NOSAVE>
    <b>
     <font size=-1>
      Questions Regarding the PTSO:
     </font>
    </b>
   </td>

   <td>
    <font size=-1>
     Art Villarreal,
     <a href="mailto:villarreat@yahoo.com">
      villarreat@yahoo.com
     </a>
    </font>
   </td>
  </tr>

  <tr>
   <td>
    <b>
     <font size=-1>
      Questions or Problems with the Web site:
     </font>
    </b>
   </td>

   <td>
    <font size=-1>
     Tom Schenk,
     <a href="mailto:tschenk@techdog.org">
      tschenk@techdog.org
```

LISTING 7.5 Continued

```
      </a>
     </font>
    </td>
   </tr>
  </table>

</body>

</html>
```


The newsletter page was only slightly more complicated, owing to the fact that the PTSO wanted to keep old issues of the newsletters online, but didn't want the user to have to click through two links to get to the current issue. This was accomplished by using a server-side include that included the current edition of the newsletter and a dynamically built listing of the other files in the directory. This meant that some rules had to be followed by the maintainers. These rules were the following:

- Newsletter files had to use a standard template.
- Newsletter files used a standard naming scheme.
- The current newsletter file was identified by a symbolic link.

The standard template was enforced so that a Perl script could parse the edition date from the HTML file. The standard naming scheme was used so that the same script could build a table of links to the older editions. By having a symbolic link that pointed to the current edition, the script also could be written so that the table of previous editions did not include a link to the current newsletter. The end result can be seen in Figure 7.3. Listings of the server-parsed HTML file, and of the Perl script, can be found in Listings 7.6 and 7.7, respectively.

LISTING 7.6 Newsletter SSI Source (index.shtml)

```
<HTML>

<HEAD>
 <TITLE>PTSO Newsletter</TITLE>
</HEAD>

<BODY BGCOLOR="#FFFFFF">
<BR>
<!--#include virtual="/ptso/newsletter/current.html" -->
<!--#include virtual="/ptso/newsletter/parsedir.cgi" -->
</BODY>

</HTML>
```

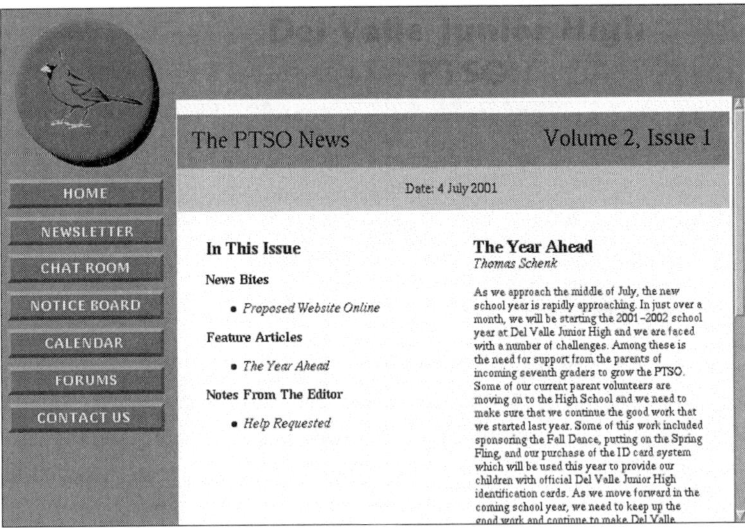

FIGURE 7.3

The newsletter page.

LISTING 7.7 Newsletter Perl Source (parsedir.cgi)

```
#!/usr/bin/perl

# Get a list of the html files in the directory and determine the
# current edition.

@files = `ls -1F vol*_issue*.html | grep -v "@"`;
$current = `ls -l current.html |sed 's/^.*curr/curr/' |cut -d ' ' -f3`;
chomp $current;

# Build a table listing all of the files other than the current edition
# with links to the actual files.

print "Content-type: text/html\n\n";
print "<CENTER>
  <P>Previous editions of the newsletter are available online
  by following the links below:</P>";

print "  <TABLE BORDER=0 WIDTH=\"50%\">\n";

foreach (@files) {
  chomp $_;

  if ("$_" ne "$current") {
```

LISTING 7.7 Continued

```
    $volume = $_;
    $volume =~ s/^vol//;
    $volume =~ s/_issue.*html$//;

    $issue = $_;
    $issue =~ s/^vol._issue//;
    $issue =~ s/.html$//;

    $issue_date = `grep Date: $_`;
    chomp $issue_date;

    print "  <TR>
    <TD ALIGN=LEFT>
     <A HREF=\"/ptso/newsletter/$_\">Volume $volume, Issue $issue</A>
    </TD>
    <TD ALIGN=RIGHT>
     $issue_date
    </TD>
  </TR>\n";

  }
}

print "</TABLE>\n</CENTER>\n";

exit;
```

Note that the Perl script in Listing 7.7 was a quick-and-dirty hack used to get the PTSO site up and running. It is in the process of being replaced with an equivalent, but more elegant, solution that will have the same functionality.

After the static parts of the Web site were completed, the next step was to integrate the tools selected for the dynamic parts of the site.

Installation and Configuration of the Support Tools

To support the selected applications for this Web site, several packages needed to be installed and configured. These tools included

- Apache with PHP4, mod_perl, and server-parsed HTML support
- PHP4 with MySQL support
- MySQL
- Perl and several Perl modules

For each of these tools, we look at the configuration file changes required for the applications being used and how I went about collecting these tools.

Apache—The Web Server

Most Linux systems already come with Apache. However, I decided, when building the PTSO Web site, that I wanted to get the latest version of Apache from the Apache Web site and include the option for supporting SSL with the mod_ssl package. I started by looking for a recent RPM of Apache with mod_ssl support that I could use as a starting point. I found one at the RPMFind Web site (`http://www.rpmfind.net/`) that was only one revision out of date with the current versions of Apache and mod_ssl. I downloaded the current versions of Apache from the Apache Web site at `http://www.apache.org/` and the latest version of mod_ssl at the mod_ssl home page, found at `http://www.modssl.org/`. A quick hack of the RPM spec file to use the newer versions I had downloaded, and a rebuild resulted in a RPM package that I could install on my Web server. If I had been less ambitious, I simply could have installed the RPM that I downloaded from RPMFind and then configured the software. The RPM I installed included an Apache configuration file in `/etc/httpd/conf/httpd.conf`. If you are interested in seeing the entire package, you can download the RPM I used for this site from `http://www.techdog.org/downloads`. If you are interested in learning more about Apache, the best place to start is the Apache Web site at `http://www.apache.org/`. At this site, you will find a wealth of information about this excellent Web server.

The changes required for my application were relatively simple. The first change was to allow CGI programs to run from within the HTML document tree and to allow for server-side includes. This was accomplished by changing the following lines from httpd.conf shown in Listing 7.8 to look like the lines shown in Listing 7.9.

LISTING 7.8 Excerpt from Original httpd.conf

```
<Directory "/home/httpd/html">
  Options Indexes FollowSymLinks MultiViews
  AllowOverride None
  Order allow,deny
  Allow from all
</Directory>
```

LISTING 7.9 Excerpt from Modified httpd.conf

```
<Directory "/home/httpd/html">
  Options Indexes FollowSymLinks MultiViews ExecCGI Includes
  AllowOverride None
  Order allow,deny
  Allow from all
</Directory>
```

I also uncommented the lines in Listing 7.10 from the section of the httpd.conf file that began with the `<IfModule mod_mime.c>` directive.

LISTING 7.10 Excerpt from Modified httpd.conf

```
  AddHandler cgi-script .cgi

  AddType text/html .shtml
  AddHandler server-parsed .shtml
```

Finally, I added index.cgi and index.shtml to the DirectoryIndex directive so that I could have index files of these two types, as well as the default of index.html. After these changes were made, I could begin the installation of PHP4.

PHP4 with MySQL Support

PHP is a complicated package to build, and many options exist, such as support for various database management systems. I opted to take the easy way out on this package and download prebuilt packages from a site that I found while searching RPMFind. The site I used was `http://rpms.arvin.dk/php/`. Several people in my local Linux user group who had upgraded to PHP4 recommended this site. The owner of the site is a Linux enthusiast who builds RPMS for Red Hat systems from the latest PHP releases with separate packages for most of the popular options, including MySQL support, PostgreSQL support, and much more. If you will be running a Red–Hat-based system, I recommend that you take a look at this site, which has not only the PHP packages, but also most of the packages you will require to support the various PHP modules, such as the various shared libraries. If you are not using a Red Hat system, your task will be more difficult. I would recommend a visit to the PHP home page at `http://www.php.net/`, which contains not only the source code for the current version of PHP, but a multitude of documentation and links to sites that can get you started with PHP. After installing the packages I obtained from this site, I added the lines in Listing 7.11 to my Apache httpd.conf file, and after Apache was restarted, PHP support was up and running.

LISTING 7.11 Additions to httpd.conf for PHP4 Support

```
LoadModule php4_module /usr/lib/apache/libphp4.so
AddModule mod_php4.c

<IfModule mod_mime.c>

  AddType application/x-httpd-php .php
  AddType application/x-httpd-php-source .phps

</IfModule>
```

Again, I modified the DirectoryIndex directive, adding index.php to the list of filenames to use as directory indices.

MySQL

After I installed PHP, I moved on to MySQL. For those unfamiliar with MySQL, it is an open source database management system. It was designed to support applications in which a database such as Oracle would be overkill. The MySQL home page at `http://www.mysql.com/` is where you can learn more about this software; if you are new to MySQL, I highly recommend it. I assumed that because MySQL was a very large package it would be difficult to install; however, I was pleasantly surprised. I opted to download the source RPM for MySQL from SourceForge at `http://sourceforge.net/projects/mysql`. After the file downloaded, I built the binary RPMS and installed them on my system. I did this before getting Perl because I realized that I would need the header files from the MySQL package to build the MySQL module. The first step after installation was to set the root password for the database. This password is unrelated to the system root password, but it is important to set this password after installation—so much so, in fact, that the installation of the RPM includes a reminder to do so. Setting the password is a simple matter of running the `mysqladmin` command as follows:

```
mysqladmin -u root -p password 'mypasswd'
```

`mypasswd` is what you would like the root password to be. When you install MySQL, the root password is empty, so when you enter this command for the first time, you should press the Enter key when prompted for a password. One additional step I took was to drop the test database from the system. This was accomplished by issuing the following command:

```
mysqladmin -u root -p drop test
```

and entering the root password I previously had set. The test database is installed during the installation, and on development systems, it might be appropriate to keep it. On my production system, however, I thought that it was not only unnecessary, but undesirable to have a database not being used by an application.

After MySQL is installed and the root password is set, I highly recommend that you install one of two additional packages to make administering your MySQL databases easier. These packages are phpMyAdmin and xmysqladmin. The phpMyAdmin package is a Web-based interface to the administration functions of the MySQL software. It requires PHP with MySQL support, but it makes administering your databases much easier and enables you to do so remotely via a Web browser. You can obtain phpMyAdmin from the PHP Wizards Web site at `http://phpwizard.net/projects/phpMyAdmin/`. This software enables you to create and drop databases, manage the database schema, dump data from a database, and manage database access. The other package is xmysqladmin. This is a GUI application that enables you to easily manage database access, test connectivity to the database, and perform other administrative functions. This package is available from Freshmeat or from the contributed software directory at `http://www.mysql.com/`.

Perl and Perl Modules

I was now ready to move on to the installation and configuration of Perl. Perl was already installed on my system, but some of the modules I needed to support the notice board feature of the PTSO Web site were not. To correct this, I read through the documentation that came with the application and determined that I needed to install the following modules:

- CGI::Carp
- Apache::CGI
- DBI
- DBD::mysql

The documentation also indicated that these modules were all available from the Comprehensive Perl Archive Network, or CPAN. For those unfamiliar with Perl, one of the things that makes it so useful is the Perl community. Perl enthusiasts from around the globe have built up a collection of add-on modules to Perl, such as those listed previously. These modules add functionality to the base language and allow Perl coders to reuse the work of others. These modules are collected and distributed from a series of sites referred to as CPAN. A visit to `http://www.perl.org/` to obtain Perl also will provide you with pointers to this network of sites and other resources that will make using Perl easier. To obtain the modules that I required, I used the CPAN Perl module that comes with Perl to retrieve, compile, and install the modules. The CPAN Perl module is designed to simplify the task of retrieving modules from Comprehensive Perl Archive Network sites and building them on your system. Use the following command:

```
perl -MCPAN -e shell;
```

This command starts an interactive shell that enables you to install modules from the CPAN sites. For example, to install the DBI module, I typed

```
install DBI
```

at the prompt and the CPAN module did the rest. I retrieved the current version of the module from the FTP site, resolved any dependencies, and proceeded to compile and install the DBI module. I did this for the remaining modules that I required and Perl was all set.

Installing the Applications

The key to making this site work was to integrate the applications that were selected for the PTSO site. These applications were

- A Really Simple Chat (ARSC)
- My Classifieds SQL Version
- WebCalendar
- Phorum

Each of these applications required some modifications to make them fit in with my overall site design, so we will look at each one and discuss what was done to each.

A Really Simple Chat

The first application I installed was the chat software, ARSC. The PTSO wanted to provide a way for the members to chat with each other without having to rely on a separate client. They wanted to be able to have multiple chat areas, so to begin with, the group decided to create a general discussion chat room, a homework chat room, and a volunteers chat room. Fortunately, ARSC supported all the features the PTSO wanted, so after we downloaded the software from the author's home page at `http://www.kiessling.net/home/manuel/projects/software/arsc/`, we proceeded with the installation procedure, which consisted of the following steps:

1. Extract the files into a directory in the HTML document tree.
2. Edit the config.inc.php file and provide the information required to connect to the MySQL database.
3. Run the installation script by loading the install.php file from the archive in a browser.

I decided to extract the files into a directory called chat under the directory containing the PTSO Web site home page. For this discussion, I will refer to this directory as HTDOCS/ptso/chat. After this was completed, I needed to configure the database access. Using mysqladmin, I created a database called chat using the following command:

```
mysqladmin -u root -p create chat
```

I was prompted for a password, which I supplied, and the chat database was created. I then created a user account for accessing this database. This step is not strictly required, because I could have used the root user; however, I thought that this would be a bad idea for a couple of reasons. First, if the Web site was compromised and someone was able to read the config.inc.php file, it would have contained the root database password, which meant that all databases on the system would be compromised. Second, by creating a separate user, I could grant that user enough privileges to work with the ARSC application without giving full access to other application databases. Therefore, I created a file containing the SQL commands, found in Listing 7.12, to create a user account for the chat database and to grant that user appropriate privileges.

LISTING 7.12 SQL Commands for Chat User Creation (chatuser.sql)

```
INSERT INTO user (Host, User, Password)
  VALUES ('localhost', 'chatmaster', password('chatwithme'));

INSERT INTO db (Host, Db, User, Select_priv, Insert_priv, Update_priv,
        Delete_priv, Create_priv, Drop_priv)
  VALUES ('localhost', 'chat', 'chatmaster', 'Y','Y','Y','Y','Y','Y');
```

LISTING 7.12 Continued

```
INSERT INTO host (Host, Db, Select_priv, Insert_priv, Update_priv,
        Delete_priv, Create_priv, Drop_priv)
  VALUES ('localhost', 'chat', 'Y','Y','Y','Y','Y','Y');
```

Please note that the password and username shown previously are not the actual ones used on the working Web site, but are for illustration purposes. After I created this file, I issued the following command:

```
mysql -u root -p mysql < chatuser.sql
```

The next step was to modify the config.inc.php file. Loading this file into an editor, I modified the `$arsc_dbhost`, `$arsc_dbuser`, `$arsc_dbpasswd`, and `$arsc_dbdb` variables found at the top of the file to contain the values shown in Listing 7.13.

LISTING 7.13 Changes to the config.inc.php File

```
// Change these values to your needs

$arsc_dbhost   = "localhost";
$arsc_dbuser   = "chatmaster";
$arsc_dbpasswd = "chatwithme";
$arsc_dbdb    = "chat"; //must already exist!

///////////////////////////////////////////////
```

After these changes were completed, I could perform the next step in the installation; running the install.php script. This script creates the tables in the chat database that are needed by the ARSC application. I examined the file and following the instructions in the README file that comes with the software. I modified it to create the chat rooms that the PTSO had requested. The modified file is shown in Listing 7.14.

LISTING 7.14 Modified install.php File for ARSC

```
<?php

include("config.inc.php");

if ($result =
  mysql_query("CREATE TABLE arsc_room_general (
    id int(11) DEFAULT '0' NOT NULL auto_increment,
    message varchar(255) NOT NULL,
    user varchar(64) NOT NULL,
    sendtime time DEFAULT '00:00:00' NOT NULL,
    timeid int(11) DEFAULT '0' NOT NULL,
```

LISTING 7.14 Continued

```
    PRIMARY KEY (id),
    KEY timeid (timeid)
    )")
  &&
  mysql_query("CREATE TABLE arsc_room_homework (
    id int(11) DEFAULT '0' NOT NULL auto_increment,
    message varchar(255) NOT NULL,
    user varchar(64) NOT NULL,
    sendtime time DEFAULT '00:00:00' NOT NULL,
    timeid int(11) DEFAULT '0' NOT NULL,
    PRIMARY KEY (id),
    KEY timeid (timeid)
    )")
  &&
  mysql_query("CREATE TABLE arsc_room_volunteers (
    id int(11) DEFAULT '0' NOT NULL auto_increment,
    message varchar(255) NOT NULL,
    user varchar(64) NOT NULL,
    sendtime time DEFAULT '00:00:00' NOT NULL,
    timeid int(11) DEFAULT '0' NOT NULL,
    PRIMARY KEY (id),
    KEY timeid (timeid)
    )")
  &&
  mysql_query("CREATE TABLE arsc_users (
    id int(11) DEFAULT '0' NOT NULL auto_increment,
    user varchar(64) NOT NULL,
    lastping int(11) DEFAULT '0' NOT NULL,
    ip varchar(15) NOT NULL,
    room varchar(32) NOT NULL,
    language varchar(32) NOT NULL,
    PRIMARY KEY (id),
    KEY lastping (lastping),
    KEY user (user)
    )"))
{
 echo "ARSC is installed.";
}
else
{
 echo "Something went wrong. You can mail me, maybe I can help you:
 <a href=\"mailto:manuel@kiessling.net\">manuel@kiessling.net</a>.";
}

?>
```

When my modifications were complete, I loaded the install.php file in a browser and saw the message `ARSC is installed`, indicating that the database table creation was successful. As you can see from an examination of the install.php file, ARSC uses a table for each chat room and a table to keep track of users. The table names for the chat rooms are important because they determine the names that are presented to the user when the user loads the application. For example, if you create a table named arsc_room_i_like_to_chat, the user would see a room called I Like to Chat as one of the rooms that he or she can enter. If you created a table called arsc_room_game_cheat_codes__walkthroughs (note the double underscore between codes and walkthroughs), the user would see Game Cheat Codes / Walkthroughs. The code that does this conversion between table names and what is presented to the user is found in the config.inc.php file. If you chose, you could modify this to define your own conversion rules.

After I had completed this step, I could customize ARSC to better fit with my site. I started by loading the application to see what the default setup looked like. I was presented with the screen shown in Figure 7.4.

FIGURE 7.4
Default ARSC interface.

This screen enables the user to select the language in which buttons and message are presented. The application currently supports English, Portuguese, and German. After you select your language of choice, clicking the OK button takes you to the login page. On this page, you can select a nickname by which you will be known in the chat room, and you can specify whether your browser supports JavaScript and the room you want to enter. With English selected as the language, this page appears as shown in Figure 7.5.

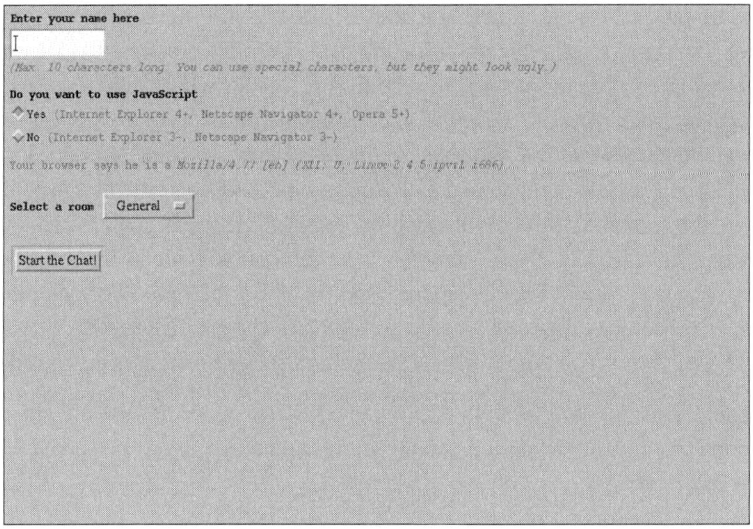

Enter your name here
(Max. 10 characters long. You can use special characters, but they might look ugly.)
Do you want to use JavaScript
Yes (Internet Explorer 4+, Netscape Navigator 4+, Opera 5+)
No (Internet Explorer 3-, Netscape Navigator 3-)
Your browser says he is a
Select a room
General
Start the Chat!

FIGURE 7.5
ARSC login page.

After you select the appropriate options from the login page, you finally get to the chat interface. This interface appears as shown in Figure 7.6. This interface requires a frames-capable browser.

User Thomas enters the room General
<Thomas> Hello gentle readers.
<Thomas> I wish there was someone here to chat with. :)
Users in room General
Thomas
Send
Leave the chat

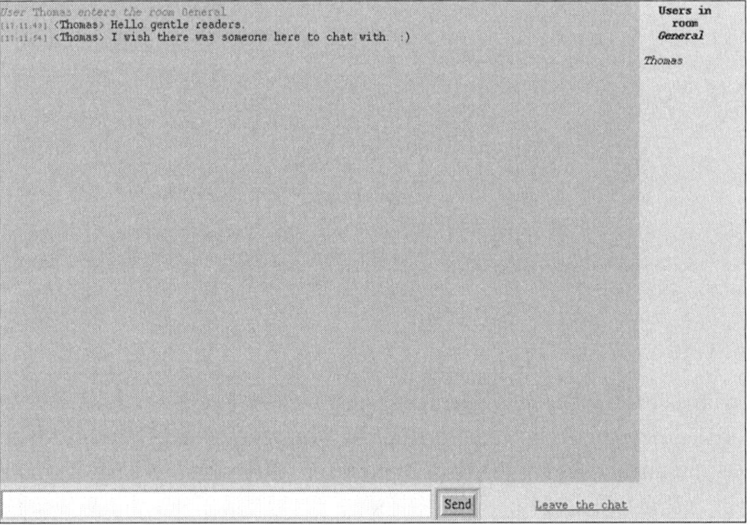

FIGURE 7.6
ARSC chat interface.

As you can see, the default configuration is rather plain and the color scheme is to use various shades of gray for everything. When I presented this to the PTSO executive committee, the members questioned the need for selecting a language, and asked if the application could be modified so that it defaulted to English. They also wanted the login page to have a white background to match the rest of the site. An examination of the source code revealed that these changes would be trivial.

One defect was discovered during the testing of my modifications. A link on a chat page showed the text `Leave the chat`. This link returned the user to the login page, but did not log out the user. In addition, the user could not rejoin the chat using the same nickname until a timeout period had expired. This defect was corrected by adding some code to delete the username from the arsc_users table when the link was followed. To remove the language selection option, the index.php file from ARSC was replaced by a symbolic link to the home.php file. The differences between my version of ARSC and the default installation are shown in Listing 7.15.

LISTING 7.15 Customizations to ARSC (diff output)

```
diff -urN defchat/config.inc.php chat/config.inc.php
--- defchat/config.inc.php    Tue Jul 10 16:46:28 2001
+++ chat/config.inc.php       Wed Jul 4 01:28:33 2001
@@ -6,38 +6,30 @@
 $arsc_dbuser   = "chatmaster";
 $arsc_dbpasswd = "chatwithme";
 $arsc_dbdb    = "chat"; //must already exist!
+$arsc_language = "english"; // hard-coded language

 ///////////////////////////////////////////////

-
-
-
-
-
 // Hack around here only if you know what you are doing

 // Connecting the db
 mysql_pconnect($arsc_dbhost, $arsc_dbuser, $arsc_dbpasswd);
 mysql_select_db($arsc_dbdb);

-
 // How long do we wait for a users 'ping'?
 $arsc_logoutbuffer = 30;

-
 // After how many entrys will the db be emptied? Dunno if this is a
```

Listing 7.15 Continued

```
 // good value... find out under your conditions
 $arsc_rowlimit = 5000;

-
 // You are expected to understand this ;-)
 if ($arsc_language == "")
 {
 $arsc_language = "english";
 }

-
 // Templates for the messages
-$arsc_template_normal = "<font face=\"Arial\" size=\"2\">
<font color=\"#666666\" size=\"1\">[{sendtime}]
</font> &lt;{user}&gt; {message}</font><br>";
+$arsc_template_normal = "<font face=\"Arial\" size=\"2\">
<font color=\"#333333\" size=\"1\">[{sendtime}]
</font> &lt;{user}&gt; {message}</font><br>";
 $arsc_template_me = "<font face=\"Arial\" size=\"2\">
* {user} {message}</font><br>";


@@ -55,7 +47,14 @@
 {
 $arsc_result = mysql_query("SELECT language from arsc_users WHERE
  user = '$arsc_user'");
 $arsc_a = mysql_fetch_array($arsc_result);
+ if ($arsc_a["language"] == "")
+ {
+ return $arsc_language;
+ }
+ else
+ {
 return $arsc_a["language"];
+ }
 }


@@ -84,7 +83,7 @@
             $arsc_posting = $arsc_lang_enter;
             $arsc_posting =
               ereg_replace("{user}", "</i>".$arsc_sysmsg[1]."<i>",
               $arsc_posting);
             $arsc_posting =
               ereg_replace("{room}", "</i>".$arsc_sysmsg[2]."<i>",
```

LISTING 7.15 Continued

```
                $arsc_posting);
-              $arsc_posting = "<font face=\"Arial\" size=\"2\"
color=\"#666666\"><i>".$arsc_posting."</i></font><br>";
+              $arsc_posting = "<font face=\"Arial\" size=\"2\"
color=\"#333333\"><i>".$arsc_posting."</i></font><br>";
              break;
  }
 }
diff -urN defchat/home.php chat/home.php
--- defchat/home.php   Fri May 11 06:36:24 2001
+++ chat/home.php      Tue Jul 3 23:41:30 2001
@@ -1,9 +1,15 @@
 <?php

 include("config.inc.php");
-include("shared/language/".$arsc_language.".inc.php");
+include("shared/language/english.inc.php");

 $arsc_timebuffer = time() - $arsc_logoutbuffer;
+
+if ($action == "leave")
+{
+ mysql_query("DELETE from arsc_users WHERE user = '$arsc_user'");
+}
+
 mysql_query("DELETE from arsc_users WHERE lastping < '$arsc_timebuffer'");
 $arsc_result = mysql_query("SELECT user from arsc_users");
 ?>
@@ -14,7 +20,7 @@
  ARSC - ARSC Really Simple Chat - Login
  </title>
 </head>
- <body>
+ <body bgcolor="#ffffff">
  <font face="Arial" size="2" color="#FF0000">
  <b>
   <?php
diff -urN defchat/shared/chatusers.php chat/shared/chatusers.php
--- defchat/shared/chatusers.php      Fri May 11 06:35:52 2001
+++ chat/shared/chatusers.php Tue Jul 3 20:39:52 2001
@@ -1,7 +1,7 @@
 <?php

 include("../config.inc.php");
-include("../shared/language/".find_language($arsc_user).".inc.php");
+include("../shared/language/english.inc.php");
```

LISTING 7.15 Continued

```
 $arsc_room = find_room($arsc_user);
 if ($arsc_enter == "true")
diff -urN defchat/version_header/chatinput.php
  chat/version_header/chatinput.php
--- defchat/version_header/chatinput.php     Fri May 11 06:36:07 2001
+++ chat/version_header/chatinput.php Tue Jul 3 23:43:12 2001
@@ -1,7 +1,7 @@
 <?php

 include("../config.inc.php");
-include("../shared/language/".find_language($arsc_user).".inc.php");
+include("../shared/language/english.inc.php");

 ?>
 <!DOCTYPE HTML PUBLIC "-//W3C//DTD HTML 4.0 Transitional//EN"
  "http://www.w3.org/TR/REC-html40/loose.dtd">
@@ -19,8 +19,8 @@
  <input type="submit" value="<?php echo $arsc_lang_sendmessage; ?>">
  <font face="Arial" size="2">
          
-   <a href="../home.php?arsc_language=<?php echo
    find_language($arsc_user); ?>" target="_parent">
    <?php echo $arsc_lang_leave; ?></a>
+   <a href="../home.php?action=leave&arsc_user=<?php echo
    $arsc_user; ?>&arsc_language=<?php echo find_language($arsc_user);
    ?>" target="_parent"><?php echo $arsc_lang_leave; ?></a>
  </font>
  </form>
 </body>
 </html>
diff -urN defchat/version_header/chatmsg.php chat/version_header/chatmsg.php
--- defchat/version_header/chatmsg.php       Fri May 11 06:36:10 2001
+++ chat/version_header/chatmsg.php   Tue Jul 3 20:40:42 2001
@@ -1,7 +1,7 @@
 <?php

 include ("../config.inc.php");
-include("../shared/language/".find_language($arsc_user).".inc.php");
+include("../shared/language/english.inc.php");

 $arsc_room = find_room($arsc_user);
 if ($arsc_lastid == "")
diff -urN defchat/version_header/index.php chat/version_header/index.php
--- defchat/version_header/index.php Fri May 11 06:36:09 2001
+++ chat/version_header/index.php     Tue Jul 3 20:35:17 2001
@@ -6,9 +6,9 @@
  </title>
```

LISTING 7.15 Continued

```
 </head>
 <frameset cols="*,120" border="0" framespacing="no"
  frameborder="0" marginwidth="2" marginheight="1">
- <frameset rows="*,40" border="1" framespacing="no"
   frameborder="0" marginwidth="2" marginheight="1">
+ <frameset rows="*,80" border="1" framespacing="no"
   frameborder="0" marginwidth="2" marginheight="1">
  <frame src="chatmsg.php?arsc_user=<?php echo $arsc_user; ?>#end"
   NAME="msg" scrolling="auto" noresize marginwidth="2" marginheight="1">
-  <frame src="chatinput.php?arsc_user=<?php echo $arsc_user; ?>"
    name="input" scrolling="no" noresize marginwidth="2" marginheight="1">
+  <frame src="chatinput.php?arsc_user=<?php echo $arsc_user; ?>"
    name="input" scrolling="auto" noresize marginwidth="2" marginheight="1">
  </frameset>
  <frame src="../shared/chatusers.php?arsc_user=<?php echo $arsc_user; ?>
   &arsc_enter=true" name="users" scrolling="auto" noresize marginwidth="5"
   marginheight="5">
 </frameset>
diff -urN defchat/version_javascript/chatinput.php
  chat/version_javascript/chatinput.php
--- defchat/version_javascript/chatinput.php Fri May 11 06:36:15 2001
+++ chat/version_javascript/chatinput.php    Tue Jul 3 23:29:49 2001
@@ -1,7 +1,7 @@
 <?php

 include("../config.inc.php");
-include("../shared/language/".find_language($arsc_user).".inc.php");
+include("../shared/language/english.inc.php");


 ?>
 <!DOCTYPE HTML PUBLIC "-//W3C//DTD HTML 4.0 Transitional//EN"
  "http://www.w3.org/TR/REC-html40/loose.dtd">
@@ -27,7 +27,7 @@
  <input type="submit" value="<?php echo $arsc_lang_sendmessage; ?>">
  <font face="Arial" size="2">
          
-  <a href="../home.php?arsc_language=<?php echo
    find_language($arsc_user); ?>" target="_parent">
    <?php echo $arsc_lang_leave; ?></a>
+  <a href="../home.php?action=leave&arsc_user=<?php echo $arsc_user; ?>
    &arsc_language=<?php echo find_language($arsc_user); ?>"
    target="_parent"><?php echo $arsc_lang_leave; ?></a>
  </font>
  </form>
 </body>
diff -urN defchat/version_javascript/index.php
```

LISTING 7.15 Continued

```
  chat/version_javascript/index.php
--- defchat/version_javascript/index.php     Fri May 11 06:36:16 2001
+++ chat/version_javascript/index.php Tue Jul 3 20:35:39 2001
@@ -6,10 +6,10 @@
  </title>
 </head>
 <frameset cols="*,120" border="0" framespacing="no" frameborder="0"
  marginwidth="2" marginheight="1">
- <frameset rows="1,*,40" border="0" framespacing="no" frameborder="0"
   marginwidth="2" marginheight="1">
+ <frameset rows="1,*,80" border="0" framespacing="no" frameborder="0"
   marginwidth="2" marginheight="1">
  <frame src="jsupdate.php?arsc_user=<?php echo $arsc_user; ?>"
   scrolling="no" noresize marginwidth="0" marginheight="0">
  <frame src="chatmsg.php" NAME="msg" scrolling="auto" noresize
   marginwidth="2" marginheight="1">
-   <frame src="chatinput.php?arsc_user=<?php echo $arsc_user; ?>"
    name="input" scrolling="no" noresize marginwidth="2" marginheight="1">
+   <frame src="chatinput.php?arsc_user=<?php echo $arsc_user; ?>"
    name="input" scrolling="auto" noresize marginwidth="2" marginheight="1">
  </frameset>
  <frame src="../shared/chatusers.php?arsc_user=<?php echo
   $arsc_user; ?>&arsc_enter=true" name="users" scrolling="auto"
   noresize marginwidth="5" marginheight="5">
 </frameset>
diff -urN defchat/version_javascript/jsupdate.php
   chat/version_javascript/jsupdate.php
--- defchat/version_javascript/jsupdate.php  Fri May 11 06:36:19 2001
+++ chat/version_javascript/jsupdate.php     Tue Jul 3 20:41:04 2001
@@ -1,7 +1,7 @@
 <?php

 include ("../config.inc.php");
-include("../shared/language/".find_language($arsc_user).".inc.php");
+include("../shared/language/english.inc.php");

 $arsc_room = find_room($arsc_user);
 $arsc_result = mysql_query("SELECT * from arsc_room_$arsc_room
ORDER BY timeid DESC");
```

For readers unfamiliar with the diff command, the lines in Listing 7.15 that begin with a minus sign (-) are lines that exist in the original files that do not exist in the modified files, and lines that begin with a plus sign (+) are lines that exist in the modified files that do not exist in the original. This diff output can be used by the patch command to make the original source code match my modified version. If you are interested in the changes I made to the ARSC software, you can download the version used at the PTSO site at `http://www.techdog.org/downloads`. After my changes were made and the chat application was incorporated into the PTSO site, the end result appeared, as shown in Figures 7.7 and 7.8.

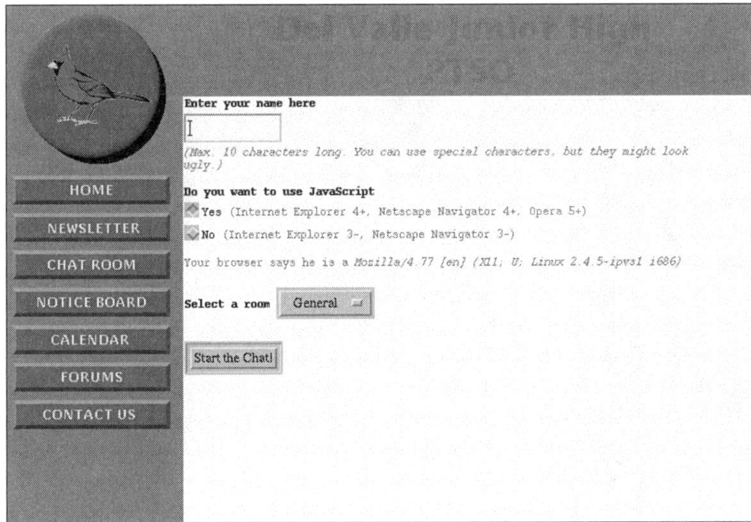

FIGURE 7.7
The ARSC Login page with my modifications.

As you can see from the figures, the changes were mostly cosmetic. The only change of any significance was the change to the action taken when you click the Leave the Chat link.

When chat was working to the satisfaction of the PTSO members, the next application I worked on was the notice board.

My Classifieds, SQL Version

For the notice board, I opted to use an application called My Classifieds, which is a Perl application that can be used to keep track of classified ads. Two features of this application that made it a good fit for the notice board function, are that it enables categorizing notices, and it is largely self maintaining. By this, I mean that no work would be required to remove notices. The application includes a user-definable timeout, and notices older than that timeout are automatically deleted from the database. This application comes in two versions: one that requires no database, and one that can use a MySQL database as the repository for notices. I opted to go with the SQL version because I already had MySQL installed. To install this application, I downloaded the source code from the author's home page at `http://www.fuzzymonkey.org/perl/`. After I unpacked the files under my Web server's CGI directory, I could begin configuring. This application consists of three Perl files and a SQL file that is used to build the database. Incorporating this application into the PTSO site was relatively painless. The steps required are

- Creating a classifieds database
- Creating a user account to access the database
- Defining the categories of notices that the PTSO wanted
- Adjusting the look of the interface

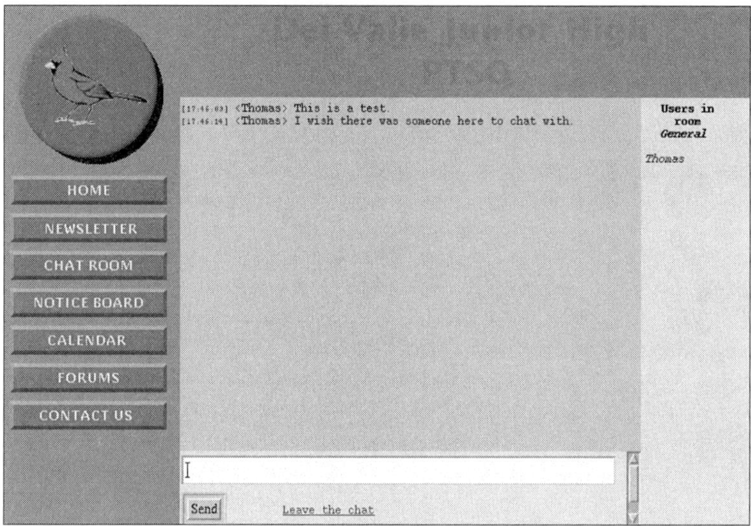

FIGURE 7.8
The ARSCChat interface with my modifications.

The first step was accomplished by using mysqladmin to create a database called classifieds by issuing the command

```
mysqladmin -u root -p create classifieds
```

and entering the root password for the database when prompted. I then created a user account to access this database for the classifieds CGI script. This was done using the SQL file, shown in Listing 7.16, and using the mysql command.

LISTING 7.16 SQL Commands to Create Notice Board

```
User Account (noticeuser.sql)

INSERT INTO user (Host, User, Password)
  VALUES ('localhost', 'notices', password('NoT1C3$'));

INSERT INTO db (Host, Db, User, Select_priv, Insert_priv, Update_priv,
        Delete_priv, Create_priv, Drop_priv)
```

LISTING 7.16 Continued

```
  VALUES ('localhost','classifieds','notices','Y','Y','Y','Y','Y','Y');

INSERT INTO host (Host, Db, Select_priv, Insert_priv, Update_priv,
        Delete_priv, Create_priv, Drop_priv)
  VALUES ('localhost', 'classifieds', 'Y','Y','Y','Y','Y','Y');
```

After I created this file, I issued the following mysql command to create the user account:

```
mysql -u root -p mysql < noticeuser.sql
```


Having created my database and the appropriate user account, the next step was to define the categories that the PTSO wanted for its notice board. To accomplish this, I modified the classifieds.sql file that came with the application so that it contained the SQL commands shown in Listing 7.17.

LISTING 7.17 Modified Contents of the classifieds.sql File

```
create table adds(
  add_no                int not null primary key,
  category              char (255) not null,
  email         char (255) not null,
  name          char (255) not null,
  subject               char (255) not null,
  data          char (255) not null,
  price         char (255) not null,
  picture               char (255) not null,
  url                   char (255) not null,
  phone         char (255) not null,
  password              char (255) not null,
  time          char (255) not null
);

create table categories(
  cat_no                int not null primary key,
  category              char (255) not null,
  category_picture      char (255) not null,
  description           char (255) not null
);

##########################################################################
# You will want to edit the categories below.
# the first value is the category name, second is the picture associated,
# third is the description of the category
##########################################################################
INSERT INTO categories
```

LISTING 7.17 Continued

```
 VALUES (1,
     'PTSO Announcements',
     '/images/pencil1.jpg',
     'Announcements from the PTSO Executive Committee.');
INSERT INTO categories
 VALUES (2,
     'Services Offered',
     '/images/pencil1.jpg',
     'Tutoring, child care, and other services.');
INSERT INTO categories
 VALUES (3,
     'Organization News',
     '/images/pencil1.jpg',
     'Announcements from campus approved organizations.');
INSERT INTO categories
 VALUES (4,
     'For Sale',
     '/images/pencil1.jpg',
     'Items for sale or trade.');
INSERT INTO categories
 VALUES (5,
     'Congratulations',
     '/images/pencil1.jpg',
     'Birthdays, anniversaries, and other special happenings.');
INSERT INTO categories
 VALUES (6,
     'Miscellaneous',
     '/images/pencil1.jpg',
     'Anything else.');
```

One change that was made to the schema was the addition of a category number to the categories table. This number was added so that the categories could be sorted and presented in a specific order. This schema and data was loaded by issuing the following mysql command

```
mysql -u notices -p classifieds < classifieds.sql
```

and entering the password for the notices user when prompted. The next step was to define the variables required for the Perl script to talk to the database. These variables were found in the file called sitevariables.pl that came with the software. In this file, you define the database name, the database user, the database password, and where the script resides on your server. In addition, in this file, you can define the timeout period for notices. I changed this from the default of fourteen days to thirty days.

The final step was to alter the appearance of the application by editing the classifieds.cgi script to change colors and some of the text and to add some logic to suppress the printing of a price field for notices that did not contain a price. The differences between the altered script and the original are shown in Listing 7.18.

LISTING 7.18 Modifications to classifieds.cgi

```
--- /usr/local/src/classifiedsSQL/classifieds.cgi   Sun Jun 10 16:01:21 2001
+++ classifieds.cgi   Tue Jul 3 23:52:22 2001
@@ -77,16 +77,16 @@

 sub printmainmenu {
        print <<HTML;
-<table><tr><td bgcolor="blue" valign="top" width=200>
+<table><tr><td bgcolor="#C0F0F0" valign="top" width=200>
        <table width=100%>
-       <tr bgcolor=#FFCC00><td><b>$title</b></td></tr>
-       <tr><td><a href="classifieds.cgi">
<font color="#FFCC00">View Ads</font></a></td></tr>
-       <tr><td><a href="classifieds.cgi?mode=placead">
<font color="#FFCC00">Place Ads</font></a></td></tr>
-       <tr bgcolor=#FFCC00><td><b>User Login/Modify Ad</b></td></tr>
-       <tr><td><a href="classifieds.cgi?mode=printdeleteform">
<font color="#FFCC00">Delete Ad</font></a></td></tr>
-       <tr><td><a href="classifieds.cgi?mode=printmodifyform">
<font color="#FFCC00">Modify Ad</font></a></td></tr>
-       <tr bgcolor=#FFCC00><td><b>Help</b></td></tr>
-       <tr><td><a href="mailto:$webmasteremail">
<font color="#FFCC00">Contact Us</font></a></td></tr>
+       <tr bgcolor=#C0D0D0><td><b>$title</b></td></tr>
+       <tr><td><a href="classifieds.cgi">
<font color="#C00000">List Categories</font></a></td></tr>
+       <tr><td><a href="classifieds.cgi?mode=placead">
<font color="#C00000">Submit Notices</font></a></td></tr>
+       <tr bgcolor=#C0D0D0><td><b>Modify Your Notices</b></td></tr>
+       <tr><td><a href="classifieds.cgi?mode=printdeleteform">
<font color="#C00000">Delete Notices</font></a></td></tr>
+       <tr><td><a href="classifieds.cgi?mode=printmodifyform">
<font color="#C00000">Modify Notices</font></a></td></tr>
+       <tr bgcolor=#C0D0D0><td><b>Help</b></td></tr>
+       <tr><td><a href="mailto:$webmasteremail">
<font color="#C00000">Contact Webmaster</font></a></td></tr>
        </table>
 </td>
 HTML
@@ -95,17 +95,17 @@
```

LISTING 7.18 Continued

```
 sub printcategories {
        #categories are stored in a separte database. Eventually, this should be
        #easily edited via
        a manager's interface with capability to remove offensive adds also.
-       $sth = $dbh->prepare(qq(select category,category_picture,description
+       $sth = $dbh->prepare(qq(select
cat_no,category,category_picture,description
                                        from categories
-                                       group by category))
+                                       order by cat_no))
                                        or dienice("Could not select from table");
        $sth->execute;
        print "<center><table>";
-       while (($category,$category_picture,$description)=$sth->fetchrow_array)
{
+       while (($cat_no,$category,$category_picture,$description)=
               $sth->fetchrow_array) {
                print<<HTML;
 <tr>
        <td><img src="$htmlurl/$category_picture"></td>
-       <td><a href="classifieds.cgi?mode=viewcategory&category=$category"><font
color="#FFCC00">$category</font></a></td>
+       <td><a href="classifieds.cgi?mode=viewcategory&category=$category"><font
color="#C00000">$category</font></a></td>
        <td>$description</td>
 </tr>
 HTML
@@ -265,21 +265,29 @@
 <tr><td>
 <table bgcolor=#FFFFFF width=500 border=0 cellspacing=0>
        <tr>
-               <td colspan="2" bgcolor="#FFCC00"
align=middle><b>$subject</b></td>
+       <td colspan="2" bgcolor="#C0F0F0" align=middle><b>$subject</b></td>
        </tr>
        <tr>
 HTML

-       print "<tr><td bgcolor=#dbdbdb>Name</td><td>$name</td></tr>";
-       if($email) { print "<tr><td bgcolor=#dbdbdb>Email</td><td><a
href=\"mailto:$email\">$email</a></td></tr>"};
-       if($phone) { print "<tr><td bgcolor=#dbdbdb>Phone</td><td>$phone
</td></tr>"};
-       print "<tr>
-               <td bgcolor=#dbdbdb>Price</td><td>\$$price</td>
```

LISTING 7.18 Continued

```
-       </tr>";
+       print "<tr><td bgcolor=#dbdbdb>Posted By</td><td>$name</td></tr>";
+
+       if($email) {
+      print "<tr><td bgcolor=#dbdbdb>Email</td><td><a href=\"mailto:$email\">
$email</a></td></tr>"
+    }
+
+       if($phone) {
+      print "<tr><td bgcolor=#dbdbdb>Phone</td><td>$phone</td></tr>"
+    }
+
+       if($price) {
+      print "<tr><td bgcolor=#dbdbdb>Price</td><td>\$$price</td></tr>"
+    }

        if($picture) {
                print "<tr><td></td><td><img src=\"$picture</td></tr>\">";
        }
+
        print<<HTML;
        <tr>
                <td valign="top" colspan=2>$data</td>
@@ -537,6 +545,7 @@
                print MAIL <<MAIL_MESSAGE;
 Subject: Your classified ad at $title
 To:$toemail
+Cc:$webmasteremail
 From: $fromemail
 $name,
```

The primary changes to the script were to change the word "Ads" to read "Notices" and to alter the color scheme. The end result incorporated into the PTSO Web site is shown in Figure 7.9.

The notice board was now functional; the next application was the calendar.

WebCalendar

The calendar function of the PTSO Web site was provided by a PHP calendar called WebCalendar. The challenge in getting this application to work was to allow multiple people to use the calendar without giving access to site visitors. WebCalendar was selected because it allows you to "stack" calendars. This means that you can define a user account such that the calendar for that user account shows not only the entries for that user account, but also the entries of other calendars in a single view. This was desirable because the PTSO then could allow the school staff, the community liaison, and the executive committee to have their own calendars and then create a public calendar that stacked all these calendars together. This application required no customization to get it working, and by following the instructions that came with the application, I quickly had the calendar function up and running. The steps required to install this software are the following:

- Create the calendar database.
- Define a user account to access it.
- Modify the configuration file.

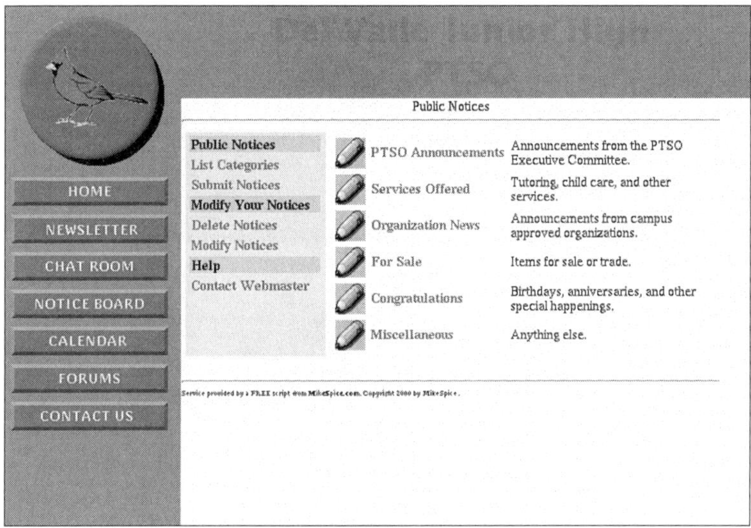

FIGURE 7.9

PTSO notice board.

Like the other applications, I accomplished the first step by using mysqladmin and issuing the following command:

```
mysqladmin -u root -p create ptsocal
```

Then I created the calendar user by using the SQL commands shown in Listing 7.19.

LISTING 7.19 SQL Commands to Create Calendar User

```
(caluser.sql) ***

INSERT INTO user (Host, User, Password)
  VALUES ('localhost', 'caluser', password('CaLU$eR'));
```

LISTING 7.19 Continued

```
INSERT INTO db (Host, Db, User, Select_priv, Insert_priv, Update_priv,
        Delete_priv, Create_priv, Drop_priv)
  VALUES ('localhost','ptsocal','caluser','Y','Y','Y','Y','Y','Y');

INSERT INTO host (Host, Db, Select_priv, Insert_priv, Update_priv,
        Delete_priv, Create_priv, Drop_priv)
  VALUES ('localhost', 'ptsocal', 'Y','Y','Y','Y','Y','Y');
```

These values were inserted into the database by issuing the following mysql command:

```
mysql -u root -p mysql < caluser.sql
```

After these steps were completed, the tables required by the WebCalendar software were created by using the following command to load the tables-mysql.sql file that comes with the application:

```
mysql -u caluser -p ptsocal < tables.mysql.sql
```

I now had my database and could proceed with configuring the software. The only changes that were required were to the configuration file, config.inc, found in the includes directory when the application was extracted into the HTML document tree. The variables that I changed for this application are shown in Listing 7.20.

LISTING 7.20 Changed Variables in config.inc File

```
// MySQL example
$db_type = "mysql";
$db_host = "localhost";
$db_login = "caluser";
$db_password = "my$calendar";
$db_database = "ptsocal";

$readonly = true;
$single_user_login = "ptsomember";
$allow_color_customization = false;
$STARTVIEW = "month";
```

These changes made my calendar a read-only calendar, and a single user was defined to access, negating the need to login each time you wanted to view the calendar. This was exactly what the PTSO wanted for the site visitors, but the question now was how to add events to the stacked calendars to create the public calendar. This turned out to be relatively easy. To accomplish this, a second instance of the WebCalendar software was installed in a different directory. This instance was configured to access the same database as the first one, but the config.inc file instead was modified, so that the calendar was not read-only and multiple users were supported. Those people who were permitted to change the calendar were given a different URL to visit to access this second instance of the WebCalendar software, where they could make changes to the calendar. Because they were accessing the same database as the first instance, their changes showed up in the read-only copy that site visitors viewed. Figure 7.10 shows the end result.

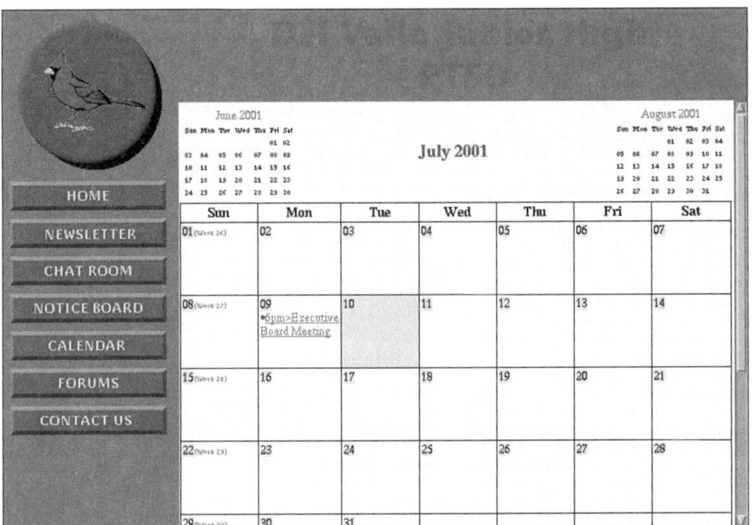

FIGURE 7.10
The PTSO public calendar.

One application remained to be installed: the forums software.

Phorums

Two versions of the Phorum software are currently available: the development branch and the stable branch. I was tempted at first to select the development branch of the software; however, because this software is considered an alpha release, I opted instead to go with the most recent stable version. This software, like the WebCalendar software, was not modified to incorporate it into the PTSO Web site. It was obtained from the Phorums home page at `http://phorum.org/`. Installation consisted of the following steps:

1. Unpackaging the software in the HTML document tree
2. Creating a directory to contain the configuration files
3. Creating the database and database-user account
4. Using the administration interface to create the forums

The first step is self explanatory. I simply created a directory called forums and extracted the software into it. For the next step, I created a directory, called phorum, outside of the HTML document tree and moved the files forums.bak.php and forums.php from the software distribution into it. Following the instructions in the documentation, I made these files writable by the user account of which Apache runs. Now I was ready to create the database and database-user account. This was accomplished by creating a file, forumuser.sql, shown in Listing 7.21 and then issuing the following two commands:

```
mysqladmin -u root -p create forums
mysql -u root -p mysql < forumuser.sql
```


LISTING 7.21 SQL Commands to Create Forum User (forumuser.sql)

```
INSERT INTO user (Host, User, Password)
  VALUES ('localhost', 'phorum', password('Ph0RuM$'));

INSERT INTO db (Host, Db, User, Select_priv, Insert_priv, Update_priv,
        Delete_priv, Create_priv, Drop_priv)
  VALUES ('localhost','phorums','phorum','Y','Y','Y','Y','Y','Y');

INSERT INTO host (Host, Db, Select_priv, Insert_priv, Update_priv,
        Delete_priv, Create_priv, Drop_priv)
  VALUES ('localhost', 'phorums', 'Y','Y','Y','Y','Y','Y');
```

After I completed these steps, I modified the forums.php file to point to the database I had created. This was accomplished by setting the values shown in Listing 7.22.

LISTING 7.22 Configuration Variables for Phorums

```
$dbName='phorums';
$dbUser='phorum';
$dbPass='Ph0RuM$';
$dbServer='localhost';
```

After these changes were made, I loaded the administrative page for the Phorum software in my browser, and using the Web-based interface, created a couple of forums. The end result is shown in Figure 7.11.

I now had the whole Web site built. The site then was submitted for review to the PTSO executive committee, who received it with enthusiasm. It was now time to discuss with them the challenges that they would face as they started publicizing their new site.

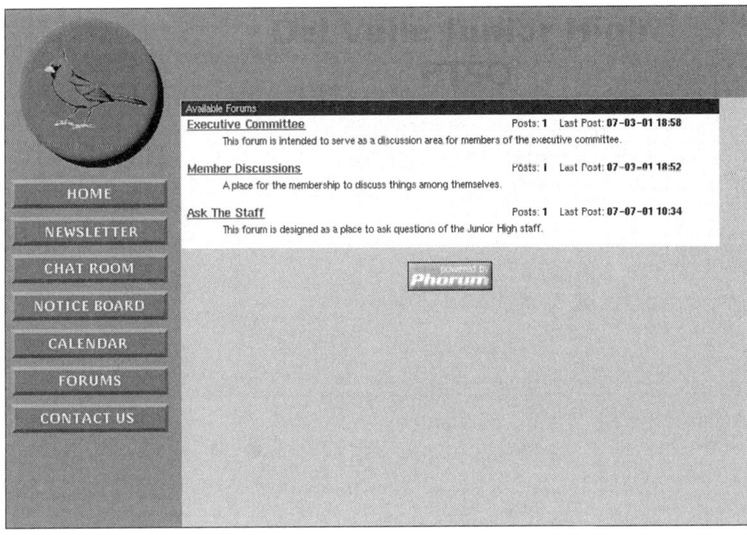

FIGURE 7.11
Phorums at the PTSO Web site.

Challenges

When creating a community site such as this one, the PTSO faces a number of challenges. These challenges include

- Publicizing the site to the community
- Keeping the site up-to-date and preventing stagnation
- Dealing with unruly users

In this section, we look at each of these areas and discuss some of the ideas that were put forward to deal with these challenges, starting with publicizing the site to the community.

Publicizing the PTSO Web Site

In the past, the parent/teacher organization at the junior high was a PTA, and it had a single page on the junior high's Web site that listed officers and how to contact them. There were no interactive features and the page fell into disuse and was grossly out of date. This was one of the motivations for building a new PTSO Web site. The executive committee of the PTSO decided that because more and more parents in the school district were getting online, a more compelling Web presence would be beneficial. The challenge, however, was how to publicize the fact that the new Web site was online. To meet this challenge, the PTSO decided to take the following actions:

- Announce the new Web site to all the members who submitted their e-mail addresses to the PTSO.
- Create a flyer to be handed out at the open house that the junior high has every year prior to school starting.
- Seek permission from the junior high to put the URL on the marquee at the entrance to the school.

The PTSO hoped that through these three actions, the word would get out about the Web site. During the first three months of the school year, log analysis will be done to determine their effectiveness. This issue will be revisited at each monthly meeting of the PTSO, and if it is determined that the Web site is not being used, a new plan of action will be considered. Fortunately, because the PTSO is using a free hosting service, no cost is associated with this course of action.

Preventing Stagnation

Because the Web site has only a very few static pages, the task of keeping them up-to-date is rather easy, but a problem faced by many community sites is that they become stagnant through disuse. Assuming that the publicity efforts for the Web site are effective and all the parents become aware of the site, the executive committee decided on a few actions that it hopes will draw parents to the site and keep the site from becoming more of a burden than a benefit to the community. Some of these actions include

- Using the Web site as one of the primary methods of communication among the executive committee
- Sponsoring chat sessions with various members of the staff, such as the principal, sponsors of other organizations, and members of the faculty
- Periodically seeding the forums with new topics of discussion in which the membership might be interested

The first of these actions is what developers sometimes like to refer to as "eating your own dog food." The PTSO executive committee wants the Web site to succeed; however, if committee members do not use the site to the greatest extent possible, it is unlikely that the other members of the community will, either. The other actions are intended to encourage people to make use of the features that were incorporated into the site. By scheduling events that make use of these features, the committee hopes to encourage people to make use of the site. If these actions are successful, the community will begin to grow around the Web site and eventually, it will become self sustaining, which is the key to running a successful community site. If the site never becomes self sustaining, then no amount of seeding or scheduling of events will prevent the site from stagnating.

Dealing with Unruly Visitors

One of the problems with sites that are publicly visible on the Internet, is that you sometimes attract unwanted attention. Unfortunately, some people have nothing better to do with their time than to try to get attention by disrupting the activity of sites such as the PTSO site. As the site was initially designed, not many measures are in place to restrict the activities of visitors. It is expected that people will follow the guidelines of civil behavior and that it will not be necessary to police the Web site too much. If this proves not to be the case, the PTSO has considered the following actions:

- Force users to register with the site and login each time they visit.
- Remove features that prove to be too difficult to police.

The executive committee believes that forcing users to register will discourage people from using the site and hopes that this course of action will not be required. The other action—removing features too difficult to police—is more likely, with some candidates for removal being the chat feature and the forums. Given the nature of the calendar and the notice board, it is likely that these features could remain without creating too much of a burden on the Web site maintainers.

Summary

In this chapter, we have demonstrated the building of a community site. We covered the goals of the community the site was designed for, and the design decisions that were made in support of these goals. We also covered how the site was created, from the installation of the supporting software to the customization of the applications incorporated into the site design. Finally, we discussed some of the challenges that the PTSO faces in making this site successful and self sustaining. If you would like to visit this site, you can see it at `http://www.techdog.org/ptso/`. Please remember that this is not a demo, but a live site serving an actual community, and act accordingly. If you are interested in obtaining a copy of this site that you can download and experiment with, contact me via the site contact page at `http://www.techdog.org/ptso/contact.html`.

E-commerce Sites

CHAPTER

8

IN THIS CHAPTER

- Characteristics of E-commerce Sites 162
- Desirable Features 163
- Some Tools to Consider 168

Electronic commerce, or e-commerce, is the selling of merchandise via the Internet, which is one of the most common reasons why businesses are creating Internet sites. Before the explosion of the Internet, one of the ways in which retail businesses could expand beyond their local markets was to get into the mail or phone order catalog business. This meant that the retailer would have to decide which items of their product line would be made available, have catalogs printed that described those items—usually with pictures—mail out the catalogs to potential customers, and then process orders as they were received either by phone or by mail. The problem with this type of business is that for the small-business owner, the costs were usually prohibitive because of the cost of printing and mailing the catalogs and the advertising required to make potential customers aware that the catalogs were even available. Now with the popularity of the Internet, this is no longer the case. For substantially less cost than a single issue of a printed catalog, a small-business owner can create an electronic commerce site. This chapter takes a look at the electronic commerce site, describing some common characteristics and desirable features to have at such a site and then looking at some of the tools that you can use to create a site of this type.

Characteristics of E-commerce Sites

E-commerce sites differ in several significant ways from the types of sites described in Chapter 4, "Content and Media Sites," and Chapter 6, "Community Sites." Some of the ways in which e-commerce sites differ are

- Content is usually derived from a database.
- A preponderance of the pages are dynamic.
- The state of extended transactions must be maintained.

These characteristics are shared by most e-commerce sites and in this section, we will examine each of these areas, discussing why this is true. So let's get started with a discussion of the first characteristic of e-commerce sites: database-derived content.

Database-Derived Content

As we have stated, the e-commerce site is analogous in many ways to the mail or phone order catalog business. The primary focus of the e-commerce site is to display your wares to potential customers. These customers visit a site, browse or search through a selection of products, and then, you hope, place an order. In the context of this discussion, to browse means to go through the catalog looking at everything that is available, whereas to search is to look for a specific item using the most direct method available to find it. Unless the number of products is very small, the most common way in which to store this online catalog of products is in a database. This is important for several reasons. First, by storing the product information in a database, you have an easy method for updating the list of products and related information.

If you did not use a database, you would be forced to manually create a new page for every product that you are selling online. Another reason is that databases allow for searching, which means that depending on the query that you use, you can accommodate searchers who know what they want as well as the browsers who want to look at everything.

Dynamic Pages

Because the bulk of the content that visitors to the e-commerce site are interested in will reside in a database, you most likely will have very few static pages on your site. Pages will be built on-the-fly based on customer queries against the database of products. In addition, as customers view products in the catalog, most e-commerce sites allow them, using a shopping cart metaphor, to tag items for purchase. Customers are likely to periodically check the contents of this virtual shopping cart, again requiring that pages be built dynamically. This requirement to build pages dynamically from content stored in a database means that page-loading times will be longer, and that you likely will require more powerful systems if you do not want database query times to adversely affect page views. Experience has shown that if a Web site visitor is forced to wait for a page to be constructed, the visitor quickly loses patience and either leaves the Web site or attempts to reload pages, which can lead to transaction problems.

Need to Maintain State

Another characteristic that e-commerce sites exhibit is the need to maintain the state of transactions. The shopping cart metaphor implies that as customers wander through your site, they will be adding items to a list for purchase. A mechanism must be used to keep track of each visitor to the Web site and each visitor's list. The most common mechanism used is cookies. A cookie is a piece of data generated by a Web site and stored on the visitor's computer; it is requested by the server on each subsequent page visited. The cookie enables the site to remember who you are, what items you have placed in your shopping cart, and various other information about you. Although many people do not like cookies, they are a necessary evil because of the way that the HTTP protocol works. Because the HTTP protocol does not maintain a constant connection between the client and the Web server, mechanisms, such as cookies, are required to enable the server to maintain state information.

Desirable Features

Now that we have briefly covered some of the characteristics of the e-commerce site, let's take a look at our desired feature list. This feature list is relatively short and includes the following:

- An online catalog of available products
- A shopping cart to keep track of customer orders
- A mechanism for allowing credit card orders
- A customer feedback form

se features is relatively self-explanatory, but we will examine each of them briefly ting at some of the available open source tools that implement these features.

Catalog

Because we are interested in selling merchandise, it is only natural that we need a way to display to the user the merchandise that we have available. An online catalog is usually just a database with a set of tools for manipulating the data stored in it. So what features should an online catalog have? Here are some that I consider important:

- Tools for updating the database schema
- A Web interface or utility for managing the products in the database (adding, updating, and deleting)
- A mechanism for tracking inventory

To understand why these features are important, let's examine each of them in a bit more detail, starting with tools for updating the database schema.

Schema Management Tools

Because developers of online catalogs have no idea what products you will be selling, it would be very difficult to predict the exact data that you will need to store about each product in your line. At a bare minimum, you likely will need to store the name of the product, a product ID number, and pricing information. Depending on the type of merchandise, you also might need to store information about color, size, unit of measure, weight, and availability. Other information that you might want to keep could include a product category, supplier information, and shipping costs. This is why you need the capability to modify the database schema of your online catalog.

For those of you unfamiliar with databases, a *schema* refers to the way in which data is stored in the database; specifically, it defines what fields are stored in each database record, the names of tables, indices, triggers, stored procedures, and other information regarding how the data in a database is organized. The capability to modify the schema of the database allows you, as the Web site developer, to decide what information to store about products. If the online catalog you select does not include tools for modifying the schema, you probably should reconsider your selection. The capability to modify the schema of your online catalog gives you the flexibility to add missing data fields to the default schema as you need them, and a good schema management tool not only allows you to modify the schema, but also allows you to make adjustments to the catalog application, as well.

Database Population Tools

After you have an appropriate schema defined, you need to start populating your database with the products that you sell; thus, your online catalog should include one or more methods for managing the product database. You can approach this in two ways. For the initial loading of a database, command line utilities can take a product data file and import it into the database. For example, if you have a spreadsheet that lists all your products along with the details regarding each product, it would be helpful to be able to export from the spreadsheet to a file that then can be loaded into the database. After the initial loading is done, another desirable feature is a simple interface, such as a Web form, that can be used to update records in the database.

Inventory Tracking Mechanism

Although not strictly required, if you maintain your own inventory, it would be nice to store information regarding it in your online catalog so that if customers make a query about a particular product, they can find out immediately if it is in stock. This is where the inventory tracking mechanism comes into play. There is nothing more frustrating to a potential customer than to try to purchase an item, only to be told that it is on back order and not currently available. When this happens, you have probably lost that sale. If customers can see, while browsing or searching the online catalog, that an item is not currently in stock, or better yet, if customers have the option to filter their queries based on availability, the disappointment that comes from finding out after the fact that a product is not currently available is lessened, and although you might still lose the sale, you keep the customer.

Shopping Cart

The next feature that our shopping site should have is a shopping cart, which is merely a mechanism for keeping track of the items a person wants to order. Before we describe the shopping cart feature, let's consider what it would be like to not have this feature. A visitor to our e-commerce site begins browsing through the online catalog. They find a product they would like to purchase and click a button to buy it. They then are prompted to enter the information required to complete the order, such as shipping address, payment information, and a shipping method. After you validate the information, the order is sent to the order fulfillment stage. Now if the customer was interested in purchasing only this single product, this is fine, but suppose that the customer wants to purchase other items. In this case, the customer starts all over again, and unless you store all the data about shipping address, shipping method, and payment method, the customer will have to enter this data again for each item he or she wants. As you can imagine, this could become quite tedious, especially if your product line is such that people typically purchase several items, such as at an online book store. The shopping cart eliminates this problem by allowing customers to do all their browsing and product selection prior to completing the transaction. After customers have made all their selections, they then can enter the ordering information just once and complete the transaction. So what features should a shopping cart application include? Here is a short list of a few that you might find useful:

- The capability to add items without leaving the online catalog
- A View Shopping Cart function with the capability to modify quantity and other details such as size or color from the View function
- The capability to maintain shopping cart state across sessions
- Resistance to spurious updates or orders if a person reloads a page

Let's now look at each of these in more detail to see why they are desirable and useful features of the shopping cart application.

Adding Items Without Leaving the Catalog

Some e-commerce sites use shopping carts that require you to leave the online catalog each time you select an item. These sites usually dump you into the view shopping cart interface each time you click a Buy button or Add to Shopping Cart button. This might not seem like a big deal, but it is an unnatural way to shop for most people. When people are shopping at a grocery store, for example, they wander through the merchandise and add items to their cart as they go. They normally do not stop each time and review the items in their cart as they are shopping. Instead, they add the item and continue wandering through the merchandise until they have everything they want. The online shopping cart should work the same way. The person finds an item in the online catalog, tags it for the shopping cart, and continues browsing through the catalog. When customers are ready to stop shopping, they use the next feature—the View Shopping Cart function.

A Shopping Cart View Function

After customers have made their selections, they will want to verify that they have everything they asked for in their cart. Your e-commerce site should therefore have a way to look at the contents and not only view, but also modify quantities, sizes, or colors, as appropriate. This is typically a tabular form that lists each item, the quantity and other parameters, and the price for that item along with a total so that customers can see how much they have spent so far. Also desirable are options to delete items, either by setting the quantity to zero or using a check box.

Maintaining Shopping Carts Across Sessions

One way in which you can better serve your customers is to allow flexibility in how they shop online. Some e-commerce sites implement sessions in such a way as to force the customer to select the items they want and check out within a predetermined time period. They do this by implementing timeouts so that if the customer doesn't request a page from the site within the timeout period, that session is lost and the contents of the shopping cart are lost with it. Although this might seem a reasonable thing to do, consider the following. A customer shopping from home visits your site and starts adding items to a shopping cart. He has added two or three items when the doorbell rings. The customer goes to answer the door and ends up listening to a Girl Scout cookie sales pitch. He makes a purchase from the scout and comes back to find that your site has timed out his session and he must start all over. Depending on how easy it is to repopulate his shopping cart with the items he wants, this can be quite an annoyance—and you might end up losing the customer. If, on the other hand, you allowed this customer to save the cart, he could have handled the interruption to his online shopping and come back to your site to complete the transaction at his leisure. This makes for more satisfied customers, and satisfied customers are usually repeat customers.

Avoidance of Spurious Updates and Orders

One of the facts of life is that no matter how many times you tell customers not to reload a page or to use only your buttons or links to navigate your site, they will use the browser Reload or Back buttons instead. This has a tendency to cause problems for some shopping cart applications because they interpret a reload as an update request, and might end up modifying quantities ordered or replacing orders when that was not the intention of the customer. You should consider this when selecting your shopping cart application and look for one that is resistant to this type of behavior. In addition, a good shopping cart application should give customers feedback so that they know their transactions were processed. If the application doesn't provide for it, you also could consider customizing it so that in addition to immediate feedback, the customer receives e-mail indicating that the order has been received and/or shipped.

Credit Card Processing

One of the trickiest problems to solve for any e-commerce site is the problem of how customers are going to pay for their purchases. The retailer has several options. Some of these options are

- Ship to your customer C.O.D. (cash on delivery).
- Require a check or money order from them before shipping.
- Use an online payment service, such as Paypal.
- Accept credit card orders.

Pros and cons exist for each of these options. For example, if you ship items C.O.D., you are trusting that the customer will accept the merchandise and that you will not go broke trying to collect restocking fees from those people who don't. The problem with requiring a check or money order before shipping is the time delay, which, in today's instant-gratification society, many people will find unacceptable. This leaves online payment services and credit card orders. Both of these are good options and the online payment services are gaining in popularity among consumers because they don't have to give their credit card numbers to every online vendor they use. Small businesses might find this option especially appealing because the fees for most of these online payment services are very reasonable, based on a percentage of the payment being requested.

Your final alternative is, of course, to use a credit card verification suite. A *credit card verification suite* is an application that takes credit card information, either via a network connection or as a file, and communicates with a credit card clearing house to process the payments. The factors that affect the cost of such a suite include the number of merchant accounts supported, the number of servers you can install it on, and the number of connections supported. There are a couple of different packages supported on Linux from different vendors, including Red Hat. Most of these packages require a server with a modem which is used to connect to a credit card clearing house, although this is changing and some packages also support secure connection over the Internet via an SSL connection.

Customer Feedback Mechanism

One other feature that is important for an e-commerce site is a customer feedback mechanism. This is usually just a Web form that sends an e-mail. These are trivial to write, so if you prefer, there are hundreds of CGI programs or scripted versions of this type of form available that you can download from sites such as Freshmeat at `http://freshmeat.net/`. The reason for including this feature is so that customers can communicate problems they experience with the Web site, problems with orders, or just make a comment. The alternative to a CGI form is to simply provide an e-mail link that invokes the mail function of the customer's browser. One reason why the e-mail form approach is preferable is that some browsers do not support e-mail links.

Some Tools to Consider

In Chapters 4 and 6, when we started looking at specific tools to use for creating a site, we looked at tools that implemented a specific feature that we were required to glue together to create a total Internet site. For the e-commerce site, however, because of the complexity of the application and the need for security, we will be focusing on complete electronic suites that implement the entire feature set that we desire. We will look at two such suites:

- Symphero
- Interchange

We will examine each suite for feature set, ease of customization, and ease of administration. Hopefully, after looking at each of these suites, you will be able to determine which one you could use for your e-commerce site.

Symphero

Symphero is a suite of tools that has been developed by Brave New Worlds, a consulting firm that specializes in developing e-commerce sites. The requirements for using this suite are fairly light and all the software is easily obtainable. These requirements include the following:

- Apache 1.3.x, with mod_perl and mod_include support
- MySQL 3.22
- Perl 5.003
- Error 0.13 (Perl module)
- DBI 1.13 (Perl module)
- Msql-Mysql 1.2210 (Perl module)
- Business::CreditCard (Perl module)

The version numbers supplied are the earliest versions that can support the Symphero software and that reflect the requirements for the 3.1.x versions of the software. If you are running a later version of Symphero, you should refer to the documentation for the version number details. Documentation is available at the Symphero Web site found at `http://www.symphero.com/` in the developer support area. The supporting software listed previously can be found any number of ways, but one of the easiest is to obtain Apache, MySQL, and Perl via Freshmeat at `http://freshmeat.net/` and the Perl modules via CPAN at `http://www.cpan.org/`. Now that you have an idea of what is required to get started with Symphero, let's take a look at how it compares with our feature list.

The Online Catalog

Symphero stores product data in a database and groups products into categories, which are typically listed on the site's home page. When a customer selects a category, the database is queried and matching products are presented to the customer. By default, frames are used so that the list of categories are always available in one frame and the database query results are presented in another frame. You have the option to display only a list of products or to display a picture of the products along with a text description. The results frame also includes a button that enables you to select the item for addition to your shopping cart. Products in the database usually are added when the site is created. Unfortunately, because the developers of Symphero have no way of knowing how the product information is currently stored, there are no tools for doing this. Instead, users of the Symphero suite must develop their own. This means that you must translate the data into a form that is compatible with the Symphero database schema. The basic steps you would be required to take are

- Export the data from the current data store
- Convert to a format that corresponds to the Symphero database schema
- Read the converted data and insert it into the Symphero database

To better understand this process, let's consider an example. Suppose that you run a small toy store. You keep all your product data in an Excel spreadsheet. Using the export facility of Excel, you would export the data to a comma separated values text file, which is sometimes called a CSV file. After you have done this, you could use Perl to parse the CSV file, extract the product information that would go into the Symphero database, such as product name, category, optional subcategories, product description, and price, and insert it into the MySQL database using the Perl interface for MySQL. After you have loaded the initial data in this manner, you then can use the Symphero software to edit it through their remote administration interface, using a Web browser such as Netscape Communicator or Internet Explorer.

Some of the areas of weakness in the Symphero online catalog include the lack of schema management tools and the lack of tools for bulk loading of catalog data. Although the documentation explains this lack of bulk loading tools as the result of not knowing what format the data is stored in to begin with, the package could include a script that takes a CSV file and loads the database from it. The person implementing the Web site would then be required only to extract the data from the current data store to that format and run the provided script. Another area of weakness on the part of Symphero is that it does not include inventory availability data in the database schema. In fact, there does not appear to be any inventory management functionality at all. Fortunately, if you are fluent in Perl and SQL, these deficiencies can be overcome. A much harder deficiency to overcome is the lack of schema management tools. Because the default schema for the database does not include variables for factors such as color or size, which you might need for clothing items, you must store each color and size combination as a separate product. This can lead to such problems as price information mismatches if you forget to update every one of these combinations. This problem is compounded as the number of combinations increases.

The Shopping Cart

The shopping cart functionality of Symphero is pretty good. Although it does not allow you to add items to your cart without leaving the catalog interface, it does provide a button to take you back to the page in the catalog you just left, which is the next best thing. When you select an item to be added to your cart, a cookie is used to keep track of the state information. The confirmation page that you see when you select an item includes information regarding the number of items in your cart and a note about the requirement for cookies. It even includes information on how to enable cookies in some of the more popular Web browsers. The View Shopping Cart feature lists all the items you have selected in tabular format with a total row. From this interface, you can adjust quantities of each item, but little else. This is sufficient in most cases; however, if your inventory includes items for which color or size are factors, the inability to modify these parameters could be viewed as a limitation. Another area of deficiency in the Symphero product is the inability to maintain shopping cart state. One area where Symphero is not lacking is in the resistance to spurious updates. Even if you sit on the confirmation page after selecting an item, or sit on the View Shopping Cart page and continually reload it, you do not end up with multiple items being added to your shopping cart by mistake.

Symphero Credit Card Processing

Symphero does not include the software required to process credit cards. You must obtain this separately. What it does provide is credit card number validation. What this means is that when a customer enters credit card information on the ordering page, that number is run through an algorithm that determines if the card number is valid. This is possible because the last digit of the credit card number is a checksum for the remaining numbers.

Other Features of Symphero

Some of the other features that Symphero provides includes mailing list support, a Specials tool, and an affiliates program. The mailing list management is done via Majordomo, and if you would like to be able to market to current customers of your e-commerce site, this can be a big win for you. By allowing your customers to subscribe to a newsletter, you can keep them up-to-date on special offers, changes to inventory, and other events designed to keep them as customers. The key to success with mailing lists of this type is to make the customer actively choose to participate, or to "opt in." There is no method guaranteed to anger customers more than to automatically subscribe them to a mailing list unless they say no. Customer are basically lazy and often overlook the fact that you might be giving them the opportunity to subscribe to your list with the default being automatic subscription. These same customers will then flood your e-mail system with complaints about receiving spam until you go in and remove them.

The Specials tool is a tool that allows you to designate a product as a special item. This item is featured on the site's home page and it is intended to entice customers to make an immediate purchase even before they begin browsing the catalog. This has been proven to be an effective tool for many e-commerce sites, and updating your specials frequently is one mechanism for bringing customers back to your site. The affiliates program is interesting in that it can be used to allow other Web site owners to link to your site and to earn a commission on any sales that result. This is one way that you can advertise your site with minimal effort. The program works by having the link to your site trigger some code, which you send to the affiliate, that keeps track of the fact that the customer came to your site via the affiliate. When the customer makes a purchase, you would pay the affiliate a percentage of the sale.

Ease of Administration and Customization

Administration of your Symphero site is done primarily through a Web browser using the Symphero remote administration features. This facility is primarily designed to allow you to keep the product database up to date, to view orders, and to manage the specials. This is all done via a secure Web interface and like the rest of Symphero, it is customizable. Other tools that you might consider adding to this interface are management of the mailing lists and the affiliates program. The options are limited only by your ability to code them. If you would like to see the amount of customization that is available to you, you should visit the Symphero Web site and look at some of the case studies. Included at `http://www.symphero.com/casestudies/15misc.html` are links to some sites built using the Symphero software.

Interchange

Another e-commerce package that is available through Red Hat is Interchange. This product is the evolution of two projects that once competed with Symphero: Tallyman and Mini-Vend. A visit to either the Mini-Vend Web site at `http://developer.akopia.com/minivend3/` or the Tallyman Web site at `http://tallyman.akopia.com/` will direct you to the Interchange site. Development of these older projects is no longer being done. Interchange is like Symphero in that it is open source software, but it is in some ways more featureful than Symphero. Some of the ways in which Interchange differs from Symphero is in its database support. Whereas Symphero uses only MySQL out of the box, Interchange supports several databases, including MySQL, PostgreSQL, and Oracle. You also can use other databases that have an ODBC interface, such as Sybase, MS SQL, or even MS Access. Other ways in which Interchange differs from Symphero is that it incorporates support for some of the leading online payment sources, such as CyberCash, which allows you to process credit card data immediately while the customer is online. Now let's take a look at our desired feature set and see how Interchange stacks up.

The Interchange Online Catalog

As previously noted, the Interchange online catalog can be stored in several types of databases, and you are free to choose the one you are most comfortable with. By default, Interchange uses DBM files, support for which is standard on most Linux-based and Unix systems. This means that if you do not require a database for some other part of your Web site, you don't have to install one just for Interchange. It also means that if you already have one of the supported databases installed to support some other Web application, you can use it instead of having to install some other database application. This is a big win if your Web server services other sites besides your e-commerce site. In addition, the online catalog of Interchange is fairly flexible and you, as the Web site creator, are allowed to define the schema as long as it contains the minimal items that the Interchange software requires. These minimal items are a unique product ID, a product name, and the price. This flexibility is because the schema is defined in the file that is used to load the product catalog. Another win for Interchange over Symphero is that Interchange includes scripts with the tool suite to create the catalogs from simple text files. This means that importing data into the Interchange database from another data source is simplified.

The Interchange Shopping Cart

The shopping cart functionality of Interchange is very similar to that of Symphero. When you select an item from the catalog, you are taken to a page where you can see the state of your cart. One difference is that unlike Symphero, which includes a button to take you back to where you left off in the catalog, clicking the button to continue shopping at an Interchange-powered site does not. You are usually just dropped back onto a default page. This can be frustrating if you intended to select several items, and this is one of the areas where a large number of Interchange users focus their customization efforts. One such customization is to provide a list of products on a page and instead of including individual Buy buttons for each product, you include a check box by each product listed and a single button to add checked items to the cart in one fell swoop. This is a good compromise and, depending on the type of merchandise you are selling, might be a better interface than the one provided by default. Like Symphero, Interchange is resistant to spurious updates from users who reload pages or use the Back and Forward buttons on their browsers.

Credit Card Processing with Interchange

Unlike Symphero, whose only direct support for credit card processing is to ensure that the number entered is valid, Interchange includes support for some of the more popular online payment services, including CyberCash. Instead of having to maintain a separate credit card processing server, Interchange sites can do online credit card verification by using this built-in functionality. The drawback is that if you are using some payment method other than the ones supported by Interchange, you are on your own.

Other Interchange Features

Like Symphero, Interchange supports more than our basic feature set and includes support for affiliate programs, search capabilities, and support for multiple catalogs. Some of the features that are missing from Interchange are the mailing list software that is included with Symphero and the remote administration pages. Details of the features and capabilities of the Interchange software are detailed at the Interchange Web site found at `http://interchange.redhat.com/`. This site includes product documentation, tutorials, and information on services available from Red Hat for setting up an Interchange site.

Ease of Administration and Customization

Interchange, which is written in Perl and available under the GPL, is very customizable. You are limited only by your coding ability. One nice thing about Interchange is that all the Perl modules required to build an Interchange site are available as a single bundle from CPAN as Bundle::Interchange. Interchange is somewhat more complex than Symphero, but help is available through mailing lists and via Internet Relay Chat. Naturally, if you are willing to pay, Red Hat would be glad to assist you in setting up and customizing your Interchange site.

Summary

In this chapter, we have taken a look at what it takes to build an e-commerce site, starting with a look at the characteristics of such a site, followed by a look at the desired features set, and finally an examination of some tools that can be used to create a successful e-commerce site. In the next chapter, we will present a case study of a site built using one of these tools. Hopefully, by combining the information contained in this chapter with the practical example in the following one, you will be able to duplicate this effort for your own site.

E-commerce Sites: Two Case Studies

CHAPTER

9

IN THIS CHAPTER

- Introduction 176
- A Brief History of E-commerce 176
- Open Source E-commerce Systems 179
- What Is an E-commerce System? 180
- What Is a Web Server? 180
- What Is Apache-SSL? 180
- What Is Perl? 181
- CP Commerce 182
- The Case of Mia Casa 183
- Firebreath.com 190
- Preparing Your Business for E-commerce 196
- Notes on Hosting an E-commerce Site 196
- Summary 197

Introduction

In the previous chapter, we took a look at the characteristics of e-commerce sites and at a couple of open source tools that can be used in their development. In this chapter, Brian DeSpain, whose e-commerce consulting company created Symphero, provides us with his view of e-commerce along with a discussion of two sites built using these tools. These case studies show how his firm used open source tools to create effective sites for two of their clients. The first of these clients, Mia Casa, is a firm that started out as a more traditional, catalog-based retailer that wanted to move into the Internet space. The other, Firebreath.com, was from the very beginning a strictly virtual business designed for the Internet. The case studies differ from the ones in Chapters 5 and 7 in that they ignore the details of the implementation and focus on the decision-making process and the rules you must follow to create effective e-commerce sites.

A Brief History of E-commerce

Over the last several years, small and mid-sized businesses have often been forced to stand idly by and watch larger or better-funded rivals carve up cyberspace. These rivals have spent hundreds of thousands—even millions—of dollars developing Web sites with advanced electronic commerce capabilities. Small businesses have had to settle for little more than an online brochure.

Some would say that e-commerce sounds impersonal, but it is actually more personal in several important ways. Good e-commerce systems are database driven and include tools that enable the site administrator to easily keep product information up to date. With fresh information, the site becomes a powerful customer service tool. Customers are able to access the information they need on demand. All product information is available based on customer demand. There is no more holding on the phone, no more incompetent or rude operators, no more phone tag.

Well-designed e-commerce sites are flexible enough to deliver the information the customer wants in the way the customer wants it. Because most of these sites are database driven, customized search tools become possible. The customer can demand product information in a certain way, and that content is pulled from the database, compiled into a Web page on-the-fly, and delivered to the customer in a format tailor-made to the customer's wishes. This capability is yet another way that e-commerce means superior customer service.

Good sites are also a tremendous sales support tool. Salespeople no longer have to spend their time faxing out the same information to prospect after prospect. It's all on the Web site. They can focus on selling. What's more, the site will handle many of the less complex sales, freeing up salespeople to work on more complex transactions where they are adding more value.

With all the opportunities that e-commerce embodies, why have small and mid-sized businesses, traditionally more innovative than their larger brothers, been slow to capitalize on e-commerce? The barriers to entry in e-commerce have traditionally been twofold. The potentially tremendous expense of an e-commerce site has kept many businesses at bay. The unfamiliar nature and complexity of the Internet has put many business owners in the position of feeling unqualified to make Internet business decisions. The medium can be quite overwhelming to the uninitiated.

Launching any e-commerce site is a complex endeavor, requiring many elements of business, IT, fulfillment, and accounting. It can be a frustrating experience if the wrong choice of consultant or technology is made. When choosing technology, especially relatively new technology such as Web software, making the wrong choice can be costly, so there are some key things to be aware of. Previously, many IT managers took a look at the number of years a company had been in business and financial indicators such as quarters of profitability and track record. Although these are important criteria in evaluating a vendor, the license of the software being used to create the e-commerce system must be evaluated along a separate set of criteria with the license being a key component. The size of the company is often not an indicator of stability of a product. Another factor to consider is that many businesses are ignorant of the Internet and do not have a clear picture of what they would like to accomplish.

NOTE

In July 1999, Intel Corporation bought ICat—at the time, one of the leading e-commerce packages with close to 40,000 deployments worldwide. With an extensive channel program, ICat was widely recognized as a leader in e-commerce catalog software. Forty-five days after the acquisition of ICat, Intel discontinued the e-commerce software product. Forty thousand customers were left in the cold, including companies such as Boeing and Hewlett-Packard, without any support or upgrade path. The situation was compounded by the fact that Intel refused to release the source code for the product. Companies that had bet on the safe but "closed source" option found themselves marooned. Companies that had invested hundreds of thousands of dollars in this software, and even more money in the knowledge of employees, the business processes, and everything involved in bringing an enterprise piece of software into a business, were left with nothing—no recourse. This is one of the worst possible situations for a company to find itself in and one of the most compelling reasons to chose an open source e-commerce system.

Many companies have found open source e-commerce systems compelling solutions without sacrificing any features at all. In fact, most find the experience quite pleasant.

So, how do you succeed at e-commerce? You should follow a few general rules to increase the odds of succeeding at marketing on the Web. These rules apply to both nonprofits and business efforts. Although these are in no way magic bullets, they are good rules to follow.

- Have a clear plan for your e-commerce site—Many people believe that this should be left in the hands of the consultant hired to design the site. Be aware that the consultant works best with a clear plan in hand. Furthermore, the consultant might be a programmer and will not have your expertise in selling your product and might not know the details of your audience demographics. By working as a team, you are sure to achieve the best of both worlds.
- Carefully choose the products in your catalog—You want to present your products in the best possible light. Carefully think about placement within the site. You don't want to frighten people away with a big ticket item at the outset, but you do want to draw them into the site so that they will see it eventually. Alix Olavarria, president of MiaCasa.com notes, "Make sure your product offer is solid and specific for easier marketability."
- Make sure that you can update your database yourself—The key to getting return visitors and business is to keep your site fresh and dynamic. To make your site dynamic, you need the flexibility to add or remove products at a moment's notice and update information quickly. Make sure you have the essential updating skills in-house.
- Listen to your consultant—Although some people might like a particular graphical image because of their attachment to a company or organization, not everyone will have the same opinion. Make sure that your Web pages load quickly, and then ask people for their opinion of the site. More important than simply getting their opinion is to listen to it. Paul Mayville of Firebreath.com noted that when looking for a designer for his e-commerce project, "I wanted creative thinking. Possibly outside the normal boundaries of conventional wisdom. And while I wanted that creativity, I also was looking for solid technology."
- Examine the traffic reports on your site—Traffic reports will tell you how many people are going to your site, as well as what times they go there and what they are looking at on the site. This information is critical for planning new developments and can help you examine the way people are using the site. Do you have donation information buried so that no one is finding it? Put a link in from one of the main pages to make sure that people can find it.
- Keep the bells and whistles down and focus on selling your product or service—Remember that animations slow down a page. As a general rule, if a page takes more than 20 to 30 seconds to load, people will leave your site because they find it too slow.

- Treat your Web site as additional retail space—If you treat your Web site as an additional storefront operation, you'll be less likely to use poor design and cutesy toys. Make it an extension of your existing service and information efforts, and you'll be much more successful.
- Return e-mail and customer service questions promptly—Imagine going into a store asking the clerk a question and waiting twenty minutes for him to respond. Taking more than one day to respond to customer inquiries on a Web site is generally a bad idea. One possibility is the use of auto responders to e-mail inquiries, followed up by a response from a real person.

With these rules in mind, let's take a look at some of the options available from the open source community when you create e-commerce sites.

Open Source E-commerce Systems

Quite a few open source e-commerce systems are available. A quick look using the Freshmeat search engine reveals 29 e-commerce software projects. Most companies should be looking for a product that is open source and also has the standing of a committed company behind it. This narrows the field somewhat because there has been some consolidation in the market. As you read this case study, keep in mind some of the choices that these companies were faced with when deploying an e-commerce Web site.

For people interested in an open source e-commerce package, I would recommend Red Hat's Interchange and Xao's ClearingPoint Commerce, also known as CP Commerce. Both products are backed by quality companies and are offered under the GNU Public License. Both have been deployed in numerous Web sites and business models. You can find more information about these products at the company Web sites, `http://interchange.redhat.com` and `http://www.xao.com`.

NOTE

ClearingPoint Commerce is the product formerly known as Symphero. In addition, all the open source components of Symphero are available on SourceForge at `http://sourceforge.net/projects/opensymphero/`.

You should also conduct some research on your own to find the product that best fits your needs. For a comprehensive listing of open source e-commerce software, check Freshmeat.net and the open source directory at `http://www.opensourcedirectory.org/`.

What Is an E-Commerce System?

An e-commerce system is a system that works with your existing Web server, such as Microsoft's IIS, Apache, or IBM's Websphere Web server. It is a middleware product with features that can display product information, change that product information, manage online catalog information, and calculate price, shipping, and handling. It has tools for taking credit cards or purchase orders and tools for managing customers and customer information. Most e-commerce software packages provide tools for managing all these business elements as well as integrating Web orders into an existing CRM and order management environment. Let's take a look at a sample e-commerce system and some of the features of the product. This system example is CP Commerce.

The Database: Heart of an E-commerce System

At the heart of every e-commerce system is a relational database. The database stores information about products, customers, inventory, and so on. Relational databases can also be open source (MySQL and PostgreSQL, for example) or expensive and proprietary, such as Oracle and IBM's DB2. CP Commerce can use any of these databases to manage information. CP Commerce, remember, is the important middleware piece that provides the end users their buying experience. Very often, open source developers use MySQL to support their e-commerce effort. This isn't the only choice, but it certainly is free. All the sites in our case study use MySQL. By contrast, Red Hat has integrated PostgreSQL into its Interchange product because this is the database that Red Hat has chosen to support. The choice of RDBMS is up to the developer.

What Is a Web Server?

The Web server is the piece of server software that serves the Web pages to the Web customer. The e-commerce software works with the Web server to provide content for the Web page while the server software serves the page. CP Commerce uses Apache (the world's most popular Web server) and the SSL (secure sockets layer) extensions of Apache. The SSL extensions encrypt the transactions, especially during the all-important check-out process when credit card information is taken. Apache/SSL provides strong encryption.

What Is Apache-SSL?

Apache-SSL is a secure Web server based on Apache and SSLeay/OpenSSL. It is licensed under a BSD-style license, which means, in short, that you are free to use it for commercial or noncommercial purposes. It is based on SSLeay implementation by Eric Young and provides open source munitions-grade security.

What Is PERL?

PERL is a scripting language that has become one of the most popular open source projects of all time. It is heavily used in the Internet space because of its flexibility and expandability of the language. In this section, we will take a look at some of its features and why it is well suited to Web application development.

Perl Features

- Perl takes the best features from other languages, such as C, awk, sed, sh, and BASIC, among others.
- Perl works with third-party databases such as Oracle, Sybase, Postgres, and many others through the abstract database interface called DBI.
- Perl can work with HTML, XML, and other markup languages.
- Perl has Unicode support.
- Perl always has been and always will be Y2K compliant.
- Perl supports both procedural and object-oriented programming.
- Perl can interface with external C/C++ libraries through XS or SWIG.

Perl Is Open Source

- Perl is developed by the perl5porters, or p5p for short. Perl 5 is extensible, and more than 400 third-party modules are available from the Comprehensive Perl Archive Network (CPAN).
- perl (the interpreter of Perl) can be embedded into other systems.

Perl and the Web

- Perl is the most popular Web-programming language because of its facility with text manipulation and rapid development cycle.
- Perl has been called "the duct tape of the Internet."
- Perl's CGI.pm module makes handling HTML forms easy.
- CGI.pm is part of Perl's standard distribution.
- Perl can handle encrypted Web transactions, including e-commerce situations.
- Companies such as Amazon.com and Deja.com use Perl to run their sites.
- Perl can be embedded into Web servers to speed up processing by as much as 2000%. See `http://perl.apache.org`.
- The Apache Web server can use mod_perl to embed a Perl interpreter.

- The Netscape Web server can use nsapi_perl to embed a Perl interpreter.
- Using Perl's DBI package, Web-database integration is easy.

CP Commerce

CP Commerce is a middleware e-commerce package designed to be deployed on any modern Unix. It is written in Perl, uses the Apache Web server, and can use a variety of databases to support the back end of the Web site. The following are the features you'll find in CP Commerce.

- Provides search and search results—When using the Web site search facility, multiple parameters in the database can be searched on simultaneously.
- Variable search results templates—After a search, CP Commerce can provide search results in a variety of formats, tuned to the customer's needs.
- Flexible database structure—CP Commerce supports a highly flexible database structure designed around the needs of businesses.
- Multiple category structure—CP Commerce supports a highly flexible database category structure so that additional category elements can be added.
- Inventory tracking and control—CP Commerce tracks inventory and inventory location and can auto-decrement inventory from multiple locations.
- Online credit card and address management—Business customers can manage multiple locations, multiple lines of credit, and multiple credit cards.
- Modular—Additional software modules interact with CP Commerce, providing XML translation, B2B functionality and so on.
- Integration with various shippers—CP Commerce is integrated with UPS, Federal Express, and all other major carriers for global shipping.
- Online CRM features—CP Commerce features online CRM features, allowing customers to check their order status and shipping location.
- Support for multiple currencies—CP Commerce supports transactions not only in U.S. dollars, but in foreign currencies as well, and it supports multiple currencies on the same site.
- Support for variable VAT and sales tax.
- Web-based administration of database and static content—CP Commerce includes modules for managing all the content associated with a Web site.
- Electronic mailing list—CP Commerce includes the capability to create mailing lists based on customer criteria and generate multiple or one-time mailings to customers in the database based on those criteria.

- Webalizer 2.0—CP Commerce includes a complete log analysis tool, tracking hits, unique visitors, and files served. This is an essential element in any site for measuring the success of the site.
- Affiliates program—CP Commerce includes an automatic mechanism for tracking referrals from other Web sites with a commission-based system in place for rewarding the referring affiliate site with a percentage of the sale or on a per click-through basis.

Xao, the company backing the CP Commerce package, provides a set of modules that interacts with CP Commerce and extends the functionality of the system. These modules are described in the following list:

- CP Foundation Server—Provides storage, search and retrieval facilities for all other Clearingpoint modules
- CP XML Translation Filters—Translate from existing document format to standard XML formats for knowledge sharing.
- CP Exporter—Enables data stream from foundation server to servers using other formats for batch processing external system archival.
- CP Application Construction Classes—APIs and objects to rapidly develop client/server applications using a Web-based front end.
- CP Reporting—Tools for collecting statistical data from the foundation server, including templates for visualizing in popular layouts.
- CP Application Adaptors—Pipe data from foundation server to online applications such as ERP shipping and accounting systems.
- CP Messaging Server—Handles message flow between partners, including data type and frequency of communications updates, including document flow and business process information.

As noted previously, CP Commerce is the product formerly known as Symphero. The CP Commerce package is available from `http://www.xao.com`. You can find out more about the modules described previously by following the links to the Products/Service pages.

In the following section, we will take a look at some businesses that have deployed open source e-commerce systems and what the results have been.

The Case of Mia Casa

If it has to do with home décor and can be characterized by the term "relaxed elegance," you'll find it at Mia Casa. Since its launch in April 1999, MiaCasa.com has focused on selling unique home decorative accessories and gifts. However, as Mia Casa expands, the company will feature an even greater assortment of high-quality goods for the home, including furniture, textiles, and an unmatched product line of gifts and accessories. Mia Casa's mission is to become a leading electronic and catalog retailer by offering substantial product selection, aggressively priced merchandise, and unparalleled customer service to individual consumers, corporations, and institutions.

The Mia Casa Product Line

Currently, Mia Casa offers more than 300 distinctive home décor items, lifestyle accessories, and gifts that are difficult—if not impossible—to locate elsewhere, either online or off. The average order at MiaCasa.com is approximately $150.

The best-selling product line at MiaCasa.com is the collection of fine decorative picture frames. Customers looking for traditional home accents or gifts for corporate events, weddings, holidays, and special occasions favor these frames. The picture frames are available in a variety of sizes and materials, including sterling silver, silverplate, recycled aluminum, and inlaid woods. They range in price from $15 to $200 per frame. Customers can also take advantage of special gift services, such as custom engraving, elegant gift wrap, and hand-written gift cards to personalize their selections.

The Mia Casa Home Décor collection also includes lines of hand-bound albums, journals, guest books, handmade silk flower bouquets and candles, aromatherapy candles, imported bath products, and other home accents in polished aluminum, leather, and silver. All the Mia Casa product lines have a high perceived value and practical appeal, meeting today's demand for a sophisticated, yet casual, lifestyle.

MiaCasa.com also offers a unique line of specialty gifts, including premade themed gift baskets and gift sets for customers seeking easy and impressive gift solutions. Products include unique packaging such as bamboo chests, sinamay satchels, and chipboard boxes filled with imported soaps, vintage bath products, or handmade candles. Prices range from $30 to $140. Mia Casa's high standard for distinctive gift solutions compels the company's buyers to continually expand and change the gift line. Today's online shoppers want interesting, hard-to-find gifts for their colleagues, friends, and family, but they also want to find these gifts easily and without hassle. Mia Casa exists to fulfill this need.

The unique services currently offered by Mia Casa complement the style and quality of existing merchandise. Custom engraving, leather stamping, hand-written gift cards, and special-order fulfillment give customers the full service they might not expect to find at an online boutique. In addition, the Web site offers an Executive Gift Program, which gives discounts and custom order assistance to corporate buyers who purchase items in bulk, and a Wedding and Gift Registry for special-occasion gift shoppers.

The Mia Casa Customer Base

Mia Casa currently enjoys a varied customer base. The home/office décor shopper wants stylish, functional, top-quality products that go with everything they already own. The wedding gift shopper desires classic, high-quality gifts that will last through the years. The corporate gift shopper looks for impressive, yet practical, gifts that are cost effective. And finally, the special-occasion gift shopper expects to find anything from easy and predictable to fun and unusual.

Mia Casa's product base is designed to appeal to customers in search of exceptionally produced, high-end goods at competitive prices. In other words, Mia Casa allows customers to obtain products of a type and quality associated with a particular lifestyle (products found in homes featured in a magazine such as *Architectural Digest* or *Elle Décor*, for example) at a reasonable cost. Currently, a customer in search of a traditional sterling silver picture frame, for instance, would easily be able to find and purchase one from MiaCasa.com at a rate significantly lower than the cost of a similar item at a retailer such as Tiffany & Co. The high perceived value of Mia Casa's product line allows the company to carry higher margins on cost than many competitors selling goods of lesser perceived value.

Additionally, MiaCasa.com offers services that give customers the opportunity to customize an item with a personal touch. Fine engraving on a silver picture frame, stamping a monogram on a leather album, hand-written gift cards, and in the near future, the inclusion of a digital photograph (sent electronically through the site) inside a frame are just a few examples of special features that distinguish MiaCasa.com from other e-tailers in the same market.

Mia Casa strives to evoke the relaxed atmosphere and feeling of an intimate Old World boutique. Unlike the enormous, hard-to-navigate, and impersonal department-store-style shopping destinations, when customers click through the MiaCasa.com Web pages or browse the Mia Casa catalog, they find just what they are looking for quickly and easily. Customers can browse the Web site using specific category links, or they can be more specific using a product keyword search or style search function.

Mia Casa shoppers will always find products beautifully photographed and displayed. Above all, the Mia Casa customer will experience personalized attention that will set them at ease and make them feel welcome. Policies and FAQs are readily available on every Web page with one click of the mouse and real-time, informed customer care agents will soon be on hand to assist Web site and catalog shoppers 24 hours a day, 7 days a week. These features distinguish Mia Casa from other shopping destinations and enable Mia Casa to build enduring relationships with customers.

The Mia Casa Business Model

Mia Casa's business model is to offer individual and corporate consumers a unique range of quality products with an emphasis on classic, European designs that are available 24 hours a day, 7 days a week over the Internet and through the Mia Casa catalog. Operating as an "Internet Boutique" supported by a quarterly mail-order catalog, Mia Casa fills an important niche in the marketplace as an appealing alternative to large, ineffectual retail giants by offering elegant, exceptional goods at affordable prices along with convenience and superior customer service. Additionally, Mia Casa offers unique personalization options to customers, including engraving, leather stamping, and hand-written gift cards, not easily available elsewhere in the marketplace.

Mia Casa's greatest strength is its cost-effective, disciplined approach to building and maintaining its customer relationships. While other e-commerce companies have come and gone, spending millions of dollars on flashy Super Bowl ads along the way, Mia Casa has maintained a more conservative strategy: gradually building recognition and a satisfied customer base.

Business Challenges/Objectives

As a cataloger with higher end products, Mia Casa faced some unique challenges in its catalog presentation. The company needed a system flexible enough to accommodate its merchandising and branding needs and customizable to its business needs. It needed a solution that would scale as the business grew. In the words of Alexandra Olavarria, President, "We looked for a one-stop, total e-commerce solution: a company that offered design, hosting, security, tech support, and a degree of marketing expertise."

Mia Casa, like many small catalogers, was looking for a single shop that could provide the full range of services, including software, support, hosting, and some marketing expertise to help launch the site. The Internet was relatively new territory for them, and like many traditional businesses, the company was looking for an experienced partner to help with the deployment.

Mia Casa was also looking to use the Web site to gauge demand for a extended version of its print catalog.

The flexibility of the electronic commerce software chosen was also important to MiaCasa.com. As cataloger, it was looking for more flexibility than an out-of-the-box solution would provide. Accordingly, an open source software package appealed to them. Olavarria stated, "Knowing that we had access to e-commerce software specifically designed for us and our needs was a definite plus when considering e-commerce providers. We wanted the flexibility to change our code and add features, further customizing the site as our business grew."

Mia Casa's budget also didn't allow for six figure e-commerce software for what was essentially a test of the market online. Mia Casa needed to effectively test the market without making a major investment in technology. Olavarria notes, "We wanted to build a business that would capitalize on the reach of the Internet and make our products and services available to millions of potential customers affordably."

Approach

Mia Casa approached Xao in 1999 about developing the site on CP Commerce, an open source e-commerce solution. Xao interactive questionnaire assessment methodology was led by a Xao business process consultant (BP) and an engineer.

The methodology was designed to gather information about the existing Mia Casa business process and the business logic Mia Casa has built around fulfillment. Xao BP consultants also worked with Mia Casa customer service representatives, asking key questions about customer behavior and how to best address customer concerns within a Web-based solution.

Xao design engineers worked closely with the executive staff of MiaCasa.com to make sure that their branding goals were met. Colors and Web presentation were designed to match Mia Casa's unique brand, as shown in Figure 9.1.

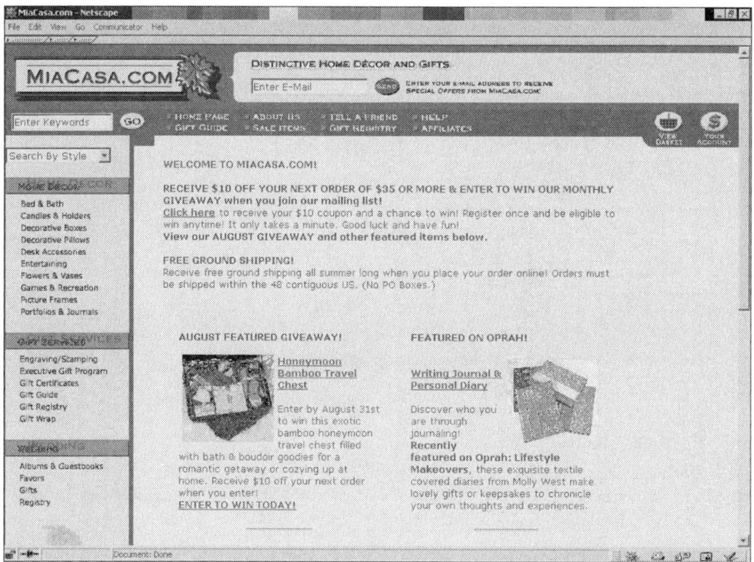

FIGURE 9.1
The Mia Casa home page.

Solution

The information gathered in the assessment was used in deployment of the software, enabling Xao to customize the deployment to match Mia Casa's needs. To minimize the impact of Mia Casa's Web site on the internal IT staff, Mia Casa decided to use Xao's Managed Hosting solution, which allowed Mia Casa to focus on its business strengths, such as customer service and order fulfillment.

Next, the Xao user interface engineer began the process of meeting with the customer, discussing branding and design issues. In the case of Mia Casa, the presentation motif matched Mia Casa's offline image with a framed design so that navigation would persist for the users. Xao prepared multiple design comps, and Mia Casa provided feedback and further revisions. The final choice was a match for both Mia Casa's branding and customer experience goals.

Xao also deployed a series of browser-based tools called Paginators, which allowed Mia Casa to update content on the non-database-driven portion of the Web site. This would allow the relatively nontechnical staff of Mia Casa to update content without worrying about mastering a new set of office tools, such as Microsoft FrontPage. This simple browser-based tool, shown in Figure 9.2, allowed the site administrator to edit the site without developer intervention.

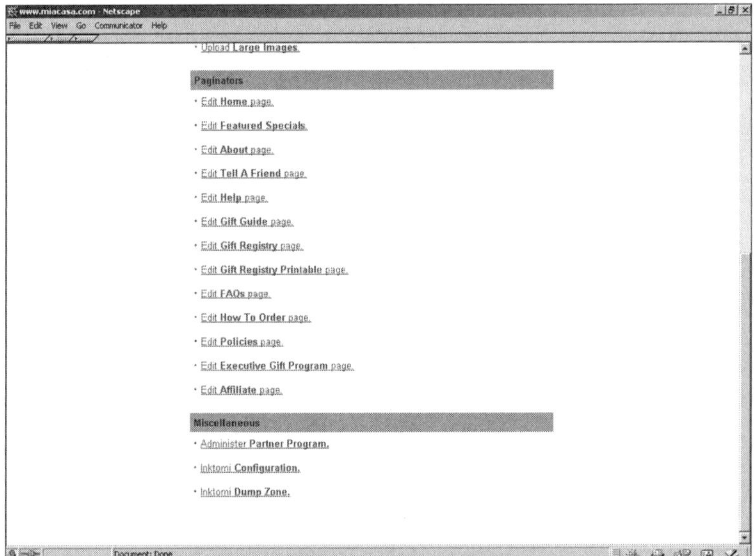

FIGURE 9.2
The Mia Casa site management interface.

While the User Interface engineer worked, other engineers customized CP Commerce and Clearingpoint CP XML filters. For Mia Casa, a discount and coupon management system was developed, enabling them to manage coupons and promote special relationships with online portals and Web sites.

The installation of the CP XML filters allowed Mia Casa to share its product catalog with various portal partners, including Inktomi, Iwon.com, Cnnfn.com, and others. The CP XML filter used was Product Mark-up Language (PML), a standard used by Inktomi for cataloging consumer products.

Results

The Mia Casa Web catalog launched on time and on budget in fewer than ninety days. Xao marketing specialists handled initial site launch and search engine marketing. The result was an online catalog that was easy to use and got rave reviews from customers. With Xao Managed Services, the Mia Casa Web site has been up three years with fewer than two days of downtime.

The Client Perspective

Alexandra Olavarria sums up the experience of working with an open source e-commerce package as follows:

"We've been able to add customized features to help maintain the 'stickiness' of our Web offering, such as an electronic discount code database that is integrated with our site and managed by us using paginators in an administration area on the site. We can offer specific discounts to customers and easily manage the codes, add new ones, etc. The Mia Casa Web site offers a registration page so that visitors can request to be part of our mailing list and enter to win our monthly sweepstakes while we can easily collect and manage the data. Additionally, visitors can search for products by style such as: French Provençal, Italian, traditional, contemporary, natural, etc. if they have a specific taste in mind. All these features help to personalize our offering and keep our visitors coming back for more. Open source e-commerce has enabled us to stretch our IT dollars while at the same time we have sacrificed nothing in terms of the features."

I asked Alix if she had any advice for young entrepreneurs going online. She recommended four points:

- Have and maintain realistic expectations for your business and the Internet.
- Make sure your product offer is solid and specific for easier marketability.
- Have strong financing in place before you launch your site. Remember, it takes money to make money.
- Try to set up your business so that your online and offline systems, data, and so on are well integrated, complement each other, and are easily manageable.

The case of Mia Casa illustrates one of the ways in which the Internet is changing the way people do business. An established firm, seeking to grow its business, used the Internet to expand and market its products to a wider audience. The next case we will look at is different in that it discusses a business that is e-commerce at its purest—Firebreath.com.

Firebreath.com

Our next case study came to Xao Inc. because of our award-winning Web site, hothothot.com. A perennial best of the Web award winner, Hot Hot Hot sells a variety of hot sauce online. Paul Mayville, the founder of Firebreath.com, thought this was a great idea and was a lot more fun than selling insurance.

How Firebreath.com Got Started

Firebreath.com is a virtual, Internet-only "retail store" selling hot sauce, salsa, and chile pepper-related products. The idea for the site came to a middle-aged guy named Paul Mayville in 1998 who, at that time, was an independent health insurance agent.

Paul originally wanted to take advantage of the Internet to offer health insurance across the country. But insurance is a real old-school kind of industry. Each state requires its own separate license. The cost of licensing fees alone (averaging $125/state) made the project extremely expensive, and after trying to meet the licensing requirements of just five states, Paul threw his hands up in disgust and gave up. So what could Paul sell on the Internet that wouldn't be regulated by each state independently? Hot sauce! Inexpensive, fun, small, easy to store, easy to ship, almost completely unregulated…and Paul knew nothing about the stuff. So there you have it. Firebreath.com is the home of inexpensive fun with chile peppers and other hot stuff.

Paul Mayville, founder of Firebreath.com, says, "My original reason for starting Firebreath was to get some kind of business going using the Internet. The insurance industry still doesn't understand what to do with the Internet. When it finally does, it won't be to sell insurance."

Paul continues,

"What (I thought) I knew:

- I knew e-commerce would work if consumers had the confidence to use it. It would simply take time.
- I knew that the Internet was the great equalizer when it came to marketing and advertising.
- I knew the Internet was 'the next great thing' in computers, and I had seen a lot since the mid '70s. I wasn't prepared to watch it become 'the next great thing' to human history. I am now.
- I knew I wasn't going to grow my company (Insurance Masters) to the size I wanted using the Internet like I wanted to. So I gave up on ever growing the company past its current size.

- I wanted not to miss the ground floor on this one. I saw the Internet as a way to grow a company reasonably quickly (1 to 2 years) to the level I was at with insurance ($2–$3 million/year). I wanted to establish a brand that was easily recognizable and well liked. I also wanted to be in an industry that didn't take itself as seriously as insurance does. I didn't want to wear a tie."

As pure self-founded start-up, Paul had the luxury of starting his business while already owning an existing business that he could fall back on. For Paul, this represented an opportunity to transform not only his business interests, but his personal interests as well.

Business Objective/Challenge

As pure startup, Firebreath.com didn't face the integration issues that Mia Casa did. Of course, it faced a challenge that many startups face—money and the lack of it. Paul states that he chose CP Commerce (formerly known as Symphero) for the following nine reasons:

- The cost was within my budget.
- Symphero (now known as CP Commerce) was proven technology.
- The product was a turnkey system.
- The cost was within my budget.
- The people I was dealing with appeared to know what they were talking about.
- The people I was dealing with knew a lot more about e-commerce and the Web than I did. (This wasn't always the case with companies and products I rejected in favor of Xao.)
- The cost was within my budget.
- Symphero (now known as CP Commerce) was open source, created using open source tools and executed on an open source OS.
- Oh, and did I mention that it was within my budget?

As you can see, cost was the driving feature for Paul, as it is in many businesses. Not having to invest thousands of dollars with a software deployment, especially on a new venture, is one reason why open source solutions and software are so compelling.

Approach

Xao took a similar approach with Paul's Web site as it did with Mia Casa. Again, strong branding elements were a consideration for Xao user interface engineers. The hot sauce market is fun, boisterous, with each sauce claiming to be the hottest, with each label more outrageous than the next. With products named Blair's Death Rain Hot Rub, Blair's Sudden Death Sauce, and Ass Blaster Hot Sauce, the site was fun experimentation for designers to discuss branding with Paul. Because Paul's only piece of existing collateral was his logo, Xao had more discretion with site design.

Xao interactive questionnaire assessment methodology was lead by a Xao business process consultant (BP) and an engineer. In this case, the methodology was used to help develop business processes for Firebreath.com, working closely with business process engineers to develop the logic for fulfillment and shipping and handling.

Working with Mayville, Xao BP recommended a combination of CP Commerce and Xao's Managed Hosting Solution allowing Mayville to focus on the fulfillment part of the operation. Mayville, although an experienced programmer, felt that outsourcing to Xao was the best solution. "Don't try to do everything yourself. Contract out as much of the work as you can."

For Mayville, the fact that CP Commerce is open source was the reason that he eventually chose Xao Inc. to develop his e-commerce system:

"I realized that open source played an important role in my decision to choose Xao and CP Commerce. In fact, as I look at it, it appears that it was the final determination, the thing that put me over the top as it were. I have an affliction, an unabiding loathing for anything Microsoft. I came to be infected slowly over the years while writing code and creating software from whole cloth (meaning I started with nothing but my imagination and a compiler). It was both my vocation and avocation from 1978 to 1994. While I starved to death making everything work right the first time, Microsoft got rich while doing everything half-assed. Like someone was making the same decision over and over: 'Hell, it's good enough. Don't bother with those revisions now. It's good enough as it is.' The fact that CP Commerce was open source was the icing on the cake. It allowed me to spit in the eye of Emperor Bill and his Evil Empire (something I probably enjoy too much) while building a strong e-commerce site with a robust infrastructure. Now, how does an aging dinosaur of a programmer turn down an opportunity like that?"

Xao design engineers worked closely with Mayville to make sure that their branding goals were met. Colors and Web presentation were designed to match Firebreath's fun yet fiery site, shown in Figure 9.3.

Solution

The information gathered in the assessment was used in deployment of the software enabling Xao to customize the deployment to match Firebreath's needs. To minimize the impact of Firebreath's Web site on the internal IT staff, Firebreath decided to use Xao's Managed Hosting solution, which allowed Firebreath to focus on development of the business.

Next, the Xao user interface engineer began the process of meeting with the customer, discussing branding and design issues. In the case of Firebreath, the presentation motif was the Dragon of Firebreath.com with a matching frameless interface to maximize search engine response. Xao prepared multiple design comps and Firebreath provided feedback and further revisions. The final choice was a match for both Firebreath's branding and customer experience goals.

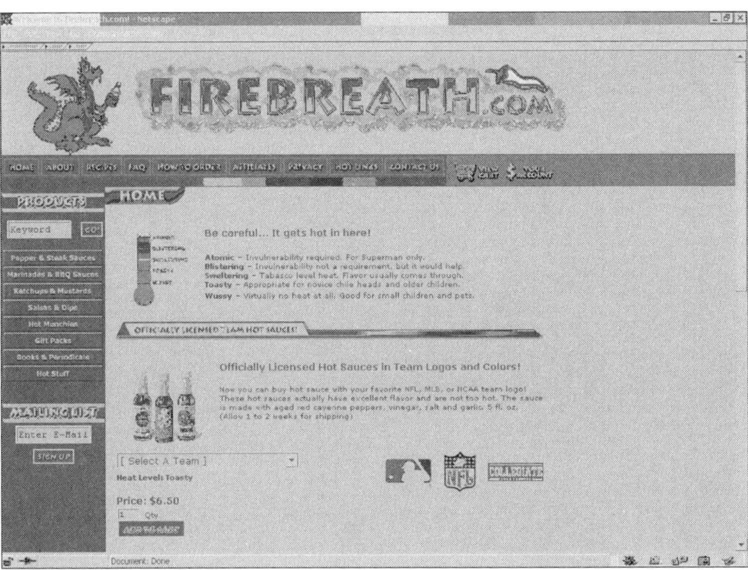

FIGURE 9.3
Firebreath.com home page.

Xao also deployed a series of browser-based tools called Paginators, which allowed Firebreath to update content on the non-database-driven portion of the Web site, as shown in Figure 9.4. This would allow the relatively non-technical staff of Firebreath to update content without worrying about mastering a new set of office tools, such as Microsoft FrontPage (especially not Microsoft FrontPage). This simple browser-based tool allowed the site administrator to edit the site without developer intervention.

Results

Even though Firebreath is less than three months old, traffic to the site is growing more rapidly than expected, with Firebreath averaging 174 shoppers per day in August of 2001 (see Figure 9.5).

Mayville notes that product selection is probably one of the reasons for early success. “From the very beginning, I knew the product had to be right or it just wouldn't work in a virtual world.

Here are the three (IMHO) reasons to pick a product for sale online:

- The price should be low enough so visitors can buy on impulse without too much trepidation.
- It needs to be light enough to ship without killing profits. Customers have a low cost threshold when it comes to shipping and handling.

- The product needs to be fairly well understood. It's much better to spend your money on bringing customers to your site than it is educating them about what your product actually is and why they should want one.

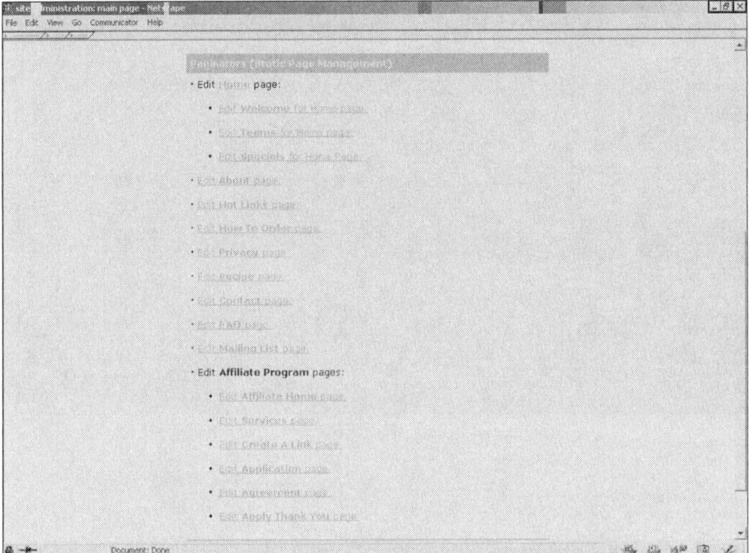

FIGURE 9.4
Firebreath.com Site Management Interface.

Not only did hot sauce meet those three guidelines but it offered other really good benefits as well:

- It's a fun product that doesn't take itself seriously.
- It's easy to write interesting and entertaining copy.
- It's small and easy to store.
- There are no special handling or storage requirements. It can be stored in a wide temperature range and has a long shelf life.
- The product is topical. Hot sauce is current and ensconced in pop culture, probably for quite a while.
- Nobody ever goes back to bland food after acquiring a tolerance for capsaicin—not quite like an addiction, but close enough that it's scary.

I'm quite happy I chose the product I did. And I did use those first three criteria."

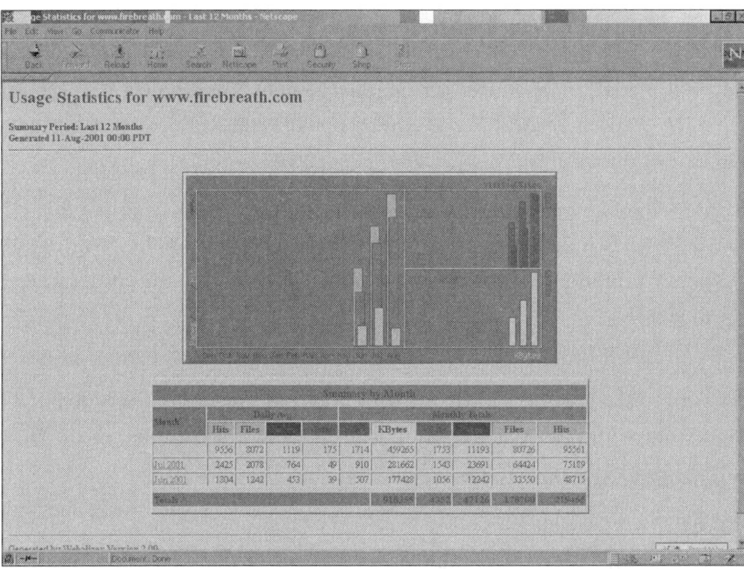

FIGURE 9.5
Site usage statistics for Firebreath.com.

Mayville offers this advice for anyone launching an e-commerce site.

- Follow Paul's three laws of choosing a product.
- Follow Brian's advice on advertising.
- Advertising is expensive so have lots of money.
- Do listen to the pros. If you know more about it than they do, why aren't you doing it yourself?
- Be patient. Start slowly and build the business as profitably as you can.
- It's going to take a long time so have lots of money.
- Take real good care of your customers.
- Make the site as interesting and entertaining as possible to encourage visitors to share their discoveries with others.
- Make your GUI as easy to navigate as you can.
- Don't try to do everything yourself. Contract out as much of the work as you can
- Contractors are expensive so have lots of money.
- Pay attention to your site and keep it up to date. Stay on top of what is going on in your industry.

Preparing Your Business for E-commerce

In both examples, these companies used an interactive questionnaire for preparing for electronic commerce. In preparing your own e-commerce site, the following points are some things to think about.

- What is your edge against your competitors? In other words, what is your selling proposition and how does it differentiate you from your competition? Is it price, service, quality, selection, availability, or purchasing terms? Emphasize your competitive advantage on the Web site.
- How will you fulfill orders? Will you outsource fulfillment or handle it in-house?
- What sort of physical world marketing will you do to promote the web site? Direct mail, cross-marketing with physical location, business cards, brochures, or radio?
- Who will maintain the Web site?
- Who will handle customer service from the Web site?
- How often will you respond to e-mail?
- Are your customer service reps comfortable with using e-mail?
- How will you integrate with your accounting package?

As you can see, there are a number of questions that you should think about when launching an electronic commerce system.

Notes on Hosting an E-Commerce Site

In both case studies, the businesses went with the solution providers hosting option for ease of deployment. In most cases, you might want to host your e-commerce Web site with a local ISP or own your own Web server colocated in a Internet Data Center. Installing an e-commerce system requires more access than a standard Web user, so be prepared to work with your local ISP if you are using a hosting service. Consider the following:

- Make sure you can install a database such as MySQl or PostgreSQL on your hosting account.
- Make sure you can install executable scripts.
- Make sure the ISP will allow you to modify your Apache Virtual Hosts file.
- Make sure that Apache/SSL or other Secure Sockets Layer (SSL) software is installed.

In most cases, it is easier to install on a machine you own; in fact, most major distributions will install everything you need except the e-commerce software. In that case, you will want to colocate the server with a local ISP to save on costly T1 connectivity charges. Most local ISPs have affordable rates.

Summary

In this chapter, we have concluded our coverage of e-commerce sites with the help of Brian DeSpain, cofounder of Xao Inc, a successful e-commerce consulting and Web development firm based in Southern California. Using some site examples that were developed using his product, CP Commerce, we have examined some of the items that must be considered when contemplating building such a site. Sites of this type are by their nature difficult to build, and for the companies contemplating building them, can represent a significant expense. It is incumbent on Web developers to work closely with their customers to fully understand their business model and needs prior to starting work on a site. This means doing a thorough analysis of the customer's business and employing the talents of people from all parts of the business, including marketing, sales, and order processing—all the way down to the shipping department so that the customer experience when visiting an e-commerce site is satisfying. Remember that the objective is not only to sell a product but to build a customer relationship.

Growing Your Site and Keeping it Running

IN THIS PART

10 Keeping the Site Running 201

11 High Availability and Scalability 243

12 Architecture for High Availability and Scalability 255

13 Hardware Reliability 271

14 Selecting Software Components 289

15 Site Management Issues 299

16 Open Source High Availability and Scalability 315

17 Commercial Load-Balancing Alternatives 359

Keeping the Site Running

CHAPTER

10

IN THIS CHAPTER

After Completion 202

The Care and Feeding of Internet Sites 202

Monitoring Tools 205

Web Site Log Analysis 217

Issue Tracking Software 227

Content Management 231

The Dangers of the Live Hack 234

Content Management Tools 235

After Completion

Your site is installed, deployed, and humming. So now what? Software engineering lore tells us our development costs will be small compared to operations and maintenance. Good design can lower our maintenance costs, but the one-time costs of design and development are inevitably replaced by a long, long string of nickels and dimes that hound our code over its lifetime. Every restart, every upgrade, every trouble ticket, and every page update mean someone must be paid.

Your server now becomes the daily concern of operations and content-management people. Site monitoring and maintenance become significant business processes, not only for technical review, but also for business and editorial review as everyone seeks to make certain the site is serving your business needs as well as it could. Because you would no more leave your Web server in the hands of your programmers than you would leave your storefront sales counter in the hands of the building's architect, your New Media department must become a serious business unit staffed by appropriate talent; as with any business unit, the bottom line must be, "Is it worth the bother?"

You already know what you want your Web services to say and do; in this chapter, you will learn about

- Uptime—How to ensure that your site stays up.
- Performance—Open source approaches to gathering and reporting server performance data.
- Evaluation—How to interpret Web site statistics and apply them in your technical operations.
- Review—Metrics and their applications in marketing and design, and the usability of your Web site.

The chapter concludes with a survey of content management and some strategies on how you can coordinate your New Media groups to keep your site vital without your developers stepping all over each other.

The Care and Feeding of Internet Sites

Your Web site is not a capital asset, and it is not a product to be purchased or outsourced. An effective Web site is a dynamic process, a vehicle for the conversation we call "doing business." Your Web site is not a marketing tool to present or illustrate your business strategy, it *is* your business strategy. Like any business strategy, what you get out of it is in direct measure to what you put in. Unless you send your advertising company to proxy for you on business trips, you will want your Web site to represent you. The services you conduct online are not promotional materials; they are a way of doing business. Anything less is missing the point.

One thing that is certain is that your site will change. It will change with your business and with your customers. Upgrades will change your technology and the services you can provide, and every few seconds, visitors will add more lines of critical customer data to your logs. Care and feeding of your site means attention to a dynamic system.

Business Requirements

What you watch, and how closely you watch, depends on what you need. We all like to think that our service is the most vitally important event in our visitors' lives, but we must be realistic and focus on what we really need to accomplish rather than what we want. Itemizing these needs leads to a list such as the following:

- Uptime—Your acceptable limits of availability.
- Rapid response—How long you can wait before your site is serviced and how long you can bear before you are alerted to a problem.
- Server performance response—Your minimum requirements for visitor transactions and the turnaround speed for a *reasonable* traffic load.

Setting realistic performance goals can make the difference between a return on your investment or a large bowl into which you pour money and flush.

Uptime

Uptime is the percentage of time your site is online and actually serving customers. Downtime can mean a server that is offline, a network outage on your upstream provider or some other Internet backbone, a misconfigured network service that prevents access to your site, or even a buggy data-access script that acknowledges receipt of a lengthy sales order with an error code.

How much uptime is enough? If you are selling snowboards, a two-hour downtime may mean lost sales, but unless you are selling huge volumes, will the loss of these sales justify the wages of a full-time system administrator? Will this downtime be as critical in July as it might be in the depths of winter? A banking, telco, or emergency response service may be able to justify "five-nines" (99.999%) uptime, but very few of us mere mortals can expect this. Fortunately, most of us don't require it.

The cost of uptime is really the cost of avoiding its complement (downtime). The formula is very simple: If the reasonable probability of downtime would inflict costs in excess of the extra costs to ensure higher availability, you go for it. For example, if an hour's loss of access would throw millions of customers into the dark, you might justify redundant servers in different geographic locations, or if you would have to beg the key and drive 30 miles to reset your server after every lightening storm, the gasoline costs alone might justify adding an uninterruptible power supply or a watchdog system.

A completely proactive plan targeting five-nines reliability requires massively redundant services and full-time human resource expenses. This is generally way beyond the reach of most Web site budgets and way beyond what they actually need. Most of us settle for rapid response.

Rapid Response

Rapid response is like your bricks-and-mortar security system. If the potential cost of any losses is high enough, you will hire full-time security staff. For a less critical loss, you might employ one security officer monitoring a sensor panel, and less than that, you might use sensors that trigger alarms at an outsourced security company call center. At the bottom of the pool is when a neighbor passing by noticed that your store had burned down (the true story of the demise of my first business venture).

For Web servers, this translates into the costs of having someone actively monitoring the panel lights on your rack servers or using automated pager and e-mail notifications of system problems. As in the bricks-and-mortar world, the role of the on-call, pager-chained technician can be a full-time in-house assignment, a staff rotation, or be outsourced to an ISP.

Server Performance

Server performance is a balance of two metrics. On one side, you want to withstand the sudden surges in your Web site traffic on the day when CNN features your site, and on the other side, you also want assurance that each customer will have a reasonable response time under most operating conditions.

Server capacity is a design issue, but keeping it there is an issue for operations. A client recently asked me to assure the delivery of 100,000 Web connections per second. The client was serious, but backed off considerably after learning how expensive it would be just to touch the "C10K" club—but staying there would be another story.

How much load can you expect? To put this into perspective, during the Nagano Olympics, the busiest news site in Canada measured sustained loads of 50 simultaneous (overlapping) Web site connections with average response times of 10 seconds for a dynamically generated news page. They were running the Apache Web server on a Sun 450. The very first Web site we built for the famous Groundhog Day groundhog (Wiarton Willie (`http://www.wiarton-willie.org`)) ran on a Pentium I desktop computer using Linux 1.0 and served more than 10,000 static pages per day during the festival weekend. With modern hardware prices, it is often far too easy to forget just how fast even modest hardware can be.

Those examples are extremes of unusual peak load. A more pragmatic issue for site maintenance is to set a realistic criteria for the level of performance that must be maintained. During the 2000 Canadian federal election, what would be a landslide Liberal win had been pumped by the conservative press to appear to be a close race. The election's Web sites, designed for typically apathetic traffic, were deluged in traffic way beyond their design metrics. Some failed over connections per second, some because of inappropriate technologies, and others failed because their base operating system simply ran out of file handles. No one was truly prepared, but the smart ones had seen the statistics build during the day and sat by their server right through the crucial endgame. The moral of this story is that unless you are paying attention, you may not see the flood until it's too late.

Monitoring Tools

Unlike desktop applications, Web applications can run for weeks, months or even years between restarts. Like other software applications, your Web site is also (hopefully) bound for ever-increasing loads. Ongoing monitoring is not just about keeping the site running or managing surges; it is your most important planning tool for predicting load patterns.

You have three ecologies to watch: the server itself, your server network (in the case of a server farm or distributed applications), and your connections to the outside world. Each tells its own story, and together they give you the complete picture of how well you are reaching the world.

Server Monitors

The most basic server monitor is the red LED on the front panel; it is so basic, we often overlook it, but the hardware designers put it there for a reason. Don't laugh. We were once called by a client who was seeing horrible performance, but only on initial access bursts. The problem was instantly solved when we asked the status of the panel light. The slow pulsing indicated power management software that was taking their disks offline during quiet periods; the disks were unable to start up fast enough when the load resumed.

Other indicators include keeping an eye on your server security logs, watching for strange system-log messages, directly monitoring the hardware subsystems and the generation of reports from automated polling of systems metrics. The next sections will show you just a few of the ways we can apply open source software to aid in our vigilance.

Security Monitors

You could fill many large books talking about security audits. You need only one incident to throw your entire enterprise into the dark for days, and you should keep abreast of every means possible to monitor your system software, suspicious port activity, and permissions and access anomalies. Many annual conferences and workshops address this subject, as do Web sites, courses, and books of all shapes and sizes—and someone at your shop should be assigned to them.

Security software should be considered as only one tool in your site security policy. Despite the media attention given to network intruders, virus writers, and worms, security watchdogs still report the overwhelming majority of security problems do not come from these sources. The biggest risks to your network security come from more mundane causes, such as people posing as system administration and requesting user passwords, system users having trivial passwords, and inside attacks.

A good security policy does not rest on the firewall or restrict its search to known system exploits. A good policy must throw an alert for any suspicious activity. In the long run, two hundred false alarms are far cheaper than just one confirmed failure.

Detecting Attacks

At the time this chapter was written, the Linux world was still in a bit of shock and denial over the overnight appearance of three "worm" attacks specifically targeting this platform. These attacks exploit known security holes in packages such as Red Hat's LPRng. The damage can be considerable: Intruders are able to gain root access, transfer files, and basically do what they like with your system. A client of ours stung by the original Ramen attack first noticed what appeared to be benign vandalism of the index.html pages of its staging server, only to later discover the intruder had installed trojan editions of the openshh tools to harvest passwords.

As with any security breach, protection against these attacks is partly a policy of following the vendor security patches, subscribing to alert services such as CERT, and mostly a matter of staying awake. Periodic sweeps of your servers, specifically watching for signs of intrusion, should be as natural as a coffee break. Had my client employed these simple processes, Ramen would have been a minor glitch in an otherwise productive day.

Keeping ahead of the latest intrusion methods can also be an effective ounce of prevention. In addition to CERT (`www.cert.org`), many blogs and news sites are devoted to security issues; you can find many of these at `www.moreover.com`.

Samhain: File Integrity and Intrusion Monitors

Most Linux distributions come preinstalled with scripts to perform security audits of key files, reporting huge amounts of data in daily e-mails to the system administrator. I don't know about you, but I would rather know what has changed rather than wade through 20KB of what has stayed the same. E-mail security monitors are also difficult to manage if you must watch over many hosts.

Security audit software, such as Satan, are also geared to the signatures of known exploits and can be fooled by new intrusion techniques. These are the administration problems that lead to Samhain.

- Web Site: Samhain Labs (`http://la-samhna.de/samhain/`)
- License: GPL
- Version: 1.1.10

Samhain maintains a database of cryptographic checksums on your files and provides a highly tamper-resistant system for verifying your filesystem integrity, complete with audit trails to report what changes have occurred, when they occurred, and a list of who was logged on at the time. Other features include

- Central monitoring of multiple hosts
- Encrypted client connections
- Ports for Linux, FreeBSD, AIX, HP-UX, Unixware, Solaris, and DigitalUnix

Other Security Resources

Your security tool kit should also include port/file monitor software such as TripWire (`http://www.tripwire.com/`), which is bundled with most Linux distributions, and the Snort (`http://www.snort.org`) network sniffer. Snort, Tripwire, and LogCheck are described in detail in Trevor Warren's excellent article, "Intrusion Detection Systems for Your Network" (`http://freeos.com/articles/3404/`). You can also find a large collection of security software and related resources at the Purdue University COAST Security Archive (`http://www.cerias.purdue.edu/coast/archive/`).

Log File Monitors

`/var/log` is your friend. The files in this directory will scream at you at the least hint of danger, and all you have to do is to pay attention. For a large network of servers, paying attention to dozens or hundreds of log files is starkly nontrivial.

Placing alerts on these files is properly the domain of the monitor kits, which are discussed later in this chapter in the section "Server Network Monitors." The modules you write for NetSaint or PIKT should always take into account what can be learned by watching log files.

LogCheck

The most often overlooked detail in system security is the security of your system logs. When intruders do gain access, their first step is usually to cover their tracks and hunt for more holes by messing with your system logs. LogCheck is specifically designed to watch this security hole.

- Web Site: Psionic (`http:!//www.psionic.com`)
- License: GPL
- Version: 1.1.1

LogCheck is part of a suite of security tools offered by Psionic. It features

- The capability to parse TCP Wrapper log files
- Support for TIS Firewall Toolkit logs

- E-mail alerts on any suspicious behavior
- Ports for Linux, SunOS, Solaris, HP/UX, Digital OSF/1, FreeBSD, BSDI, OpenBSD and NetBSD.

You can read an excellent essay by Trevor Warren on where and why to apply LogCheck at Intrusion Detection Systems, Part IV: LogCheck (`http://www.fr!eeos.com/printer.php?entryID=3540`).

Linux /proc Files

Statistics gathering under Linux can be done by reading pseudo files in the /proc/ sysctrl interface. The format of these files is often human readable and can be used in a pinch to gain immediate insight into the system status. Most of the tools mentioned in this section are basically just pretty-print methods applied to these files.

The /proc interface files useful for system monitoring include

- `/proc/net/dev`

  This pseudo file gives a cumulative total of the throughput on each of the network interfaces.
- `/proc/net/sockstat`

  Shows the number of TCP and UDP sockets in use and the high-water mark for each.
- `/proc/meminfo`

  Shows current counts of free and shared memory, buffer use and swap totals.

Detailed information on the Linux sysctrl interface can be found in the linux/Documentation/sysctl directory of the Linux source code.

SAR Reports

The System Activity Reporting package (SAR) is a toolkit for gathering and reporting low-level system statistics on Unix servers. The package can track disk access and access errors, inode request rates, transfer rates between system buffers and block devices, system calls, CPU usage, paging activity, kernel memory allocation, and swapping activity. These statistics are collected into a file on a polling schedule and can then be read back and reported in a Web page or parsed and used to generate graphical charts of system activity.

Although SAR is bundled as standard with most Unix platforms, it has only recently become available for Linux. A complete Linux implementation, sysstat by Sebastien Godard, is available from IBiblio Linux System Status archive (`http://metalab.unc.edu/pub/Linux/system/status`). This kit includes the sar, sa1/2 and sadc tools, three general diagnostic utilities, mpstat for CPU statistics on MPU systems, iostat to view disk activity, and isag, a simple SAR data-plotting program.

For the most basic use of the SAR tools, you need to generate the system data log. A system command `/usr/lib/sa/sadc 1 10 -` would log 10 records at 1 second intervals to the fs18/var/log/sa/saNN spool file (in which NN is the day of the month). To log the same information in a less compact but parsable format, use `sar`. Collected system statistics can then be plotted by running `isag` and selecting the data source log file and the parameters to plot. Binary log data from `sadc` can also be extracted by using `sar` and then parsed and reformatted to feed custom scripts, for example, as input to `gnuplot`.

The usual method for collecting system data is to run the `/usr/lib/sa/sa1 interval count` command from a crontab; this is a wrapper on the `sadc` program, which will spool data samples to the default date-named log file. The companion `/usr/lib/sa/sa2` command does a similar job to the straight `sar` and mines the binary data file to produce an ASCII report; `sa2` also manages the daily files, removing reports more than one week old.

TIP

In an emergency server situation, you can take a fast, one-shot overview of disk, CPU, and network activity with the `sar -A` command.

Stephen Tweedie, best known as one of the core members of the Linux kernel memory-management team, has also ported SAR to Linux; his package and the patch can be downloaded from `ftp.linux.org.uk` (`ftp://ftp.uk.linux.org/pub/linux/sct/fs/profiling/`). A complete guide to performance monitoring using SAR can be found in any of the online mirrors of the Solaris Systems Administration Guide, Vol. II (`http://ab2.cs.uiuc.edu:80/ab2/coll.47.5/SYSADV2/@Ab2TocView/67662`).

Other Server Monitors

The IBiblio Linux system status archive (`http://metalab.unc.edu/pub/Linux/system/status`) holds a large collection of tools for assessing server performance. These include SAR and ps/top style monitors for watching specific server process metrics as well as lm_sensors monitors to place alerts on hardware sensors and report on CPU temperature, voltages, and fan speeds.

Server Network Monitors

Faced with a pool of machines, network administrators need to be aware of what is running where and be especially aware of what is not. Network monitors are an essential part of this process, providing real-time displays of the overall health of the network and timely alerts via e-mail, pager, or messaging to inform operations of sudden or impending failures.

Many very good open source network monitor tools exist; Big Brother and OpenNMS are only two examples of what you might find with a quick scan of any open source archive.

Big Brother

Big Brother was originally developed by a coop student working at Bell Canada. Initially conceived as a simple Web-based display of server status for use in a server farm, Big Brother has become a full alert system for monitoring local and remote machines and is often bundled with commercial server products such as Caldera's OpenServer Suite. In the author's words:

Big Brother is a combination of monitoring methods. Unlike SNMP where information is just collected and devices polled, Big Brother is designed in such a way that each local system broadcasts its own information to a central location. Simultaneously, Big Brother also polls all networked systems from a central location. This creates a highly efficient and redundant method for proactive network monitoring.

- Web Site: BB4.com (`http://bb4.com/`)
- License: Big Brother License (`http://bb4.com/license-text.html`)
- Requirements: C compiler, Web server, e-mail MTA for e-mail and paging alerts, Qpage or Sendpage for alphanumeric paging, Kermit for numeric or European SMS paging.

Features

Big Brother (BB) is a mature open source project that has been in production use for more than five years and has a huge installed base. Two good reasons for this are simplicity and flexibility. The Web-based console display can be rendered in HTML for browsers or WML for access by WAP-enabled devices. The monitor also uses a combination of push and pull to collect statistics from remotely deployed clients or by directly testing server ports from the central location. The BB control station supports failover redundancy to assure the availability of the reporting.

Notifications on preset alerts can be configured based on time of day, specific servers, or by the particular test that has failed. BB can also be set to delay before paging (to cut down on late-night false alarms) or to restrict paging to specific intervals. Paging can be assigned to paging groups and configured for acknowledgement and escalation. BB also supports e-mail paging, alphanumeric paging, and numeric and SMS pages.

Warning and alarm levels can all be modified, and the page template can be customized for your site. BB also provides the hooks to integrate other monitor products—for example, using MRTG for bandwidth monitoring. Monitor and reporting functions are extensible through plug-ins, and a large corpus of community-written plug-ins are available (`http://www.deadcat.net`), and, of course, you have the source.

Client programs are available for Unix, Windows, and Mac servers, and the central monitor station code currently runs on any Unix platform with an NT port planned for Q3 2001.

Client/server communications between BB components has been assigned by IANA to use port 1984 (of course).

Installation

Big Brother is distributed as a C-language binary that must be configured and compiled for your reporting server. The files are highly portable, and stock configurations are supplied for most flavors of Unix and the popular Linux distributions. The compiled data-collection daemon is then run from an init-script under a dedicated bbuser userid, with a companion CGI script that formats the daemon data into a Web display. Installation requires root access and careful attention to permissions, but a basic monitor can be installed in less than an hour.

Downside

One small downside to BB is the license, and this is not really much of an obstacle. The agreement essentially says that it is free only when used on your own servers and for nonrevenue purposes. Compared to the proprietary alternatives, even if you must take a commercial license, BB is well worth the investment; BB mediates this demand with Clause #4, whereby 10% of your license fees will be donated to the Canadian charity of your choice and on your behalf.

Conclusion

The BB mailing list has more than 1,500 active subscribers, and that alone is not only an endorsement but a convincing sales pitch. The product is mature and widely deployed, and for most situations, it has everything needed to assure a fair degree of rapid response.

OpenNMS

At the opposite end of the complexity and muscle-power spectrum, OpenNMS is a serious attempt to throw the full weight of open source software at the problems of network monitoring. The authorship roster includes Shane O'Donnell, principle architect of one of the world's largest private networks, Brian Weaver, a co-developer of IBM's RMON/6000, and Steve Giles, who served 10 years at Hewlett-Packard.

Strongly influenced by OpenView, this is a package for enterprise network administration that goes beyond the simpler push/pull and alert model of Big Brother. OpenNMS reports malfunctions, records trends, and configures network hardware; it is intended for networks of hundreds of seats spread across many locations.

- Web Site: `http://www.opennms.org/`
- License: GPL
- Requirements: Java 1.3, Postgres

Features

Like Big Brother, OpenNMS uses a combination of port polling and deployed client programs to collect and report on your server network, but this is a full network admin station and it goes much further than Big Brother. Major features include

- Automatic discovery of TCP/IP addressable devices
- Distributed architecture
- Extensible polling set, which includes HTTP, SMTP, DNS, FTP, and ICMP polling
- Secure, policy-based partitioning of the network
- Scheduling for service windows, system backups, and maintenance

Installation

Installation of OpenNMS is done through a downloadable installer; those familiar with Ximian Gnome will already know what this is about. The installation process is initiated by fetching and running the install script; this can be done in one command line with

```
$> lynx -source http://install.opennms.org/ | sh
```

For those who prefer to roll their own, binary rpm packages are available for Red Hat 6 and 7 and Mandrake 7.2, with others on the way, and the system can also be compiled from source for Solaris 80x86.

Downside

The main problem with OpenNMS is its size. This is really a general-purpose network-management station and may be overkill for monitoring a Web server farm.

Conclusion

If you need advanced reporting and need to monitor a large network, including routers and workstations, OpenNMS is worth some serious consideration, but be aware that it is a nontrivial, Web-deployed application in its own right.

NetSaint Network Monitor

From a purely featureset point of view, Ethan Galstad's NetSaint is very similar to Big Brother. Both are portable C-language programs with Web-display components. Both monitor server processes in much the same way, using combinations of port polling and deployed clients, and both can send alerts. The primary differences from Big Brother, apart from a very different interface style, is the addition of authentication-based tiers of access to the network statistics and the capability to modify the configuration on-the-fly without restarting the data-collection daemon.

- Web Site: NetSaint Homepage (`http://netsaint.sourceforge.net/`)
- License: GPL
- Requirements: C compiler; Thomas Boutell's gd library is required for some of the reports.

NOTE

At the time this chapter was written, NetSaint was involved in a trademark infringement over the name of the application, and because this name is also the domain name of the home site, if NetSaint loses its court case, you may need to do some digging to find it.

Features

The fundamental innovation of NetSaint is a clean break between the configuration and reporting controls, the event-notification processing model, and the view. By adhering to the familiar MVC design pattern, NetSaint is exceptionally flexible.

The architecture of NetSaint uses plug-ins to extend the polling and reporting engine and community-contributed add-ons to extend the console reporting station. Optional add-ons include

- An ncurses console display mode
- A Perl-based Web admin interface
- Webmin admin interface
- Audio alerts
- Remote execution of "local" plug-ins

Installation

The project is distributed as a core tarball with the C language core and a separate tarball containing the statistics-collection plug-ins. The plug-ins have also been spun off into a separate SourceForge project with a separate project page (`http://sourceforge.net/project/showfiles.php?group_id=644`).

Installation is a bit of an adventure. The program is shipped with sample configuration files preset to an imaginary bank of machines, and although we can appreciate the working example, pandemonium breaks out if you try to run the program without carefully checking everything in the /etc/netsaintf0 directory. Unfortunately, the Red Hat RPM binary installations conclude the installation by running the data collection process; be prepared to run a fast `/etc/init.d/netsaint stop` command!

Downside

Unlike Big Brother, NetSaint is still a somewhat immature program, humbly versioned at 0.7, and although the response and participation of the open source community has been surprisingly strong, NetSaint is still not widely deployed. This will change.

The install process also needs some work, so do your bit—keep notes of your adventures, and then submit your notes to the developers or contribute what you can to the installer.

Conclusion

Although it is a young project with a name in limbo, NetSaint is rapidly growing in features, stability, and popularity. NetSaint also sports a friendlier license and an excellent support Web site hosted through SourceForge. For the medium-to-large enterprise, it is well worth the effort to check it out.

Other Network Monitors

Because network monitoring is such a general itch that spans everyone from small ISPs to globally distributed enterprises, many very good network monitor projects are available, any one of which could be the subject of a book. Some of the better known are Transmeta's MON (`http://ftp.kernel.org/software/mon/`), the highly programmable PIKT (`http://gsbwww.uchicago.edu/pikt/`), Sysmon (`http://www.sysmon.org/`), and Angel (`http://www.paganini.net/angel/`). The NetSaint Web site provides a fairly complete list of links on its About page (`http://netsaint.sourceforge.net/docs/0_0_7/about.html#othermonitors`).

Offsite Monitoring

Your site may be running, your network humming, and your log file registering hits, but are you really accessible? The Internet is a tricky thing. We tout it as being "nuclear war proof," and the architecture of the TCP/IP technology does route around problems, but in reality, the public Internet we know and love has not been deployed as a grid, but as a tree. One small outage can cut you off from a huge branch.

The problem is a shortage of peering sites—network hubs where several backbones are joined to provide alternate paths. In Canada, the two dominant networks, UUNet and CANet, have very few peering sites; an e-mail sent from my home in Sauble Beach to a client 30 kilometers away in Owen Sound might travel through a peering site in Toronto or Chicago. In Mexico City, an e-mail sent across town may need to route through Boston.

Because of this topology, the quality of service to your site will vary greatly by geography. Your first point of potential failure will be the peering provided by your ISP (see Chapter 15, "Site Management Issues," on choosing an ISP), but even if you use a host with redundant feeds, countless other potential failure points exist. Depending on your business needs, keeping watch over your availability can be done by colocating and cascading NetSaint stations or by outsourcing your offsite monitoring.

Outsourced Monitoring

Several offsite monitoring services are available, ranging in cost from free to hundreds per year. The cost trade-off is in response time and coverage: The free services will poll your site from one location and alert you by e-mail, whereas a commercial service will poll from multiple locations, include other port monitoring, and page you immediately when problems are detected.

The Internet Seer (`http://www.InternetSeer.com`) is an example of a free monitor, offered as a promotional teaser for its more extensive site-monitoring services. With the free service, your site is periodically polled from its MAE East (Philadelphia) hub. In the event of an outage, the alarm escalates to its false-alarm protection to verify the error, and if the outage is confirmed, an e-mail report is sent to show the time of the probe and the error code.

CAUTION

When installing site monitors, be aware that each polling HTTP probe will register as a hit in your Web site logs. You should always exclude the IP addresses of the polling stations from your site log analysis reports and choose an appropriate probe page.

Stress Testing

Although system monitors are vital in the day-to-day operations of your Web applications, you need to know the limits of your server and whether your applications meet the performance criteria you have set. One way to test these limits is to become fabulously famous (aka "being SlashDotted"), but a far less stressful method is to probe your performance limits in advance through stress testing.

Web-loading programs spawn simultaneous clients aimed at one or more URLs within your site. When used in tandem with server and network monitors, these tools provide a rich data set to quickly pinpoint breaking points such as memory leaks and serialization (code which causes simultaneous access to queue) and can clearly identify bottlenecks in disk access or network throughput. No one wants to overspend on server configurations, and to this end, it can make a big difference knowing that $150 for a second NIC will buy more firepower than a $1,000 RAID array.

Web traffic is a difficult scenario to simulate. If you have dynamic content that depends on visitor input, browser agents, or other stray variables, your test suite must simulate these scenarios to assure sufficient branch coverage of your applications. Web visitors also come in many speeds and from many networks. You can get some indication of your server limits through simple load testing using concurrent client simulations with the ab utility bundled with your Apache server (see your Apache manuals in /usr/share/docs or in the /manual section of your

Web server), but to gain any reasonable measure, you will need a scriptable load generator, and you will need to run these load generators with varying intensities and from varying locations.

Siege

- Web Site: Freshmeat (`http://freshmeat.net/projects/siege`)
- License: GPL
- Requirements: Perl5

Features

Siege will stress a Web server with repeated accesses by multiple clients and records the duration of the test and of each single transaction. Reports include the number of successful transactions, elapsed time, total bytes transferred, server response time, and the transaction rate. Originally written for Linux, it has been ported to HP-UX, AIX, Solaris, and BSD. When used with the openssl (`http://www.openssl.org`) package, Seige can also run tests against a secure server.

Installation

The package is distributed as a C program configured with the GNU autoconf tools. Installation is simply a matter of running `configure`, followed by the usual `make` commands.

Downside

Seige is designed to assail your site from one location, although it is scriptable enough to simulate varying loads. You can get a better result running Seige from different locations, but you are on your own for correlating the reports. The program can also be scripted for URLs to access, but it supports only `GET` requests and does not simulate `POST` actions or access password-protected services.

Conclusion

For a small and simple load test tool, Seige is just about perfect. Unless you have need to simulate multiple networks or to test forms and restricted access pages, it's an essential part of your server testing toolkit.

Site Monitor Services

In lieu of having paid professionals keeping watch over your site, a number of automated services are available that will ping some page on your Web site and send an alert via e-mail when the page is unavailable. Several services will do this from one or more locations as a for-fee service, and a number of free services are also available, which, although they may not check as frequently, can still give you a timely indication that your site is having problems.

Web Site Log Analysis

When we launch any media campaign, whether in print, on television or by hosting an event, we consider it irresponsible to expend our resources without a follow up. Unless we are spending from the marketing budget for humanitarian causes, every dollar spent needs to assure at least a dollar in return business—hopefully more. Why should a Web site be any different?

Similarly, when we deploy any computing system, we want to know if our assumptions for the server technology and the interface were valid, and we always seek user feedback to help us improve our products. In assessing the impact of your site in these technical, design, and marketing dimensions, your Web logs are a gold mine of information.

Business Requirements

What you can extract from your server logs depends on what you record and what resources you have to sift the results. What you record, on the other hand, is a trade-off between what you need for your business use and the network and server resources you can spare.

For example, most sites record only their page counts, treating the Web site as a black box where changes to a page can either result in more hits, less hits, or no change. This sort of log is small and easy to process, and most small Web-hosting ISPs provide this level of statistics for their customers for free.

On the other hand, if you need a measure of the geographic appeal of your site—the classic list of server traffic versus top-level domain (.com, .net, .us, .ca)—this information is latent in the IP numbers recorded by the server software, but it requires some processing and network traffic to be resolved from numeric IP addresses to human-readable domain names. Other common business requirements include reports on the distribution of browser agents and operating systems of the visitors, or reports on the external sites linking to your page (referrers). Each additional item adds bulk to the log, requiring more resources to store and to process the file. As a worst-case scenario, the monthly full-detail log files recorded by our proxy server at the 1995 Ontario Science Center Information Highway Internet café exhibit totaled more than 600MB of data that had to be processed using an SGI Onyx supercomputer. For all this extra expense, these results can also be misleading (see the section "Interpreting Web Server Logs" later in this chapter) and care must be taken to assure that the reported results have some correspondence to reality.

Web server log files are not just marketing tools but are also important to evaluating the design and performance of your Web server, and especially in evaluating changes to the design and performance. Post-process evaluations should be part of everyone's Web strategy; without them, debates on "what works best" can never be resolved.

> **What Works: The Art of Web Design**
>
> Three conversations to avoid are politics, religion, and what works online. Our industry has no shortage of pundits and self-appointed Web-marketing gurus who will line up to sell you their tome on what is best for your Web site. Although each has grains of good common sense, the final word is that we just don't know.
>
> There are no magic formulas. Sites that violate every tenet of good design and taste have done magic for their owners; other sites with arm's length lists of awards go bankrupt. The only certain rule in Web site design is that no one knows what works. No one can tell you the direction to head, but what we can tell you is how to tell if you are going anywhere near where you want to go. This is through a continuous rigor of Web site revision followed by log analysis.
>
> Be aware that even this formula is not without problems. One recent revision to our TCI Web site (`http://www.teledyn.com`) resulted in an overnight 40% drop in our Web traffic; this was because the update had been designed to dramatically decrease the number of reentrant include files requested during the display of each page. In this instance, the success of the revision was still measured by appealing to the log files, but without the explanation of the revision, it might have alarmed our marketing unit.

The following checklist may provide some guidance in planning your Web server reporting requirements and choosing an appropriate reporting tool:

- Target Audience—Reports for marketing and for technical audiences are very different. By selecting a reporting format and content appropriate to the target group, you can avoid a great deal of misunderstanding and misrepresentation of your site performance.
- Distributed Processing—Reports run on the Web server can result in significant strain on the server and can impact your Web site performance. This is especially important on busy sites where log files can grow considerably over the course of a day. Reverse DNS lookups to resolve geographic distribution can also impact your network throughput.
- Technology—Although Perl is a popular technology for text-file processing, each instance of the Perl interpreter can add megabytes to your server memory footprint. This can be mediated using `mod_perl` or FastCGI, but only if the design of the reporting engine is cleanly divided between persistent and transient data. Reporting tools also differ in the technologies they use to cache data, and while a `dbm` hash-file may be easy to implement, the performance may suffer as the file grows. Relational databases can mediate this strain by allowing you to move the data across the network, but you need to know if the cached data will automatically expire or if your database administrator will need to periodically flush out old records using manual SQL scripts.

- Extensibility—No one knows your requirements. You will probably change your requirements as you become comfortable with the reporting tools. Reporting software should grow with you and should allow you to configure your own reports and add to the reporting engine. Your definitions of core concepts such as "pages" may also change with time, so a reporting engine that can only map HTML files to pages may not suit your purposes if you move to dynamic pages using JSP or PHP.
- Participation—Just because a project is open source does not mean that anyone is invited to participate, nor does it mean that anyone is actively participating in the project. Before you commit to any open source technology, you should check the revision history and project pages to assure yourself that there are other contributors and that development is active. You may also want to peek at the structure of the code to see if it can be modified.

Interpreting Web Server Logs

Web site log analysis is the single-most ignored and most abused aspect of the Web. Few non-technical people understand these metrics, and as a result, many make absurd assertions about their site reports. To understand the Web server logs, you need to understand how your analysis defines these metrics, and you must understand the audience that each metric serves.

Hits

If anyone quotes the hit counts of their Web site, unless they are a network or server technician, you should smile politely and walk away. Hit counts record the number of TCP requests made by browsers as they seek to assemble the pages of your Web site. A page with 10 icons, a style sheet link, a background image, page text, and an included JavaScript library file registers 14 hits for each visit by a JavaScript-enabled CSS-aware browser, 11 hits for alternative browsers, and one hit for an audio desktop or text browser.

This difference in per-browser hit counts can greatly skew your results; for example, the server analysis software AWStats, because of the small graphics used to create bar graphs, weighs in at 53 hits for every view of the statistics report, so if your staff are hitting this page daily with Mozilla under Linux, but your target audience is accessing pages from monochrome handhelds, your browser share statistics will be practically useless.

Pages

Pages is a more useful term for site designers and for marketing research because it gives the more human statistic of the number of accesses to a given screen of information, which is what people generally associate with the URL. The reliability of this metric is somewhat assured because the Web analysis software will generally (but not always) allow you to specify the filename extensions that are considered as "pages." Although reliable in the general case, the statistic can be misleading if the analysis software is unaware of dynamic HTML processes, such as having one page include another page via URL. For example, if a page using PHP or some other embedded scripting language includes other pages from the site, such as RSS files or news pages, and the filenames of those other pages are also in the set of extensions classified as pages, the count will be inflated.

Another example of where pages reported and the actual pages read can differ occurs when using Java Server Pages (JSP) where one page may redirect to another through an HTTP call (using `request.sendRedirect()` or through page chaining (using `<jsp:forward>`; the former case will result in two pages being counted whereas the latter, because it happens within Jasper and does not involve the Web server, will register as only one read of the first page.

Visits

Visits is another voodoo item that can give insight into the useability of your site but that needs to be taken cautiously. Log analysis software generally gives some minimum cutoff session period where multiple page reads occurring within that period are assumed to originate from the same browser session. Thus, in the ideal case where this assumption is true, comparing the number of pages read per visit can provide a measure of the "stickiness" of the site, of your ability to hold the attention of your visitors and lure them further into your Web presence.

Browser Agent and O/S

Browser agent does track requests per browser but can be so far from a useful truth as to be useless. With each TCP request to your Web site, the headers of the request will include an identifying string issued by the visiting browser; the intended use of this string is to allow Web page designers to detect and accommodate the variant behaviors of different browsers with respect to JavaScript and other browser features. This statistic is very often naively interpreted by Web site owners to assess the market share of these browsers within their visitor population.

The problem here is with the counting method. This statistic is most often measured in hits, which we already know have very little correspondence with the human experience of Web surfing. The same warning applies to those analysis programs that attempt to map the browser agent to the host operating system to show the relative market share of desktop platforms visiting the site.

You may argue that all browsers will be viewing the same content, and therefore, proportionally will see the same number of hits per page, but take care—one of our clients was surprised to see a high percentage of Linux browsers until it was pointed out that access of the Web site report, a page with an abnormally high hit count, was exclusively by the Linux desktops within their development crew, whereas the normal viewing pages were very light on graphics and amounted to only three hits each.

Referrers

Referrers are the URLs where the visitor clicked the link to arrive at your page. Unlike the other metrics, this is an exact and reliable measure, but because of the added bulk of recording complete URLs in the logs, this logging option is turned off by default. This is unfortunate because referrers are one of the most useful items in any Web statistics report.

From a marketing perspective, referrers tell you who out there considers your site important enough to include in their own. Web search indexes such as Google (`http://www.google.com`) often rate a page proportional to the number of referrers, and with some report engines, you can even track those keywords that were used to find your page through the search engines.

Web designers are interested in the ratio of inside to outside links—the relative frequency of referrers from this same Web site. This gives an accurate measure of the "stickiness" of the site and the site's capability to retain the attention of the visitors.

The discrepancies between the hit and the page and the pages per visit should be noted when looking at all the metrics reported by your analysis software. When viewing per-country counts, perhaps a third-world country is near the bottom of the list because they are using older browsers that cannot incur the extra hits of DHTML, or perhaps the visitors are being drawn to light hit-count pages. Another region may show long sessions because of overlapping sessions by indistinguishable hosts coming in from behind the same NAT firewall. Before you base any serious business decision on your Web log analysis, be certain you understand what the figures really mean.

Webalizer

Bradford Barrett's Webalizer is a low-overhead log file report generator that produces annual, monthly, daily, and hourly usage reports in a pleasant Web display, complete with bar charts and pie graphs.

- Web Site: `http://www.mrunix.net/Webalizer/`
- License: GPL
- Requirements: C compiler, libgd

Features

One strong feature of Webalizer is speed; the program can chew through a large log file very quickly but can also keep cumulative statistics for incremental update. One distinguishing feature of Webalizer is the capability to resolve DNS lookups by launching many parallel lookup processes.

Another very strong feature of Webalizer is the fine control over the definition of a page; page extensions can be explicitly specified in per-server configuration files allowing you complete control over what is and is not counted among the page totals.

Installation

Webalizer is a portable C language program and is also available in binary format. Installation only involves making the binary file available and creating a configuration file set to read from your log files and write to a Web-accessible directory.

At TCI, we have an outsourced Web site on a hosting service that gives us access to raw logs. Using the following script and our local configuration files, we have automated the collection and processing of this log:

```
#!/bin/sh
# fetch the stats archives from the host web site (using lftp)
# and run webalizer once to resolve domain names and a second
# time to generate the report.
cd /home/garym/public_html/stats
cat <<EOF | lftp ftp://USER:PASSWD@www.teledyn.com/
mget access_[0-9]*.gz
mrm access_[0-9]*.gz
EOF
for F in access_*.gz; do
        gunzip -c $F | webalizer -N 12 -c webalizer.teledyn
        gunzip -c $F | webalizer -c webalizer.teledyn
        mv $F stats/
done
```

Our webalizer.teledyn config file is set to resolve page types, to filter out our own internal access of the site, and to process the records incrementally:

```
OutputDir /var/www/stats/superb
ReportTitle     Usage Statistics for
HostName        www.teledyn.com

# filename to cache DNS resolutions
DNSCache        webalizer.dnscache

# file extensions to be counted as 'pages'
PageType        shtml
PageType        html
PageType        jsp
PageType        php
PageType        cgi

# Incremental means you can run the script
# several sessions in a row, each with new
# or overlapping data, to produce a report
Incremental yes
```

```
IgnoreHist      no

IndexAlias  index.htm
IndexAlias  index.jsp
IndexAlias      index.phtml
IndexAlias      index.shtml
IndexAlias  index.cgi

#Grouped URLS will combine all stats under
# one listing
GroupURL        /cgi-bin/*
GroupURL        /.gfx/*                 # all images are grouped

GroupSite       *.netscape.com  # group dialup accounts
GroupSite       *.bmts.com
GroupSite       *.wave.home.com
GroupSite       *.home.com
GroupSite       *.symapatico.ca
GroupSite       *.sprint.ca

HideSite        maya.linux.ca

HideReferrer    www.teledyn.com
# This one hides non-referrers ("-" Direct requests)
HideReferrer    Direct Request
```

Downside

Webalizer is an English-only report generator and primarily targeted at the technical Operations audience. The reports do include important details for marketing and other non-technical readers, but the free mixing of hits and pages in the file tallies can easily mislead the less-savvy reader.

Because the data is kept in files, Webalizer may not be appropriate for extremely large log files. This can be mediated by frequent runs to incrementally process smaller log files. Report generation is also geared to the technical Web server audience and may not be appropriate for your executive presentations.

Conclusion

For medium traffic Web sites where reporting is primarily for load monitoring and other technical issues and where you do not need consolidated reports across multiple servers, Webalizer is an easy solution, quick to set up, and effortless to run.

Perl Webstats

- Web Site: Gallant Technologies (`http://webstats.gallanttech.com/webstats/`)

- License: GPL
- Version: 3.1
- Requirements: Apache, Perl5, Template Toolkit

Features

Perl Webstats provides the usual kit of reports for daily summaries, browser agents, referrals, and server traffic. The per-server reports are particularly useful for ISPs or servers using virtual named hosts. Unlike many reporting packages, the Webstats use of Andy Wardley's Perl Template Toolkit (available through any CPAN archive; see `www.cpan.org`) means that your presentation pages can be easily branded and arranged by editing only two template pages.

The distribution kit also includes a Perl redirector CGI script that enables tracking outbound traffic; by referring all outbound links through this script, the package can record the selected URLs before redirecting.

One final feature worthy of note is the architecture: Webstats is coded in object-oriented Perl, making it very easy to extend and modify. For example, to change report qualities, you need only to subclass the nearest report, providing only those methods you want to change.

Installation

Like the other CGI-based reporting programs, Webstats requires a data repository directory with write permissions for the Web server. The package also includes an option to store DNS lookup information in a relational database through a vendor-neutral Perl DBI interface; this is recommended for sites where the level and diversity of traffic is likely to exhaust the capabilities of a hash-based lookup file.

To use the outbound traffic reporting, you will also need to modify your content-management process to prefix all URLs with a call to the redirection CGI `http://www.domain.org/cgi-bin/redirect.pl`.

Downside

The biggest downside for Webstats is the naive use of Perl for the redirection script. On a busy Web site, the Perl load from this script will crush your server. This can be mediated by using (or abusing) mod_perl, and it would be very little trouble to recode the script or reimplement it using FastCGI or C. A much greater problem is the data store for the DNS resolution. As with Webalizer, we cannot hope to mirror every DNS on the Internet, and there does not appear to be any facility to expire hostname mappings.

Conclusion

Perl Webstats is the easy winner for flexibility of reporting. The package also has the minimum server requirements, making it painless to install and possible to install even on ISP-hosted Web accounts, but the overall architecture would require some work to deal with large log files.

AWStats

- Web Site: `http://www.awstats.com/`
- License: GPL!r-
- Requirements: Perl5

Features

AWStats splits your Web site statistics collection into two phases: a crontab-run log file compiler to create the structure of the statistics and a CGI program that uses the accumulated statistics from the cron edition and updates the numbers to show up-to-the-minute counts.

The cautions I gave on server resources in the previous product descriptions might suggest that real-time report would place an unreasonable load on your server, but this is not the case with the awstats.pl; it does inflict the load of a Perl instance to run the script, but it reduces the overall impact of computing the statistics by computing these incrementally.

When first run, and during the subsequent crontab runs, the script will read through and delete log records, optionally spooling the deleted lines into another file for later processing by other software. Because of this, the CGI reporting mode must parse only those few lines that have accumulated since the last run of the cron job. The frequency of running the cron mode script can be set to achieve a balance between the rate of growth in your logs and the speed at which the CGI can parse the remainder and issue the report.

AWStats reports include the top referrers, browser agents, top downloads, and geographic origin of your visitors, with a pleasant graphic display suitable for delivery to your business unit. All reports are also available in foreign language versions.

Installation

AWStats is painless to install. The program needs a cache directory, a cron entry to run the log processing, and one CGI to do the page display. Configuration is done by hand-editing the awstats.conf file, but the defaults are reasonable for most small Web sites.

One installation detail worth mention is the definition of a page; to track our JSP- and PHP-based Web applications, the main Perl script required one small change to expand the regexp defining the valid page extensions.

Downside

AWStats gives none of the usual daily totals, such as hits or KB/day, and although it compensates with instant live reports, daily totals over the month are often needed to assess the impact of marketing efforts. The program is also another monolithic procedural Perl script, neatly laid out but awkward to extend in any manageable way. The load of the CGI mode would be difficult to adapt to effective use of mod_perl or FastCGI without a great deal of reverse-engineering effort.

As shipped, AWStats also has a naive definition of what constitutes a page and must be hacked to extend this definition to include JSP and other dynamic HTML files. The reporting engine is also locked into measuring most statistics, such as top level domain and browser distributions in terms of hits rather than pages, resulting in skewed data. If `lynx` browsers are unable to view graphics and JavaScript, the hit counts registered by this browser agent will be dramatically less than the same pages being viewed by modern GUI browsers.

Conclusion

AWStats is not for everyone, but in its niche of real-time reporting, it is a clever and effective solution. The incremental approach avoids the load problems associated with other Perl CGI-based reporting tools.

OpenStats

- Web Site: OpenStats.Net (`http://www.openstats.net/`)
- License: GPL
- Version: 1.0
- Requirements: Apache, Perl5, PHP4, MySQL, libgd

Features

Unlike most of the other open source log parsers, OpenStats is a truly distributed, database-enabled reporting tool. Web servers send their log data directly to a central relational database. This not only saves the Web server the strain of processing the statistics, but also allows reporting of the whole server farm from one location and allows for creating comparison and ad hoc reports. Because the data is held in a relational store, site statistics can also be exported to other applications via JDBC or ODBC.

Installation

The distribution file is a small (96KB) tarball containing the PHP code for the administrative and public interfaces, the Perl script for statistics collecting, and the SQL scripts for creating the data tables. Installation involves the set up of the reporting station Web site, altering the Apache logging to direct output through a preprocessing Perl script, and creating the MySQL data store with appropriate permissions.

Downside

Unfortunately, there are a few potential show-stoppers with OpenStats, but nothing that can't be solved by your involvement in the open source development. In the 1.0 release, OpenStats does not yet do hostname resolution; this is a serious obstacle for large sites, and the program could probably benefit from the Webalizer approach of running parallel hunts for DNS results.

The second serious problem is the architecture of the code. The author has chosen a monolithic procedural Perl paradigm complete with global variables, a design choice that may frustrate those who would try to help the project.

Conclusion

Despite its shortcoming, OpenStats is a promising project and worth watching as the versions develop.

Issue Tracking Software

The process of managing a large Web site requires that issues are not lost in the shuffle. Even in relatively small shops where revisions may all pass through one Webmaster, issue tracking can save a great deal of distraction while people are awaiting a fix.

The purpose of issue tracking is to record problems and feature requests and to assign these to the officers in charge of those site elements. Tracking also allows those who log these problems to check on the status of the request. Issues may be logged by the public, your staff, or restricted to the Web development team, and can be submitted by e-mail, Web forms, newsgroups or Post-it notes stuck to the Webmaster's console.

All issue-tracking software will timestamp the trouble ticket and allow you to assign and reassign the ticket to different staff as you escalate or resolve the issue. Other features to look for include

- Multiple interfaces, ideally with an open API that will let you insert or retrieve ticket status from e-mail, WAP devices, or anything else that may come around later.
- An open database API, again so that you can adapt your database to unforeseen changes in technology.
- Multiple project areas with permission systems to prevent teams from altering items outside of their domain.
- Task dependencies, so that administrators can prioritize and critical-path their task list items.
- Ticket searching through multiple interfaces or an open API, so that you can create a simplified view for your public, and a detail view for team leaders.

Business Requirements

Issue tracking is traditionally seen as a developer or beta-tester thing, as a means to catalog problems with your code and to log them so that you can track your progress on solving them. This is definitely one use of issue tracking.

Like everything else about your Web site, who issues these trouble tickets—and the detail and process behind those tickets—depends on your business needs, and like everything else, there is a distinction between what you might want and what you actually need to provide acceptable service within your margins of cost. But what you do need may be more than you expected.

Do you need to provide customer support? Absolutely. You would never consider opening a storefront with no sales staff or running a service with no call center, yet most Web sites provide only a bare contact e-mail address to the Webmaster, or perhaps list sales and information contacts. Isn't this the digital equivalent to handing out brochures and business cards at a trade show but refusing to engage anyone in a conversation? Would you keep a receptionist this helpful?

Web applications are also notoriously difficult to test. You need to track browser differences, OS differences, several conflicting proxy server standards, dozens of flavors of JavaScript, and odd combinations of legacy Java jar files. The list keeps getting longer and no one has the resources to test all variations. Every time your site disappoints a visitor, that visitor is going after one of the thousands of competitors they saw listed in that search-result page. The greatest gift they could ever give you (aside from a hefty purchase) is to grace you with their time and effort to log a trouble ticket.

How important is customer satisfaction? So important that we now have a buzz word for it—Customer Relations Management (CRM). How do you know your Web site is working? You may have the server logs, but they may show only that people walk in, look around, and leave, with no record that they left because it was broken. You have an infinitesimal opportunity to speak with them, to ask them why they didn't buy or what they expected. The only way you are going to track that feedback is with smooth, seamless issue tracking.

The tracking tools you choose depend on your resources, but you should still plan for some sort of issue tracking. At a minimum, all server error pages should lead to trouble-ticket entry in which your server collects as much information as it can and then respectfully asks your visitor to complete the picture.

You can also go much further in your CRM strategy, and for a manageable cost. Alternatives include newsgroups, live operators, instant messaging, and chatterbots as ways to invite the visitors to your site to help you refine your business to better serve their interests.

As with other human interfaces to your servers, you will find that no one solution will do for every stakeholder, but you will want to minimize disjointed data collections. An important criteria in choosing these tools is to ensure that all trouble tickets are eventually logged in to the same database.

Mail/Web-Form Issue Tracking

The first rule of enticing user feedback is K.I.S.S: If you throw the average layperson into a BugZilla page, you are not very likely to get any responses, let alone useful responses. Unless your audience is a technical crowd, trouble-ticket pages should be clean, well-lit pages, clear and painless to complete, and should automatically fill in as much detail as possible.

One clean and flexible issue-tracking kit is Jesse Vincent's RT (`http://fsck.com/rt2/`). This is a Perl and MySQL/Postgres-based tracking system that provides an easy e-mail gateway and a Web-based administration console. RT can also define default actions to e-mail requests, allowing you to respond with custom acknowledgements (for example, to send your current network status report) or to filter and/or escalate tickets based on keywords. Personally, for automated trouble tickets, I'd use RT until I was certain I needed more firepower.

Live Operator Issue Tracking

You are probably thinking that I'm off my rocker even suggesting that you should have a live operator standing by your Web site. I'm not. Prior to the "Please press one" DSP-driven voice-mail support line, all businesses used live operators on their company access lines. Everyone has a receptionist or at least shares one with other offices or departments. It's just good business to have a human being as your first line of problem solving; they are better at this than any machine.

Whether you do this is not an option; the only question is how you do it. How depends largely on the frequency of trouble reports. For example, my Web-hosting ISP maintains an ICQ technical support handle that is live almost 24 hours every day. Messages sent to this address do not always receive an instant response, and the line does not accept requests to chat (except by invitation), but the line is there and it is dependable. If there is a serious problem with the e-mail service, I know that even if my message does not receive any immediate reply, it was received, and the "panic" button right there on my contact list is very comforting to have.

Other means of personal (or semipersonal) issue tracking include using newsgroups or IRC, which in both cases can be supplemented by automated support and can leverage your customer community for peer support.

In considering live-operator issue tracking, keep in mind that this lacks the critical component of the tracking. With the exception of chatterbots, these methods are an adjunct to a trouble-ticket reporting system; they are means to obtain more and better trouble reports, which would then be entered into your traditional ticket database.

Using ICQ

For those who don't know, ICQ is the original instant messaging client. It doesn't stand for anything: The acronym is meant to be spoken as "I Seek You." The client-side program is a small desktop utility window listing your personal contacts and their current online status. When a "buddy" is online, you have the option of sending a short message, URL, or file, which your buddy will receive immediately. ICQ also provides a simple chat facility, broadcast messages, and file transfers.

ICQ is also not the only means of instant messaging. AOL has its own AIM system, and a new, decentralized peer-to-peer system called Jabber is emerging as a means of unifying all the instant-messaging protocols under one free open source application.

ICQ and AIM are not open source, but many open source messaging clients are available that emulate ICQ and AIM. The popular LICQ and GAIM clients interact with the official servers with varying degrees of success, providing most services such as messaging, chat, multiperson chat, and file transfer. The Jabber system also has these features and can use plug-in modules to interact with all the other popular message networks (including IRC).

As a business CRM tool, ICQ is useful but not flawless. The biggest obstacle is the first connection. To offer your support services via ICQ or AIM, you provide your account number to your site visitors, but they must download and install the client software to use it and then request your authorization; it is not something you can do for them. Unlike e-mail, newsgroups, or even IRC, no URL protocol exists for placing a link on your page to automatically launch the ICQ client to send a message to your account number.

Using IRC

Internet Relay Chat (IRC) is an old technology that is having a renaissance. Like ICQ, IRC relies on server hubs to connect individual clients, but unlike ICQ, IRC is very distributed, with many internationally deployed servers relaying the same channel globally and avoiding single points of failure.

Support via IRC requires special client software. You open your support channel by signing on to an IRC server and simply joining the channel; if the channel exists, you join it, and if it was undefined, your joining it will create it. Some IRC hosts offer services where you can register your channel and have the name reserved and the channel kept live by a simple help chatterbot.

As with ICQ, a big obstacle to effective business use of IRC is the lack of direct support by the common desktop environments; IRC also requires obtaining and installing the client software, although there are very effective Java and JavaScript clients to effect an IRC experience directly in a Web page; relay chat may also become more mainstream after browsers support it directly, as is now done with the chatzilla module of the Mozilla browser.

Bots and Chatterbots

Every help desk knows that the majority of the trouble reports are for the simplest of reasons. Many of these basic trouble reports and support queries can be handled by a machine, or in IRC terms, by a bot.

Although they have been around for more than a decade, bots are a much-neglected technology in the business world. This is primarily because of the business world's obsession with HTTP and e-mail to the exclusion of nearly all other Internet protocols. Bots have been very effectively deployed in education as training and tutorial agents and are extremely popular in the online gaming world.

Deploying a bot requires only a full-time Internet connection, a friendly IRC server, and some effort to program the bot with the query schemas and access to your data. IRC bots can be simple help agents with highly structured query languages, or they can be elaborate natural-language "chatterbots" that can interject themselves into a conversation, relay messages, consult FAQ lists, and perform database lookups.

Newsgroups

If you have the network resources, Usenet newsgroups can be a very effective means to attract trouble reports and communicate with your audience. Usenet servers are reasonably easy to install and maintain and have several advantages over e-mail for customer support and issue tracking:

- Postings can be moderated so that only authorized messages are made public. This allows people to post to the group to log their issues and let your technical support staff post updates as summaries.
- Postings are threaded, and previous messages can be retrieved.
- News-to-e-mail bridging can be installed to connect the newsgroups to your e-mail or Web-form trouble-ticket system.
- Almost all browsers recognize the `news:` URL prefix. Directing Web page visitors to your support newsgroup is no more trouble than adding a hyperlink.

Content Management

The overall intent of content management is to coordinate your content providers in the care and feeding of your Web site while ensuring that your visitors are never denied its service or are misled because of a content error.

Depending on your role, the mechanics of content management can mean very different things. A Web server is a complex application, typically involving the craftwork of many people. These stakeholders will include

- Systems administrators who maintain the operating system and installed utility software.
- Web applications developers who extend and maintain the services of the Web server software.

- Web designers who create the visuals and templates used in the display; this group is often concerned with site usability and effective branding.
- Content providers; for example, the staff in charge of specific pages or applications that feed pages within the site.

Although some process of content management must be applied to every link in this chain, no one system is going to please everyone. For example, your system administrators will need to update systems software, which may require services to be suspended and software installed in single-user mode; Web applications teams may update projects that require a restart of the Web server; editorial, design, and marketing staff may update the message your site delivers. If you are particularly progressive in your use of this technology, you will also need means for the producers of information to retain ownership of their content. Obviously, CVS is not going to work for everybody.

All Content Is Not Equal

In designing a content management plan, I try to divide all content into three categories: systems software, active pages, and passive content. The boundaries between these are fuzzy but are roughly drawn first at the interface between the Web server software and the applications deployed on it, and then between those applications and the content they carry. The rigor and care of the content-management process is then proportional to the position in that list, with systems software being most critically important because even a small error can result in a denial of service for all visitors.

Where any given piece of content fits into this scheme is a matter of acceptable risk. For example, if you deploy a forum or Web log application where all but the most rudimentary HTML is filtered from posting, it is probably safe to allow anyone to update the content without much process; the highest risk here is legal: Famed Weblog SlashDot (`www.slashdot.org`) was forced by court order to remove references to the banned DVD-decryption code during the DeCSS affair. If you allow your Web designers use of CGI scripts or Active Server Pages, their risk of bringing down the entire server through evoking a halt or error condition is a much higher risk and needs to be managed accordingly.

Managing Updates to the Site

The purpose of content management is to minimize risk within an acceptable cost. How you do this depends entirely on the relation between the probabilities of that risk and the impact it may have on your business. This section describes processes for promoting active and passive content from concept to publication, giving checkpoints for this risk management.

Business Requirements

Your definition of risk will depend on the service you provide and on your corporate culture. For example, an emergency-response service may easily justify redundant production servers to permit low-level systems upgrades without service downtime, or a political party Web site may need to be especially careful of potential implications of everything said or implied on its pages. Your checkpoint plan will therefore be constrained by an upper bound of what you can afford and a lower bound of what you can accept.

Staging Servers

Every Web service should use a staging process, if for no other reason than to avoid pandemonium on the main server. Even if the staging server doubles as the development server, and even if the staging server is some tiny commodity white box computer, many heartbreaks can be avoided by having one breather space where new content can be proofed before being deployed.

In an ideal situation, staging is identical to the production environment in every way. Same hardware resources, same operating system software and server versions, same network connectivity. Not only do you have maximum assurance that what works on the staging machine really will work on the production machine, as well as a suitable test environment where you can conduct heavy load testing without jeopardizing the production environment, but also, in a pinch, you have built-in redundancy that allows you to swap staging for the production hardware during catastrophic failures.

Identical hardware is not always practical, for example, where the production machines are clustered or where the data being handled is of a unique or secure nature. Still, the objective is to make these machines as similar as is practical.

Production Is Sacred Ground

Your production servers are your storefront, your receptionist, your phone lines, and your fax lines, TELEX and pagers. Every time it is down, you are out of business until it comes back up. Every time there is a glitch, a hiccup, or even just a mistake, you've just thrust it at hundreds of potential customers. Your visitors were kind enough to grace you with their attention, and you repaid them with inattention; this is not a very good recipe for business success.

Preserving the sanctity of your production machines may be the hardest act of self-discipline short of walking on hot coals. Can't you just change a typo or an icon? No. That one phrase or icon, misspelled or incorrectly transferred, could be catastrophic. A thousand things can go wrong. When operations people guard their machines and passwords, when they insist on proper process and signing authorities before they flip a few files across the network, they are not being egotistical turf lords or arrogant net gods, they are looking out for your business. We should respect that.

Production Process

The objective of content management is to collect the creativity from many sources and to channel it into the customer's hands with the minimum risk to your business. It is a process of access restriction. At the outermost layer, content providers create content, typically on their own machines. After they have what they like, be it a spreadsheet result or a Flash graphic, they "sign-off" on their own work by delivering it directly to the staging machine or to a business process, such as technology or legal reviews. For active content, this may mean that each component is unit tested and peer reviewed over e-mails or SourceForge, passing from design to implementation, and then entered into the CVS and tagged for release. Page design and layout work may follow a similar path from concept to realization, but in both cases, everyone's work eventually collects on the staging server.

Staging is an integration phase where the total design is proofed and tested. If your staging server is accessible to the public, you may offer a sneak preview to solicit design and usefulness feedback. We often give our staging servers hostnames prefixed like `beta.ourdomain.com` so that our visitors will not mistake this for the real thing and must explicitly act to try the test environment. Our customers appreciate early involvement, and as application designers, we can never have too much advance feedback from our stakeholders.

When staging is production ready, a signing authority for the project promotes the content to the production servers. This can be one complete update of the entire site (especially where many components must interact and must avoid version conflicts) or as a daily process where different components can be replaced on an ad hoc basis.

NOTE

Although some Web applications will have tightly interrelated components and demand full-site updates, your workload and general stress levels are much less when you can update your production servers in smaller segments. Modular updates let you keep your site fresh, and distributing the signing authorities reduces operations bottlenecks. Aim for a clean design that allows module updates a minimum of cross-talk and external coordination. Careful attention to operations' use cases early in design can save a lot of trouble down the road.

The Dangers of the Live Hack

You already know this: What can go wrong usually does; what cannot go wrong also does. Yes, sometimes it is necessary to `ssh` in to the live server to make a quick hack just to get the site operational. Before you do, though, remember that the risks are tremendous, and you, or someone else, is someday going to forget to back propagate the least obvious of those fixes, resulting in an expensive day spent trying to rediscover the cause of the problem and reinvent the solution.

You already know this, and we all still do it. With every upgrade, I always dread having forgotten to note some small change made to a site during a crime of passion, or more often, having forgotten to notify my clients in such a way that they will remember to reapply my hack should the situation revert. This is especially dangerous where the staging and production servers are not identical and differ in core configuration details.

Where I must hack, I use the following convention: Knowing that software package updates, for example .rpm packages, often overwrite tweaked configurations without notice, I make a copy of the changed file in the same directory, giving the copy an added filename extension of the server hostname. Thus, a modified /etc/services file, extended to allow some other port definition, would be copied to /etc/services.whitemoon. The only information I must relay to my successors are to be mindful of any *.whitemoon files when doing any kind of system upgrade.

Which Root Is Root?

Closely related to the live hack is losing your grip on root access. Unfortunately, with the new generation of dynamic Web processes, root access is often required for restarting Web servers or clearing out generated files, and the temptation exists to give this out like candy to your developers. This is a mistake.

It's not that you shouldn't trust your developers, because you should. It's just that should your system become compromised because of some other problem—for example, if your server was hit by the Ramen Worm and the attacker gained root access, no one would notice because the server is generally bubbling with root sessions. Even when root access is restricted to non-login **su** use, no one will notice changed files or strange commands in the command-line history, and your root compromise can go unnoticed.

Unfortunately, the converse of restricting all root access is generally counterproductive. Time spent trying to contact that one officially sanctioned someone and then explaining what and why you need the change can stall the production process and result in expensive logjams; at best, it creates a bottleneck to getting these privileged operations done. Because you probably must allow root access, remember `sudo`.

Content Management Tools

Content management is a buzzword phrase, and like its sister term, knowledge management, there are as many definitions as there are practitioners. A simple SlashDot-like message board is content management, and so are full-blown publishing systems, such as Typo3 (`http://typo3.sourceforge.net/`), OpenCMS (`http://www.opencms.com/servlets/opencms/`

index.html) or ArsDigita (http://www.arsdigita.com/products/), but all your Web-publishing engines belong to design, not to deployment.

For deployment, regardless of your applications, content management means applying process to the motion of all digital content from the author's concept to the visitor's browser. Contact management is the process of publishing to the production server, whether the content is images, text, script code, or binary server application components.

Managing updates to Web sites is a common itch, and many young programmers have made their start in the IT world by contracting out as Web developers. As a result, there is no shortage of open source software to move files through the production process. This section describes a few of the more readily available systems found on just about every Unix Web host, but this should not be considered an exhaustive list. Before you commit to any content management tools, do a search on Fresh meat (http://freshmeat.net) and compare feature sets with your requirements.

Also, don't expect to find one application that suits your whole process. Different content and different content producers will have different needs; the goal is to manage the content, not to frustrate those people on whom you depend to keep your Web site vital. For example, if your design department is Mac based, they may appreciate access to layout and image files using AppleTalk to the staging box, whereas the developers of Java Beans will likely prefer a versioning system. There is nothing wrong with a patchwork approach; it may cost a little more in maintenance, but it will pay back far more in productivity. Remember: Technology should serve the body, not enslave the mind!

Business Requirements

The best plan for content management is to leave nothing to chance. Many organizations install a Web-page application server and define a process for filling the pages, and then assume everything else will fall into place. It won't. Content management must plan for the needs and issues from all the content stakeholders, including

- Staff—Those who provide information
- Editorial staff—Writers and copy editors
- Design staff—Graphic arts and layout
- Developers
- Operations—Systems administration

Your objective is to preserve the sanctity of the production server while providing for the content-management use cases of each of these roles. Your exact criteria depends on your resources, your needs, and your infrastructure, but unless the system serves the needs of these actors, you're headed for a revolution—or at least stark apathy. Questions to consider when selecting content management systems include

- Can it handle all your digital content? No one tool is likely to do everything for everyone, so you will need to partition your plan with an eye to using the smallest possible set of tools.
- Can you add new types of content? If a content-management process is geared to publishing static HTML and images, can you later add streaming video or XML? Can you add ASP or JSP?
- Can you delegate responsibilities? Unless you are a very small shop, you will assign those different roles to different people. For example, customer account updates may be the responsibility of your accounts staff, but the layout of the display page will fall to design, the display engine to development, and database software itself will fall to operations or your DBA.

As with server monitoring, streamlining content management is a common goal for all those open source hackers working for tiny startups and underfunded labs or who pay their way through college by building Web sites. As a result, a quick look on Freshmeat or SourceForge is likely to give you enough leads to fill an entire book.

The applications in this section are those most fundamental to the content publishing process and those with the widest application across all the content management roles. The first, CVS, is a means for controlling the parallel development of abstract content, such as your templates, dynamic code, and software systems. It probably does not apply to the actual words on the published Web page but is more geared to controlling how those words get to the production page. The rest are utilities that are generally considered as tools for content mirroring but recast as a means to manage updates from your staging to your production environment.

CVS for Web Masters

CVS, the Concurrent Versioning System from Cyclic Software, is the de facto standard in the Linux world for version control and can easily be applied to Web site management. The particular strengths of CVS over other versioning systems, apart from being open source and widely available, is its capability to allow simultaneous updates from multiple developers.

Although the need to revert Web content to a previous version is almost never needed in Web development, CVS is most useful for managing multideveloper work on modern dynamic Web pages. With technologies such as PHP and other embedded scripting languages, the page designers are most often not programmers, and the developers of the active page behaviors would rather not be concerned with the visual and political aspects of the pages. Because these page elements rarely overlap the same lines on the source file, page designers can be working on the layout elements of the page while developers are working at the embedded control language, and both can check their work into the version control repository without undoing other persons' changes.

For example, if I change the block of JavaScript or embedded JSP code between lines 32 and 60 of the file while the designer had concurrently checked in changes to the tags in the page footer, when I update the repository, my changes will be merged with their changes, and the composite file will be left on my machine. The only cultural discipline required is for the developers to realize that their files may change without notice and to call for an update before they make their next change; in practice, notification of changes are made between team members via e-mail.

CVS also accommodates cross-platform development, with clients available for Windows, Unix, and Mac. These client programs also adjust for the different linefeed conventions of the three platforms, allowing pages to be freely moved from one platform to the other.

One final advantage of CVS in today's security-conscious computing environment is its capability to run over secure socket connections using the open source ssh tools. For example, the following Linux shell script wraps the CVS commands into the secure access required by projects using the SourceForge:

```
#!/bin/sh
# secure CVS to a sourceforge project CVS tree
# c. 2001 by Gary Lawrence Murphy <garym@teledyn.com>
# usage: sfcvs PROJECT cvs-command
# example: sfcvs kernelbook commit porting.xml
P=$1
SFUSER=garym
shift
CVS_RSH=ssh cvs -z3 \
  -d$SFUSER@cvs.$P.sourceforge.net:/cvsroot/$P $*
```

CVS and Web Publishing

Although useful for the development process and for publishing content to the staging environment, CVS is not a particularly good choice for publishing content to the production server for a number of reasons:

- CVS access on the production machine requires shell access to effect the command.
- The structure of the CVS packages would be required to mirror the structure required by the deployed Web application.
- CVS is relatively slow, leading to a longer period when the Web site content is unstable.

Except for benign passive content, it is rarely wise to automate the process of promoting content from staging to production. We have seen sites where cron processes were used to effect

CVS commands to do incremental updates of production servers, but this places significant network load on the server while the files are compared, and using the CVS export command requires removing all content before the publishing can begin. If the process fails, the site can be left in an unstable state.

Content Publishing Using rdist

At the bottom of the food chain of content management is venerable old `rdist`. Originally a means to synchronize systems software across nodes on a network, `rdist` is a simple to configure and effective tool for transporting updated files from staging to production, even across secure channels.

Basic use of `rdist` is to provide a descriptor file listing files and directories to be promoted to the target server. The program compares time stamps on both servers and will transfer only those files which are newer than the production copies.

The trick is to create `rdist` update scripts for each server module; each script is then bound to a module publish command allowing different officers to control all updates to their templates, software, and other application files, preserving the ownership of files as they are transferred.

```
######################################################################
# Filename: tomcat
#
# usage: rdist -P /usr/bin/ssh -f tomcat
#
# synchronize the staging tomcat configuration and library files
# with the production website on whitemoon
#
# Created: Tue Jan  9 15:22:54 EST 2001
#
# Author:  Gary Lawrence Murphy <garym@canada.com>
# Copyright:  2001 TeleDynamics Communications Inc
#             (www.teledyn.com)
######################################################################

FILES = (
        /opt/tomcat/lib
        /opt/tomcat/conf/server.xml
        /opt/tomcat/conf/web.xml
        /etc/httpd/conf/mod_jk.conf
        /etc/httpd/conf/jserv/cocoon.properties
        /opt/tomcat/webapps/admin.war
        /etc/profile.d/tomcat.sh
        /etc/profile.d/jdk.sh
)
```

```
# list of hosts to sync
HOSTS = (whitemoon.teledyn.com)

# rdist commands -oyounger means do not replace any files on the
# webhost which are newer than the distro files
${FILES} -> ${HOSTS}
        install -oyounger;

# 2001 by TeleDynamics Communications Inc
```

`rdist` provides a simple, easily deployed, and completely secure solution. Officers can sign off on updates on their own initiative. For example, one `rdist` script could list all the configuration files for the Apache server software, another for Tomcat, and other scripts for each Tomcat Web application. Each development or application admin team, after they have proofed the update on the staging server, promotes their new content by running `rdist` with their module script.

RSync

RSync might be considered an advanced `rdist` to transfer files between servers over a secure connection. Whereas `rdist` updates changed files from corresponding locations, `rsync` is able to move files from your staging host to any other host location, transferring only the *diffs* of the files.

- Web Site: Samba RSYNC (`http://rsync.samba.org/`)
- License: GPL
- Version: 2.4.6
- Requirements: C compiler

Features

The advantages and features of `rsync` are too numerous to even outline completely. It will transfer files by transferring only the differences between files; it allows for anonymous access to package modules within a server archive, and it accepts a URL specifier that can be used in Web pages. It also can include or exclude files by file lists or by pattern expressions—the list goes on and on. If you need to synchronize files between servers, `rsync.samba.org` is your first stop.

Installation

Use of `rsync` requires running the program as a server (`rsync --daemon`) on your local and remote machines. The daemon process can be run as needed through `inetd` or used in standalone mode to provide a persistent network service similar to a Web server. Just as with Web servers, there is considerable overhead in using the `inetd` method, but it does save on the memory footprint of keeping the daemon live and makes one less port to guard.

Each peer server must be configured by creating an /etc/rsyncd.conf file to describe the paths available for remote updates and the security parameters. A sample rsyncd.conf file is listed next:

```
# rsync daemon login message and runtime files
motd file = /etc/rsyncd.motd
log file = /var/log/rsyncd.log
pid file = /var/run/rsyncd.pid
lock file = /var/lock/rsyncd.lock

# the block name identifies the context for the
# rsync command
[public_html]
        path = /home/teledyn/public_html
        comment = configuration for TCI website
        uid = nobody
        gid = nobody
        read only = no
        list = yes

# logins authorized to run the service
        auth users = webmaster
        host allow = maya.teledyn.com
# plaintext key/value pairs
        secrets file = /etc/rsync.secrets
```

To run as an `inetd` process, you must add the following to /etc/services:

```
rsync          873/tcp
```

and add a definition of the executable to /etc/inetd.conf:

```
rsync    stream   tcp      nowait\
        root    /usr/bin/rsync    rsyncd --daemon
```

To run the update from the preceding script, preserving permissions and update times, you would issue the command

```
rsync --progress --stats --compress \
        --rsh=/usr/bin/ssh --recursive \
    --times --perms --links --delete \
    --exclude "*~" --exclude "CVS" \
    /var/www/www.teledyn.com
    www.teledyn.com:public_html
```

Downside

Installation and configuration is a complex and delicate matter involving proper installation of openssh and the rsync servers, and you need to be mindful that you haven't provided a security hole where any arbitrary Internet site could clear your machine with a deft use of `rsync --delete`. The requirement to run a daemon process may also prohibit your use of `rsync` on Web-hosting ISPs.

Conclusion

The `rsync` command is included with most Linux distributions and is portable to most other platforms. Although it takes a bit of preparation to install, it is easy to operate, provides fine-grain permissions control, and is light on network resources. You can get fancier server-mirroring kits with GUI consoles, but you are not likely to get much more update power.

Summary

Many Web servers have an option to do the IP lookups but strongly recommend against enabling this feature because the extra network activity to resolve every server request would severly impede the server performance.

Visitor tracking through making assumptions about IP addresses over some time interval is an indicator, but can be frustrated by NATed address (hosts hidden behind firewalls). A more exact method of tracking users is to use a session cookie within the Web pages themselves and to log this information elsewhere, but care must be taken that the data you collect does not violate your national or state privacy laws. In most locations, collecting any data that can be used to identify the surfing habits of any specific person is classified as stalking and carries stiff penalties.

High Availability and Scalability

CHAPTER

11

IN THIS CHAPTER

- **High Availability 244**
- **Scalability 247**

In this chapter, we take a look at two of the concerns you will face in building a commercial Internet site: high availability and scalability. We look at the different aspects of high availability, including a formal definition of high availability, a discussion of the areas of concern when architecting a solution, and a look at the costs associated with implementing a high availability solution. We then take a look at the issue of scalability and discuss vertical scalability, in which capacity is added to a system by adding resources to a single system, and horizontal scalability, in which a service is scaled by adding additional servers and load balancing between them. This discussion includes a look at the different areas where capacity can be increased and also at some of the available load-balancing algorithms. So let's get started with a look at high availability.

High Availability

If you are running your Internet site as part of your business, especially if you rely on it for a significant part of your income, keeping it up and running is of paramount importance. In some cases, each hour of downtime can translate to thousands of dollars of lost income. If this is the case for your Internet site, you will be concerned with making sure that your Web site is up and running twenty-four hours a day, seven days a week. In this section, we look at the components of high availability, starting with a look at some of its aspects.

Aspects of High Availability

If you ask a group of IT professionals to define high availability, you might be surprised at the number of different answers you receive. This is because there are several aspects to keeping systems up and running on a 24/7 basis. These areas include

- Redundant hardware
- Backup power
- Reliable software

Let's take a look at these areas in a bit more detail.

Redundant Hardware

The first area we will look at is redundant hardware. If you look at a typical home PC, you will find that it usually has a single power supply, and unless the person is very dependent on the system, it usually will not be connected to a uninterruptible power supply (UPS). In addition, it usually will not have features such as RAID controllers or other redundant hardware components. Servers, on the other hand, are usually equipped with dual power supplies, use hardware RAID controllers with highly reliable disk drives, and have hot-swappable components, including disk drives, power supplies, and cooling fans. If your Internet service is your business, making the investment in hardware of this caliber is insurance that you will want to have. We discuss hardware issues in much more detail in Chapter 13, "Hardware Reliability."

Backup Power

Another area of concern is power in the event of the loss of commercial power. For small Web sites, this usually means at a minimum the use of a UPS. For larger sites, however, you will have to rely either on the redundant power features offered by your colocation provider or build your site to include not only backup battery power, but also a backup generator system. In addition, if you are building your own facility, you should look into the possibility of locating it in a place where you can get commercial power from multiple sources. Power issues are covered in the discussion of colocation facilities in Chapter 15, "Site Management Issues," and in Chapter 13.

Reliable Software

Vendors of server software often make claims of reliability about their software. This includes vendors of server operating systems, Web servers, and database systems. It is incumbent on you to take these claims into account when selecting the software that runs your site. Unfortunately, with open source software, often no vendor exists to back it up and, therefore, no one makes this information available. You need to carefully investigate the claims of software vendors to ensure that their claims of reliability are not overstated. The software features you want to look for in your server software depend on the type of software it is. For example, if you are looking for database systems, you probably will be interested in features such as transaction support and replication support. For further discussion of software reliability, refer to Chapter 14, "Selecting Software Components."

Defining High Availability

Now that you have an idea of some of the factors that can affect availability, let's take a look at a more formal definition. You need to determine two factors to calculate availability. These factors are:

- Mean time between failures (MTBF)
- Mean time to repair (MTTR)

Using these two factors, we can calculate the availability of a system using the following formula:

Availability = [MTBF / (MTBF + MTTR)] * 100

The resulting number is expressed as a percentage, with the obvious goal of getting as close to one hundred percent as possible. You often might hear vendors make claims of "five nines availability," which means 99.999% availability. This translates to a little more than five minutes of downtime during a year. To better understand how you can improve the availability of your systems, let's take a look at the two factors that determine availability.

Mean Time Between Failures

The mean time between failures (MTBF) is defined as the average time between the failure of a large number of like components over a long period of time and is expressed in hours. Hardware vendors usually do these calculations, and you can find the MTBF numbers for a piece of hardware in the specifications that come from the manufacturer. Where your decision making comes into the picture is in selecting components to put into your servers. One approach to increasing availability is to increase the overall MTBF of your system by building it from components with the highest possible individual MTBF.

Mean Time to Repair

The mean time to repair (MTTR) is defined as the total amount of time required to repair a system divided by the number of repairs. This is something you must determine for yourself and is the reason why it is important to fully document downtime. An alternative approach to increasing availability is to reduce the MTTR by selecting systems that are easy to repair or replace. This is why hot-swappable components are so popular in servers, because these types of components reduce the MTTR.

Weighing the Costs

As you might guess, high availability is not cheap. Hardware and software components that are the most reliable also are typically the most expensive. Adding components, such as hot-swappable power supplies and disk drives, to servers and adding software features that minimize downtime all add to the cost of keeping your Internet servers up and running. The thing to remember when considering whether to spend the extra money to purchase this level of reliability is how much it will cost for your systems to be down. Many studies on the cost of downtime have been done, and some of them indicate that the average cost of downtime is about $1,300 per minute. This figure is arrived at by taking into account the many contributors to downtime costs. Some of these contributing factors are

- Lost sales and customers
- Lost opportunity
- Costs of replacing failed hardware or software
- Costs associated with support personnel

Let's take a look at each of these areas in more detail and see how each of them contributes to the cost of downtime.

Lost Sales and Customers

If you run a high-traffic Web site that supports extended sessions, such as an online store, a hardware or software failure can result in an interrupted transaction for customers. This in turn can result in a lost sale because customers can be unforgiving of site problems and might decide to look elsewhere if your site fails during a transaction. As you might guess, frequent failures of your site will not only cost you the transactions that are lost directly, they also can have the effect of giving your site a reputation of unreliability and cause people to avoid your site. Unless you are the only source of the products and services you offer, an unreliable Internet site can drive your customers to your competition.

Lost Opportunity

Another way in which downtime for your Internet site can cost you is through lost opportunities. Customers who are unable to access your site during downtime might be lost forever as they seek out other sources of the products or services you offer. In addition to losing your customers, excessive downtime might cause problems with your investors or shareholders, resulting in the loss of opportunity to expand your business or to get working capital.

Replacement Costs

The previous two categories of costs are often difficult to measure because of the problems of determining how many sales and potential sales could be lost during downtime. On the other hand, some costs easily can be measured. These costs include the costs of replacing defective hardware and software. If a disk drive fails, a fixed cost is associated with replacing it. If a piece of software must be replaced, a fixed cost is associated with purchasing and installing the new software.

Personnel Costs

Another cost associated with maintaining your site is the cost of the personnel you must hire to do this support. The thing to remember is that the more your support personnel are idle, the greater the cost. This sounds backward; however, if you consider that you are paying people to be idle, it makes sense. In addition, if you choose to hire less-skilled employees, such as college students who will work for lower salaries, you are likely to have higher costs anyway because of the need to properly train them and the higher turnover rates that these lower-paying positions usually have. Even if you choose not to hire full-time support personnel and to outsource the support of your Internet site, you will have to pay one way or another.

As stated earlier, high availability is not cheap. The thing that you, as the proprietor of an Internet site, must do is to weigh the cost of maximizing your availability against the cost of downtime at your site.

Scalability

Having tackled the issue of high availability, we now take a look at another concern that will come up in the running of your Internet site—the issue of scalability. Scalability is the capability of your systems to grow as the demands on them grow. For example, if you run a Web server that can handle one million hits per day, scalability might be defined as the capability to grow your Web site to handle two million hits per day. In this section we take a look at some of the ways in which you can scale your Internet site. We begin looking at one of the two traditional approaches to scalability—vertical scalability.

Vertical Scalability

Vertical scalability is one of the approaches to increasing the capacity of servers. This approach relies on the capability to add resources to a server to allow it to handle additional load. Figure 11.1 is a conceptual diagram that illustrates this type of scalability solution in which the increased size of the server indicates increased capacity to handle load. Examples of the types of resources are

- More processors
- More memory
- More storage capacity
- Increased network bandwidth

Which of these resources you add to scale your systems depends on the type of services that you will be offering on them. Let's take a look at each of these and discuss when adding them would be appropriate.

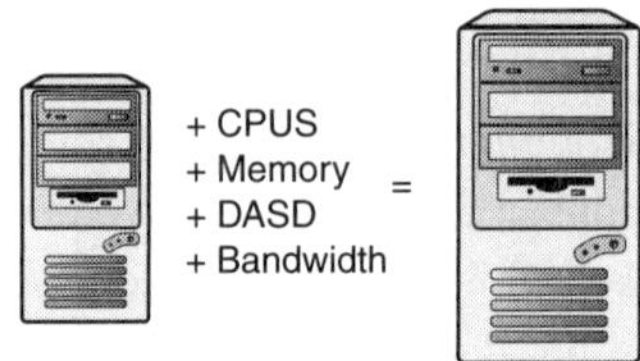

FIGURE 11.1
Vertical scalability.

Adding Processors

For some classes of computing problems, adding processors gives the greatest return in scalability. These types of problems are those that can be parallelized to take advantage of the extra computing power that you get when you add processors to a multiprocessor system. An example of a problem that would likely benefit from an increase in the number of processors is graphics rendering, such as is done by computer animation and game companies. Because of the complex mathematics and because most rendering jobs can be broken up into many smaller tasks, these problems usually can be parallelized to take advantage of additional processors. In general, if you have a CPU-intensive task that is not serial in nature, adding processors usually can help you to scale.

Adding Memory

You also can scale your systems in the area of system memory. By analyzing the memory usage characteristics of your systems, you can determine whether adding additional memory to a system would be a good approach to increasing the load-bearing capability of the system. An example of a system that can benefit from increased memory can be found in the Apache Web server. Some versions of the Apache Web server handle extra loads using a model where a new server process is forked for each new connection. Each of these processes is not very processor intensive. However, each requires some amount of memory, and eventually you will hit the limit of the system's memory resources. In my experience, you typically hit this memory limit before you reach the limits of your processors, so adding processors in this case would not help much. On the other hand, by increasing the amount of memory in a server, more child processes can be forked off, thereby increasing the maximum load that the system can handle.

Adding Storage

For some applications, growth of a system depends on having more storage capacity. An example of this is a database system. To grow the database, more and more storage is required. In addition, not only do these types of systems typically benefit from having more storage, but having faster storage is useful. This is the driving force behind hardware manufacturers continually increasing the speed at which data can be transferred to and from disk drives by creating more powerful disk controllers and reducing seek times on disk drives.

Adding Network Bandwidth

One more area in which a system can grow is in the amount of network traffic coming into and out of it. As the number of visitors to your Internet site grows, you might find that you are reaching limits based on the network bandwidth. On individual systems, this might mean that you need to switch from 10BaseT network interface cards to 100BaseT or even Gigabit ethernet.

Horizontal Scalability

The other approach to scalability that is often employed when building Internet sites is called horizontal scalability. The basic idea is illustrated in Figure 11.2.

Using this approach, instead of adding components to a single system, more systems are added to the site and some form of load balancing is employed to distribute the load among them. Some of the most popular load-balancing algorithms used by horizontal scalability solutions are

- Round robin
- Least connected
- Least loaded
- Response time
- Service-level agreements
- Custom rules

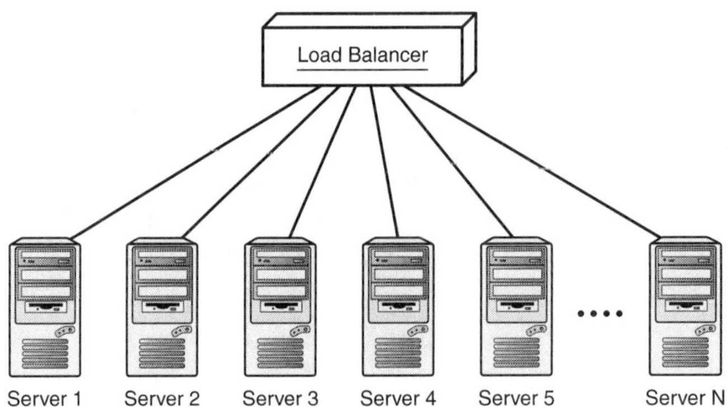

FIGURE 11.2
Horizontal scalability.

Let's examine each of these approaches with a view to their strengths and weaknesses, starting with the round-robin algorithm.

Round-Robin Load Balancing

Probably one of the most common means of load balancing among multiple systems is the round-robin method. This algorithm works by distributing the load between some number of servers one after another. An analogy that can be used to explain this methodology is that of dealing cards. The dealer, which is analogous to the load-balancing hardware or software, deals cards (connections to a service) one at a time in a specific order. One of the reasons for the popularity of this method is the ease with which it can be implemented. For example, you can set up simple round-robin load balancing using DNS, the domain name service. Most modern DNS servers can resolve a single name to multiple IP addresses. These servers answer queries with a different IP address on each subsequent query. This is the essence of round-robin DNS. The biggest drawback to this method is that it doesn't take into account variables such as server capacity or load. In addition, although the distribution method is very simple, to properly implement this algorithm, you must implement a mechanism for verifying that the servers in the load-balancing pool are available. This is one of the problems with using round-robin DNS.

Most DNS servers don't include facilities for monitoring that the servers whose addresses they resolve names for are up and running. Failure of one of the N servers in a round-robin DNS scheme means that 1/Nth of the traffic to your service will be lost as long as the service is down. In addition to strict round-robin load balancing, a popular variation exists that takes into account differences in the capacity of the servers in the load-balancing pool. This variation is called weighted round robin. In this variation, servers are assigned a weight according to their capacity to handle load. Servers with more capacity are given more of the load to handle.

Least-Connection Load Balancing

Because load balancing is typically employed to distribute network traffic to a specific service, another popular method of load balancing is to track the number of connections to that service and to distribute the next connection to the server with the fewest number of active connections. This is referred to as least-connection load balancing. One way in which this algorithm can be implemented is that each of the servers in the load-balancing pool runs a process that keeps track of the number of connections and reports it to the load-balancing system. When a connection request is made to the load balancer, it serves it to the system that has the least number of connections. This can be a very effective method of load balancing; however, it makes the assumption that all the servers in the load-balancing pool can handle the same number of connections. This might be the case if all your servers are identical and all run the same software. If this is not the case, you might want to use a variant of the least-connection algorithm called weighted least connection. Like the weighted round-robin algorithm, weighted least connection works by assigning a weight value to servers that can handle more connections. This weighting allows the load-balancing system to take into account differences between the servers in the load-balancing pool to make the load-balancing algorithm more efficient.

Least-Loaded Load Balancing

Another load-balancing algorithm that is very similar to the least-connection algorithm is the least-loaded algorithm. Using this method, each server in the load-balancing pool is monitored to keep track of system load, which is reported to the load-balancing system. Connections are distributed to the systems with the least amount of system load. This algorithm is more difficult to implement, but it has the advantage of taking into account differences in server capabilities automatically. This means that a variant in which weights are assigned to servers based on these differences makes little sense. Another advantage of this algorithm is that differences in the software running on each of the servers in the load-balancing pool also are accounted for automatically.

Response-Time Load Balancing

This method of load balancing is one of the easiest to implement. The load balancer receives a request for a connection from a client. The servers in the load-balancing pool are periodically queried, and whichever system has the fastest average response time gets the connection. This method performs in many ways like the least-loaded algorithm because the system with the lightest load is likely to be the one that responds the fastest. Problems can arise, however, because of network topology. For example, if the load-balanced servers are connected to different switches, traffic on that switch can have an impact on response time.

Service Level Agreement Load Balancing

Yet another form of load balancing is called service level agreement load balancing. This method routes traffic to the load-balanced server pool based on the source of the traffic.

Consider the following example. Company A is a parts supplier for automotive parts stores. They have several customers: Customer A, which provides seventy percent of the revenue for Company A, and the other customers, which provide the remaining thirty percent. Company A has seven servers in its load-balanced server pool, three of which are faster and have more capacity than the other four. To keep Customer A happy, Company A sets up its load balancer so that requests from Customer A always are routed to the three fast servers, whereas requests from the other customers are distributed to the four slower servers. This ensures that the most important customer always gets the fastest service.

Custom-Rules Load Balancing

A final form of load balancing that might be employed is referred to as custom-rules load balancing, in which the load is distributed among servers according to a set of user-defined rules. For example, you might load balance among an e-mail server farm based on the username of the individual making the connection. You also could distribute load based on domain name or any other criteria that you choose.

Vertical Versus Horizontal Scalability Solutions

When you begin budgeting for your Internet site, you will find that one of the major costs will be for the space to host your server systems. The cost of square footage in a colocation facility can be quite high, and you might think that buying systems that are vertically scalable is the best solution because you will be able to grow your site without having to take up any more space. This becomes less of an advantage, however, if you are paying for space based on number of racks instead of number of units of rack space.

Another thing to remember is that systems that are highly scalable are usually very expensive. In addition, currently available Intel-based systems do not compare to other architectures when it comes to vertical scalability. That is, if you find that CPU capacity is where you need to scale, Intel-based systems normally do not scale beyond eight processors. Exceptions to this occur; however, finding commodity systems that have more than eight processors is next to impossible. On the other hand, Sparc- and Alpha-based systems are available with up to 64 or more processors.

Another thing to consider when deciding whether to architect for horizontal versus vertical scalability is that fewer systems might also mean more single points of failure. For example, if you host your Web site on a single system rather than a Web farm, even if the single system is capable of handling the level of traffic you want, if you lose that system, your Web site is down. On the other hand, if you implement a horizontal scalability solution, you are spreading the load between multiple servers and while the loss of a server will reduce your capacity, it will not take out your entire site. The disadvantage of horizontal scaling is that as your site grows, so will the cost of maintaining it, because you will require additional staff to care for the additional systems. In addition, if you pay for rack space based on the number of rack units occupied, the addition of servers means additional cost.

Summary

In this chapter, we have examined the ideas of high availability and scalability. Areas of concern for high availability systems have been discussed, including redundant components, power considerations, and software reliability. In addition, we have discussed scalability and looked at the two basic approaches to scaling your systems. We also have examined some of the facets of both horizontal and vertical scaling solutions, including areas where a system can be scaled horizontally and some of the methods of scaling vertically. In later chapters, we will revisit some of these topics as we talk about specific solutions that can be employed to make your Internet servers more reliable and expandable to meet your needs.

Architecture for High Availability and Scalability

CHAPTER

12

IN THIS CHAPTER

- **Approaches for Achieving High Availability 256**
- **Scaling Your Internet Site 264**

In the previous chapter, we covered high availability and scalability and discussed, in general terms, why striving for high availability is not only desirable, but essential to your Internet site. In addition, we looked at scalability and the two classical approaches to scaling your systems to deal with increased load. In this chapter, we discuss the steps you should take while deciding on your site architecture. We start with a look at some of the approaches you can use to design in high availability for your Internet site. We then discuss how to determine where you need to target your scalability efforts by using benchmarks and stress testing. These will determine the characteristics of your site and where potential bottlenecks exist. We also will look at the role that performance tuning plays in site architecture.

Approaches for Achieving High Availability

In our previous discussion of high availability, we touched on three areas where you can focus your efforts. These areas were redundant hardware, backup power, and reliable software. In this chapter, we focus on two architectural decisions that you can make to keep your Web site highly available. These two approaches are

- Hot-swap systems
- Failover systems

You might think that these two are the same. However, as we discuss them in more detail, you will see how these two approaches are in fact different.

Hot-Swap Systems

One approach used by many Web sites to help achieve high availability is to maintain hot-swap systems that can replace critical systems with a minimum of effort. For example, when I was a system administrator at DejaNews, we had a number of front-line Web servers. In addition to these servers, which were in production serving our Web clients, there were usually at least two systems, which were kept in synchronization with them but were not serving our user base. In the event of a failure of a production Web server, one of the hot-swap systems would assume the hostname and IP address of the failed server until the failed system could be replaced or repaired. The key to success with this strategy is synchronization. You must ensure that the software and content on these hot-swap systems match the production systems at all times. Depending on how often the content on the systems is changed, this might not be as easy as it sounds. Let's take a look at a few of the options you have to accomplish it, specifically:

- Synchronization using rsync or rdist
- Network attached storage for content
- System-imaging software

Synchronization Using rsync or rdist

One way to keep systems in synchronization is to use software such as rsync or rdist. These tools are available for most Unix and Unix-like systems, and are capable of checking for differences between two systems and updating them so they match. The advantage of using these tools is that they are relatively easy to set up and can be run out of a cron job without the need for human intervention. In addition, you can target the specific areas of the file store that you want to keep synchronized instead of the entire system.

Consider the following example. For your Web servers, you have a generic operating system load plus the configuration files required for your HTTP daemon. You have developed a system that allows you to quickly install this OS load and the configuration files. All the Web content is stored in a single directory structure. To keep all your Web servers in sync, you designate one system as the master and all the other Web servers as slaves. On each of these slave servers, you run a cron job once per day (or at some other convenient interval) that runs rsync to compare the content on the slave with the master. In the event that they are different, rsync updates the slave from the master. In addition to the cron job, the system startup files call this same rsync script so that if a system is brought back from a crash or a new system is brought online, it will automatically synchronize itself with the master content server. Some other considerations are that to avoid using bandwidth that should be reserved for your users, you use an independent network to perform these updates. This also allows you to keep your content master server hidden from your users. Figure 12.1 illustrates how such a setup might look.

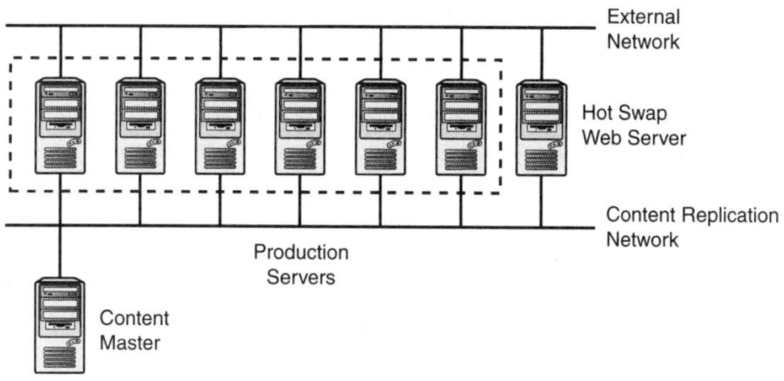

FIGURE 12.1
Synchronization using Content Master and rsync.

In Figure 12.1, each of the production Web servers surrounded by the dashed box and the hot-swap Web server has two network connections. One of these, labeled External Network, is for connections from users and the other, labeled Content Replication Network, is a network by which updates are distributed from the content master. On each of the slave servers, which are the production Web servers, and the hot-swap Web servers, the script in Listing 12.1 is run from a cron job once every four hours. The script contains comments that describe how it works.

LISTING 12.1: Script contains comments that describe how the cron job works

```
#!/bin/bash

# Set some environment variables that we can use throughout the
# script.

# The path to the rsync command
RSYNC=/usr/bin/rsync
# Document master
DOCMSTR=docsrv
# Document directory
DOCDIR=/home/httpd/htdocs
# Configuration file directory
CFGDIR=/etc/httpd/conf

# Run the rsync command with options to copy the entire contents
# of the document directory and the config file directory. We will
# delete files not found on the document master and use ssh as the
# transport mechanism. We will also exclude CVS directories and use
# compression.
$(RSYNC) -e ssh -Cavz --delete-after $(DOCMSTR):$(DOCDIR) $(DOCDIR)
$(RSYNC) -e ssh -Cavz --delete-after $(DOCMSTR):$(CFGDIR) $(CFGDIR)

exit 0
```

As you can see, this system is relatively easy to set up; after it is set up, it is very easy to maintain. Another advantage of this method is that if you choose, you can have the transfer of content secured by using ssh, a rsh replacement that encrypts what is being transmitted, as the transport agent.

Network Attached Storage for Content

Another option for keeping your Web servers in sync is to keep only one copy of the content and have your Web servers access them via NFS or some other network filesystem. This system has the advantage in that it requires the least work. You can never get out of sync, because only a single copy of the content files exists. There are, however, trade-offs to consider. One of these trade-offs is that you will see longer times to load Web documents because of the time required to transfer them from the network attached storage (NAS) system. Depending on how critical this longer load time is to you, this might or might not be a problem. Another drawback of this system is that by keeping all your content on a single system, you are introducing a single point of failure. You can solve this in a couple of ways, such as by having a failover system that replicates the content of the NAS system or by using a storage system that allows two systems to access the same disk device using a twin-tailed configuration. The diagram in Figure 12.2 illustrates a sample of this type of solution.

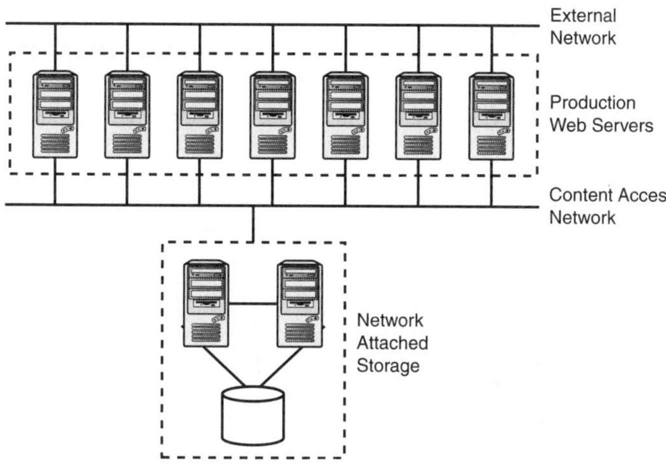

FIGURE 12.2
Network attached storage for content.

In the sample shown in Figure 12.2, we again see that a separate network is used to access the content, thus helping to reduce the network latency problem by separating user traffic from the traffic related to content distribution. The network attached storage subsystem in this figure consists of two systems that share a single storage device that is twin tailed and is connected to the two servers using a fiber channel connection. The two servers in this setup are configured to use a heartbeat protocol between them, and in the event of the failure of the primary, the backup system takes over the network identity of the original to ensure high availability of the files on the storage device. The Web servers use NFS to access the storage device using the virtual IP that identifies the NAS subsystem.

System Imaging Software

A final approach that might be used is system-imaging software to enable you to quickly synchronize a system. Using this approach, the production systems are imaged every time an update to any of them is made. Using this methodology, the failure of a system is handled by replacing the server with a fresh one and then updating it from the image server to make it match the system that failed. This approach can be implemented using software such as System Imager, which is available at `http://systemimager.sourceforge.net/`. Using this method, you create an image server where the snapshots of the system are stored. After you have installed one of your servers the way you want it, you run a client program to copy an image of the entire system to the image server. You then can use that image to build the remaining servers, and with the exception of the network configuration information, the systems will be identical. After you have System Imager set up, it also can be used to distribute updates to all the imaged systems. One of the key advantages to this methodology is that you do not have to maintain a separate system to load the operating system and to keep it in sync. In addition, systems maintained as hot-swap systems do not have to be kept in sync all the time, and if you have different types of servers that use the same hardware, you can keep a blank system and just install a different image on it to replace a failed server. Figure 12.3 illustrates this type of setup.

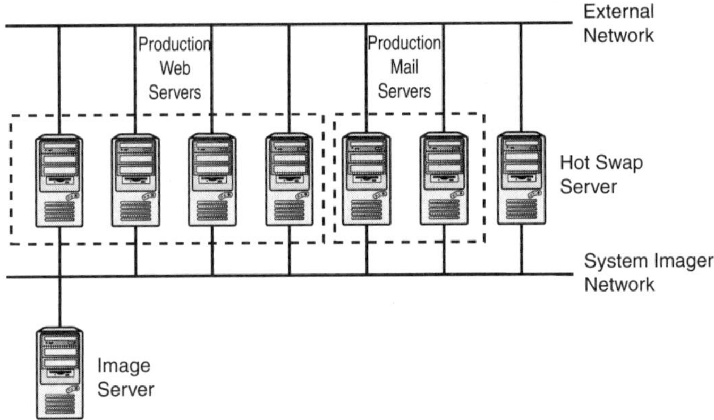

FIGURE 12.3
System-imaging software.

In this figure, the site contains two types of servers that use the same hardware. The system image host contains images for each of these servers taken from the initial installation of the first Web and first mail server. In the event of a system failure, the hot-swap system is overwritten with the appropriate image from the system image host.

Failover Systems

In addition to hot-swap systems, another strategy employed to make your site highly available is to use failover systems. A failover system differs from a hot-swap system in that a failover system is designed to take over automatically when the primary fails. Failover systems are best employed where you find that you have a single point of failure. Some examples where this might be true include firewall systems, load balancers, database systems, or a NAS system, as described in the previous example. Typically, configuration is done with two systems, as illustrated in Figure 12.4.

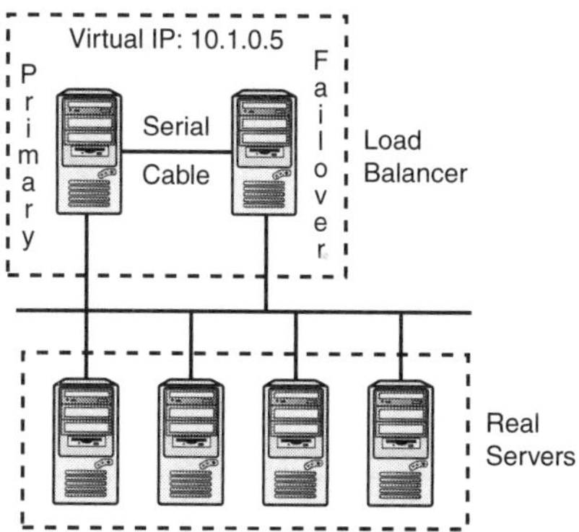

FIGURE 12.4
An example of a failover system.

The figure shows a set of real servers—for example, Web servers on an intranet. Load-balancing software is running on each of the load-balancer hosts. These two systems use a serial connection as well as their network connection to run a heartbeat protocol. As long as the primary system is up and running, it sets up a network interface with a virtual IP address by which clients access the real servers, and this primary system does load balancing between the real servers on the back end. In the event that the primary system fails, the failover system takes over the virtual IP, and it now serves as the load balancer for the real servers. When the primary system is brought back online, it resumes its duty and takes back the virtual IP. As you will see in Chapter 16, "Open Source High Availability and Scalability," this technique is used in the Ultramonkey product, and the time between primary failure and the failover system taking over can be a matter of seconds. In addition, this process is automatic, requiring no operator intervention. This goes a long way toward achieving the goal of five nines availability.

Combining Approaches

Because hot-swap systems and failover systems are not mutually exclusive, the best approach for your Internet site might be a combined approach. When you begin designing your network, look for places where you have single points of failure or where you have multiple systems that are common. At these places, look at the viability of using hot-swap and failover systems. To illustrate how this is done, let's take a look at an example.

A Combined Approach Example

Suppose that as a network designer, you are approached to help a company, which we will call WebNews.com, develop a network to support its Web design. This company plans to build a site that provides a Web interface to Usenet newsgroups. They require servers to run the Web front end, news servers, name servers, load balancing, mail servers, and database servers. You start by drawing an initial diagram of how you envision their network incorporating all these servers. This picture is shown in Figure 12.5.

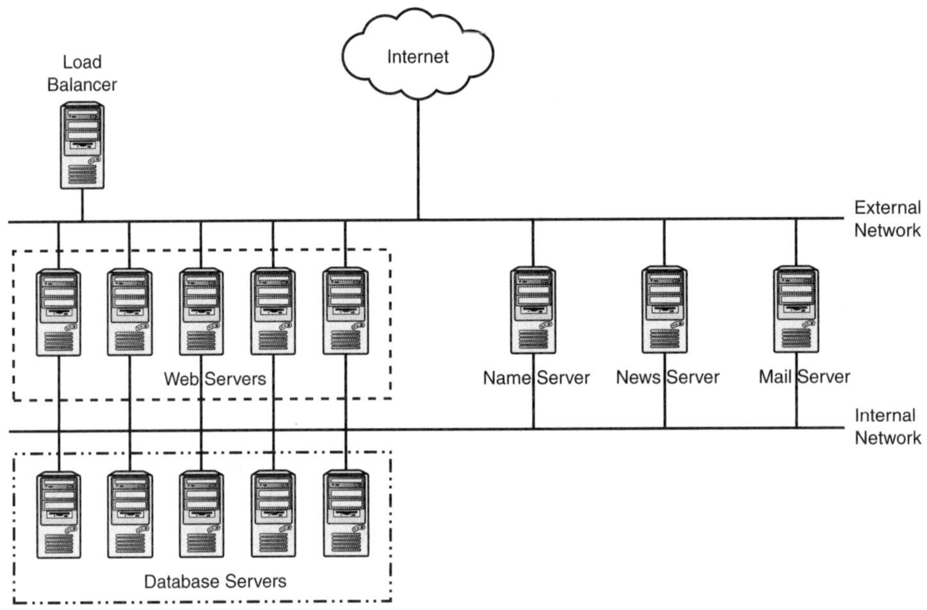

FIGURE 12.5
Initial network design for WebNews.com.

From the diagram in Figure 12.5, and based on our previous discussion of hot-swap systems and failover, you should see several places where we could use these strategies to improve on the design. Let's start with failover systems. In our network, there are three places where we might be able to do so. Starting from the left, the first place where a failover system might be appropriate is the load balancer. By adding a failover load balancer, we eliminate this single point of failure. The same could be said of our name server. In fact, because name service and load balancing are typically low-impact services, you could consider combining these two services onto the same set of servers. This would still have the advantage of being more reliable, and because you could retask the name server in the original diagram as the failover for the load balancer, you would not be incurring additional cost.

Two more servers where you might want to consider implementing a failover system are the news and mail servers. Where these systems differ from the name server and load balancer systems is that both of them require semipersistent storage for their spool directories. One way in which you could address this problem is by using a network attached storage device for these directories. On the other hand, the Web servers and database servers do not lend themselves to failover systems. So let's update our diagram to incorporate the changes we have thought of so far. This update is illustrated in Figure 12.6.

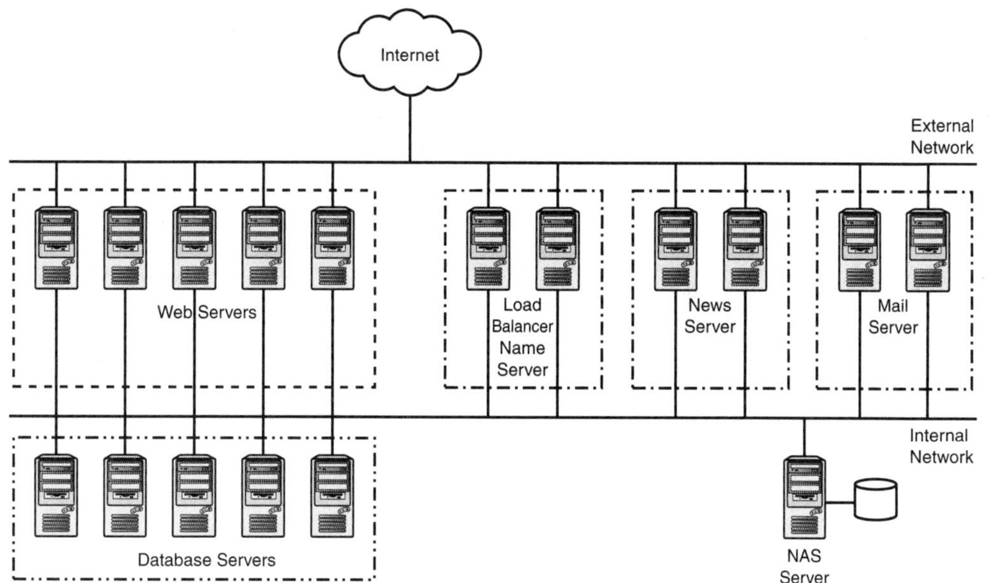

FIGURE 12.6
Updated network design incorporating failover systems.

Now that we have addressed the single points of failure, we can take a look at where hot-swap systems would give the greatest return. In our network, the servers were of three basic classes. First is the Web class, which is a dual-processor system with 1GB of RAM. These servers are used for the Web servers only. Second is a slightly less powerful system that is used for the mail, news, and name servers. This class of server, which we will call the mail class, has a single processor and 512MB of RAM. Third is the database class—the most powerful system. This is a quad processor system with 2GB of RAM. The synchronization method that is best suited to this configuration is probably the system-imaging method, which means that we will need at least three hot-swap systems and an additional host as the system image host. We will now update our diagram again to add our hot-swap systems and the system image server. This updated diagram is shown in Figure 12.7.

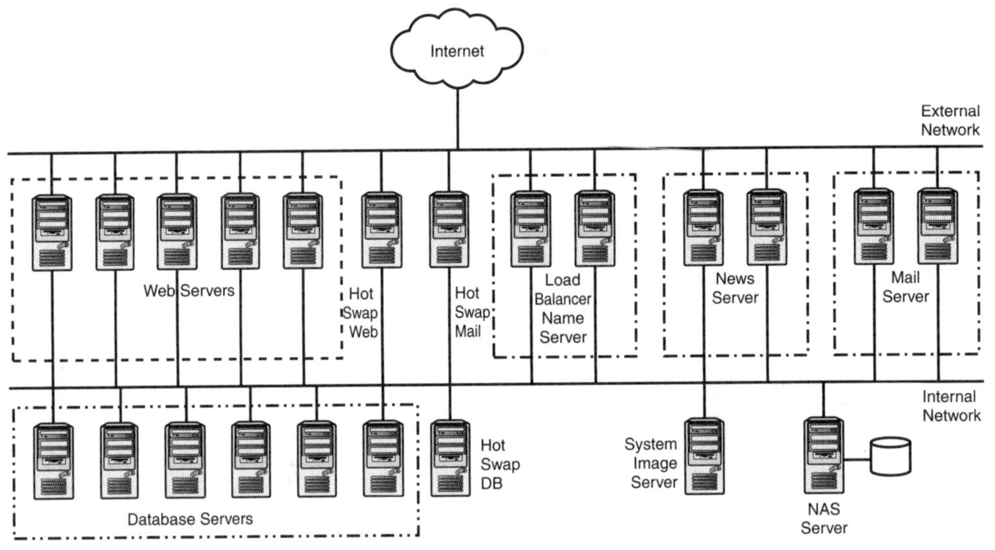

FIGURE 12.7
The final network design.

In this final design, you can see that we have three hot-swap servers, one for each class of machine. The system labeled hot-swap mail acts as a hot-swap server for the load balancer, mail, and news systems. In addition, you can see that we have added the system image host. In total, we have added seven systems to our original design. Two systems were added to provide failover for the mail and news servers. Three systems were added as hot-swap systems. The NAS server was added as part of the failover for the mail and news system. And finally, the system image server was added to support the hot-swap architecture. Naturally, this will add to the cost of your network. However, when you consider the cost of downtime for your Internet site, you will see that the investment is well worth it.

Now that we have covered how to build high availability into your architecture, we are ready to move on to the next topic—planning for Web site growth.

Scaling Your Internet Site

After you have addressed the availability of your network design, you should consider how to address growth or scalability. Unless you have no plans for your site to grow, you should begin planning on how to scale your site during the design phase. Failure to do so means having to redesign your site later, when design changes mean costly downtime. In this section, we take a look at what you need to do to ensure that you will be able to grow your capacity as your site traffic increases.

Benchmarking to Determine Limitations

To plan for growth, you must first determine where the bottlenecks in your system exist and your current capacity. The way to do this is by running benchmarks. Unfortunately, to effectively test your site capacity, you probably will have to build these benchmarks yourself. Although plenty of benchmarks are available to test Web performance, such as SpecWeb, these tests probably won't accurately reflect the limitation of your system, because they do not simulate your traffic patterns.

If feasible, you should try to run a beta test of your site with a controlled audience to see how they interact with your site. Although you probably have an idea how you would like people to interact with your site, there is no guarantee that they will do so. For example, you might provide links to go back and forth between pages, but your users might all decide that they prefer to use the Back button on their browsers. Depending on the nature of your site, you might find that this causes unexpected problems, especially if you don't take this into account during your planning.

After you have assembled your test group and studied their traffic patterns, you can begin constructing your test software. Starting with a test system, you now should begin to simulate traffic while monitoring the system load. You should pay special attention to disk usage patterns, memory usage, network throughput, and CPU use. Gradually add more simulated users to your system and watch for bottlenecks to occur in one of these areas. You do not need to do any tuning during these tests; the purpose is only to determine the limitations. When you reach a limit in one of the areas you are monitoring, you should try adding additional capacity in this area and run the tests again. The purpose here is to determine how adding capacity in this area affects the limitations, because you may find that the growth in capacity is not linear.

Suppose, for example, that you run a Web server, and during your initial test, you top out in the CPU use area. Your system is capable of supporting two CPUs and your operating system is SMP capable, so you add a second CPU. Although you might think that adding a second CPU will double your capacity, you might find that this is not the case. This can be true for a number of reasons, such as the nature of the Web server software, which might not be well suited to running on a SMP system. Another reason why this might not be true is that the operating system might not support SMP effectively. Whatever the reason, you should start your test over and determine how adding a second CPU to a single system contributes to your capacity. If you find that dual-processor systems do not add adequate capacity, you might try adding a second system and load balancing between them. This method works not only for CPU, but also for other areas such as memory or disk drives. Some of the things you might try during your benchmarking runs include adding more memory to a system, adding additional drives, and spreading frequently accessed filesystems across multiple drives to improve read times.

As you run these tests, you might determine that bottlenecks exist in areas such as disk access time or network throughput. Some of these areas might be tunable, which brings us to our next topic—performance tuning to reduce limitations.

Performance Tuning to Reduce Limitations

After you have identified the bottlenecks in your system, you can look at ways to address them. This is the definition of performance tuning. Linux is unusual in the world of operating systems in that it is designed to run efficiently without a lot of tweaking. This is not to say that there is no tuning that you can do to make your Internet servers run more efficiently. However, you might find that there is little that you have to do to get the best performance from your systems. The following are some areas where you might want to concentrate your tuning efforts:

- Disk access time
- Swap behavior
- Server response time

Let's take a look at each of these areas and see how they might be tweaked to improve the performance of your systems, starting with disk access time.

Improving Disk Access Performance

The disk input/output system is typically one of the first places that people try tuning their systems. You can do a number of things to access your data quicker. Some of these are related to selecting the hardware, and others are strategies that you can try to speed things up.

Starting with hardware, let's first consider the issue of IDE versus SCSI drives. Although IDE drives are usually much cheaper to buy, there are some definite disadvantages to using IDE instead of SCSI drives in your servers. The first of these disadvantages is that the IDE drivers in Linux are usually much less verbose in reporting problems than their SCSI counterparts; thus, it might be harder to detect errors early and avoid problems by being proactive in your maintenance. Another disadvantage is related to the nature of IDE controllers. You might have heard recommendations about spreading files across multiple drives to improve access times. With IDE drives, this is true only if the drives are located on separate buses. For example, if you have a system with two IDE buses, each of which supports two drives, spreading files between two drives connected to the same bus will not gain you anything, because access to the drives on a single controller is sequential—that is, while you are accessing the first drive on the bus, you cannot access the second drive and vice versa. The only way that you could get any performance increase is if you attached the second drive to the second bus.

This is not true of SCSI drives. Spreading files across multiple SCSI drives can increase performance. One method by which you can achieve this is to use the Linux software RAID drivers to create a RAID 0 device that spans multiple drives. The diagram in Figure 12.8 illustrates how this works.

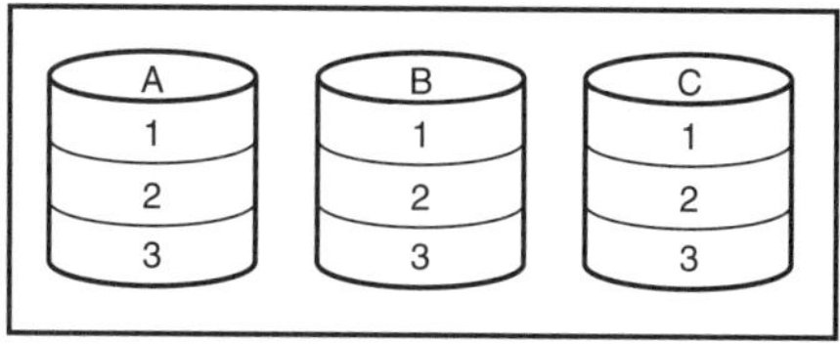

FIGURE 12.8
RAID 0 conceptual diagram.

In Figure 12.8, each disk is divided into a number of chunks, which are labeled A1, B1, C1, and so on. As data is written to the RAID 0 device, it is written first to A1, then to B1, then to C1, then to A2, B2, C2, and so on. This method of spreading data across multiple drives that appear to applications as a single drive is known as striping. RAID 0 does not provide any redundancy, and if a drive in the array is damaged, you have to rebuild the array from scratch. (You do keep backups, don't you?) To improve reliability at the cost of a slight write penalty, you can combine striping with RAID 1, or mirroring. This results in what is sometimes called RAID 0+1, in which you create two or more striped drives and then mirror the data between them. This can give you even better performance because data reads can now be spread between the mirrors. This can be accomplished under Linux using both software and hardware RAID. If you choose to implement this technique and want to use hardware RAID, be sure that the controller you select supports it. Other tuning can be done on your filesystems, such as changing block sizes, bytes per inode, and other parameters. It is up to you to determine the best values for your application.

Tuning Swap Behavior

Another area that might require tuning to get the maximum performance is swap behavior. Some believe that if your servers are swapping, you should add more physical memory. This is a good rule of thumb because RAM is much faster than using swap. If you are unable to follow this rule, you should at least follow some of these simple rules for swap space:

- Always use swap partitions instead of swap files.
- Use multiple swap partitions and distribute them among multiple physical drives.
- Assign priorities to swap partitions with higher priorities given to partitions on the least-accessed drives.

As for how much swap space to use, this is the subject of some debate. In the Unix world, one general rule that has long been proposed is that your swap space should be at least twice the amount of physical RAM. Part of the reason for this was the nature of swap under systems such as Solaris and AIX. This rule, however, does not apply to Linux systems because the virtual memory system is implemented very differently. On Linux systems, the virtual memory system is optimized for the situation where swap equals the amount of physical memory; on systems with less than 1GB of physical memory, this is a good rule. However, on systems with 1GB of RAM or more, you can make your swap space much smaller and optimize your applications so that swapping is avoided.

Server Response-Time Tuning

In addition to tuning the operating system, it is important to optimize the applications—specifically, servers such as Web servers, for performance. In the case of Web servers, this might mean using one server for static pages and another for dynamic pages, such as using the kernel space Web server in Linux 2.4.x for static pages and Apache for dynamic pages and scripting. It is this combination that has been used to set new records in SpecWeb benchmarks. Other things that you can do to tune your servers include limiting the number of children that Apache can start up so that they don't cause swapping, or you can set specific flags, such as the noatime flag, when mounting spool directories on NNTP servers to increase performance. Tuning is an art that requires a lot of in-depth knowledge of the application and the operating system. You would be well advised to do your homework before attempting to tune your systems. Some sites that you should visit if you are interested in Linux tuning include `http://www.linux.com` and `http://www.linuxperf.org`. You also should visit the sites of specific applications, such as Apache, at `http://www.apache.org`, for tips on application-level tuning.

Planning Is Key

As we stated earlier, planning is the key to success. The time invested in creating a detailed plan up front will be well worth it when you don't have to redesign your network later. If we go back and consider our example of WebNews.com, you can see that we already have included some scalability features in our design. These include the use of a load balancer to provide horizontal scalability in our Web server and database server classes. Other areas where we could address scalability include tuning the disk access times on the news and mail servers because these applications are by their nature input/output oriented. Some other optimizations that might be considered are the use of RAID 0+1 for the database filesystems, providing both reliability and improved read performance.

Summary

In this chapter, we have looked at the importance of proper analysis in the design phase of creating your Internet site to ensure high availability and scalability. These techniques are more expensive initially; however, considering the cost of downtime and the level of effort that would be required to redesign a poor initial design, this expense is almost always worth the effort. We also have taken a look at how tuning, testing, and proper planning are necessary steps if you will be building and maintaining large-scale Internet sites or if you are ready to move beyond the small site stage.

Hardware Reliability

CHAPTER

13

IN THIS CHAPTER

- Mean Time Between Failures (MTBF) 272
- Maintaining Spare Systems and Components 274
- Sales Pitches—Separating the Wheat from the Chaff 275
- Hardware Technologies Used to Achieve Reliability 277
- Hot-Swappable Components 279
- Infrastructure Requirements 280
- Choosing Hardware Vendors 283
- The Importance of FCC and UL Ratings 286

Regardless of the stability of your operating system and software, it won't mean anything if your hardware is substandard. Given a stable software environment, there should be minimal downtime due to failed hardware, although most subsystems have a limited life expectancy. With the right hardware downtime should be at most a few minutes per year or should not happen at all. When selecting your hardware, keep in mind the requirements for the system, allowable downtime, quality of service contracts you have with your clients (and contracts with your hardware vendor), and any other factors that relate to the reliability of the system. Proper preparation in the face of all known factors will result in a system that is reliable in general and, at the same time, prepared for the eventual hardware failure.

Depending on the environment, reliability can have different meanings. Failure rates are the predicted rate at which your hardware will fail, whereas failover hardware refers to the components that are in place to swiftly (and possibly transparently) handle failure situations.

Over time, nearly all hardware is going to fail, although this varies based on the technology involved. Memory chips tend to have long lives but are a little more susceptible to damage from electrical fluctuations. Drive technology is now fairly resistant to shock damage, but because of the construction of the drive, a point in time exists when the physical mechanics are going to give out. By using reliable hardware and factoring normal failure rates with spare systems, your system should be relatively resistant to hardware failure situations. Let's take a look at some of the factors involved in making sure that your system is reliable.

Mean Time Between Failures (MTBF)

Any system component is going to fail eventually. Steps can be taken to extend life in certain situations, but assuming off-the-shelf components (Intel or otherwise), nearly everything is going to die eventually. As mentioned, drives tend to die first, and components without moving parts last longer. But for the most part, MTBF rates should exceed the lifespan of the system. For example, you might deploy a normal IDE drive on a Web server. The MTBF rate for that drive is most likely in the 500,000 hour range. In real terms, this works out to about 57 years, which is obviously longer than the expected lifespan of the system. (Who really thinks that we'll all still be using the rotational drives in the late 2050s, let alone the same IDE interface?)

Even though most components should outlast the system, you should figure on having a subset of the parts fail over the system's lifespan. Although the MTBF rates of drives seem like an absurdly long time, many drives turn out to be bad within a few months of their introduction. Many times in the field, a drive is deployed, and it works fine for several months, but then it fails without warning shortly after that. This is actually more common than thought and is usually tied to a specific set of drives from the manufacturer. For example, all drives from a given plant during a two-month interval could have ended up with bad parts. Although they might have passed internal burn-in periods, the drives aren't up to sustained field usage. This can happen anytime, either because of a new shipment of parts at the manufacturer or as a result of a new drive construction method (such as a new platter layout scheme). The manufacturer should do complete burn-in tests, but in reality, this can't catch everything.

In the end, it's a good idea to be ready to replace drives on a normal basis, assuming the worst. It is also a good idea to track what drives are deployed in what machines, noting each one's manufacturer, fabrication location, date of construction, and other factors noted on the drive's label. In the event that you did receive all your drives from a bad group, it's handy to know where these drives are located, so that you can replace them all in one pass. This is especially helpful if your machines are located in a colocation facility, which might not be physically convenient. Otherwise, you either need to sit back and wait for the other ones to die (which can be catastrophic) or take each machine apart and look at the drives. Either way, it damages your system's availability rating.

Other than drives, MTBF rates shouldn't be much of a factor in your system, although if you have custom hardware, refer to the vendor for applicable data. Memory chips, motherboards, network cards, and so on tend to live almost indefinitely. Because there are no moving parts, little can go wrong. The exception to this is if your local power is not clean. By this, I mean that the power source either is not constant or fluctuates greatly. In most server environments, though, especially in hosting facilities, the power is centrally managed to ensure that it is constant and nonfluctuating. It might be beneficial to get a separate Uninterruptible Power Supply (UPS) to ensure that power is cleaned before entering your system, just to be safe. This provides an extra layer of insurance between your system and the provider, to handle the situation in which the hosting site might inadvertently disrupt service. In most situations, there should be a guarantee by the service provider that power will be provided and that they assume responsibility for any losses, but it's still a good idea for your customers' sake (and your reputation) to place a safeguard wherever you can.

It is tempting to take a look your machine's power-supply safeguards and your provider's infrastructure and decide that it's not worth the extra cost of dropping in a UPS. In some cases, it might not be worth it. But keep in mind that power fluctuations can have a devastating effect on your system's hardware, and a UPS can handle nearly anything that comes down the line before it gets to your servers. Although your server will have a power supply that can handle a large disruption and should block the hit before it gets to the motherboard and components, this is an unnecessary risk to your operations because it is not guaranteed that the spike will be completely handled at the power supply. (Although, on one occasion, I have seen a power supply take a spike that loaded the capacitors to the point of explosion and blue flame, cutting the circuit and saving the motherboard. And yes, this was at a hosting facility that provided supposedly stable power.) Also keep in mind that in most situations, turning your hardware on is the most violent act you perform, because of the sudden flow of electricity, the heat fluctuation, and so on. Anything that can be done to maintain a constant, even flow of electricity is good for your server's uptime and good for the health of the components involved. In addition to this safety benefit, a UPS will also monitor temperatures, tell your machine when to shut down in a real emergency, and can notify administrators by e-mail when the situation is looking bad. This helps you manage downtime caused by power failures and provides you with data that can be used to analyze your service provider's performance.

As you can see, MTBF rates, although important, tend to live outside the range of your system's expected lifespan, and it is generally more important to ensure clean usage of the components involved. This way, you can rest safely. You've done all you can to ensure that the system is being used in a stable electrical environment, and that most hardware failures that do occur will most likely be due to faulty hardware, not physical mismanagement. (This can be helpful in ensuring the place of blame when handling the hardware warranty.)

Maintaining Spare Systems and Components

A good way to ensure reliability in the face of a server failure is the practice of maintaining spare systems and components. The level of redundancy depends on your hardware needs, of course, but it is important to have a good idea of what needs to be swappable in the event of a failure. For example, the complete failure of a core database server would require the presence of an identical machine that could swap in immediately to handle the load. For something like a drive array, the failure of a drive would require only a spare drive or two to be kept on hand.

Regardless of the type of work the system does, probably some components end up being more important than the others. If your system is database-centric, your database servers are going to be more important to your operations, compared to the farm of Web servers involved at the front end. The loss of a Web server from the cluster might increase the load slightly on the others, but without your databases, none of the Web servers will have anything interesting to serve. Because of this imbalance, it is very important that you step back and analyze the system according to two factors: which systems are most important to overall operations and which components are most likely to fail over time.

Spare Storage

As mentioned earlier, drives tend to be the most failed pieces of any system, so your failure contingency plans should account for this. Any system that heavily relies on drive subsystems should have spare parts ready to be swapped in as needed. With any high availability system, a Storage Area Network (SAN) or Redundant Array of Inexpensive Disks (RAID) should be in place to ensure continued support in the face of most failures. In these situations, the drive replacement shouldn't cause any kind of system downtime.

Spare Systems

At the system level, it might be worth keeping a full spare system around to replace an existing one. As previously mentioned, this is generally useful for database systems, but it has applications elsewhere, too. In Chapter 16, "Open Source High Availability and Scalability," we discuss the concept of Web serving farms. The technical points are discussed in detail there, but the concept in general is that a load-balancing machine handles requests for the cluster. Machines in the cluster handle requests as given and generally answer back directly to the client. In these systems, the cluster is often made up of many machines with the same hardware and software configurations. Should one of these boxes fail, the load balancer will rebalance the load among the remaining servers. In this scheme, because the servers in the cluster are usually standard off-the-shelf machines, it makes sense to keep an extra box laying around, ready to be rotated in. Because the machines all keep the same configuration except for network address, it becomes very easy just to keep a box online and ready to rotate in if one of the existing boxes dies unexpectedly. Depending on your configuration, you might need to drop some data on the drive to make sure it's up to date with the rest of the cluster. However, this is generally trivial to do, and in the case of a purely dynamic site, it might not be needed at all.

Cost Considerations

Depending on your budget, the idea of having a spare system around that does absolutely nothing might seem like a waste of money. But given that the cost of a low-end Web server for a cluster might be less than $1,000, the benefit of being able to swap in a full system in a matter of seconds becomes evident. Balanced against the cost of downtime to your business, having the spare is definitely worth it. Although full systems for a database server might be more costly (much more so, in many situations), it is again balanced against the potential loss of customers because of downtime. For many applications, the backup database server can replicate against the primary one, allowing for load balancing during normal situations and providing insurance in the face of a failure on the primary. Having extra components on hand is an even simpler decision. Individual components are, of course, much cheaper than a full system and can be used in most of the boxes present. Having a few drives, network cards, and other components handy can greatly reduce downtime in the face of a failure, in contrast to waiting until parts die and then going out to look for replacements.

Sales Pitches—Separating the Wheat from the Chaff

Let's face it—not all the hardware offerings out there are equal. Even among different vendors targeting the same customer base, the products in question might vary widely in their capabilities and reliability. It is important for your system and your budget that you are able to effectively select the right solution for your needs.

An important factor in choosing the right vendor is making sure that the vendor can adequately handle your needs. If you have a large amount of requirements that depend on high-quality hardware, it probably doesn't make sense to question a smaller vendor. The smaller shops might not be able to provide the level of service you need in an emergency. On the other hand, they might be local enough to be able to handle situations faster than it would take a larger vendor to show up. Balance these factors with the reliability of the vendors over time and whether they will be able to meet your unique requirements as the system advances in the coming years. Choosing the right vendor is one of the more important decisions to be made when planning; make sure that every factor is taken into account. Everything from hardware availability, driver support, support contract levels, and so on have a direct physical impact on your system's viability in the marketplace. Software can be reconfigured, replaced, rewritten, and so on, but it is difficult to recover from bad hardware choices on a running system.

Although it is important that you choose your vendor carefully, the larger issue at hand is understanding what you are looking for. It is not enough to know what you need the system to do. When it comes down to making a real decision, it is important that you know exactly what you want in terms of raw specifications, hardware technologies involved, and standards relating to the technologies. Don't take this to mean that you need to be a hardware god in every aspect of your system; if it did, you might as well do the hardware work yourself. But it does mean that you should know what you're looking for when you're going to a vendor for hardware. Then you can be sure that you are getting what you need—not being fed a line. For example, you might need a certain throughput from your disk subsystem to keep the system from bottlenecking. Here, it is important that you select the right types of drive and bus from the manufacturer and that you select them based on the right information. The hardware might be presented as being capable of performing at a given rate that fulfills your need, but it might not be noted that the speed rating is burst speeds only and that normal sustained rates are lower on average. Make sure that the vendor provides as much detail as possible about the hardware in question to ensure that the right parts are selected for the system.

In most situations, vendors are going to tell you that they can perform the job you need them to do. After all, sales is their job. But in some cases, either the vendor's support line might not be equipped to handle your needs or the salesperson might be misinformed about the company's capability set. In nearly all situations, it is good to work both with a sales support person and a technical support person to balance all your needs. This way, you can be sure that your budgetary needs are considered by knowledgeable people and that your technical needs will be handled by those who know the vendor's current capabilities and where things are headed in the future. This also provides a good conduit to getting detailed technical answers to all your questions, making for a more defined decision matrix when considering different vendors.

Realistically, every sales situation will be different, and you will likely need to ask different questions of everyone to get the level of detail you need to select a vendor. Because corporate image is so important, it is unlikely that you will be given incorrect answers to your questions just to get your business. However, it is possible that you will get inaccurate responses because of misinformation within the vendor's internal informational pipeline. Therefore, you should make sure that you know exactly what you want and get as much detail as possible when selecting a vendor. Check specific vendor support for your detailed needs and verify them if possible against open source congregation points. These points vary by need, but freshmeat.net, sourceforge.org, development lists, newsgroups, and so on can give you some real hands-on explanations of what works and what doesn't. More information can only help in deciding which sales pitch is really delivering the product that is right for your situation.

Hardware Technologies Used to Achieve Reliability

In most situations, reliability should be built in to the system. Downtime is expensive and damaging both to the system and your business; reliability shouldn't be defined as always having someone on hand to take the machine apart. Rather than keeping someone around and ready to spring on a dead machine, failover and reliability should be inherent to the system. This could be done within the scope of the operating system, but software configuration adds an extra layer of management to an already complex picture. In many cases, these factors are built in to the hardware so that not even the operating system needs to manage it. This is the case for most failover hardware, such as RAID. If a drive dies, the hardware transparently handles the failure, and the operating system and applications never know the failure occurred. Next, we'll take a look at some of the ways of using hardware techniques to prevent downtime on your system.

Redundant Arrays of Inexpensive Disks (RAID)

RAID is the most common means of ensuring reliability in the face of a hardware failure. Put simply, RAID is a mechanism for distributing your data across several disks and storing summary data across others to ensure that if a disk fails, the data that was on that disk can be reconstructed from the remaining information that lives on the remaining drives. RAID has many levels of support, some of which are built to provide speed gains rather than failover. Listed here are the common types found in practice and a summary of their approach:

- RAID 0—Although it's not technically RAID because it is not redundant, RAID 0 stripes data across multiple drives present in a set. By distributing the write (and read) load, drives can provide data to the bus faster because each one is acting independently. If you need speed but not redundancy, this is the path to take. Also make sure to use stripe sizes that are larger than the average requested records so that queries can be completed against the set in one request.
- RAID 1—This is a simple mirror set. For each drive, one counterpart exists that has its data constantly updated with the master. In some situations, there can be more than one mirroring drive. Throughput is not as fast, because the bus is handling two write operations for every write from the system, but redundancy is maintained.

- RAID 5—This is the most common balance of redundancy and distributed data. In this case, a parity drive exists for the sole purpose of maintaining parity status for the data on other drives in the set. The other two drives have data distributed between them. Writes to a RAID 5 array can be slower using striping because there needs to be two writes on disk per system write. RAID 5's write performance isn't perfect, but it offers fast reads and can survive the death of a drive in the set. However, the loss of a drive will impact performance. Performance during the rebuild is also degraded, although the rebuild can be done online. Make sure that this degradation of performance is permissible in your environment. If the normal throughput of the RAID set is just above what you need, performance during a rebuild is going to severely impact system throughput. If it's handled correctly by either hardware or software, a RAID 5 failure should never cause an interruption in service or a loss of data.
- RAID 10—This is a hybrid of RAID 0 and 1 (as you can tell from the name); it performs striping across sets of mirrored drives. In this system, sets of drives are set up to be mirrors of each other, and then a stripe set is built across them. This requires more drives to be present because each drive needs to be duplicated. Data availability is very high, and overall interaction, such as reads, writes, and rebuilds, is very good. If RAID 5 doesn't offer quite the right performance during a rebuild and you have the drives to spare, RAID 10 is probably the right choice.

Other types of RAID not mentioned here are RAID 2, 3, 4, 6, 30, 50, and JBOD (Just a Bunch Of Disks) configurations. These aren't very common, though, and they generally don't offer much more in performance aspects for most situations. If none of the options listed fits your needs, however, you might want to check out the other levels. For most uses, if the extra storage is available, RAID 5 and RAID 10 are the most recommended because they provide both good performance and redundancy. Check with your hardware vendor concerning bundled RAID configurations; nearly any vendor these days ships a Linux-supported RAID system. If they don't, a card can be easily obtained from any of the normal RAID vendors. This was not always the case, but as Linux has become a staple in the server room, many vendors have developed drivers for it.

For the most part, RAID support is handled in hardware. The drivers for the RAID card are loaded into the kernel, and the card presents the RAID drive set to the kernel as a block device that a filesystem can be constructed on. This way, file operations are handled through the kernel and to the card as if it is a regular disk, and the card handles the distribution of reads and writes as needed by the configured RAID level. But it should be noted that Linux has long had support for software RAID in which the drive set is configured from within the system. In this situation, the kernel is configured to view multiple drives as components in a RAID set and is responsible for doing the read, write, and other operations on its own.

Although the software approach is known to work (very well, actually), a hardware solution is preferred in most situations. If the kernel is responsible for maintenance of the RAID set, it has to do a fair amount of bookkeeping to handle the drive interaction. For example, writing data to a RAID 5 set in software forces the kernel to do the normal file write and also to perform the checksumming operation needed to prepare for another write to the parity disk. This causes extra work for the kernel and keeps it from doing other system work. This performance hit is usually significant enough that a hardware solution is used instead. Also, with the hardware solution, the card can keep requests in a local memory buffer that is not susceptible to power loss; therefore, unfinished operations can be rolled back in the case of a power failure. Recovery from a power failure is also possible in a kernel-level RAID configuration, but it is generally not as failsafe as a hardware configuration. Refer to the Software RAID HOWTO at `www.linuxdoc.org` for more information on kernel-level RAIDs.

Hot-Swappable Components

If you can't get failover within hardware, you might need to settle for being able to swap components in and out on-the-fly. Some buses were built to handle this type of operation. Universal Serial Bus (USB) is one of these. Others support hot swapping in some form, but weren't necessarily built with this in mind. SCSI, PCI, and IDE are some of these.

In a server environment, however, USB is not likely to be much of a player. In general, it is prevalent on the client side because it connects peripherals easily, but it is generally a low bandwidth bus compared to something like PCI. In the case of PCI, IDE, and SCSI, which are prevalent on the server side, ways exist to allow for hot swapping, but it might not be allowed by your specific hardware. IDE hot swapping is generally viewed as a shaky proposition, whereas SCSI swapping is fairly straightforward. In general, most RAID situations come with hot-swap drives so that in the case of a drive failure, a new one can be plugged in and merged into the array to reestablish the integrity of the RAID set. As a side note, it is a good idea to test the hot-swap and RAID-rebuilding capabilities of your system while it is in testing by pulling drives from the RAID during a period of heavy activity and monitoring the effects on the system.

PCI is commonly the bus by which most peripheral cards interact with each other and the rest of the system. It is a fairly high-speed bus and fulfills the needs of most operations. But for a long time, cards using PCI weren't able to be swapped in and out on-the-fly. These days, however, many vendors are selling machines with at least a subset of the PCI slots capable of allowing live swapping of cards. This can be a great help in the event of a card failure, such as a network card. Generally, the hot-swap slots are easily accessible; the machine can be opened, the card swapped, and operations can continue while the machine is up. Combined with a second network card, this can yield a decently fault-tolerant machine. There are generally some caveats to keep in mind with this system, such as the fact that the slot with the card being swapped out has to be replaced with another of the same type of card because of resource allocations. But in general, because this hot swap is used for failure contingencies rather than for adding new capabilities to an existing system, PCI hot swap can be very helpful in maintaining uptime.

Apart from buses, other components of the system, such as power supplies, should be hot swappable. In general, most hot-swap components can happen without the operating system dealing with it or even knowing it is happening, as is the case with hardware RAID and power supplies. In the case of power supplies, the machine comes outfitted with at least two separate power supplies, each with its own interface to a board that coordinates the power with the rest of the system. In the event that one power supply goes bad (or someone yanks the wrong cord out), power is drawn from the other supply. Each supply should be built to be easily withdrawn from the system so that another one can be brought in. Depending on the system architecture, the power draw might go back to the first supply, but that can vary. Either way, the part can be easily replaced, and in minutes you're back to having a backup power supply, all without ever interrupting services on the machine.

Infrastructure Requirements

As previously mentioned, it is always important that you have a good hold on what your requirements are. Without understanding where you're trying to go, it is unlikely you'll ever get there. So, the first thing that should be done is a detailed analysis of what the system needs to do.

Routers, Switches, and Hubs

Network capacity is generally one of the most important factors in system planning, second to disk subsystem planning. Nothing will leave a user more dissatisfied with the system than slow access time, and because the network interface is most likely the user's only interface with your system, you need to make sure it meets or exceeds their expectations. In most situations, however, the speed of the uplink interface to the Internet is going to be more of a bottleneck than the network speed of the local network. We will leave that problem between you and your network provider. Instead, we will focus on requirements of the local network as it would apply to a network-heavy application or a network application that is only used by people within the organization.

Hubs

First, let's take a brief look at hubs. These days, hubs are generally a second- or third-rate solution. Let's step back for a minute to see why. With an ethernet interface, packets are transmitted to the wire according to the wire format specified by the ethernet standard. The network card watches the local wire and checks for transmission breaks on the line so that it can transmit a frame. If it determines that it can send, it will push your packet out as an ethernet frame. If a collision occurs during this transmission, it needs to back off and try again. The more traffic it encounters, the more time it needs to back off, waiting for a good chance to transmit. As you can easily guess, the more time it spends waiting, the less data is transferred, cutting into the bandwidth of your network. Hubs provide common bandwidth between all nodes connected to it. So for every machine connected to the hub, it must coordinate all its transfers with those around it. The more servers you have on there, the more time each one will have to spend sitting around waiting for a chance to transmit. Commonly found in 10Mb and 100Mb configurations, hubs tend to cap performance at levels well below what they advertise. Getting 3.3Mb/sec out of a 10Mb hub is considered a fairly decent rate. This won't scale well to a server farm of 20 or 30 nodes serving millions of hits per day, all using the same underlying bandwidth.

Switches

Switches are similar to hubs, with the exception that they don't share the same bandwidth. A 100Mb switch with 8 ports will give a 100Mb channel to each machine involved. Within the switch resides hardware that handles the coordination of traffic between the ports and to the uplink port. So a machine on port 1 talking to a machine on port 8 will cause traffic to flow through the fabric (another name for the interconnect) directly, without the machines on ports 2 through 7 to coordinate their transfers around this conversation. Although the uplink can still cause contention, coordination of traffic can be done so that most machines talk to others on their local switch and rarely have to use the uplink. This allows for a more scalable framework for deploying server farms, especially because at this point switches cost only marginally more than a standard hub and are available in the 1Gb range. With a local network based on a switched 1Gb fabric, you can compete against what used to be solely the domain of Asynchronous Transfer Mode (ATM) networks. For most server farms, 100Mb switches are good enough to handle the internal network activity, and because most uplinks become the bottlenecks anyway, this level of switch provides a good way to have a reasonably powerful and scalable local network without laying out a large amount of cash.

Routers

When it comes down to it, the subject of routers could easily fill a volume of books. There is a large industry making use of this fact. Routers essentially serve a couple of purposes. They link physically separate networks, whether they are 100 feet apart or 1,000 miles apart, and they provide a simple layer of security between the external world and a local network. The actual details in planning, deploying, and maintaining routers is well beyond the scope of this book, and so we'll just touch on the subject lightly. Essentially, you should deal with routers in coordinating use of your uplink, whether it is a local uplink into the rest of the corporation or your connection to the rest of the Internet.

In general, the bandwidth of your router is going to be much less than that of your local network, and care should be taken to make sure that the bandwidth you do have there is used wisely. Even in these days, where bandwidth is considered to be plentiful, the average connection that a router handles can be swamped pretty easily if enough thought isn't going into the plan. The best way to get a starting point on finding the right solution for your need is to determine the amount of bandwidth your application uses, both from the client and the server. This should be done at the local network level, too, but because things are generally tighter at the router level, more care needs to be taken. For something such as HTTP serving, this process is fairly simple because the protocol is fairly easy to watch, and it is very easy to tell how much data is going across the wire in a given transfer. To get a rough estimate of what you need, perform some tests to figure out how much data is being sent and received by the client during a normal transfer. Then multiply that number of bytes by the number of users you intend to have and the number of requests anticipated by each user. This will give you a basic estimate of how much bandwidth you will need for your uplink, although you should take steps to anticipate future needs and other factors specific to your situation.

As previously stated, your network is very important to the health of your system and business. A few years ago, independent machines did large amounts of work, but these days, it's difficult to build a system that is dependent only on a set of local machines.

NOTE

Great care should be taken in determining what will need to be handled over the network, both locally and externally, to effectively plan for the right amount of bandwidth to serve you today and tomorrow.

Uninterruptible Power Supplies

Earlier in the discussion on MTBF rates, we touched on the concept of an Uninterruptible Power Supply (UPS). Let's take a closer look at what they are and how they apply to your system's reliability.

The precise purpose of a UPS is pretty easy to determine simply from the name—it provides an uninterruptible power supply. It regulates the power supply between the wall and the servers it is handling and at the same time provides a short-term power supply in the event of a power failure. The length of this temporary supply is determined by the capacity of the UPS and the number of components depending on it. Because it is only a temporary supply, the power supply to your server is technically interruptible, but a solid UPS should help you weather most outages.

Given the context of this book, you are most likely hosting your machines within a larger hosting facility that provides guaranteed power for you. So why bother with a UPS? As we discussed earlier, it offers an extra layer of insurance in the event of a problem with the hosting site, both from outages and from spikes in the power supply. Most sizable hosting facilities offer several days of generator power even in the event of a power loss from their provider. However, even they are run by ordinary people, and there could be mismanagement resulting in an unscheduled power loss or spike for your systems. Although you might be insured for this, it is still a risk for your customers that can be avoided with minimal cost to you. Also, an outage can be caught and give you enough time to hop into your systems and perform an orderly shutdown, rather than trying to recover from an unclean shutdown later on when power is restored and customers are screaming. Your UPS software should be able to trigger this clean shutdown itself, in most situations. In these days of journaled filesystems on Linux, this is less of an issue, but getting an extra few minutes to perform a clean shutdown of your databases and other applications can save you a large amount of work trying to ensure integrity later.

One important factor to remember when selecting the right UPS is to make sure that you get enough power to handle everything you need to keep up in an emergency for the amount of time dictated by your needs. Refer to vendor data for specific sizes for your needs, but make sure to look specifically at what will be plugged into the UPS and what kind of power requirements the components have. For example, you might want to ensure power for your database servers but allow your Web servers to go down during an outage. This will allow a clean shutdown of the database, and it is assumed that the 3-second filesystem rollback on the Web servers is worth the savings from not purchasing an extra group of UPSes.

You should also make sure that only your servers are plugged into the UPS and not any peripherals that don't need it. For example, monitors draw large amounts of power and will drain the UPS's battery in short order if they are left plugged into the UPS itself. It might be worth checking through your lines occasionally to make sure that no peripherals have been inadvertently plugged into your UPS. Waiting to find this out during an outage can be a painful experience for all those involved. Only machines that are deemed critical should work off the UPS, and nothing else. (Nothing is more annoying than having a power outage and watching your UPS go offline almost immediately because too many unneeded peripherals are plugged into it.)

Depending on your needs, the Keyboard/Mouse/Video (KVM) switch might need to be plugged in so that an operator can attach and work on the machines by hand during the emergency. For most UPSes, the client-side software can be configured to listen for the UPS's notification of a depleting battery and perform an automatic shutdown. These values are generally configurable so that the machines will continue to run during an outage but will trigger a shutdown when fewer than five minutes of battery life is left. This policy should be handled by the administrator; combined with good usage of UPS power, your system should be able to gracefully handle nearly any type of electrical disturbance that comes down the wire.

Choosing Hardware Vendors

We've already mentioned some of the issues involved in choosing the right hardware vendor. Back in the section "Sales Pitches—Separating the Wheat from the Chaff," we looked at a few ways to make sure that you're dealing with the right vendor for your needs. But this focused only on making sure that you avoided vendors falsely offering solutions (intentionally or not) that don't fit your plans for future needs. Now let's take a larger view of the issue and analyze more of the factors that should be taken into account when selecting a hardware vendor.

Questions to Ask

First, it should be noted that if you are building anything but the most simplistic system, it is highly unlikely that you will be able to go with only one vendor. In most cases, there will be many—some for the server, some for the client, some providing certain hardware components (networking hardware, for example, or custom hardware for your analysis work). All these vendors might have different approaches to selecting solutions, causing you to keep track of different purchasing procedures and different points of contact for each one. Although having multiple vendors is nice from the perspective that each is focused on getting the right solution for their subsystem, it does cloud the issue of responsibility during troubleshooting and greatly complicates the issue of warranty and service contracts. When possible, a single vendor should be chosen for groups of components, such as going with a single hardware vendor for the server and client hardware. This is preferred over building a large number of machines from individual components bought around the Net, even though it might be cheaper up front. In the end, the costs incurred because of the maintenance confusion will greatly outweigh the few dollars saved up front. Although you might have saved a few dollars on the drives, you now have seven or eight dealers to contend with, all with different warranty and service expiration dates, rather than having a single vendor with a constant point of contact and a single connection to a consolidated warranty and service plan. In some situations, vendors might have joint service agreements, simplifying troubleshooting by creating one informed point of contact where there might have been many, with each knowing only part of the picture. In many situations, it makes sense to follow this consolidated route when it is available, but as always, it depends on your unique situation and needs.

A primary factor in the minds of most management is budgetary concerns. The smaller and newer the vendor is, the cheaper the hardware is, whereas larger, entrenched companies tend to have significantly higher costs. With the cheaper costs can come some hardware scalability issues, and the higher end usually comes through with extremely high-end hardware, although this is not always the case. It is important that you find a vendor that adequately fits your budgetary and system needs. These days, most vendors break their support into different business sizes and can help you align your needs with your budget by offering the right technology for your size and discount rates based on specific buying practices made by your company. All of these can come with different benefits. It is important to try all vendors in your range that might be applicable to see which one offers the right set of incentives and pricing deals for your needs.

Although it might seem obvious, the vendor you select should have a support contract that fits your needs. Every business, from the smallest shop to the largest industry leader, has a specific set of needs and goals. The vendor selected should not only be able to fulfill these needs now but also in the future. Although it is your job to move forward in your industry, you should be able to work with your vendor to move your solutions forward, even if that means going into areas that aren't as clean cut as doing normal Web services or storage management. Sometimes your vendor is the best source to keep on top of budding developments, and if you know that you are going to be pushing the existing limits now, make sure that you look for a vendor that will likely be able to push things even farther tomorrow. The vendor should also have a history of meeting expectations. Looking forward is one thing, but it is important to have a solid track record of managing existing solutions well. Without a solid platform to stand on today, the chances of successfully moving forward tomorrow grow slimmer. Although the vendor will be glad to extol its own virtues, most of this data should be obtained through external sources who are less partial to the vendor's success. Companies with existing solutions are one good way to get a bird's-eye view of how the vendor deals with customers, although accurate information might be difficult to get. Various independent (relatively) entities exist to provide impartial data on these issues and can be a good way of getting your hands on raw numbers about vendors that you are considering. One example is the Gartner Group, although it is a good idea not to trust external parties implicitly, without some research specific to your situation. Research companies, even though they make their living analyzing data, cannot predict the future, and are known to be wrong on occasion. Always balance their knowledge with your own specific needs.

Choose a vendor with a good technology base and also a good path for scalability. This takes some planning skills both on your part and the part of the vendor. You should be confident in your planning skills so that you know how much you are going to need to scale in the future, and you need to know that the vendor has the resources to scale along with you. This applies to the vendor's support infrastructure and the hardware it is trying to sell. As your system grows, your support needs will probably increase dramatically—not necessarily because of the number of machines but because of the importance of the system. In the beginning, an hour or two of downtime for a system might have been acceptable, but as the system grows in importance, you might be able to handle only a couple of minutes of downtime per year. In this case, your vendor needs to be able to scale its support appropriately. Likewise, the vendor's hardware needs to be able to scale at the same rate. Your hardware requirements are going to jump up along with your customer base, and you need to make sure that as you grow, your vendor can keep pace with those needs. Look for a vendor that can handle your needs now but that won't force you to switch to a larger vendor down the road as your needs grow.

Now let's take a look at a vendor factor that slips many customers' minds but, in reality, is a very important point. When you are checking around with various vendors for the right fit for your business, note how well each one is at effectively answering your questions. The salesperson you deal with directly is not likely to be able to answer your technical questions in any real depth, but he or she should be connected to at least one technical person when working with you. Depending on your needs, there could be several people because a single technical representative might not have all the answers to all aspects of your needs. It is important to note the way that these questions are handled. If the queries are handled effectively and you are consistently connected to the right people internally, that is indicative of an effective internal resource matrix. This also indicates that when you really need support down the line, the vendor is likely to be able to effectively connect you to the people and resources you need.

We mentioned in passing that it can be important for different vendors to have relationships with each other because it can simplify your support needs. Let's take a closer look at how this affects the selection process. In general, it might be better to put this lower on the list of priorities—if you know that you can get the support you need elsewhere and that the other factors we have discussed are handled well by the vendors you have worked with. But if you do decide to include this in your selection process, it usually makes sense to consider the following factors: First, make sure that the hardware end is covered well because this is your primary reason for dealing with the vendor in the first place. Coordination with other vendors on the hardware end should be considered first priority. Second, operating system support might be important to you. Keep in mind that even among the larger vendors, Linux support is still being grown in-house and between vendors, and you might need to use other standard open source channels to get effective information on your needs. Because so many ways exist to get useful information other than from the vendor, specific vendor support should be considered a much lower priority than consolidated hardware support among vendors. Third, joint support for your particular application set should be considered. This is a rarer situation, except in cases where larger applications meet larger vendors, where it makes sense for the vendor to join up to handle customer demand. Because most of your work will likely be a custom situation, these agreements are not as likely to affect your vendor choice, but if you know that you are going to be pushing a particular application very hard on a particular platform, it might help to have an agreement with a hardware vendor that has worked with your software provider. The vendor could have already dealt with many of the problems you are likely to face.

As you can see, many factors are involved in selecting the right vendor. In your specific case, there are likely to be even more, based on your own particular set of needs. Of course, every factor should be taken into account, but the importance of each is going to vary. If you have a large amount of software expertise or even hardware expertise in-house, it might make sense to place less emphasis on the vendor helping in the planning process and use the vendor more for ensuring quick turnaround in the event of a disaster. Whatever your needs are, to find the right vendor, balance all the vendor information available with the amount of in-house expertise and support you need.

The Importance of FCC and UL Ratings

Nearly any vendor you work with is going to provide systems that pass the Federal Communications Commission (FCC) and Underwriters Laboratories (UL) standards. If they do not, you should shift to another vendor because nearly every component made today complies with the standards put forth by these bodies.

The UL organization is a nonprofit group that performs safety testing in all types of product ranges. The UL mark is prevalent on electrical devices found throughout the home. In general, it is a sign that the product has passed the group's safety tests and should be safe for your use.

The FCC deals with communications issues, and its stamp of approval is important in making sure that your machine is safe to operate either in a residential or commercial setting. For most uses, the FCC ratings apply to hardware that interacts with various pieces of the broadcast spectrum, and ensures that the hardware is not going to interfere with other portions of the spectrum. For example, a piece of hardware might be certified for radio transmission or for receiving capabilities. By making sure that your hardware is properly certified, you won't run into interference problems at your hosting facility, either between your own hardware or with the other hardware in the proximity.

Regardless of the type of work you are doing, it is important that these standards are met, if only to ensure proper operation of your hardware. Failure to meet basic safety standards could open the system up to disastrous electrical situations in the future. Likewise, failure to meet communications standards will likely cause problems either within your system or with other systems in the area. Either way, this is not a good situation and is one that can be easily avoided; nearly all hardware available to you should be properly certified already.

Summary

Selecting the proper hardware is no simple task. It requires planning up front to make sure that you know what you will need down the line and careful selection among the various vendors to get the right fit for your needs. If you don't know what your hardware needs are going to be, there's really no way to accurately plan for the future. There's also no way you can reliably believe what vendors say if you don't have a clear picture of what you're talking about. That is why education and planning should be first and foremost in the process of selecting hardware. After this is done, it becomes a much simpler process to select a vendor; you know what you want, and you have a reasonable way of determining which vendor is capable of delivering what you need.

Selecting Software Components

CHAPTER

14

IN THIS CHAPTER

- Determining Software Reliability 290
- Stress Testing 291
- Benchmarks 292
- Factors That Affect Software Reliability 293
- Dealing with Software Vendors 295

After you've decided on your hardware, you need to choose the right software to run on it. This varies widely, depending on your specific needs, but you should follow some basic guidelines when selecting software. When it comes down to it, this decision depends mostly on your knowledge of the current problem, and you should never go for a package without fundamentally grasping the situation at hand and how the software choices will help solve it. Many times, software solutions are chosen without any real thought about the various possibilities involved, resulting in a system that doesn't do the job as well as it could and that is less likely to face future challenges well. The simple approaches presented here will help you avoid making this mistake. Remember that above all, your situation is going to have specific needs, and the responsibility of being completely prepared and knowledgeable about those needs is up to you. There is no such thing as a completely "normal" situation—one that is going to require no software planning at all.

Determining Software Reliability

In theory, software should be perfectly reliable, right? It's assumed that hardware, because it is a physical device, has a given lifetime before it begins to break down. Software, on the other hand, is basically doing the same process repeatedly, with minor variations depending on what data is presented to drive the code. In a perfect world, this would mean that if the product works fine in all the situations you need it for, it will always run perfectly.

Wrong. In any complex system, bugs are likely to exist. Either they will occur during testing or they exist as a memory leak. This will cause resource starvation over time, and might not become visible until the system has been up and running for days and has processed large amounts of requests. Most bugs can be found during testing, if the test cases are rigorous enough. But particularly in the case of services that are network aware (as most useful ones are), exploits and bugs might not be found for months and cannot be accurately predicted. A product that has been thoroughly tested against all known types of requests and deployed to the field might be brought down in an instant three months later when someone finds a new way of constructing a request against it. This can result in a simple service outage until the problem is fixed, or it could open up your network and data to anyone who wants to view it. As cracking tools become more prevalent on the Internet, when new vulnerabilities are found, attacks become more probable and occur more quickly. These days, after a vulnerability is found, it is usually a matter of hours before a set of automated tools is developed to attack large sets of servers.

The following sections outline some factors in determining the reliability of your software, but all factors hinge on a simple fact, especially when you're choosing third-party software: It is important to get an idea of how the track record of the software components have fared over time. This sounds obvious, but as already mentioned, solutions are repeatedly chosen using products that are well known for having a poor security and stability track record. In nearly every sector, some historical data should be available showing how often flaws are found in the system and how long these flaws take to get fixed.

Consider the question of choosing a Linux distribution. Take into account how many security violations are found for the distribution's configuration and how long it takes the distributor to release patches. Interestingly, some vendors are good at turning around patches in minutes or hours, whereas others take months, even though the fix is out there for the package already because of the nature of the open source paradigm. Be sure to take these tendencies into account if you are intent on getting all your fixes directly from the vendor. The larger vendors, such as Red Hat, are known for pushing out fixes usually in a matter of hours, whereas others, such as Corel, have been known to wait months, even though the source has been fixed in the public domain.

Stress Testing

Assuming the system works as needed, the question of scalability and speed under load should always come up. There should have already been some planning or predictive analysis done to determine what the expected usage patterns of the system will be. Hopefully, this attempts to predict some of the growth patterns in the future, as well. Based on these numbers, you should be able to construct a test environment that simulates this usage.

As always, the actual implementation of the stress testing will vary widely by the needs of the application and the overall system. In the case of a database-heavy application, you might have some application or code that tests the database, but that is only one fragment of the overall system. In our case, Web servers are involved, probably some application servers, and maybe some custom servers are in place for your specific needs. As these pieces come together, they interact in many ways, and the matrix of possible interactions grows with every addition to the configuration. It is important that you have code that stresses the system in all possible ways, especially in the way that the system is supposed to be used in the real world. This is not meant to disparage unit testing of each component—that is obviously important to ensure that each piece operates as it should—but the real test of any system is how all the parts work together as a whole.

Now that this point has been sufficiently driven home, how do you do all this? Probably, some commercial or open source applications exist that will serve your basic needs well, although understand that your specific system will probably need at least some custom testing. In the Web-serving arena, the problem of stress testing has been known for a long time, and many applications are out there that will do a good job of making sure that your site is up to the task required of it. Apache Jmeter (`http://jakarta.apache.org/jmeter`), which is free, is one example, and there are many like it. These applications simulate the effect of many users hitting your server simultaneously, with varying requests and varying download speeds. The statistics gleaned from these tools can be invaluable in seeing how your system responds to various load environments.

If you have other components in your system, such as databases, these should also be tested thoroughly on their own. For example, a simple mistake would be to not have the maximum connection count on the database set high enough. Simple bugs such as this will easily be picked up during stress tests. Tuning also comes into play on the Web server end and on the database end as the system load rises. For the most part, however, in this case of assuming a Web-based system, your primary point of interaction should be through the Web site. Stress testing this end will probably cause problems in the unseen back end to pop up immediately, because the Web server is going to stress the rest of the systems involved. Note that if you have other types of clients hitting the same systems, such as native clients using the database from another network and not through the Web site, this load needs to be accounted for in testing.

Stress testing, by default, also tests your hardware. Therefore, as you are testing each software component, you are also testing the underlying operating system and physical components. This is obviously a good thing because you can tell how prepared the overall system is for the predicted load, but it might cloud your judgment of the software if you're not careful. Some bottleneck checking needs to occur to make sure that you're using your hardware efficiently. For example, it might appear that your database is operating very slowly, when in reality it's just a matter of the drives not being tuned correctly for optimal use, or you might need to distribute your data files over different disks.

If it is at all possible, try to use hardware identical to what will be used in production. Don't use a slower, cheaper disk for testing and attempt to guess how much more speed you'll get out of the faster disk in production. Because the hardware and software end up being so intrinsically linked, it is important that they are tested together, exactly as they would be configured in a production environment, with a load proportional to what they would see in the real world.

Benchmarks

This is probably one of the most controversial aspects of software selection. Although benchmarks can be useful in getting an idea of how well system components will perform, they should not be a determining factor in making software decisions; performance under your specific type of system load is likely to vary greatly. This point is brought forward almost any time that a performance benchmark is made, even as a disclaimer to the benchmark itself, but people inevitably forget this fact.

The most famous example of this is the Mindcraft study. This found that Linux performed poorly in a server role, whereas in reality many people had moved to Linux to get better performance (and more stability). The way that a benchmark stresses the system is in all likelihood going to be very different from the way a real system is stressed. In many situations, it is difficult to get a benchmark to accurately test the system with respect to all the ways that a real system will be hit. Although the benchmark might do the same test repeatedly with many clients, a real-world situation is much more likely to have many clients doing different activities, and these activities will vary by the client and by the specific needs of that moment. The combination of variables here is difficult to replicate in an automated test.

This is not to say that all benchmarks should be discounted. If a benchmark's activities closely model your own, it might be worth looking at the results of the various systems it has tested. But even in this case, don't accept it as gospel. Slight variations between the benchmark's system and your own can have large performance implications. To really understand which software component is right for you, you should test it in your environment with your specific type of work.

Factors That Affect Software Reliability

Let's step back a moment and look at specific elements that affect the reliability of your software. As mentioned earlier, in theory software should be a repeatable process, and there should never be any reason why it would break down in practice. Although this is a nice ideal, it rarely works this way in practice, for several reasons.

Traditionally, reliability in large (or even small) systems is affected by memory leaks over time.

Resource misuse and failure to accurately track memory internally to the application will eventually cause resource starvation on the system, both through memory leaks and other resources. This can result in performance degradation, or more often, a crash of the application involved or another one on the system looking for more memory. Memory leaks are usually indicative of software that hasn't been tested well enough, although they do tend to show up even in complex systems, regardless of the amount of testing. In many situations in which complex applications are used, the software vendor even recommends that the application be restarted regularly, whether daily or even once a year. This is a rare situation, but it does occur. The reason it happens is fairly simple—the leak might be extremely minor and pops up only in very rare implementations of the system (especially if you are using a new or rarely used aspect of the software package in question). For the vendor, it would take a large amount of development time and effort to track this leak down, and rather than spending the internal effort, the vendor might recommend that restarts are done when possible. This factor should be taken into account when selecting the right vendor for your needs. Thankfully, these days many system components are written using interpreted languages, which usually handle all the reference counting and internal memory usage within the interpreter or virtual machine and help to simplify the problem of resource leaks.

Reliability is also likely to be affected by the system resource load. A common reason for systems to fail is that they simply can't handle the resource requests asked of them. This can be a result of both software and hardware involved. In the case of a software problem, it usually indicates poor system design. Scalability, at least to some degree, should have been designed into the system from the start, and failure to scale means that somewhere in the code a component is acting as a bottleneck. Failure to handle large loads can also be the result of lack of hardware. This is usually a very simple problem, such as not having enough memory for the software, and can be solved by throwing more hardware at the system.

Note that high resource load can affect reliability in other, more subtle ways, too. Performance degradation at high load levels might not cause failure of the system components, but the increased load is likely to cause significant slowdowns. This loss of performance might as well be considered a loss of reliability, especially in the case where you have a specific agreement in place that requires you to get requests handled in a certain amount of time. Failure to respond in the allotted time is a failure of the system, as far as the client is concerned.

Hardware scalability is also a factor in determining your software's reliability. If the hardware in place cannot handle the requests made of it, the overall system is not going to make it. This is why your hardware should be wisely chosen to be able to handle current and future loads. It has always been the case that software usage will expand to push the capabilities of the hardware, so make sure that your software components have room to grow on your system. Refer back to Chapter 13, "Hardware Reliability," for more information on choosing the right hardware solution for the job.

As the system components get more usage in the field, it is very likely that bugs and exploits of the bugs will start to pop up. Regardless of how well software is tested, there is likely to be some angle that the tester or designer never considered. The more prevalent the component becomes, the more likely that certain angle will be found by someone, either through normal usage or by looking for a way to break it. In the open source community, these bugs are usually fixed in a matter of minutes or hours, so it is important to keep on top of the latest news so that you can patch your system. In general, the problems are found and fixed in the source before it is ever released, because of the peer-review process that open source is subject to. If these holes are left open, it is very likely that the process of finding vulnerable systems will be automated, and it might only be a matter of time before your system is targeted. In the case of normal system bugs that can't be exploited externally, you should use the same diligence in making sure your system is patched appropriately. It should go without saying that every known bug that affects your system's operations should be fixed as soon as possible.

Last, but definitely not least, is the fact that the interconnectedness of the system can affect reliability because the failure of a single component can ripple out and affect the usefulness of the others that depend on it. The classic example is again the database. If the database goes down, the site as a whole might not be usable at all. Even if it is just restarted, there might be an application server that ends up having handles to a database connection that is no longer valid, causing clients of the application server to fail until these are reconnected.

In any system where each component depends on another, the failure of one can have disastrous implications. Because of this problem, any component that has others depending on it should be redundant in some fashion. Databases should be replicated, probably in a live-switch fashion, so that a failure of one can force the backup to come online as the master immediately. Web servers should be redundant or in a clustered environment where the failure of one will not cause clients to lose access to their data. This goes for any kind of component in the system, whether it is an off-the-shelf piece of software or a custom application that exists only in your environment.

Dealing with Software Vendors

When dealing with software vendors, there are a few factors to keep in mind. Depending on the software model in place, there are going to be some very different things to watch for, not all of them bad. As with hardware vendors, you need to make sure that you're working with someone who fits your needs well, and it is important that you get past the sales pitches to see what content is really there. Many of the factors involved with selecting a software vendor are similar to selecting a hardware vendor. Refer to the previous chapter on hardware vendor selection for a detailed explanation of these factors. Following are other factors that are specific to the software domain.

OSS Vendors (aka Project Leaders)

These days, many vendors offer Linux support. The numbers are fairly amazing, considering that just a few years ago, the concept of commercial support for an open source system was unheard of. Undoubtedly, the industry still has some growing pains to live through, and probably new shifts will occur in how some of the work is done, but the idea of getting commercial support will continue.

Let's look first at normal commercial vendors. If you are building a Linux-based system, you might need to have commercial support for various components involved. Again, the classic example is database support. Many of the larger database vendors have commercial support these days for their products under Linux, and more are following all the time. Sometimes this support is just starting out, and the vendor might have a port of the system to Linux, but the support mechanism might not be in place yet. In this case, it might be better to get commercial support for one of the free database systems. This way you get the benefit of having access to the source and the open source community, but you have the added backing of someone who is paid to fix your problems as they occur. Because this area is rapidly evolving, however, it helps to get a good idea of how well the vendor supports Linux. For some vendors, this is a very new thing, and some of their support representatives might not be completely up to speed on all aspects of supporting the Linux port. If it is at all possible, it is a good idea to talk to some of the tech support people, ask the vendor directly how well they support the product, or try to get data from another company that uses the same technical support. In an emergency, you want to make sure that the person on the other end of the line is really up to date on how to support Linux in contrast to another system.

Now let's look at normal OSS vendors—those who specialize in support of open source products. This is still a growing market, and many companies are taking advantage of that fact. Most of these vendors make money from packaging various products for you and support the open source product in the field. For the advanced user this really doesn't offer much on a per-machine basis, but it can become important when dealing with a large number of machines and a large number of disparate technologies. With vendor support for something that is already open, at the very least, you get expertise, and you also should get extra testing of the software in question.

Many of the Linux distributors perform all kinds of testing on various components—the kernel in particular. It is rare for vendors to ship with a stock kernel—they usually have all kinds of patches applied to it either to add support for various peripherals or to sidestep problems that haven't been fixed in the main source tree yet. In addition to this testing, they do all the package management for you, preventing many kinds of installation hassles. While not a problem for an advanced user, these are a boon to someone new or a harried administrator. In addition, some vendors are now providing a support network so that individual fixes are distributed to subscribers as problems are solved down the road. Because this can greatly reduce the load on your administrative overhead, this can be a great time and energy saver.

Whether the vendor is a normal commercial vendor or an OSS one, the same rules of selection apply. Take care to make sure that vendors can fill your needs adequately and that they fit within your budget. They should have a good history of providing solid support and be able to scale with your needs. Vendor relationships can be influential in coming to a conclusion, because support matrices will simplify when things go wrong. For a more detailed discussion of these topics, refer back to the "Questions to Ask" section in Chapter 13, where we discussed these terms in relation to selecting a hardware vendor. The same concepts apply in general, if you simply replace the word "hardware" with "software." Both vendor types are serving mostly the same industry and have a lot of things in common.

Individual Leaders

Sometimes you might need a feature added to a particular application or need additional support for a certain software component. Support for new hardware can also be a factor, although this is less so in the Web-serving arena. But in some cases, there might be a new card on the market for which you need better support, or there might be some piece of physical hardware that provides data to drive your system, and it would be beneficial to make better use of it under Linux. In these cases, the vendors might not have direct support for it, but individual project leaders can help. In terms of both software and hardware, historically, many people have done the work themselves, rather than waiting for a vendor to allow them to do something. If you have a need that a vendor can't quite fulfill, finding individual open source leaders might be a better route. This is especially true when dealing with noncommercial software, because the developers are the primary means of getting work added to the source tree if you can't do the work yourself.

Usually, if the request is rational and makes sense for the project, it will be developed and worked quickly into the standard distribution of the software. (Although it will go even quicker if you can write it yourself and offer the fixes to the developers, of course, and this is greatly appreciated.) This applies to hardware, too, and usually, if the developer doesn't have access to the specific hardware in question, supplying a sample piece will usually justify their work in getting the request up and running. This is how a lot of the work got done in the open source world before the commercial players got into the arena and started doing the work themselves. Either method is effective, and if you can't get support directly from the vendor or from a standard distribution, the project leader is the next logical stop in looking for a solution. In many cases, projects are already in place to add support for specific software ideas to existing packages. These can usually be found on sourceforge.org or freshmeat.net, although some projects are done through collaboration sites such as collab.net. In the case of existing projects, a mailing list is usually available where questions for features can be placed.

Questions to Ask Vendors During the Planning Phase

As mentioned earlier, this chapter greatly parallels Chapter 13, which dealt with choosing a hardware vendor. In most respects, the software vendor selection process parallels the hardware vendor process. Refer back to the "Questions to Ask" section for what to look for when selecting software vendors. Keep in mind that the hardware process is different in that it locks you in more tightly to your solution, whereas the software side offers a little more flexibility down the road. This doesn't mean that you can make the software decisions without thought, but the decision should be considered with your hardware decisions. Because you work with open protocols, if you do need to change components down the road, it isn't a major issue.

Summary

Even though in theory software should be a repeatable process, many factors determine how appropriate it is for your needs and how well it performs in your environment. When determining the software that is appropriate for your needs, you need to make sure to actually test it under the types of loads that you expect it to perform under in the real world. Performance benchmarks are not perfect and are generally not indicative of how the software will behave in a real-world situation. In the end, you need to select a vendor to support your needs well and select software that actually works for your business. It is as simple as that. Take into account all the factors mentioned—from user communities to open source leaders—when deciding which vendor set to go with. Making the right choices up front can save time, money, and hassles down the road.

Site Management Issues

CHAPTER

15

IN THIS CHAPTER

- Self-Hosting Versus Colocation Facilities 300
- Selecting a Colocation Provider 309

In the beginning, most of us connected to the Internet over transient UUCP feeds. Connections to the upstream providers happened on fixed schedules to relay e-mail and Usenet in bulk; FTP by e-mail was commonplace, and the only "servers" we cared about were our in-house file servers. By the early '90s, most everyone was hardwired to the world by coaxial cables. Gopherspace and later the Web were at our fingertips 24 hours a day, and it truly seemed that the network was one big computer. Installing a Web server for the world to see was as easy as installing HTTP server software.

When the public dial-up Internet took over in the mid 1990s, we returned to the discontinuous connection model. Dial-up—even business ISDN connections—were expensive and metered by the minute, and bandwidth was poor. We moved from owning our servers to begging for space on shared servers; most of us lamented the loss of being online full-time, and we dreamed of a future with a server in every shop and a T1 to every door. All our Web application ideas seemed to require in-house servers, with full and instant control to keep on communicating with our online audience.

What actually happened was beyond what we expected. Naive and sheltered in our development and research shops, we never thought of security, business models, or quality of service. The real world was wrought with script kiddies and crackers, profitabilities and ROI, and a new seriousness of purpose we had seen before only in mainframe shops. Suddenly, managing your own site wasn't fun anymore—it was a 24/7 pager job, a thankless job, and a major pain. It was also the kind of tedious work that most of us seek to avoid.

We still romanticize about owning our own servers. We like that feeling of control, of being Net Gods, and it does simplify our Web applications knowing that we can tightly bind our machines with simple sockets and can tweak and twiddle to our heart's content. Unfortunately, the costs of this luxury have escalated out of control and we must now stop to ask the hard question: Do we really need to host in-house?

Self-Hosting Versus Colocation Facilities

There are varying degrees of hosting. You might have some services behind your firewall with a frontline server hosted at an ISP, or you might move the entire application to a colocation site with hooks back into your legacy or development systems. You might share a machine, share a partition of a machine, or purchase or lease your own hardware on an ISP's site, or you might run everything from one or more company sites.

Web hosting comes in many flavors, with different costs and tribulations in each. These options fall into the following spectrum:

- Virtual hosting at an ISP
- Virtual servers at an ISP

- ISP-owned colocated servers
- Customer-owned colocated servers
- In-house servers with outsourced network and server management
- In-house, staff-managed servers

This list is ordered by increasing levels of control, but also by increasing responsibility and total cost of ownership. Where you place your servers must be carefully weighed against what you actually need.

Drawbacks of Self-Hosting

One scenario exists in which you need the total control of 100% in-house, staff-managed servers: You are a Web-hosting ISP. Everyone else should carefully rethink their requirements because the gains may not be worth the bother. Self-hosting means more than spare closet space.

Self-hosting involves hardware costs and the risk of asset ownership, considerable operations costs, and taking responsibility for your own quality of service. It also involves a big responsibility as a network citizen in a hostile world.

Hardware Costs

A vendor quote on a Web-server box is not your cost of ownership. As with hardware in general, the cost of the machine is perhaps half the initial cost and says nothing about recurring costs. The following is a partial checklist of some of the other items not to be taken for granted:

- Rackmount hardware and the wiring closet are important components for future maintenance. A rack lets you keep the hardware out of the way and insert new servers or network appliances into the same space. The care you take in the wiring can mean hours or days saved when someone needs to restructure the physical network.
- Routers and switches. The quality of service you can provide inside and outside the firewall are directly influenced by your skill in the black art of selecting and integrating these components. The configuration of your switches and WAN connections is vital to the performance of your application. If you share a T1 with your office, you need to ensure that customers are not denied service while your staff does Web research.
- Firewalls are also critically important for the impact they can have by reprioritizing network traffic—for example, to give scheduling preference to customer Web traffic over staff e-mail. Firewalls and network security can be implemented by software components such as iptables or by dedicated network appliances, but both require installation and configuration.

- UPS and watchdog devices are needed to detect and act on power fluctuations or outages. These can range from relatively inexpensive devices that only ensure an orderly shutdown to auxiliary power generators to protect against unscheduled shutdowns.
- Hot swappable and redundant server components are needed to ensure uninterrupted service. A simple RAID-0 SCSI server may give the service you need today, but what happens in two or three years as the disks wear out? How much data corruption or downtime can you afford?

You must also insure your equipment and purchase service contracts, and you will probably enlist outside help to get them shipped in, plugged in, and properly configured. All these costs add up. You will have utility costs, office space costs to provide a suitable and secure environment, and amortization or interest costs. The economics of bulk buying are also a factor: If you buy 5 servers for your project, whereas a large ISP buys 50 servers every year, who gets the better price?

Operations Costs

Operations and maintenance are the largest share of the ownership cost. Qualified systems and network administrators are expensive, and unqualified administrators can cost you 10 times as much.

Far too many companies underestimate the value of systems administration. Part of this is because a good systems or network administrator is almost invisible; when the machines are working, no one remembers them. As a result, people can branch out from a well-administered shop to launch their start-up, vastly underestimating the value of the admin talent they left behind.

All we know is that the administrators are never at their desk when we need them. There is a reason why we typically find system administrators at some other terminal or in the server room, and it is not because they love their machines. System administrators are faced with the live integration of the craftwork of literally hundreds of vendors following dozens of conflicting and ill-documented standards, and they must balance this with the unrealistic expectations of a user base weaned on sweet-talking Star Trek computers. A day in the life of a system administrator can involve

- Tracing network outages or performance problems
- Installing new software, correcting or modifying installations, and evaluating new network software en route to installing and configuring it
- End-user support, also known as fighting fires that are very often caused by end users simply misunderstanding badly designed software interfaces
- Reconnaissance of the servers for capacity planning, monitoring resources, and sniffing for the smell of ozone

Monitoring

As discussed in Chapter 10, "Keeping the Site Running," system monitoring is not an intense job, but it requires constant attention and availability. Monitor software can spot many troubles, but most often the software will report the issue after the fact. A good systems administrator saves time and company money by tracking down the trouble spots in advance of the failure.

As a result, even a single server demands full-time attention, although, like preschoolers, the trouble is not additive. A colocation ISP can justify the staff and the tools to let them monitor dozens, or even hundreds, of servers.

System Upgrades

System upgrades are always an adventure. Upgrades can overwrite configuration files or render prior configurations mildly incompatible. Upgrades to one component can cause a cascading effect, which can force upgrading of dozens of other otherwise unrelated systems, and component conflicts can often go completely undetected until such time as the feature is critically needed.

If you host your own server, your operations staff are expected to become expert at installing and configuring software they may see only once. Just as an outside consultant brings expertise gained from a wide variety of business situations, Web-host system administrators have probably solved even relatively rare problems many times in the course of dealing with their clients. By contrast, your in-house staff will have only that one rare instance to learn from their mistakes.

Security

Security is no longer about protecting your data from theft; I am not certain it ever was. Crackers are not after your data, they want your machine. There is nothing more precious to the cracker community than an unprotected machine where they can insert themselves and anonymously launch fresh attacks.

Security is an active task. It involves scrupulous attention to detail and constant vigilance. It involves following incident-alert mailing lists and applying almost-daily vendor patches. It also involves sniffing for any sort of suspicious behavior. Your systems administrator can use software tools to aid in the detection of intruders and virus attacks, but a good systems security administrator prevents these costly attacks.

Firewall Issues

Because your Web site must be exposed, self-hosting gives no real advantages to your in-house developers; your server must still be secured. IP spoofing and other mindless attacks have prompted most Linux distributions to disable NFS, Telnet, and other traditional server-integration services, leaving your staff with the same ssh-based access they would have if the server was colocated.

This is probably a good thing in the long run because it also forces your content development into some sort of controllable process model and frustrates the "live hack." Because most effective LAN speeds are less than a T1, your staff may not even see any response-time improvements with an in-house hosting.

Pros and Cons of Colocation

Although colocation or Web hosting dramatically reduces your hardware and operations costs, offloading these responsibilities still involves social and procedural costs. As with any decision to leave some part of your business in the hands of some other company, you need to weigh your risks.

From a design point of view, colocation adds complexity to your applications and introduces that huge, fuzzy region called "the Internet" into the middle of your architecture. You now need to provide appropriately secure connections for all your content providers, developers, and for connections to any legacy applications that feed your Web server. For example, you may need Remote Method Invocation (RMI) or CORBA channels to move your enterprise data to and from server applications, and this requires accommodating all the scenarios of dropped connections and network outages. What might have been a simple and reliable socket to some data source may now need timeout and rollback features. It is all doable, but it needs to be considered in your design work.

In social terms, colocation means that you will rely on personalities who are not under your control, and your staff will need proper process and education to deal effectively with this new layer of administration. One criteria for selecting your colocation host is an assurance that your staff can resolve issues quickly.

Although all this extra effort amounts to extra cost, these are primarily one-time implementation costs in contrast to the recurring costs for managing your server in-house. In many cases, such as restructuring your Web applications into distributed designs, the extra effort may pay off in the long run when it comes time to scale your application.

NOTE

An excellent and simple model of a remote-sensing Web application is the camserv Webcam application by Jon Travis (`http://cserv.sourceforge.net/`). This program uses a small server process on a small desktop connected to a Linux V4L compatible video feed or Connectix camera and a second server running on the Web site. When visitors reach the camera page, the Web server component requests a single stream from the remote camera server; the camera responds over an HTTP connection by returning what is effectively an endless animated GIF file. This feed, which arrives at the Web server with a frame rate limited by the camera host's bandwidth, is then duplicated by the server and handed out, on demand, to an arbitrary number of Web site visitors, each receiving frame samples appropriate to their own bandwidth.

Intranet, Extranet, Whatever

Remember the Extranet? This term was a fad in the '90s used to describe a company server placed outside the firewall and used to link customers and suppliers to back-office legacy systems. The concept silently morphed into business-to-business {B2B) computing as we quickly realized that no one in his or her right mind wants to give out access to internal business processes, and most of us have no interest whatsoever in becoming full-time network, systems, and security administrators. Whereas Extranet, like the Web-news portal, implied moving your company into a completely new line of business, B2B just wants to connect you with your business partners.

The business case for an in-house versus an outsourced server largely depends on the application architecture. If you need to have a close integration with legacy business systems, the jump across to an ISP is going to involve new requirements for security and transport, which may be much simpler in an in-house model. For example, the Canadian Broadcasting Corporation (`http://cbc.ca`) uses a proprietary news feed that arrives on a dedicated serial-port device that is relayed via TCP/IP to news desk and Web servers. With an in-house model, this is done using a simple chatlike server; it does not violate the news provider's copyright so long as it is behind the firewall. To move this data link across to an outsourced server, the chat server would need channel encryption, host authentication, and extra code to detect timeouts and other transfer problems.

Speed can be another issue. A Web application that transfers instant data to and from legacy applications may require being hosted across the same network switch as the Web server. Extreme security can be another constraint that makes outsourcing prohibitively difficult, but these are all extreme conditions. In 90% of the applications currently running on business Web servers, all that is needed to move the server offsite is a little imagination.

The Impossible Takes a Little Longer

Things that cannot be done over colocation can often be done with a bit of ingenuity. You can still re-create the Trojan Coffee Monitor, but you will need a multitier solution where the coffee-pot camera feeds the Web site over a thin pipe, and a multiclient server process on the colocated machine rebroadcasts the images.

Most read-only business data can be relayed through similar rebroadcasting. Interactive services, on the other hand, require a bit more complexity, using pools of secure connections in a multitier architecture where your Web server, or a cluster of servers, communicate with your onsite data through JDBC or ODBC, caching repeated data where possible. Port-forwarding and "Webifying" systems, such as Tarantella, can also offload the security and interface processing to the Web server while providing clean and secure access to the back-office legacy applications. Other transport methods include SOAP or XML-RPC to transfer application objects from the Web server to some other server binding the two sites into a single unified application. An implicit advantage exists to architecting your Web applications in this N-tiered fashion in which a small low-bandwidth server is multiplied and rebroadcast by a dedicated customer interface. Multiple tiers can generally be extended by distributing the application across many servers. For example, an application that serves a directory lookup for addresses could use an intermediating layer that distributes requests from multiple Web servers to "domain authority" hosts that each manage some subset of the data; this is essentially the architecture behind DNS lookups and is the primary purpose of LDAP.

Sharing Underutilized Resources

Colocation means leveraging economies of scale. On the first layer, this means sharing some huge amount of bandwidth on the assumption that all the colocated hosts will not need all this bandwidth at the same time, but this economizing also extends to other resources.

For example, few of us can justify the expense of an Oracle database just to provide personalization services to our Web visitors. Oracle has some important advantages for CRM; it is secure and reliable, it is easy to find Oracle expertise, and applications and the server is blazingly fast, but all this comes with a hefty price tag. Because most Web services use only a fraction of the data server capacity, and because partitioning access to a relational database is reliable, secure, and trivial to implement, many colocated hosts can share the cost of the resource.

The cost savings are more than for license fees and hardware. Any decent RDBMS requires a full-time security officer, a skilled database administrator, and peculiar network and system administration skills; such individuals are not inexpensive. Just as colocation lets you leverage the accumulated experience of their systems administrations people, their in-house talents for RDBM management, streaming media, CDN, and other expensive services will have repeated exposure to these products in a variety of applications and can provide more expertise for less cost than hiring our own.

The High-Speed Universe

The growth in low-cost, high-speed Internet access also contributes to easing the disadvantages of colocation. Instead of leasing an expensive symmetrical connection, your staff and applications may be able to work their magic over an inexpensive consumer-grade connection. High-speed access to the home and a shift in our post-Boomers corporate culture also means that development, design, and content work can be done by home-based or offshore talent, and for these users, the in-house server is often more of a barrier than an advantage.

The P2P Universe

Another change is in the wind that will greatly alter our Web applications designs: Peer-to-peer (P2P) computing has come of age.

Peer to peer means shifting the network load off the server and out into the space between your clients. Content providers inject content into these community subnetworks, but from there, the clients themselves handle the expense of rebroadcasting. Most of us are already familiar with the Napster program and its capability to move files from one desktop to another, relieving the originating host from serving the same file to many people. An excellent early example—a next-generation P2P application is Swarmcast by OpenCola (`http://www.opencola.com`), where even the first download of a file is fragmented and distributed; paradoxically, as the demand for the content increases, the resources to deliver it decrease, eventually falling to zero.

Other models of P2P include distributing the processing power across many small computers, such as with the Popular Power (`http://www.popularpower.com`) supercomputing applications, or even by distributing large data sets across the clients, as is now being done by the Human Genome project. As the P2P world moves forward and out into even small handheld devices, less and less need exists for large and fragile server farms to handle popular Web applications.

Colocation Options

The cost of colocation depends on where you sit in the spectrum between sharing account space on a virtual host or rack space with a dedicated server cluster. Where you need to be depends on four factors:

- Resources—Shared virtual hosts and virtual servers will share all or some resources within the same server, so your application requirements must be weighed against the CPU load, memory image, network traffic, and other OS metrics available.
- Reliability—Shared servers are only as reliable as the weakest link. Applications on shared hosts can crash server software, causing outages for all other customers, whereas shared servers can suffer only hardware lockups.
- Security—Every OS has security holes, but the biggest risk is always from other users on the same machine. A virtual host amounts to giving login accounts to perfect strangers or spending the night in a shady hostel.
- Applications—Just as with the desktop, your choices in servers is also constrained by the applications you need. If you must run FilePro, a BDS-based hosting service is not going to be very useful.

If you can accept some degree of losses in these areas, you can move down the cost scale.

Assessing Your Risks

The first consideration must be to your level of acceptable risk in these three areas. If your application demands heavy OS resources such as file handles or memory, you need at least a virtual server. If you monopolize hardware resources, such as disk I/O or the network interface, you probably need your own server. If your site contains sensitive data where a leak might leave you liable under privacy or theft laws, you probably want an in-house server locked in a guarded room, accessible only to bonded personnel bearing a smart card.

Dedicated Server

The primary advantage with a dedicated server is freedom. You can use whatever server systems you want, and you are isolated from risks from applications owned by other parties. As with everything else in life, the most freedom carries the most responsibility—and the highest price. Dedicated server fees vary, depending on the level of service and connectivity of the ISP, but generally $cost around $300–$500/month plus machine lease costs for a reasonably connected host with reasonable support.

Like an in-house server, you must buy or lease the box, although the cost is usually mediated through ISP financing or their bulk-buying discount plan. The hosting ISP handles installing the server. They provide the UPS and watchdog systems, as well as general monitoring and network administration. You are spared network planning, WAN connections, and may even be given secure access through the ISP firewall. The ISP also provides a DNS server and may provide other network services such as e-mail, Usenet, or community applications such as data servers or LDAP. Every thing within the box, however, is your domain and your responsibility.

With the dedicated server, only your software can threaten the uptime, disk throughput, and bandwidth. You have full freedom to implement whatever statistical reporting, applications monitoring, or support software you choose, although your ISP may have recommendations to allow your machine to integrate with its network monitoring system.

Because it is your own machine, a dedicated server is easy to duplicate, and dedicated hosting can scale up for large clusters.

On the downside, you and only you are responsible for what goes on inside the machine. You will need to provide your own applications monitoring and security patches, and if some system on the machine runs amok or if you are cracked by a Raman worm attack, your ISP won't know and won't be able to do much about it.

Shared Virtual Server

A shared virtual server is almost a dedicated server: Your application runs in its own partition, with its own OS image, but on physical hardware that may be shared by others. You lease a fraction of a box for a fraction of the total cost, typically for less than $100/month.

As with a dedicated solution, you choose your own software, manage your own server security, and install and maintain your own applications. Your server has the same level of security as a separate box, and apart from applications that might lock the underlying hardware, you have the same guarantees of uptime.

How the machine is partitioned depends on the underlying hardware. For example, an IBM S/390 mainframe can run 40,000 distinct Linux images, but these images will all share the same peripheral resources, such as the network pipe. For most applications, the cost savings over a dedicated colocation server far outweigh the small availability risk.

Shared Virtual Host

The shared virtual host is the lowest in cost but also carries the fewest guarantees. Monthly fees are typically in the $20–$50 range, depending on services, and these services may include access to a relational database, access to installed applications or scripting languages, e-mail and autoresponders, and domain name hosting.

Virtual hosts are hosts in name only; your applications will share the box—and its operating system, memory, and CPU resources—and all other services and software with many other virtual host accounts.

Selecting a Colocation Provider

Although I generally recommend colocation instead of in-house hosting, I don't envy anyone who has to make the final decision. Colocation providers come in many flavors, from the small mom-and-pop shops running on a shared T1 out of a local computer store all the way up to the bandwidth guarantees of monster ISPs such as Akamai. Narrowing down that list is part investigative journalism, part networking with your peers, and part just trying a few and seeing what you get.

This section will outline a few of the things to look for in selecting a colocation provider, but like anything else, your satisfaction as a customer can come only if you have realistic expectations and demands; it could well be that the local mom-and-pop shop can do everything you need and give you a warm, neighborly experience while they do it.

Business Requirements

Before you can select the home for your server, you need to have a clear idea of what your server must actually do. Consider who it serves:

- Do you need global coverage?
- Do you need exceptional response times?
- Do you need exceptional response times from any location?

If you are serving large files to urban high-speed Internet users, you will need a host with redundant connections directly connecting them to multiple backbones. If you target a rural or third-world audience, it is probably more cost effective to design the Web site to be lean and fast or to choose multiple colocations close to your audience.

Your choices of a colocation company and the decision to use a shared server rather than your own dedicated box can be limited by the technology or operating systems you want to use. For example, Apache Tomcat is a very efficient technology for building multitiered, high-traffic applications, but it may require a shared host or a dedicated server unless one of the few Tomcat-enabled Web hosts can provide the bandwidth and coverage you need. Even if you choose a dedicated server, you may want to inquire whether the colocation company has any in-house expertise in your technology. Be aware, too, that your needs will change over time.

Narrowing the Field

A simple search on Google for colocation providers returns no less than 96,000 entries. Even the Colocation Directory (`http://www.colosource.com/`) lists more than 500 vendors. However, not all Web-hosting companies are created alike, despite what their Web sites might say.

Hidden Costs

The first and slipperiest issue to deal with is knowing what you are buying, and as you move away from the major vendors with reputations to risk, there is an increased risk of fine print. Check your contracts for bandwidth or server-space overrun costs and other incidentals; in these days of QuickTime and streaming media files, a gigabyte a day can vanish pretty quickly.

Your contract agreement should state the location being licensed, extra services such as monitoring, electricity costs, and it should differentiate between one-time setup costs and metered costs. You should also set clear performance standards and verify some recourse should those standards fail to materialize. Every piece of hardware is going to have downtime, and many catastrophes can impact your throughput beyond anyone's control, but when deficiencies are chronic, you need to have some means to resolve them and to obtain some compensation for unreasonable downtime.

Hardware Partners

Depending on your own corporate alliances, those of your colocation host may be an important consideration. This is also a double-edged consideration: Although a close partnership with one vendor may mean superior support and core competencies in that product line, there is an equal risk of having a hammer and seeing all problems as nails.

Backbone Connectivity

The first obvious difference between colocation sites is connectivity. All OC3 lines are not alike. A site several hops from a backbone will not have the throughput of an identically equipped shop wired directly to the fiber lines. A site on the West Coast may have good connectivity to China but be unable to reach Europe, and a MAE East site may have trouble reaching the Midwest U.S.A. Even if a host has redundant lines to several major networks, you need to know whether your audience will be on the networks served by those particular backbones.

Most reputable colocation companies will provide their connection details on their Web site or by request. You can also get some idea of the geographic concentration of bandwidth by looking at the Colosource Colocation Facilities map (`http://www.colosource.com/usamap.htm`) and comparing candidate sites with their list of exchange points (`http://www.colosource.com/ix.asp`).

Because the Internet is not deployed in the grid array as its designers intended—in reality, it is a treelike graph of trunks and branches—the proximity of your target host to peering exchange points is critical in achieving maximum coverage. The lack of sufficient peering is a fundamental problem with the modern Internet, and there are those who are lobbying for change, but that change will take time. At present, if you choose a site far out on some remote limb, it may serve its local area with blazing speed but crawl like a dial-up line trying to reach customers of other networks, even though they may reside in the same city!

Uptime Disclosure

When someone else runs your network, you have a loss of control. When a customer calls your office to tell you the site is down, you might experience something like road rage. We all want 100% uptime, but when that fraction of a percent happens, you want to have an answer to give to your customers.

Most colocation hosts worth their salt will publish a live Web page itemizing the state of their network and showing when the entire network is down; a forthright and honest colocation service will also give you the history charts so that you can see their reliability in action.

Security

Whether you are buying or leasing your hardware, you have a right to be nervous about the capability of your colocation site to ensure the safety of your assets. At the very least, your insurance company is going to be interested in this aspect of the contract.

Your contract provisions should include some statement of responsibility for fire, theft, flooding, or other loss of property. You will also want to know if the site itself is secure:

- Building security—Do they allow access to the premises after hours, and if so, what are the security arrangements? Are they insured?
- Environmental controls—What are the arrangements for air conditioning and humidity control? What arrangements exist for power failures?

- Fire systems—Are the sprinkler systems wet sprinklers or Halon?
- Disaster plans—Do they have any formal contingency plans for natural disasters? What are the local risks for earthquakes, flooding, or tornados?

If you have extremely valuable assets to locate in their shop, whether this is your hardware or the data it holds, you will want to inquire about closed racks, locked cage areas, or secured vaults. You will also need to know the exact access provided to their personnel and whether those personnel are bonded. Data theft from the console is far more frequent than anyone wants to admit. If your site holds 100,000 VISA numbers, you want to be pretty well assured that organized crime is not going to bribe someone to slip in a floppy disk and take off with your records.

Special Features

Special services and features are other criteria to consider, although without connectivity, security, and reliability, it doesn't much matter what special features are provided. Common offerings include streaming-media servers, content-delivery systems, and scaleable bandwidth on demand. With all these services, what looks good on paper may not pan out in practice, and you should seek to have assurances in print of the minimum performance metrics for these services and some contingency plans for when these metrics are not met.

Bottom Line

All things considered, a lot can be said for just being reasonable. The most important criteria for selecting your colocation host may be social rather than technical.

Selecting a colocation or Web-host ISP is no different from selecting any strategic business partner. Just as with any service contractor, you would ask the usual questions:

- How long has the company been in business?
- How much of their revenue comes from colocation?
- Are they stable? Do they have any unusual turnover of technical or office staff? If they are publicly traded, you can check their stock ticker on Yahoo or Netcenter, and you can check into their hiring rates with a quick scan of the job-hunting Web sites.
- Do they have the core competencies you need? If you have special server technologies, will they be able to help in an emergency?
- Do you *like* them?

As with any candidate supplier for digital infrastructure, whether it is a developer, a consultant, a hardware vendor or a Web host, your very best resource is probably the buzz on the street, or in our case, the buzz on the Web. The very simplest test for anyone claiming to support the Internet is to see if the Internet knows them, and the fastest way to do this is to just type the name into Google and see what comes back.

Customer Referrals

The S in ISP is for service, and that is one of the hardest features to ascertain before the fact. Fortunately, we live in a networked world. Markets are conversations and people like to talk. Before you sign any colocation contract, check the buzz around you.

Be aware that customer referrals are a double-edged sword. Like everything else you read online, you should always retain a grain of doubt and double-check all your facts. Even a trusted colleague may recommend a service that did fine for their purposes but that could be completely inappropriate for your own needs. A bad recommendation may be a true incident, or it may be industrial sabotage by ruthless competition (and this industry is highly competitive). Even with trusted reviews, you should greet any and all complaints and recommendations with your own list of requirements, and go for a second opinion.

Colocation Ratings Web Sites

Colosource (`http://www.colosource.com/`) is an excellent and objective resource for finding the needle provider in the great haystack of noise. Their site contains member-contributed white papers on the art and science of selecting hardware and locations, maps and conference listings, member forums and bulletin boards, and news summaries in the colocation industry.

Other online colocation review sites are the following:

- Web Hosting Directories (`http://www.dmoz.org/Computers/Internet/Commercial_Services/Web_Hosting/Directories/`)—The DMOZ page featuring a collection of Web hosting directories.
- ISP-Planet (`http://www.isp-planet.com/`)—Although not a directory or review site per se, Internet.com's ISP page is an excellent resource for news, policies, and other items directly affecting the Web hosting and ISP industry.
- BigHosts (http://www.bighosts.com/)—Contains user-submitted reviews which, although signed, make no attempt to verify the authorship and tend to attract reviews of the smaller colocation providers. Mildly useful as a second opinion.
- RATEaSERVER.com (`http://www.rateadedicatedserver.com/`)—A new service that is not yet complete but that plans to offer contributed reviews and a message board. May be worth bookmarking if they avoid the mistakes of BigHosts.

Summary

While every business will have its own criteria for keeping Internet services inhouse or outsourcing some or part of it, you need to weigh your total costs very carefully before you jump to the conclusion that inhouse is your best choice. There is an engineer's joke that says the first rule of optimization is "Don't" and the second rule, for experts only, says "Don't, yet"; inhouse servers do give you absolute control over your services, but the downside is that they also give you absolute responsibility.

The responsibilities of running an Internet service are not to be taken lightly, and even when looking at outsource vendors, you need to examine the capabilities of the each bid very carefully. You need to know that they can manage your equipment responsibly, but that they can also reach the audience you need to reach. Just as with any business service, the whole ecology needs to be assessed, and that includes your own company ecology and culture. You may look for talent, skill and infrastructure when pairing your enterprise with a provider of any publically visible service, but you ignore cultural factors at your own peril.

Open Source High Availability and Scalability

CHAPTER

16

IN THIS CHAPTER

- Two Sample Network Designs 316
- Linux Virtual Server Project 318
- Ultramonkey 332
- Piranha 341
- Super Sparrow 353

In Chapter 11, "High Availability and Scalability," and Chapter 12, "Architecture for High Availability and Scalability," we discussed high availability and scalability and how it is important to remember these two areas when designing the network for your Internet service. In this chapter, we take a look at some specific tools to implement these features. Each product is described and examples of the configuration files required to implement one of the sample network designs are given.

Two Sample Network Designs

Before we start looking at the tools in the open source arsenal for implementing a highly available and scalable network, let's take a moment to describe a couple of sample network designs. The first network design is for a small Internet site offering Web services, FTP services, and mail services. Our sample design for this site, which we call Site A, is shown in Figure 16.1.

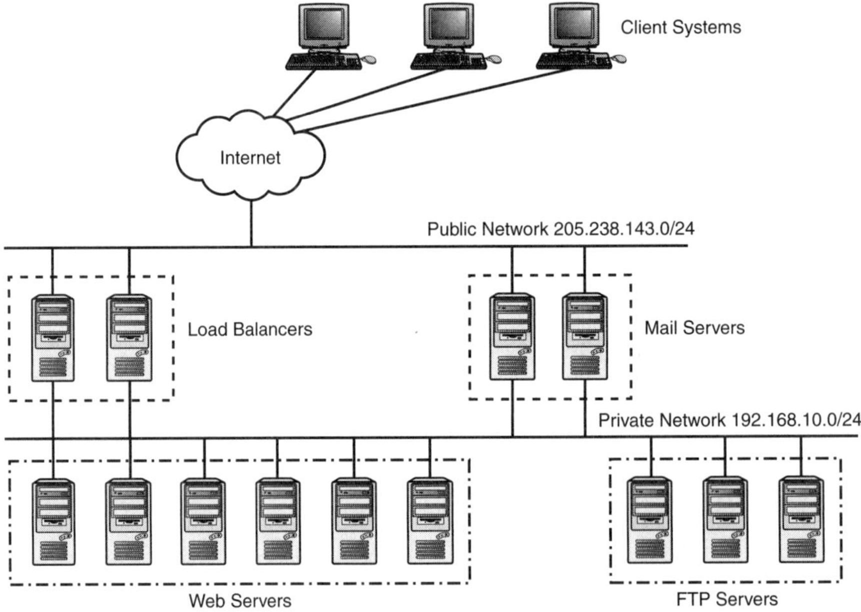

FIGURE 16.1
Sample network design for Site A.

As you can see from this diagram, we are using a load balancer to distribute the Web service load among 5 real servers and to distribute FTP service load among 3 real servers. In addition, we have added a failover mail server to ensure high availability and a failover load balancer for the same reason. In addition to load balancing, the load balancer will be acting as a gateway, providing network address translation (NAT) services for systems on the private network. NAT is a technique that allows you to use private network addresses for systems on your network that are translated to one or more public addresses when communication with the Internet is required. There are two basic forms of NAT. One maps private addresses to multiple public addresses. The other, which is commonly referred to as *masquerading*, maps all the private addresses to a single public address. On Linux-based systems, this form of NAT can be implemented using ipchains. This is the form of NAT we will focus on in this chapter.

Our second sample network design, which we call Site B, is for a larger network, which will need to support much larger traffic levels and will start out with 25 Web servers. This site will be generating dynamic pages from database back ends consisting of 8 load-balanced database query servers and a single database update server, which is fed data from a pair of news servers in a failover configuration. This network is pictured in Figure 16.2. Note that only 7 of the Web servers are pictured and the remaining 18 are represented by the ellipses.

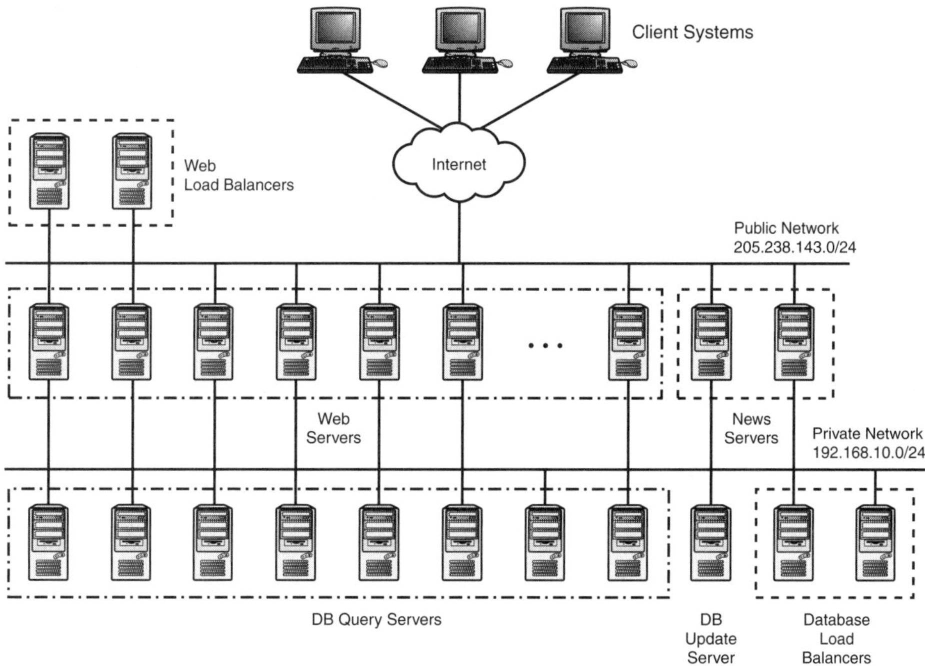

FIGURE 16.2

Sample network for Site B.

This diagram differs slightly from our previous one in that we use two separate load-balancer pairs: one for Web traffic and the other for database traffic. In addition, the Web servers are connected directly to the public network. As we get into the configuration of our networks later in this chapter, the reason for this will become clear. In addition, although not pictured here, a router that is independent of the load-balancing systems serves as the public gateway for outward facing servers. This is because unlike the Site A design, the load-balancing systems will not be doing NAT.

Now that we have described our two sample networks, we can begin looking at some of the software that is available for Linux to implement high availability and load balancing.

Linux Virtual Server Project

Most of the open source load-balancing solutions for Linux share one common component—the Linux Virtual Server, or LVS, which was developed by Wensong Zhang at the National Laboratory for Parallel and Distributed Processing. The goal of the project, as described in a paper available at `http://www.linuxvirtualserver.org/` was to provide a basic framework on which highly scalable and highly available network services using commodity servers could be built. The basic idea here was to support scalability, 24/7 availability, manageability, and cost effectiveness. Let's take a closer look at what LVS does and the tools associated with it.

What It Does

LVS consists of two basic parts. These parts are a patch to the Linux kernel that extends the TCP/IP stack of Linux and a utility to allow you to access the extended features. This patch can be applied to kernels in the 2.2.x branch and are also available for the 2.4.x branch. If you are not familiar with how to patch and rebuild the Linux kernel, you should take a look at `http://linuxdocs.org/HOWTOs/Kernel-HOWTO.html` for information on configuring, compiling, and installing a customized Linux kernel. To enable the extended features, you would select the IP:Masquerading Virtual Server Support option in the kernel configuration, specify the size of the VS table, and select one or more of the scheduling algorithms that you would like to use. These options are found under the Networking Options section of the kernel configurator, as shown in Figure 16.3.

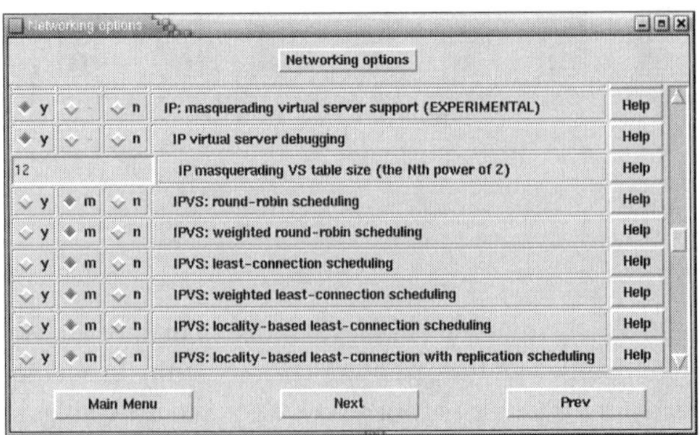

FIGURE 16.3
Kernel configurator Networking Options dialog box.

The following are some tips for building support into your kernel for LVS. First, you must select the IP:Masquerading option for LVS to be available as an option. You should also enable IP:ip fwmark Masq-Forwarding Support because this will give you more flexibility in your use of LVS. This support can be built as a module if you desire. The size of the masquerading virtual server (VS) table is specified as a power of 2 and should be determined based on the levels of traffic you expect to receive. The help information in the kernel configurator for this entry explains how you can determine this setting. If you are just experimenting with LVS, you can probably just accept the default value of 12, which gives you a table size of 4,096 entries. As you might expect, maintaining this table requires space in memory. Each table entry occupies 128 bytes, and if you select the default table size, it will use 512KB of memory. Using the same rules, increasing the value to 16 would give you a table size of 65,536 entries and use 8MB of memory. Keep this in mind when setting this value. The final suggestion is that you select all the scheduling algorithms, building them as modules. This allows you to use any of them as required and gives you the greatest flexibility because you can load or unload the desired module as you require.

After you have built and installed your kernel with LVS support, what next? What does LVS do? Basically, LVS provides the Linux kernel with the capability to define a virtual service on the LVS system and to distribute the network load among a set of real servers in a loosely coupled cluster. Various options are available when using LVS, including two methods of defining virtual services, three routing methods, and six load-balancing algorithms. Let's take a look at each of these areas, starting with methods for defining virtual services.

Defining Virtual Services

LVS supports two methods of defining virtual services. These two methods can be used simultaneously on the same load-balancing server for defining different services. The methods are

- The protocol, port, IP address method
- The firewall mark method

Which of these two methods you use is your decision, but you have this choice of methods only if you are using a recent version of the LVS patches and ipvsadm, the tools used to define services to the kernel. Let's take a look at each of these methods to see how they work.

The Protocol, Port, IP Address Method

The most common method is to define a service in terms of a protocol, a port, and an IP address. For example, your Web service could be defined in terms of protocol TCP, port 80, on IP address 10.10.10.1. Currently supported protocols are TCP and UDP, and services that work best are those that use a single port, such as HTTP, HTTPS, and so on. However, explicit support exists for some multiport services such as FTP. If you are looking to define simple protocols that use a single port, and you are defining just a few virtual services, this method will probably be all you require.

The Firewall Mark Method

The other method for defining a service is through the use of firewall marks. Firewall marks are generated by the packet-filtering software under Linux and consist of a 32-bit unsigned integer value that is added to the packet headers as they traverse the TCP/IP stack. These marks can then be used to determine where to route the packets as they leave the load-balancing system. The use of firewall marks to define a service is much less common than the other method, partially because it has been supported only since version 0.9.10 of the LVS kernel patches.

The Routing Methods

As we mentioned previously, LVS supports three methods of routing packets to the real servers in the back end. These methods are

- Network address translation (NAT)
- Direct routing
- IP encapsulation (tunneling)

Which one you select is determined by a number of factors, such as a need for persistence, the OS of the back end servers, the number of back end servers, and network performance issues. As we look at each of these routing methods, we will discuss the pros and cons with respect to these factors. A diagram showing the flow of traffic is also provided, illustrating each routing method.

Routing Using Network Address Translation

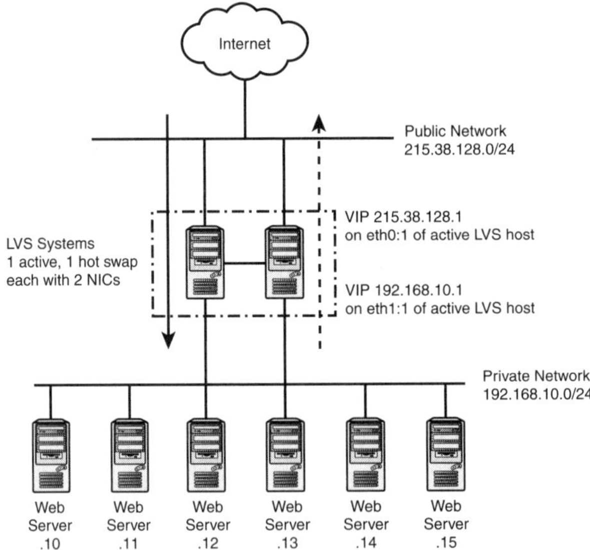

FIGURE 16.4
Load balancing using the NAT routing method.

With this type of setup, clients wanting to connect to the load-balanced service connect to the virtual IP address, or VIP, on the public network. The load-balancing algorithm is applied, and traffic is routed to one of the back end Web servers via the VIP on the private network. Traffic flow is indicated by the solid arrow and passed from the Internet to the private network via the LVS host. The Web server on the back end fulfills the client request and responds to the client via the LVS host because the VIP on the private network is the default gateway for the hosts on the private network. Traffic flow is indicated by the dashed arrow, passing from the Web server via the LVS host, which does network address translation, back to the client on the Internet. Because all traffic passes in and out through the LVS host, I recommend that you have two LVS hosts, configured as an active and hot swap, so that you eliminate the single point of failure that having a single LVS host would create.

We have already discussed some of the limitations of this method of routing—specifically, a limitation on the number of back end servers and the creation of a single point of failure in the LVS host, but one of the key advantages of this routing method is that no special requirements exist for the back end servers, which means that you could conceivably use any operating system you want behind your Linux LVS hosts. You could even mix operating systems on the back end if you chose, running Linux on one or two, Solaris on another, and Windows NT on the rest, although why you would want to do this I couldn't imagine.

LVS Using Direct Routing

If you require more servers on the back end than supported by NAT, you could select the direct-routing method. Using this method, traffic bound for the back end servers is received on the VIP of the LVS host, and after the load-balancing algorithm is applied, the MAC address in the data frame of the packets are rewritten to match the selected back end server and the packets are forwarded to that server. These back end servers share the VIP with the LVS host on an interface that does not respond to ARP requests. The back end server then responds directly to the client, bypassing the LVS host on the return trip. This is illustrated in Figure 16.5.

As the diagram illustrates, each server on the back end is on the public network and is configured to share the VIP with the LVS server. We again use a failover setup for the LVS hosts to provide high availability. The biggest difference is the traffic flow. In this configuration, the default gateway is a router that is independent of the LVS hosts. Traffic originates with a client on the Internet, travels to the VIP on the LVS host via the gateway router, is distributed to the back end server and back to the client again via the gateway router.

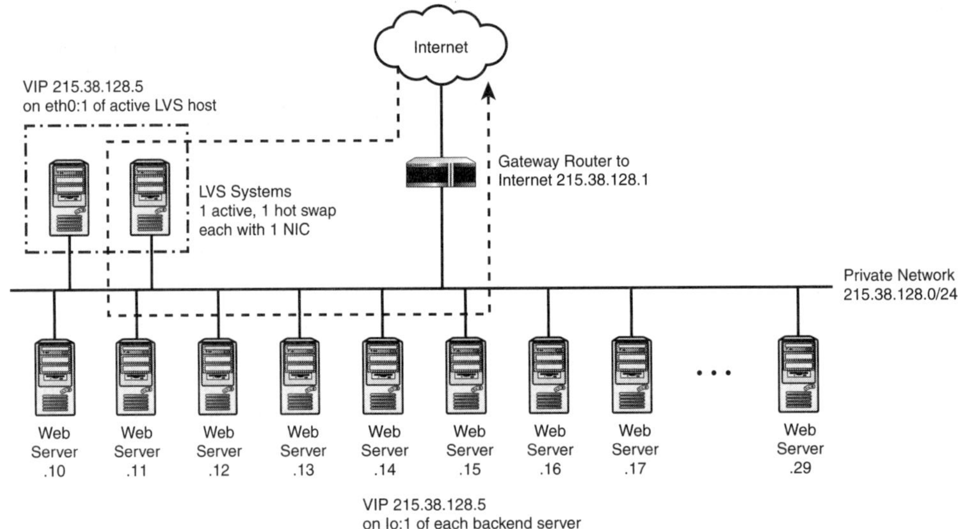

FIGURE 16.5
LVS using direct-routing method.

This method of routing has the advantage of allowing for many more back end servers. Because no bottleneck occurs at the LVS host, and because of the limitation that servers must be able to set an IP alias on the loopback device that does not respond to ARP requests, you are limited in your choice of operating systems on the back end servers. In addition, all the back end servers must be on an uninterrupted LAN segment with the load-balancing server, which is to say that they should all be on the same hub or switch. The reason why the loopback device of the back end servers must be able to ignore ARP requests is to avoid address conflicts with the LVS host, which shares the VIP with all the back end servers.

LVS Using IP Encapsulation (Tunneling)

Yet another type of routing available with LVS is IP encapsulation, or tunneling. This method is very much like the direct-routing method, but it works by encapsulating packets coming in to the VIP and redirecting them to the back end servers. Naturally, this means that the back end servers must support IP encapsulation because they must have a tunneling device configured with the VIP. Like the direct-routing method, this method allows you to have many more back end servers; however, there is slightly more overhead because of the encapsulation, which is more work than simply rewriting the MAC address of the datagrams. This setup is illustrated in Figure 16.6.

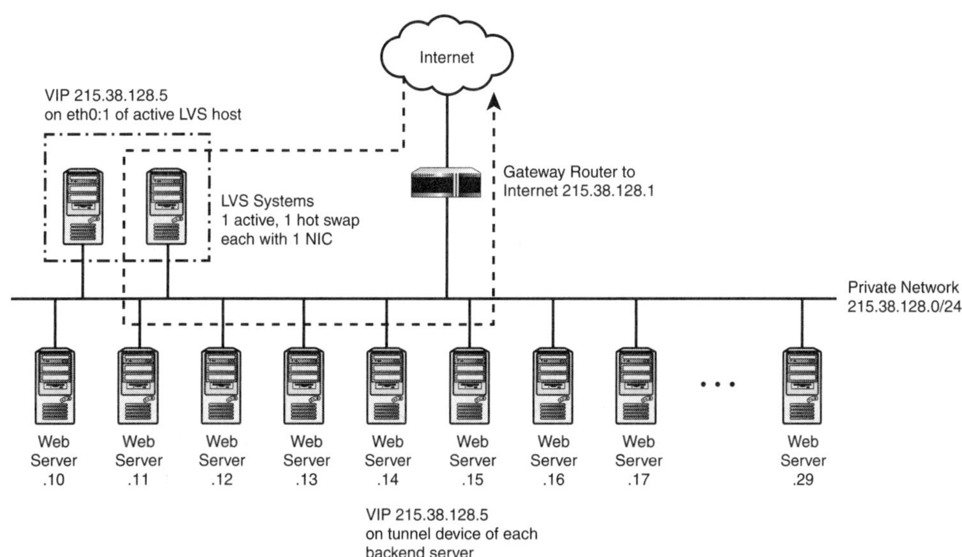

FIGURE 16.6
LVS using IP encapsulation (tunneling).

Although not shown in the figure, one of the advantages that this method has over the other routing methods is that back end servers do not have to be on a private network, as they do with the NAT method, or even on the same LAN segment, as with direct routing. Instead they merely have to be accessible via the network from the LVS host. This means that the servers could be in different physical locations from each other; however, if you are thinking that this means that you can do geographic load balancing using this method, think again. None of the load-balancing algorithms supported are designed to determine the shortest route between client and server. What it does mean is that you can have servers spread among different colocation providers if you choose.

As you can see from the diagram in Figure 16.6, the traffic flow is just like it was when we selected direct routing as the method, meaning that just as with direct routing, the IP encapsulation routing method is much more scalable than the NAT method. In addition, as more and more operating systems add support for the tunneling, they become capable of serving as back end servers.

The Load-Balancing Algorithms

At the time of this writing, the LVS patches to the Linux kernel support six load-balancing algorithms. The load-balancing algorithms are

- Round robin

- Weighted round robin
- Least connection
- Weighted least-connection
- Locality-based least-connection
- Locality-based least-connection with replication

We will take a brief look at each of these, describing how they work, starting with the simplest scheduling algorithm—round robin.

Round-Robin Scheduling

Round-robin scheduling is the simplest scheduling algorithm and load is distributed in a manner analogous to the way that a dealer deals cards. That is, if you have five servers, A through E, the order in which connections are distributed would be first to A, then to B, and so on up to E, and then back to A again. The problem with this scheduling method is that it doesn't take into account server load or the number of active connections already established. It also does not take into account differences in the processing capacity of the back end servers.

Weighted Round-Robin Scheduling

A variant of round-robin scheduling that LVS allows you to use is weighted round-robin scheduling. This allows you to take into account different load capacities among the servers in the back end server pool. By assigning a weight value to servers with more load capacity, you can direct more of the load to those servers best able to handle the load. For example, if the default weight for a server is 1, and you assign one of the servers a weight of 2, this server will get twice as much of the distributed load as the others. You can use weight values to give the lion's share of the load to servers with more memory or more processing power. Of course, if all your servers are identical, this will be of little value to you.

Least-Connection Scheduling

Yet another load-balancing algorithm available with LVS is the least-connection scheduling algorithm. This method causes the LVS kernel to keep track of the number of connections to each server and to use this information to distribute the load evenly among the back end servers. Unlike the round-robin scheduling algorithm, this is a true load-balancing algorithm. The limitation of this algorithm is that just like the round-robin algorithm, it does not take into account differences in the processing power of the back end servers.

Weighted Least-Connection Scheduling

Probably the best general-purpose load-balancing algorithm available is the weighted least-connection scheduling algorithm. Like the weighted variant of the round-robin algorithm, using this scheduling method, you can assign weights to servers based on their capability to handle the load. Differences in processor speed, memory, and network capacity can be taken into account by assigning weights to servers.

Locality-Based Least-Connection Scheduling

This algorithm is an addition to the original scheduling algorithms described in the LVS white paper. As the name implies, it is a variation on the least-connection scheduling algorithm—or more properly, of weighted least-connection scheduling. It is primarily useful in cache clusters. This algorithm works by keeping a table of cache nodes that associates them with a destination IP address. If a connection request comes in for a destination IP address that is not in the table, then based on the weighted least-connected algorithm, a cache node is selected, a table entry is made, and the connection is forwarded to that node. If an entry in the table does exist, things get a bit more complicated. In this case, if the node is not dead and is not overloaded, the connection is forwarded to that node. If the node is dead or the node is overloaded, look for a node that is under half load, create a table entry and forward the connection to that node.

Locality-Based Least-Connection with Replication Scheduling

A further refinement to the locality-based least-connection algorithm is the locality-based least-connection with replication scheduling algorithm. This algorithm differs from the previously discussed algorithm in that instead of a single server being associated with a destination IP, a set of servers is associated with each destination IP; when a connection request is made for that destination IP address, the connection is forwarded to the server in the set with the least connections. If all the cache nodes in a server set are overloaded, a new node is added to the server set. In addition, after a user-defined amount of time, if the server set is not modified, the most-connected node is removed from the server set and is available for addition to another server set. This algorithm is designed for use in cache clusters as well.

The Tool Suite

Now that we have taken a look at what LVS does and some of the aspects of using it, we can look at the tools that come with it. In addition to the kernel patch, the latest versions of the LVS patch comes with the `ipvsadm` utility, which is used to manipulate the tables implemented by the LVS patches. Also, in the contrib directory are a couple of useful utilities for monitoring the real servers in the back end. In this section, we look at the `ipvsadm` utility and how it is used as well as how to use the other utilities that come with LVS.

The ipvsadm Utility

After you have built the LVS-enabled kernel, you need a way to manipulate the LVS tables. This is done with the `ipvsadm` utility. To get started, let's take a look at the syntax of the `ipvsadm` command.

Running the `ipvsadm` command with the `-h` option gives us the usage statement, which provides us with the following output:

```
ipvsadm v1.14 2000/12/17 (compiled with popt and IPVS v1.0.5)
Usage:
  ./ipvsadm -[A|E] -[t|u|f] service-address [-s scheduler] [-p [timeout]]
➥[-M netmask]
  ./ipvsadm -D -[t|u|f] service-address
  ./ipvsadm -C
  ./ipvsadm -R
  ./ipvsadm -S [-n]
  ./ipvsadm -[a|e] -[t|u|f] service-address -[r|R] server-address [-g|-i|-m]
➥[-w weight]
  ./ipvsadm -d -[t|u|f] service-address -[r|R] server-address
  ./ipvsadm -[L|l] [-n]
  ./ipvsadm -h

Commands:
Either long or short options are allowed.
  --add-service     -A        add virtual service with options
  --edit-service    -E        edit virtual service with options
  --delete-service  -D          delete virtual service
  --clear           -C        clear the whole table
  --restore         -R          restore rules from stdin
  --save            -S          save rules to stdout
  --add-server      -a        add real server with options
  --edit-server     -e        edit real server with options
  --delete-server   -d        delete real server
  --list            -L|-l     list the table
  --help            -h          display this help message

Options:
  --tcp-service    -t service-address   service-address is host[:port]
  --udp-service    -u service-address   service-address is host[:port]
  --fwmark-service  -f fwmark           fwmark is an integer greater than zero
  --scheduler      -s <scheduler>       one of rr|wrr|lc|wlc|lblc|lblcr,
                                        the default scheduler is wlc.
  --persistent     -p [timeout]         persistent service
  --netmask        -M [netmask]         persistent granularity mask
  --real-server    -r|-R server-address server-address is host (and port)
  --gatewaying     -g                   gatewaying (direct routing) (default)
  --ipip           -i                   ipip encapsulation (tunneling)
  --masquerading   -m                   masquerading (NAT)
  --weight         -w <weight>          capacity of real server
  --numeric        -n                   numeric output of addresses and ports
```

As you can see, the `ipvsadm` command has a lot of options. Fortunately, we don't have to remember them all, because the software comes with a man page and as we will see later in the chapter, there are alternatives to invoking `ipvsadm` directly. That being said, however, let's take a look at some of the ways in which `ipvsadm` could be used if you didn't have these alternatives.

Some ipvsadm Usage Examples

For our first example, let's declare a virtual service using the port, protocol, IP address method. We will assume that we are trying to implement the network in Site A as described at the beginning of this chapter. Because LVS by itself does not provide for failover and doesn't include any of the failover software with it, we will be pretending that there is a single load balancer and will be ignoring the mail servers for the moment. We will be demonstrating the commands to set up a single load-balancing host, the Web servers, and the FTP servers.

Let's start with the Web servers because these are easier to configure. To get started, we define the virtual service. We will be using the port, protocol, IP address method and the weighted least-connection scheduling algorithm. The virtual IP address for this service will be 205.238.143.5. To accomplish this, we would issue the following command.

```
# ipvsadm -A -t 205.238.143.5:80 -s wlc
```

Breaking this command apart and using the information from the usage statement, we see that we are adding a virtual service (`-A`) using the TCP protocol (`-t`) defined at IP address 205.238.143.5 on port 80 and have elected to use the weighted least-connection scheduling algorithm (`-s wlc`).

We can now define the real servers in the back end. These servers are on a private network and we are using the NAT method of routing. For our sample group of Web servers, we will be using IP addresses on the private network 192.168.10.0/24 as shown in Figure 16.1, starting with .12 and incrementing by 2. Here are the commands required to do this for the five back end servers.

```
# ipvsadm -a -t 205.238.143.5:80 -r 192.168.10.12:80 -m
# ipvsadm -a -t 205.238.143.5:80 -r 192.168.10.14:80 -m
# ipvsadm -a -t 205.238.143.5:80 -r 192.168.10.16:80 -m
# ipvsadm -a -t 205.238.143.5:80 -r 192.168.10.18:80 -m
# ipvsadm -a -t 205.238.143.5:80 -r 192.168.10.20:80 -m
```

Again, breaking apart the command, each preceding line adds a server (`-a`) as a back end for the TCP service listening on 205.238.143.5:80 (`-t 205.238.143.5:80`). You specify the real server using a syntax similar to how you specified the address and port for the virtual service (`-r 192.168.10.2:80`). The final option specified on the command line is the routing method to use, in this case, the NAT method (`-m`).

Now we can proceed with the next part of our example and configure the virtual service for the FTP servers. For this example, we are using the firewall mark method of defining a service. This example does not exactly fit with our sample Site A network because when you use firewall marks, you are actually specifying that connections on any port to the VIP address will be forwarded to the corresponding port on the real servers in the back end. If we were actually implementing the network in the Site A diagram, we would use the ipchains utility to limit traffic to the IP address for the FTP service to just those ports required for FTP.

We will use simple round-robin scheduling and specify that we want persistence. To get started, we will add the virtual service using the following command:

```
# ipvsadm -A -f 1 -s rr -p 150
```

This command adds a virtual service for any packets marked with a firewall mark of 1; it specifies that we are using simple round-robin scheduling and that we want all connections from the same IP address that arrive within a timeout period of 150 seconds to be directed to the same server (`-p 150`). This last option deserves a little explanation. Unlike HTTP, which does not require a persistent connection to work well in a load-balanced environment, some protocols require it. By specifying that all connections from a particular IP address within a timeout period be handled by the same server, we can achieve this persistence. If we were not able to do so, protocols such as FTP and others could not be handled properly.

Now for the back end servers, we issue the following commands to add the three real servers to the back end for the FTP virtual service:

```
# ipvsadm -a -f 1 -r 192.168.10.30:0 -m
# ipvsadm -a -f 1 -r 192.168.10.32:0 -m
# ipvsadm -a -f 1 -r 192.168.10.34:0 -m
```

These commands add real servers at the IP addresses specified for packets bearing the firewall mark 1, and again we are using the NAT method of routing.

NOTE

The preceding examples are similar to those found in the manual page that was distributed with version 1.14 of the ipvsadm utility; however, the manual page contains a syntax error in that they used the `-t` option instead of the `-f` option.

Assuming that you issued the preceding commands, you could now use another feature of the ipvsadm utility to examine the tables maintained by the kernel. To do this, you could issue the following command, which would produce output as shown:

```
# ipvsadm -ln
IP Virtual Server version 1.0.5 (size=4096)
Prot LocalAddress:Port Scheduler Flags
  -> RemoteAddress:Port          Forward Weight ActiveConn InActConn
TCP  205.238.143.5:80 wlc
  -> 192.168.10.20:80            Masq    1      0          0
  -> 192.168.10.18:80            Masq    1      0          0
  -> 192.168.10.16:80            Masq    1      0          0
  -> 192.168.10.14:80            Masq    1      0          0
  -> 192.168.10.12:80            Masq    1      0          0
```

```
FWM  1 rr persistent 150
  -> 192.168.10.34:0             Masq    1      0         0
  -> 192.168.10.32:0             Masq    1      0         0
  -> 192.168.10.30:0             Masq    1      0         0
```

In this example, we use the list option (`-l`) and the numeric output (`-n`) options to look at the results of our previous commands. The previous output displays the version of the LVS patches we are using and then shows the information for the virtual services we have defined. Each virtual service starts with a line indicating whether the service is a TCP, a UDP, or an FWM (firewall mark) service, the scheduling algorithm, and persistence, if any. Following these lines are the definitions of the real servers associated with each virtual service, the routing method used, the weight assigned to the real server, and the number of active and inactive connections to each of them. This command is quite useful to determine that you have correctly defined a service and the related real servers in the back end.

Yet another very useful invocation of the ipvsadm utility is shown in this example, which clears the entire LVS table in the kernel by using the `-C` option. In the lines that follow, we will demonstrate this and show the result by using the `-ln` options as in the previous example.

```
# ipvsadm -C
# ipvsadm -ln
IP Virtual Server version 1.0.5 (size=4096)
Prot LocalAddress:Port Scheduler Flags
  -> RemoteAddress:Port           Forward Weight ActiveConn InActConn
```

Now that we have seen some examples of using the ipvsadm utility directly, we can move on to some of the contributed software that comes with LVS.

Some Contributed Software

In addition to the LVS patches for the kernel and the ipvsadm utility, the LVS software package contains a couple of pieces of software in the contrib directory that you might find useful.

The ldirectord Daemon

One of the pieces of software that comes with the LVS distribution is called ldirectord. This software has two primary functions:

- Defining virtual servers and associating real servers with them
- Managing the real server pool

The definition of virtual servers and associating real servers with them is accomplished by calling `ipvsadm` with the appropriate parameters based on the ldirectord configuration file. The more interesting aspect of ldirectord is the real server pool management. The ldirectord daemon periodically checks each real server to determine whether it is still up and running. If it does not respond to this check, it is removed from the server pool so that you don't lose traffic by routing it to a server that is not available.

The httpdMonitor Script

Yet another contributed piece of software that comes with the LVS package is a script called httpdMonitor. This script is a shell script that accomplishes the same thing as ldirectord, but is only for Web services. It is primarily useful if the only thing you want to do with LVS is to load balance for Web servers.

The configure Script

A final piece of contributed software is the configure script. This Perl script creates other scripts that you put into the init script hierarchy under /etc/rc.d to set up LVS. It relies on the use of mon, a general purpose monitoring utility, to monitor the real server pool. One advantage of using this software is that it is much more generic than ldirectord, but it relies on your capability to create the scripts used by mon to determine whether the back end servers are up and running.

Completing the Example

Now that we have an idea of what LVS does and the tools that come with it, let's go back and complete our work on implementing the sample network, Site A, as shown in Figure 16.1. We will create a single script that configures the load balancers to define our virtual servers and their associated real servers and show all the other commands required to set up our example. This solution will not include the management of the real server pool and will not include the configuration of the failover systems. If you are interested in this topic, I recommend that you read the LVS whitepaper that is included with the source code for some of the methods that can be used to perform these tasks.

The script shown in Listing 16.1, which I will call *lvs_setup*, would be run on the load-balancing host. The hosts on the back end would require no special configuration to implement this solution.

Some things to note about our load-balancing host include the following:

- There are two network interface cards. One of these, eth0, is connected to the public network and has IP address 205.238.143.5. (IP addresses are typically assigned by your ISP. These IP addresses are for example only and should not be used.)
- An additional IP address is associated with eth0 for the FTP service. This IP address is 205.238.143.10.
- The other network card, eth1, is connected to the private network along with the real server pool. It has an IP address of 192.168.10.5. (Certain IP address ranges are reserved for private networks. You can find these ranges by referring to RFC 1918 at `http://www.faqs.org/rfcs/rfc1918.html`.)

LISTING 16.1 lvs_setup

```
#!/bin/sh

# lvs_setup - a script to define a Web and a FTP virtual service and to
#             create the masquerading rules
#

# First set up the system so that it will forward packets.  This is
# required for masquerading (NAT) to work.
echo 1 > /proc/sys/net/ipv4/ip_forward

# Load the module to support masquerading of FTP connections.
/sbin/modprobe -a ip_masq_ftp

# Set up the ipchains rules to do the firewall marks and to do the
# masquerading.
/sbin/ipchains -A input -j ACCEPT -s 0/0 -d 205.238.143.10/32 -m 1
/sbin/ipchains -A forward -j MASQ -s 192.168.10.0/24 -d 0/0

# Now we can set up the LVS configuration, starting with the Web servers
ipvsadm -A -t 205.238.143.5:80 -s wlc
ipvsadm -a -t 205.238.143.5:80 -r 192.168.10.12:80 -m
ipvsadm -a -t 205.238.143.5:80 -r 192.168.10.14:80 -m
ipvsadm -a -t 205.238.143.5:80 -r 192.168.10.16:80 -m
ipvsadm -a -t 205.238.143.5:80 -r 192.168.10.18:80 -m
ipvsadm -a -t 205.238.143.5:80 -r 192.168.10.20:80 -m

# and then the FTP servers.
ipvsadm -A -f 1 -s rr -p 150
ipvsadm -a -f 1 -r 192.168.10.30:0 -m
ipvsadm -a -f 1 -r 192.168.10.32:0 -m
ipvsadm -a -f 1 -r 192.168.10.34:0 -m

# End of script
```

What is missing from this setup is the monitoring of the servers in the real server pool. For that you have a number of options, including software such as ldirectord, which is part of the Ultramonkey package. Other options include mon, a generic monitoring package, and nanny, which is part of the Piranha package that we will discuss later in this chapter. Now that we have seen the manual method of configuring LVS, let's take a look at a couple of open source products that can make the job easier and that give you additional capabilities.

Ultramonkey

If the idea of configuring LVS as we have just described sounds rather daunting, you might want to consider looking at the Ultramonkey project as described at `http://ultramonkey.sourceforge.net/`. This site includes not only the documentation for this project, but also source code and binary packages (RPM format) that you can download. This project combines LVS with ldirectord and adds heartbeat to allow you to implement load balancing in combination with failover. In this section, we look at what Ultramonkey adds to LVS and show how you would implement the networks described in Figure 16.1 and Figure 16.2 using the Ultramonkey tools. So let's get started with a description of what Ultramonkey does.

What It Does

Ultramonkey does what LVS does, but it also includes software that allows you to build failover systems. The other advantage to using Ultramonkey over plain LVS is that it pulls together into one place all the pieces that you would otherwise have to collect for yourself, and it documents using the particular suite of tools that the product comprises. And if you have an RPM-based system, such as Red Hat or Mandrake, you can use the Ultramonkey packages, eliminating the need to patch the kernel yourself.

The Tool Suite

Ultramonkey is a superset of LVS in that it includes LVS and adds to it. The two things it adds are ldirectord and heartbeat. Because we have already described what LVS does, we will now concentrate on heartbeat and ldirectord.

Heartbeat

Heartbeat is a piece of software designed to let you build failover systems. Using the heartbeat configuration files, you define one system as your primary server and another identical system as your failover or secondary server. During normal operation, all functions are handled by the primary system, but if the primary system fails for some reason, the secondary system takes over automatically. To see how this works, let's take a look at a sample configuration. We will implement the load-balancing systems for the Site A network.

As you might recall, each of these systems has two network interface cards. The first interface, eth0, is on the public network, which clients point at to connect to the services that we provide. The other interface, eth1, is on the private network that attaches the load-balancer systems to the back end servers. Take a look at Figure 16.7 for a picture of our two load-balancing systems. One thing to note is the connection via a null modem cable between the two systems. A null modem cable is a serial cable that has the transmit and receive wires crossed to enable communication. These cables typically come with network equipment that allows configuration via the serial port, or you can purchase one at most computer stores.

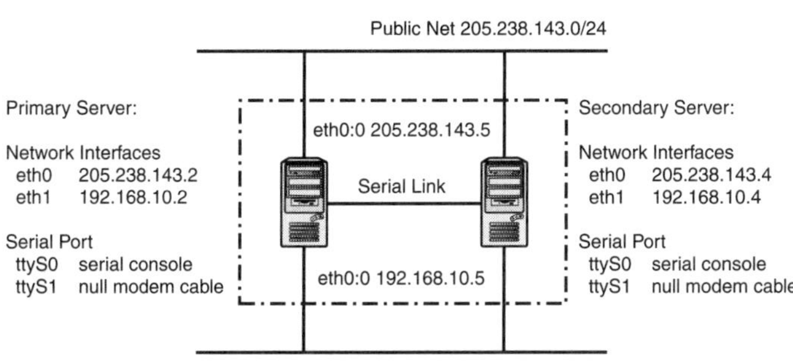

FIGURE 16.7
Primary and failover load-balancing servers.

The virtual IP addresses, which on the diagram are shown as eth0:0 and eth1:0, are created by the heartbeat software, and the system with which they are associated depends on which system is handling the load of the failover pair. The way this works is as follows:

- The heartbeat software is started on both systems.
- The primary system sets up an IP alias with the virtual IP of the services configured.
- At a user-defined interval, the primary system sends a message to the secondary system indicating that it is up and running.
- If the secondary system does not receive this message within a user-defined timeout, the secondary system uses a method called gratuitous ARP to take over the virtual IP of the defined services.
- If the primary comes back online and sends the heartbeat message indicating that it is back online, it then uses a gratuitous ARP to take over the virtual IP of the defined services, and the secondary goes back to waiting.

Now that you have an understanding of what heartbeat does, let's take a look at how you configure it.

The first step in configuring heartbeat is the creation of the `ha.cf` file—which, if you use the binary packages available at the Ultramonkey site, `http://ultramonkey.sourceforge.net/`, should be placed in the directory `/etc/ha.d`. Here in Listing 16.2 is a sample `ha.cf` file that demonstrates a sample configuration.

LISTING 16.2 `/etc/ha.d/ha.cf`

```
#
# /etc/ha.d/ha.cf
#
# ha.cf file to configure two nodes connected by ethernet (eth0) and
```

LISTING 16.2 Continued

```
# a null modem (/dev/ttyS0).
#
# Based on sample ha.cf shipped with heartbeat
#
#    There are lots of options in this file.  All you have to have is
#    a set of nodes listed {"node ...} and one of {serial, udp, or
#    ppp-udp}
#
#       Note on logging:
#       If any of debugfile, logfile and logfacility are defined then
#       they will be used. If debugfile and/or logfile are not defined
#       and logfacility is defined then the respective logging and debug
#       messages will be logged to syslog. If logfacility is not defined
#       then debugfile and logfile will be used to log messages. If
#       logfacility is not defined and debugfile and/or logfile are not
#       defined then defaults will be used for debugfile and logfile as
#       required and messages will be sent there.
#
#    File to write debug messages to
#debugfile /var/log/ha-debug
#
#     File to write other messages to
#logfile    /var/log/ha-log
#
#    Facility to use for syslog()/logger
logfacility    local0
#
#    keepalive: how many seconds between heartbeats
keepalive 1
#
#    deadtime: seconds-to-declare-host-dead
deadtime 3
#
#    hopfudge maximum hop count minus number of nodes in config
#hopfudge 1
#
#    serial    serialportname ...
serial    /dev/ttyS0
#
#    Only for serial ports.  It applies to both PPP/UDP and "raw"
#    ports
#
#    This means run PPP over ports ttyS1 and ttyS2
#    Their respective IP addresses are as listed.
```

LISTING 16.2 Continued

```
#    Note that I enforce that these are local addresses.  Other
#    addresses are almost certainly a mistake.
#ppp-udp    /dev/ttyS1 10.0.0.1 /dev/ttyS2 10.0.0.2
#
#    Baud rate for both serial and ppp-udp ports...
#baud    19200
#
#    What UDP port to use for udp or ppp-udp communication?
#udpport    1001
#
#    What interfaces to heartbeat over?
udp    eth0
#
#    Watchdog is the watchdog timer.  If our own heart doesn't beat for
#    a minute, then our machine will reboot.
#watchdog /dev/watchdog
#
#       Nice_failback sets the behavior when performing a failback:
#
#       - if it's on, when the primary node starts or comes back from any
#         failure and the cluster is already active, i.e. the secondary
#         server performed a failover, the primary stays quiet, acting as a
#         secondary.  This way some operations like syncing disks can be
#         easily done.
#       - if it's off (default), the primary node will always be the primary,
#         whenever it's powered on.
nice_failback off
#
#    Tell what machines are in the cluster
#    node    nodename ...    -- must match uname -n
node    lvs1.example.net
node    lvs2.example.net
```

This sample file contains a large number of comments and shows the possible configuration options that you have when setting up heartbeat. It is based on one of the sample ha.cf files that comes with the ultramonkey-doc RPM package available from the Ultramonkey home page at `http://ultramonkey.sourceforge.net`. As you can see, most of the options are commented out and defaults are used. Let's take a look at the minimal file that could be used to implement the failover of the Web load balancers for our Site B network (refer to Figure 16.2).

LISTING 16.3 `/etc/ha.d/ha.cf` File for Site B Web Load Balancers

```
logfacility    local0
keepalive 1
deadtime 3
serial    /dev/ttyS0
udp eth0
nice_failback off
node    lvs1.example.net
node    lvs2.example.net
```

The ha.cf file shown in Listing 16.3 configures heartbeat as follows:

- Log and debug messages are recorded using syslog using the log facility local0 (`logfacility local0`).
- The heartbeat message is sent once per second (`keepalive 1`).
- If no heartbeat is received in three seconds, which is the hard-coded minimum value for this parameter, failover occurs (`deadtime 3`).
- Heartbeat messages are sent via a null modem cable attached to `/dev/ttyS0` on both systems as well as by udp packets over eth0 (`serial /dev/ttyS0, udp eth0`).
- The primary bears the load whenever it is up and running (`nice_failback off`).
- The primary and secondary nodes are `lvs1.example.net` and `lvs2.example.net` respectively (`node lines`).

NOTE

Currently, heartbeat works only between two systems. A possible enhancement being considered is to allow for more than two nodes and to determine the primary by election among the configured nodes based on load or some other factor.

The next file that you must create to get heartbeat working is the authkeys file. This file is used to ensure that only the nodes in the failover configuration are able to respond to the heartbeat messages. It defines the authentication method to use, which is one of crc, sha1, or md5 and a key to use (except for crc). Listing 16.4 shows a sample authkeys file, which should set to file mode 600 and should by default reside in `/etc/ha.d`. The file mode would be set with the command `chmod 600 /etc/ha.d/authkeys`.

LISTING 16.4 `/etc/ha.d/authkeys`

```
#
#       Authentication file.  Must be mode 600
#
```

LISTING 16.4 Continued

```
#       Must have exactly one auth directive at the front.
#       auth    send authentication using this method-id
#
#       Then, list the method and key that go with that method-id
#
#       Available methods: crc sha1, md5.  Crc doesn't need/want a key.
#
#       You normally have only one authentication method-id listed in
#       this file
#
#       Put more than one to make a smooth transition when changing auth
#       methods and/or keys.
#
#       sha1 is believed to be the "best," md5 next best.
#
#       crc adds no security, except from packet corruption.
#               Use only on physically secure networks.
#
auth 2
#1 crc
2 sha1 ultramonkey
#3 md5 Hello!
```

This sample authkeys file defines the authentication method as sha1, which is considered to be the most secure and defines the key that the servers will use in heartbeat messages. You should, of course, define your own key, which can be any string you choose. I recommend that you use keys that follow the same general rules as those you would apply to creating a password—namely, that it should probably not be a dictionary word and that it is not easy to guess.

Now that we have the ha.cf file and the authkeys file, we can look at the final file used by heartbeat, the haresources file. This file specifies the services to transfer from the primary to the secondary system during a failover. For example, if you were using heartbeat between two systems that acted as your mail server, you could have heartbeat start sendmail on the secondary node when the primary fails. Here is an example haresources file taken from the Ultramonkey Web site. This sample file could be used for the Web load-balancer systems in our Site B network (refer to Figure 16.2).

LISTING 16.5 /etc/ha.d/haresources

```
#
#       /etc/ha.d/haresources
#
#       haresources to configure heartbeat with one resource
```

LISTING 16.5 Continued

```
#        that has a master host va4. The resource will take over
#        one IP address and run ldirectord to monitor the
#        real servers.
#
#    This is a list of resources that move from machine to machine as
#    nodes go down and come up in the cluster.  Do not include
#    "administrative" or fixed IP addresses in this file.
#
#    We refer to this file when we're coming up and when a machine
#    is being taken over after going down.
#
#    You need to make this right for your installation and then install it in
#    /etc/ha.d
#
#    These resources in this file are either IP addresses or the name
#    of scripts to run to "start" or "stop" the given resource.
#
#    The format is like this:
#
#node-name resource1 resource2 ... resourceN
#
lvs1.example.net IPaddr::205.238.143.5/24 ldirectord::ldirectord.cf
```

The file in Listing 16.5 specifies that `lvs1.example.net` is the primary in this high availability pair, that the virtual IP address to use is 205.238.143.5, and that when the failover occurs, the ldirectord script should be run to bring up the load-balancing software with a command-line argument of `ldirectord.cf`. A variation of this file that would be suitable for the load balancers in the Site A sample network (shown in Figure 16.1) is shown in Listing 16.6. Please note that although this listing shows two lines, you must enter everything on a single line in the actual file.

LISTING 16.6 `/etc/ha.d/haresources` for Site A Network

```
lvs1.example.net IPaddr::205.238.143.5/24/eth0
IPaddr::192.168.10.5/24/eth1 ldirectord::ldirectord.cf
```

This file sets up the internal and the external facing virtual IP addresses and again starts ldirectord with a command-line argument of ldirectord.cf when a failover occurs.

Now that we have seen what heartbeat does, we can take a look at another utility that comes with Ultramonkey—the Linux Director, ldirectord.

The Linux Director, ldirectord

As we discussed earlier, ldirectord is a Perl script that performs two primary functions. These functions are to define the virtual and real servers associated with a virtual service and to manage the real server pool. We will look briefly at both functions and see how using this software can make the work of using LVS much easier. To get started, let's take a look at the ldirectord configuration file that we would use to accomplish the same thing that we accomplished previously with the ipvsadm command directly. This configuration file is shown here in Listing 16.7. It differs from the example we did earlier in that this time, we will be using the port, protocol, IP method to define both the Web and FTP virtual services and will not be using the firewall mark method at all.

LISTING 16.7 `ldirectord.cf`

```
#
# Sample ldirectord configuration file
#

# Global Directives
checktimeout=3
checkinterval=1
fallback=127.0.0.1:80

# Define the Web virtual service.
# method
virtual=205.238.143.5:80
        real=192.168.10.12:80 masq
        real=192.168.10.14:80 masq
        real=192.168.10.16:80 masq
        real=192.168.10.18:80 masq
        real=192.168.10.20:80 masq
        service=http
        request="/index.html"
        receive="Test Page"
        scheduler=wlc
        protocol=tcp

# Define the FTP virtual service.
virtual=205.238.143.5:21
        real=192.168.10.30:21 masq
        real=192.168.10.32:21 masq
        real=192.168.10.34:21 masq
    fallback=127.0.0.1:21
        service=ftp
```

LISTING 16.7 Continued

```
        scheduler=rr
        login="anonymous"
    passwd="ldirectord@localhost"
    request="welcome.msg"
    receive="test"
        persistent=600
        protocol=tcp
```

Having created this file, we could the invoke ldirectord with the name of our configuration file as an argument. This would cause ldirectord to invoke the appropriate ipvsadm commands to implement the services that we previously implemented by hand on the command line. As an alternative, if we are using heartbeat and have a failover pair of load-balancing hosts, heartbeat is used to start ldirectord.

This brings us to the next function of ldirectord, which is managing the real server pool. In the definition of the HTTP service shown in the listing, there are two lines: one that specifies a file to request and one following it that specifies a string to look for in the response. These two lines are

```
        request="/index.html"
        receive="Test Page"
```

You will also notice in the section following the comment `Global Directives` that these values are defined:

```
checktimeout=3
checkinterval=1
```

What these values do is to specify how often the real servers should be checked to see whether they are up and running and how long one of them can be down before we remove it from the real server pool. Here is how the real server management works.

Once every N seconds, where N is defined by the checkinterval variable, the ldirectord requests the file /index.html from each of the real servers. The response from the real server is then compared to the value you specify using the 'receive' variable, in this case, the string "Test Page". If the server does not respond with the correct string within the timeout specified by the 'checktimeout' variable, a command is issued to remove the real server from the LVS table. In this way, if one of the real servers in the back end falls over for any reason, it is removed from the pool of servers and no traffic is lost. Contrast this with a load-balancing method such as round-robin DNS, and you can see the obvious advantage. Instead of losing the traffic that would have been directed to a server that is not responding, you lose the connection that exists at the time of the crash, but a simple reconnection attempt by the client results in their traffic being redirected to another back end server. This means that you are now free to fix the problem on the server at your leisure.

As you might guess, ldirectord is a useful utility; to accomplish the same thing without it would require that you monitor each of your back end servers and remove them from the LVS tables manually or that you write your own monitoring solution.

Now that we have seen what Ultramonkey does and the tools that it uses, we can move on to another product which does the same thing—Piranha.

Piranha

In many ways, Piranha is like Ultramonkey. However, you should be aware of some key differences. These differences are primarily in the tools that come with Piranha, but other differences exist as well. In this section, we see what Piranha does, describe the tools that make up this product, and look at some sample configuration files. So let's get started with a look at what Piranha does.

What It Does

Like Ultramonkey, Piranha is a superset of LVS in that it uses the LVS patches to the Linux kernel to do the load balancing. It differs from Ultramonkey in the tools used to control LVS and to implement failover services.

Piranha was created by developers at Red Hat and was included with Red Hat version 6.x, but with the release of version 7.0 of Red Hat, Piranha was removed from the base distribution and made a separate product. The value it adds to LVS, just as with Ultramonkey, is that it bundles into an integrated package all the utilities required to set up failover services and load balancing. Although it is not included with the 7.x release of Red Hat, it is still available as a separate product built on an updated 6.2-based system. Red Hat calls this its High Availability Server product.

Advantages of Using Piranha

One of the key advantages to using Piranha is that it includes as part of the tool suite, a Web-based configuration tool that allows you to build configuration files for the lvs and fos daemons and to manage the real server pool. The lvs daemon is a program that manages the real server pool much like ldirectord does with Ultramonkey. The fos daemon is used for failover systems. This is a replacement for the original GUI tool that was shipped with Piranha and the use of the GUI is discouraged because it is no longer being maintained. In addition to the Web-based configuration tool, the monitoring tool, nanny, included with Piranha, allows you to do weight adjustments based on server load. If you select the weighted least-connection or weighted round-robin scheduling algorithms, the weights are adjusted, if necessary, each time the monitoring process checks to make sure that the server is still online. However, this feature is available only if you use Linux on your real servers, because it relies on a software client running on them.

Limitations of Piranha

One of the limitations of Piranha is that if you want support from Red Hat, you must use Red Hat's kernel and the version of LVS that it selects. This means that you might not be able to take advantage of all the latest features. For example, the ipvsadm utility that comes with Red Hat 6.2 does not support the firewall mark method of defining virtual services, and even if you updated the ipvsadm utility to a newer version, you would find that you would also have to create your own customized kernel with a newer version of the LVS patches to take full advantage of the complete feature set. In addition, if you want to use the Web interface, you will not be able to use all the features—even if you did upgrade your kernel and ipvsadm utility—unless you are also willing to make your own modifications to the PHP source for the Web interface software. This limitation is lessened somewhat in the most recent versions of Piranha because they have removed ipvsadm from the package and you might choose to run the most recent versions.

Now that we have discussed briefly some of the features of Piranha and the advantages and disadvantages of using it, we can look at the specific tools that make up Piranha and how they are used.

The Tool Suite

Piranha is distributed as a set of packages in RPM format. Three packages that you must install come with Red Hat 6.x. These packages are

- piranha
- piranha-docs
- piranha-gui

The first of these is the piranha RPM, which contains the lvs daemon, the fos daemon, pulse, nanny, send_arp, supporting manual pages, and a few documents. This package is absolutely required to use Piranha.

The second package is the piranha-docs RPM, which contains more detailed documentation on the Piranha suite as well as supporting documentation for LVS. This package is optional, but recommended.

The final package in the set is the piranha-gui RPM, which contains the Piranha-executable (the deprecated GUI interface) and the Web-based configuration tool. If you want to use this tool, you must install this package; however, if you are willing to configure the software by hand, you can omit this package.

If you are using Red Hat 6.2, one other utility is included in the piranha package—ipvsadm. However, if you update to the most recent version of Piranha, you must install ipvsadm separately.

Assuming that you have these packages installed, we can take a look at the individual tools included and how they are configured, starting with the lvs daemon.

The pulse Daemon

One of the software tools that comes with Piranha is the pulse daemon. This daemon is a heartbeat daemon much like the heartbeat tool found in the Ultramonkey tool suite. It is used by Piranha to monitor the nodes in a failover cluster and is responsible for starting the lvs or fos daemons on the currently active node in the failover pair. This daemon is the one you start after you have used the Piranha GUI to configure your load-balancing or failover services. To keep things simple, the designers decided to use the same configuration file for this daemon as for the lvs and fos daemons—namely, /etc/lvs.cf.

One way in which pulse and heartbeat differ is in the handling of the primary and backup nodes. As we previously discussed regarding heartbeat, when a primary node fails, the backup node takes over the services as defined in the configuration files. With heartbeat, when the primary comes back online, it initiates another failover and resumes the services specified in the configuration files. This can have the undesirable effect of interrupting transactions unnecessarily. On the other hand, if you are using pulse when a primary fails, the backup node takes over, becoming primary. When the primary comes back online, it becomes the backup unless you start the pulse daemon with the `--forceactive` option, which will cause a failover to occur. The heartbeat daemon uses a configuration variable to control this behavior.

The lvs Daemon

The lvs daemon performs the same set of functions as the ldirectord daemon that comes with Ultramonkey. It works in a similar fashion, calling ipvsadm to manage the LVS tables in the kernel, and calling nanny to perform the real server management and monitoring functions. It relies on a configuration file that defaults to /etc/lvs.cf that defines the virtual services and the associated back end servers. This software can be run either as a daemon, which is its normal mode of operation, or for purposes of testing and debugging, it can be run in the foreground. The software is normally not started by itself, but instead is started by the pulse daemon, just as ldirectord is normally started by heartbeat. To get a better feel for what the lvs daemon does, let's take a look at its help statement and some of the more commonly used options. The help statement, which is obtained by running `"lvs --help"` is shown here in Listing 16.8.

LISTING 16.8 The lvs Daemon Help Message

```
# lvs --help
Usage: lvs [OPTION...]
```

LISTING 16.8 Continued

```
  -c, --configfile=configfile   Configuration file
  -n, --nodaemon                Don't run as a daemon
  --nofork                      Don't fork, but do disassociate
  --version            Display program version
  -t, --test-start              Display what commands would be run on startup,
                                but don't actually run anything

Help options
  -?, --help                    Show this help message
  --usage                       Display brief usage message
```

One thing that you will notice if you compare this help message with the manual page is that they do not match. Specifically, an extra option is indicated in the help message that is not present in the manual page. This option is the `--nofork` option, which is rarely used. As we stated, the lvs daemon performs the same function as Linux Director. To see this, let's take a look at the sample lvs.cf file shown in Listing 16.9.

LISTING 16.9 `/etc/lvs.cf`

```
primary = 205.238.143.2
backup = 205.238.143.4
service = lvs
rsh_command = ssh
backup_active = 1
heartbeat = 1
heartbeat_port = 539
keepalive = 6
deadtime = 18
network = nat
nat_router = 192.168.10.5 eth1:1

virtual www {
     active = 1
     address = 205.238.143.5 eth0:1
     port = 80
     send = "GET / HTTP/1.0\r\n\r\n"
     expect = "HTTP"
     load_monitor = rup
     scheduler = wlc
     protocol = tcp
     timeout = 6
     reentry = 15
```

LISTING 16.9 Continued

```
     server www1 {
         address = 192.168.10.12
         active = 1
         weight = 1
     }

     server www2 {
         address = 192.168.10.14
         active = 1
         weight = 1
     }

     server www3 {
         address = 192.168.10.16
         active = 1
         weight = 1
     }

     server www4 {
         address = 192.168.10.18
         active = 1
         weight = 1
     }

     server www5 {
         address = 192.168.10.20
         active = 1
         weight = 1
     }

}

virtual ftp {
     active = 1
     address = 205.238.143.5 eth0:1
     port = 21
     send = "\n"
     load_monitor = rup
     scheduler = rr
     protocol = tcp
     persistent = 60
     pmask = 255.255.255.255
     timeout = 6
     reentry = 15
```

LISTING 16.9 Continued

```
    server ftp1 {
        address = 192.168.10.30
        active = 1
    }

    server ftp2 {
        address = 192.168.10.32
        active = 1
    }

    server ftp3 {
        address = 192.168.10.34
        active = 1
    }

}
```

As you might have guessed, this configuration file is what could be used for our sample Site A network. It defines the primary and backup lvs hosts, how often to check that the primary is alive and how long before a failover occurs, the routing method for LVS to use (in this case NAT), and the VIP that is used by the real servers as their default gateway. It then defines the two virtual services, Web and FTP, and the real servers associated with them. The syntax is very straightforward, and although you could create it by hand, this file is normally generated by the Web interface. For a complete list of the keywords and their meanings, refer to the lvs.cf(5) manual page.

The fos Daemon

For simple failover services, Piranha comes with a separate program called fos, which works in a manner very similar to heartbeat. This program uses the same default configuration file as the lvs daemon, /etc/lvs.cf. Just like lvs, the heartbeat between systems is handled by pulse, and the fos daemon is usually started by pulse. The fos daemon could be used to implement the failover between systems, such as the mail servers in the Site A network example or any other set of systems where you want the capability to automatically failover to a backup system in the event of a server failure. A sample of the configuration that would be required to do this is shown in Listing 16.10. This is how you would configure fos to implement the mail server pair in Figure 16.1.

LISTING 16.10 /etc/lvs.cf

```
primary = 205.238.143.15
backup = 205.238.143.17
service = fos
```

LISTING 16.10 Continued

```
rsh_command = ssh
backup_active = 1
heartbeat = 1
heartbeat_port = 539
keepalive = 2
deadtime = 10
network = direct

failover mail {
     address = 205.238.143.50 eth0:1
     active = 1
     port = 25
     timeout = 6
     send = "\n"
     start_cmd = "/etc/rc.d/init.d/sendmail start"
     stop_cmd = "/etc/rc.d/init.d/sendmail stop"
}
```

In this example, note that the service is specified as fos instead of lvs. This tells the pulse daemon to start the fos daemon instead of the lvs daemon. The address specified in the failover mail section is the virtual IP to use for this service and the interface on which to set up this IP address. Also note that a start and stop command used to start the services to run on the failover pair are specified. You could use one set of machines and fos to provide multiple services simply by adding more failover stanzas to the configuration file. Again, this file is usually modified by using the Piranha Web interface.

The nanny Utility

The Piranha software includes the nanny utility to monitor either the real servers in a load-balancing pool or the backup system in a failover service pair. In the case of the load-balancing pool, it is the one that calls the ipvsadm daemon to modify the LVS tables in the kernel, taking servers in and out of service as required and also adjusting the weight values based on the server loads. In the case of the failover pair, the nanny utility is the one that issues the specified start or stop command as required during a failover operation. Like the rest of the Piranha utilities, nanny uses the `/etc/lvs.cf` file.

The send_arp Utility

A special purpose tool is included with the Piranha software to allow for the fast takeover of IP addresses that occurs when a failover happens. This utility is the send_arp utility, and it sends a gratuitous ARP. This forces systems that know about the virtual IP address of the load-balancing pair, or failover pair, to update their ARP tables to include the MAC address of the currently active member of the server pair. This is necessary so that a failover does not have to wait for any ARP entry timeouts and to prevent traffic destined for the virtual IP address to go to a machine that is down.

The Piranha Web-Based Interface

One of the nice features of Piranha that is not shared by Ultramonkey is the Web-based interface that allows you to create the lvs.cf file for your load-balancing or failover systems. Let's take a look at the different screens and briefly explain what they do. But before we do, you must first set the Piranha password by using this piranha-passwd utility found in /usr/sbin. The following command must be issued to set an initial password for the Piranha user, which is the owner of the /etc/lvs.cf file.

```
# /usr/sbin/piranha-passwd <password string>
```

Of course, you would replace *<password string>* with the password of your choosing. After you have done this, you can start the Web-based configuration tools by accessing your host on which you installed Piranha in a Web browser. The system you connect to must be running the Apache Web server and have PHP installed and configured. This is detailed in the readme file installed with the piranha-docs package. The following is an excerpt from that file regarding the installation requirements.

LISTING 16.11 Excerpt from README File

```
Installation Notes:
```

1. Apache and PHP must be installed on the system in order to install/upgrade piranha.
2. If you are installing Apache and/or PHP for the first time, you must remember to uncomment the PHP settings and mime types in /etc/httpd/conf/httpd.conf (and possibly in /etc/httpd/conf/srm.conf for earlier apache releases). Then (re)start Apache. You will not be able to view the piranha php files until this is done. Detailed instructions on this are covered in the php INSTALL file.
3. For the web tool (and indeed the gtk tool version) you will need to set up the intended cluster servers to allow remote login of user piranha from each other either via ssh or (less securely) rsh.
4. Connect your web browser to the primary IP on your active/master node as in `http://test.host.name/piranha`.

After you have met the installation requirements, you can start the Web-based interface by accessing `http://piranha.host.name/piranha` in a Web browser, such as Netscape Communicator. This brings up a Web page that looks something like the one shown in Figure 16.8.

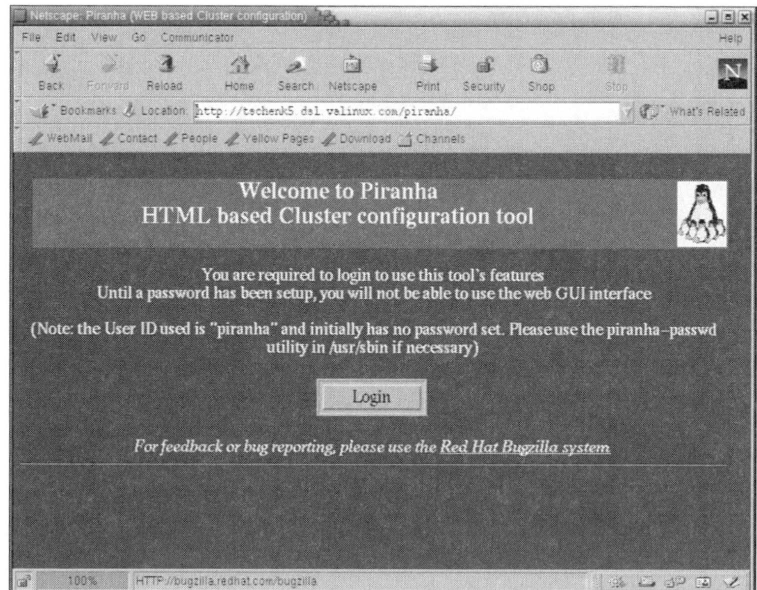

FIGURE 16.8

The Piranha login screen.

When you click on the Login button, you should see a dialog box to log in using the username `piranha` and the password that you supplied to the piranha-passwd command. When you log in, you are presented with the initial Control/Monitoring screen as shown in Figure 16.9.

The Control/Monitoring screen enables you to determine the status of the pulse daemon and if running LVS, the state of the LVS tables in the kernel. The information on this screen is updated automatically at the interval you specify. This allows you to see at a glance how the server pool is doing. If, on the other hand, you are running a failover service, this screen will have little to show you except whether pulse is running. The other option you have on this screen is the Change Password button, which, as of Piranha release 0.4.14, only displays a message telling you how to change the password with the piranha-passwd command.

The next tab of the configuration tool is the Global Settings tab, which displays the another form that allows you to choose between lvs and fos managed services, the lvs.cf synchronization method to use. The preferred synchronization method is via ssh because this is more secure than the alternative, rsh. In addition, if you are running a lvs managed service, you can select the routing method to use. You should make any selections you desire and then click the Accept button. This screen is shown in Figure 16.10.

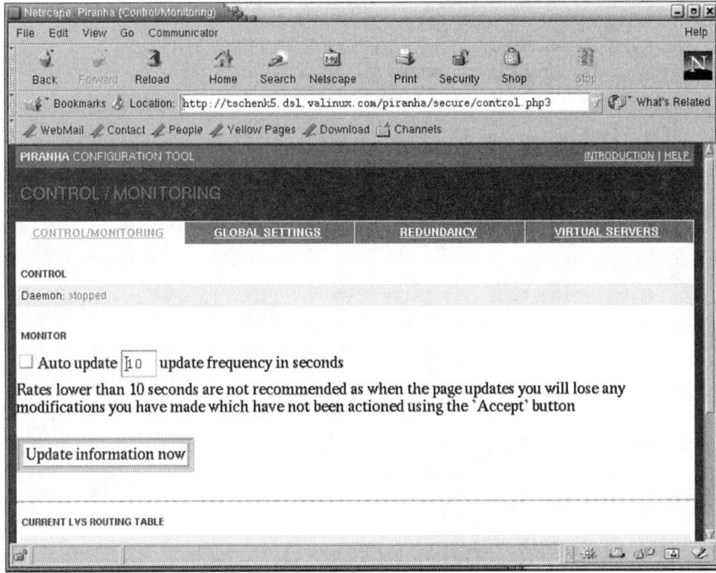

FIGURE 16.9

The Control/Monitoring screen.

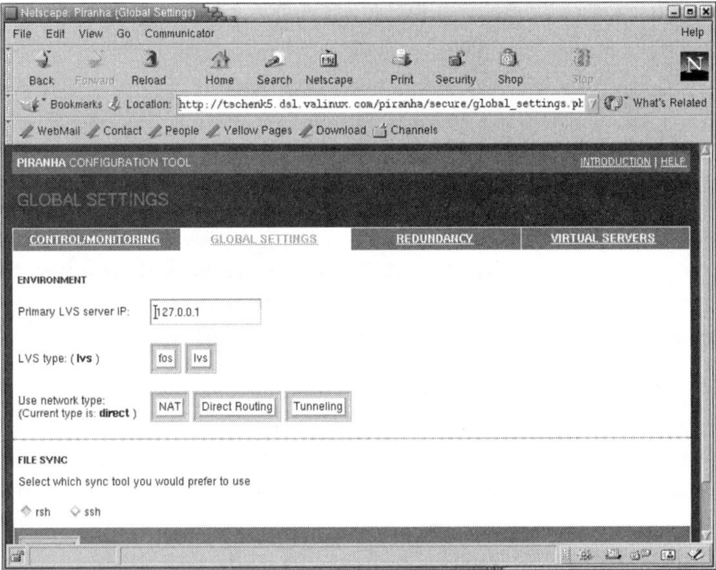

FIGURE 16.10

The Global Settings screen.

The next tab is the Redundancy screen. For lvs services, this is optional; however, I highly recommend that you run a backup load balancer to eliminate the single point of failure a single load balancer would represent. To enable a backup server, you must click the Enable button. After you do this, you should enter the real IP address of the backup server, the heartbeat interval, how long a server is dead before a failover occurs, and the port to use for the heartbeat packets. Again, you should fill in the appropriate values for your setup and click the Accept button to write the corresponding variables to the /etc/lvs.cf file. The Redundancy screen is shown in Figure 16.11.

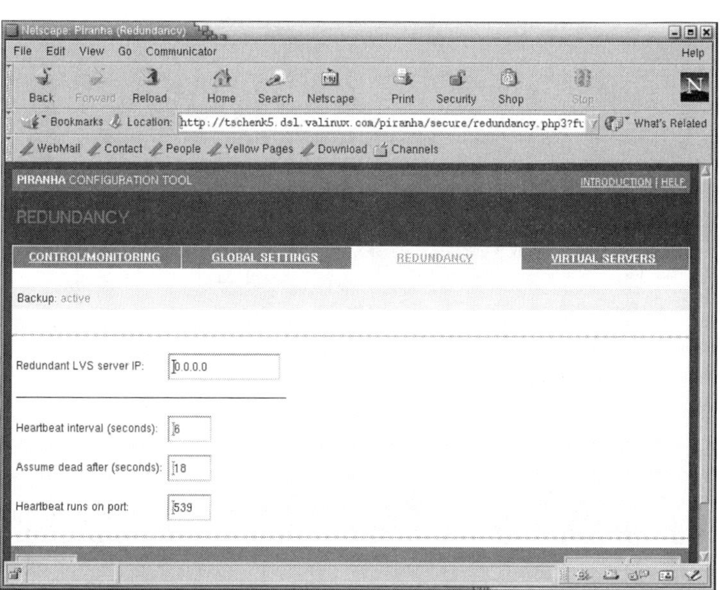

FIGURE 16.11
The Redundancy screen.

The contents of the final tab depend on whether you specified lvs or fos on the Global Settings screen. If you selected lvs, the final tab is the Virtual Servers screen, as shown in Figure 16.12. On this screen, you add virtual services by clicking the Add button. After you have done this, you should click the Edit button, which brings up another screen where you define the virtual services. On this subscreen, you can select additional subscreens where you specify the real servers and the monitoring parameters. If you specified fos on the Global Settings screen, the final tab is the Failover screen, which is similar to the Virtual Servers screen, as you can see in Figure 16.13. Again, to add a failover service, click the Add button and then the Edit button. This brings up a subscreen, which, like the subscreen from the Virtual Servers tab, allows you to define the failover services you want to run and to specify the monitoring parameters. As with the other screen, click Accept to write the changes to the /etc/lvs.cf file.

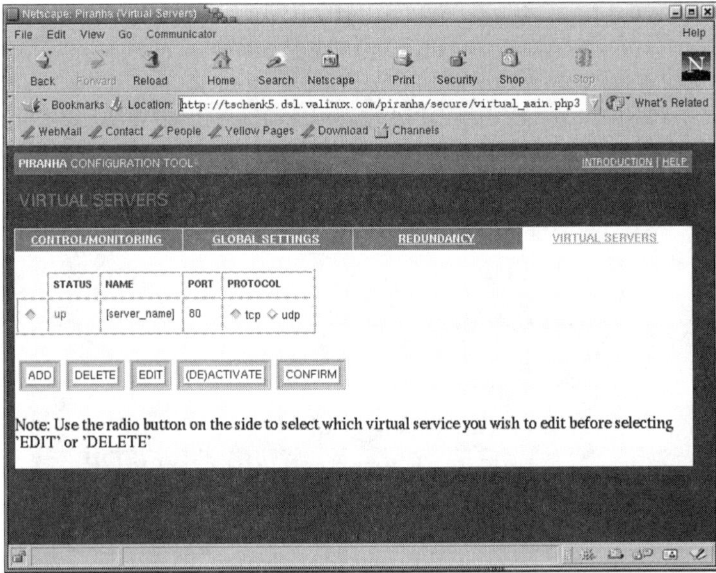

FIGURE 16.12

The Virtual Servers screen.

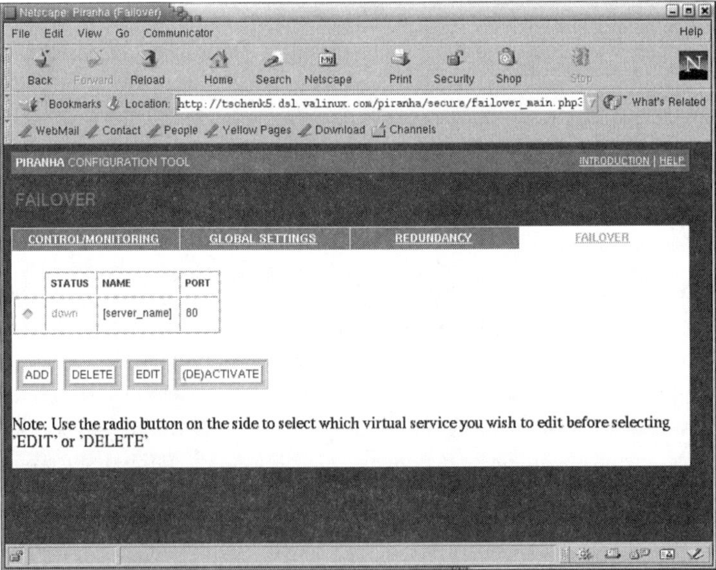

FIGURE 16.13

The Failover screen.

As you can see, using this Web-based interface is much easier than doing the configuration by hand, and as an added bonus, you are ensured that the configuration file is syntactically correct. The Web-based interface has the additional value of being accessible to multiple platforms, which is the reason why it was developed and the Piranha GUI interface was deprecated.

This completes our discussion of the Piranha tool suite. We are now ready to look at a final open source package that allows you to move beyond load balancing at a single site.

Super Sparrow

If you run a large Internet site, you might find it useful to create points of presence at multiple sites located in different facilities around the country or world. This practice gives you redundancy beyond that which can be achieved at a single site and therefore, greater availability in the event of a failure. Having thus dispersed your site to various locations, it would then be beneficial to your users if you could somehow direct them to the sites that are closest to them geographically to reduce network latency. This is where Super Sparrow comes in. Super Sparrow is a relatively new project that allows you to accomplish geographic load balancing in much the same manner as products such as Cisco's Global Director. In this section, we take a look at how this is accomplished and then look at the tool suite for Super Sparrow. We'll also see some sample configuration files.

What It Does

Super Sparrow is under active development and is the work of some of the same people as those who developed Ultramonkey. This work is sponsored by VA Linux, and you can view the Super Sparrow Web page at SourceForge at `http://supersparrow.sourceforge.net/`. There you will find the tools you need to implement this solution, as well as some documentation on the various tools. So let's take a look at what Super Sparrow is by first looking at the problem it tries to solve.

Why Global Load Balancing?

Content is the lifeblood of the Internet. People go online to look for interesting content and it behooves the content providers to make this content as easily accessible to users as possible. One of the things that makes content more accessible is to have it served from multiple locations. By distributing the content to multiple locations, users are no longer held hostage to overloaded servers or outages, because if the content is available at multiple locations, you merely have to point at one of the multiple servers that has the content you desire. Historically, this has been accomplished using mirror sites. A mirror site is basically a copy of the original site that is periodically synchronized with the master site. The user can then choose to look at the master site or any of the mirrors that are available. The problem with this scheme is that the onus is on the users, who might not know about the mirrors or who might select a mirror site that is very distant from them geographically. The solution to this is to take the decision of which server to choose from out of the hands of the user.

To understand the goal we are trying to achieve, let's imagine that we have implemented our site and have it mirrored at three locations around the country. Suppose that we have our master site located in Austin, Texas. We create mirrors of our site in San Jose, California and New York, New York. To provide our customers with the best possible response times, we want to service our East Coast users from the New York site, the customers in the middle of the country from our Austin site and those customers on the West Coast from our San Jose site. We have two options. The first is to tell our customers to select the site nearest them. The problem with this is that some people are just lazy and will always choose the default location, even if it is across the country from them. The other option—and the one that Super Sparrow allows you to implement—is to somehow determine to which site customers are closest and redirect them to that site. This is what global load balancing is all about. The advantages to global load balancing are the following: Because the packets have to travel less distance, they arrive at the client's system faster, giving them better response time. In addition, if a mirror site goes down, for whatever reason, the traffic to that site can then be directed to another site, thus improving reliability. Your customers are happy because they get better service, and you are happy because you have made your site more reliable.

How Does It Work?

The way in which global load balancing is achieved is through the use of modern routing protocols. Most modern routers are capable of finding the shortest path from one point on the Internet to another. The routing protocol that makes this possible is the border gateway protocol, or BGP. A router that uses BGP can determine the best path to take through the network to get from point A to point B. This is an over-simplification of what it does; however, for the purposes of our discussion, this definition will suffice. Because this is true, we have a basis on which to build a load-balancing solution that uses this information to distribute connection requests from clients to the server that is closest to them on the network. Super Sparrow uses two methods to distribute connection requests. These methods are

- By means of a modified DNS server
- By use of URL redirects by Apache

Let's take a look at each of these methods, starting with the DNS server method.

The Modified DNS Server Approach

For the purposes of this discussion, let us imagine the following scenario. A site, www.example.com, is located at a point of presence, POP A, and is mirrored at another point of presence, POP B. Both POPs are running the modified DNS server and are authoritative for the domain example.com. Given this setup, the basic algorithm works as follows:

1. A client sends a lookup request to its local DNS server for www.example.com, which queries either the POP A DNS server or the POP B DNS server (it doesn't matter which; both are authoritative for example.com).
2. The modified POP A (or B) DNS server uses the IP address of the DNS server of the client to query the router on its respective networks to determine the best route between either POP and the DNS server of the client.
3. Based on this routing information, an IP address for www.example.com is returned to the client, and the client makes the connection to that server.

If you think about this, you can see one obvious problem. That problem is that it assumes that the DNS server for a client is one that is close to the client, as would be the case for a local dial-up user to a local ISP. Where this assumption breaks down is if the client is pointing at a DNS server that is not local to it. If the DNS server used by the client is near the client, determining the best route between the POP and the DNS server is about as effective as would be determining the best route between the POP and the client itself. However, if the DNS server used by the client is not near, the route selected might not be the best one to reach the client. An advantage of this scenario is that if one of the POPs is down, the DNS queries to it will fail and the DNS server will direct the client to the other POP transparently.

The Apache URL Redirection Approach

Now let's consider this slightly different scenario. The site www.example.com is as before, mirrored between POP A and POP B. However, this time, instead of running modified DNS servers at each of these POPs, we run Apache with the mod_rewrite module loaded. The name www.example.com is shared by all the Web servers at both POPs. In this case, the algorithm works like this:

1. The client requests a connection to www.example.com and is sent to one of the Apache servers by means of the normal round-robin DNS algorithm.
2. The Apache server that receives the request has a rewrite rule in effect that causes all requests for a particular type of document to be passed to an external program. The IP address of the client is passed to this external program.
3. The external program uses the IP address of the client and queries the routers at POP A and POP B to determine which one has the best route to the client address. This information is passed back to Apache, which rewrites the URL to redirect the connection request to a server at the POP that has the best route to the client.

The key advantage of this method is that you are certain to get the best possible route from the client to a POP because we are able to use the IP address of the client instead of the client's DNS server. Another advantage is that the granularity of the DNS method is per host, whereas the granularity of the Apache method is per request. For example, you could load balance only requests for ad banners (*.gif files) instead of for every connection. The key disadvantage of this method is that if a POP fails, there is no way to tell the Apache servers to stop redirecting to it, because it has no way of telling that the POP is down.

Now that we have an idea of how it works, let's take a look at the individual pieces of the Super Sparrow tool suite.

The Tool Suite

The Super Sparrow project is made up of a number of tools, and which ones you require depends on whether you want to use DNS or Apache to perform the redirection. These tools fall into the following categories:

- Route servers
- Support libraries
- Router query tools

We will look at each of the categories and discuss how they fit into Super Sparrow.

Route Servers

The Super Sparrow developers had a number of choices during the design phase, and one of them was whether to develop yet another BGP implementation. They chose not to and instead decided that they would make Super Sparrow work with a number of existing route servers. A route server is either a host running a routing daemon or a dedicated piece of routing hardware. The developers built in support to be able to use Gated, the routing daemon from the MeritGated Consortium; Zebra, a routing daemon developed as part of the GNU project; and the Cisco IOS, the operating system used by Cisco routers. This means that you must choose to run one of these three if you want to use Super Sparrow as part of your load-balancing solution.

Support Libraries

The next part of the Super Sparrow solution is the support libraries. The key library is called libsupersparrow and it is available both in source code and binary formats at `http://supersparrow.sourceforge.net`. In addition, because Super Sparrow is sponsored by VA Linux, you also need to get the VAnessa support libraries, which are used to handle logging and other functions. VAnessa is the VA Linux parent project of both Super Sparrow and Ultramonkey and helps to unify the two into a total load-balancing solution. For more information about VAnessa, you can refer to the VAnessa Web site at `http://vanessa.sourceforge.net`.

Router Query Tools

Based on your decision whether to use the modified DNS server approach or the Apache mod_rewrite approach, you will need either mod_supersparrow, which is a loadable module for the Dents DNS server, or supersparrow, a standalone program that is intended to be called by the mod_rewrite modules of the Apache Web server. Dents is a modular DNS server that is intended to be a drop-in replacement for Bind, the most popular DNS server on the Internet today. The mod_supersparrow module relies on the libsupersparrow and allows Dents to answer queries based on the result of querying route servers. The standalone program supersparrow performs the same function as the mod_supersparrow, but for the Apache Web server instead of the Dents DNS server.

Super Sparrow is a relatively young solution, and using it is not for the weak hearted; however, it does provide an open source solution to a problem that continues to grow in importance. If you are interested in learning more about this product, an excellent source of information is the white paper, "Globally Distributed Content (Taking Over the World Using BGP)," written by the lead Super Sparrow developer, Simon Hormans. This white paper is available at the Super Sparrow home page.

Summary

In this chapter, we have looked at some of the open source tools that can be used for load balancing and failover. These tools allow you to implement the ideas we discussed in Chapter 11 on high availability and scalability. These solutions enable you to design your network from the beginning in such a manner as to allow for future growth without costing an arm and a leg. However, if you are interested in other options, be sure to take a look at Chapter 17, "Commercial Load-Balancing Alternatives," in which we'll discuss some of the commercial alternatives to these open source products.

Commercial Load-Balancing Alternatives

CHAPTER

17

IN THIS CHAPTER

- BigIP 360
- Cisco LocalDirector 362
- Other Products 364

In Chapter 16, "Open Source High Availability and Scalability," we examined a few of the open source tools that can be used to do load balancing for your Web site to allow it to scale up as your site grows. In this chapter, we take a look at some commercial alternatives to these products and the advantages and disadvantages of each. We will focus on two of the most popular load-balancing solutions, BigIP from F5 Networks and LocalDirector from Cisco, but we also will take a look at a few other products—both software and hardware—that are available and work well with Linux-based Web solutions. So let's get started with a look at BigIP.

BigIP

One of the popular load-balancing solutions available today is BigIP from F5 Networks. BigIP is an Internet appliance that sits between your Internet servers and the Internet. In this section, we start with an overview of BigIP and then take a look at the features of BigIP, including the load-balancing methods used, the configuration method used, and optional features. After we have completed this overview and examination of the features, we look at the advantages and disadvantages of this product.

BigIP Product Description

BigIP refers to a line of products from F5 Networks that does load balancing in a manner very similar to the products described in Chapter 16. The BigIP product line consists of a network appliance (a PC in a fancy box) running a customized version of BSDI. The basic differences in the BigIP product lines are based on the speed of the PC processor found in it, the amount of memory and disk space, and the number of systems that make up the solution. For example, the BigIP Enterprise system is a Pentium III processor running at 933MHz, with 1GB of RAM and a 15GB hard drive. It comes in a 4U rackmount enclosure, and if you request the high-availability configuration, you get two of these systems. If you contrast this with the entry-level system in the BigIP line, the BigIP Load Balancer, you see that this system comes with a slower processor, only 128MB of RAM, and a smaller hard drive.

The other differences between the products are in the software that comes with the system. For example, the Enterprise system comes with additional software for network monitoring and trending. Other products in the BigIP line are designed for special-purpose load balancing, such as a system to support firewalls, cache systems, and e-commerce solutions. For a complete look at the products in the BigIP product family, check the company's Web site at `http://www.f5.com/`.

Features of the BigIP Product Line

Now that you have a basic idea of what BigIP is, let's take a look at the features of the entry-level system—the BigIP Load Balancer. The BigIP Load Balancer is designed for load-balancing Web servers. It supports several load-balancing options, including

- Fastest
- Round robin
- Least connections
- Ratios

These are very similar to the algorithms supported by the Linux Virtual Server (LVS), with the exception that LVS doesn't support the fastest, in which a connection request is sent to the server that responds the fastest. The ratios option allows you to assign weights to servers to take into account variations in the servers, such as capacity.

To continue our comparison to LVS, let's look at the routing methods supported by BigIP. These methods are NAT and what F5 Networks refers to as nPath. The network address translation (NAT) method works just like it does with LVS, in which all packets enter and leave the real server network via the BigIP appliance. The nPath method allows you to bypass the BigIP system on the way back to the client. This routing method is the same as the direct routing method used by LVS in that you must configure the real servers in the back end and assign the IP address for the service to the loopback interface. This means that you are faced with the same restrictions as you are with LVS regarding the back end servers; you must be able to assign an address to the loopback interface and set it to not respond to ARP requests.

Other features of BigIP Load Balancer include the capability to provide high availability by adding a second BigIP Controller, SNMP monitoring capabilities, and three persistence modes so that connections that require it can be made to "stick" to a particular server in the back end. BigIP also includes VLAN support so that you can segregate traffic on a single physical network into multiple virtual networks. In addition, because the BigIP software is based on the BSDI kernel, there is full TCP/IP network support. Another result of being based on BSDI is that you have multiple methods available to configure your BigIP controller. Supported methods include a Web-based interface for those who prefer a point-and-click interface and SSH support for those who prefer to login and use the command line.

As you might expect, if you move beyond the entry-level system in the BigIP line, you get additional features. For example, if you look at the Enterprise Controller, you see that in addition to supporting Web load balancing, it supports load balancing just about any service you choose, including Web caches, firewalls, and any service you can define with a port, protocol, and IP address. In addition, this system includes the SEE-IT network management software, which allows you to monitor your entire network from the BigIP controller. Another added feature is the capability to do redirection to the back-end servers based on application-level data, such as the URL requested. This is sometimes referred to as Layer 7 switching. This is different from LVS, which does switching based on information at the protocol level, or Layer 4 switching, which also is supported by BigIP.

Advantages and Disadvantages of BigIP

As you can see from the features list, there are some advantages to using BigIP over LVS, such as the Layer 7 switching support; however, these advantages come at a price. BigIP appliances start at approximately $8,000 and can go as high as $30,000 or even higher, depending on the options selected. Contrast this with the cost of implementing a LVS solution. A system comparable to the BigIP Load Balancer appliance with a Pentium III, 256MB of RAM, a 9GB drive and dual ethernet can be obtained for less than $2,000—or about one fourth the cost. Given this, you can see that you could add failover capability to your LVS system and still pay about half the price of the BigIP system. The advantage to the BigIP system is that you are backed by its support organization. In addition, with BigIP you can call on the professional services division of F5 Networks to help you implement a BigIP solution. One of the disadvantages of using BigIP is that the appliance is just that—an appliance. With an LVS solution, you could use your LVS system for other duties, such as a DNS server, a firewall, or any other function that is supported by Linux.

Cisco LocalDirector

Another popular load-balancing solution that is available and that works with Linux servers is LocalDirector from Cisco. In this section, we take a brief look at LocalDirector and compare and contrast it with the solutions described in Chapter 16. We begin with an overview of LocalDirector and then describe the features of the product. Next, we describe the advantages and disadvantages of LocalDirector when compared with LVS. So let's get started with the overview.

Overview

The functioning and features of Cisco LocalDirector are very similar to the BigIP appliance from F5 Networks. LocalDirector, like other Cisco products, uses a proprietary operating system that is accessed by logging in to the system and using a command-line interface. For those familiar with the Cisco IOS, the command structure of Cisco LocalDirector is very familiar. Like the BigIP product line, multiple versions of LocalDirector are available to meet the varied needs of different-sized networks. Depending on your needs, you can select different memory and network interface options to allow you to scale the load-balancing services. In addition, like LVS and BigIP, Cisco LocalDirector also is capable of being configured in a high-availability configuration in which two systems are connected in a failover setup.

The Cisco LocalDirector Feature Set

The feature set of the Cisco LocalDirector system is very similar to that of the BigIP line and of LVS. The differences are primarily which load-balancing methods are supported and which routing methods are supported. The load-balancing methods are referred to as predictors in the terminology of the LocalDirector operating system. These methods are

- Fastest
- Round robin
- Least connections

Variations of these also allow you to assign weights to different servers. In this respect, LocalDirector is just like BigIP. Unlike BigIP and LVS, however, LocalDirector also has a Slowstart option that is designed to avoid bombarding a new real server added to the server pool with connections.

To understand this, consider the following scenario. By default, LocalDirector uses the least connections method of distributing traffic to the real server pool. When a new server is brought online, it has zero connections, which would normally result in it being assigned all new connection requests. If this server is added when the site is under load, this could result in the new server being inundated with connection requests that could conceivably cause it to fail. To avoid this, LocalDirector defaults to a mode of operation referred to as slowstart, which causes connections to be distributed among new servers in the server pool using a simple round-robin fashion until the network traffic is stable. After the traffic has stabilized, the connections are distributed using the selected predictor.

Like BigIP, Cisco LocalDirector uses one of two methods of routing packets between the clients and the real server pool. These two methods are equivalent to the NAT and direct-routing methods of LVS; however, in the terminology of LocalDirector, these are referred to as Directed mode and Dispatched mode, respectively. This means that the same restrictions apply to LocalDirector as to LVS and BigIP regarding the operating systems supported in the real server pool. With Directed mode (NAT) there are no restrictions, and with Dispatched mode, you must be able to assign the IP address of the virtual service to both the LocalDirector appliance and all the real servers.

LocalDirector has many other features, including integrated monitoring support for certain types of services, such as Web and DNS. One interesting feature is the capability to set up SNTP (Simple Network Time Protocol) services on the appliance so that this system can not only do the load-balancing duties but also can be used to keep the system time of the servers in sync. Persistence, failover, and support for SNMP monitoring and traps also are available.

Some of the features that differentiate LocalDirector from the competition can be realized only if the appliance is used in conjunction with other Cisco products. For example, if implemented in a network with Cisco Catalyst switches, the LocalDirector system can be configured to do what is called Accelerated Server Load Balancing. This feature uses features of the operating systems on the switches and the load balancer to streamline the traffic between them, resulting in better response times. Naturally, if you use a different brand of switch, this feature is not available.

For a complete list of features of LocalDirector and an explanation of the differences between the models, your best reference is the Cisco Web site, which can be found at `http://www.cisco.com/`.

Advantages and Disadvantages

One of the key advantages of LocalDirector over both BigIP and the LVS solutions described in Chapter 16 is the use of the proprietary real-time operating system on the appliance. Unlike the general purpose kernels of the BigIP and LVS systems, the operating system of the LocalDirector product is streamlined to perform the single function of load balancing, which means that it can do so very efficiently. This also can be a disadvantage of the LocalDirector system because you are required to learn that operating system in addition to the operating system of the back-end servers. Other advantages of using LocalDirector include the integration with other Cisco products, which allows you to use the accelerated options discussed earlier. As with BigIP, these advantages come at a price, which is again where LVS-based solutions win. Prices for the Cisco LocalDirector products range from about $8,000 to upwards of $20,000, depending on the options selected.

Other Products

As you might expect, the explosive growth of the Internet has resulted in a great deal of competition in this market. As a result, many load-balancing solutions are available. These products fall into three basic categories: software load balancers, load-balancing switches, and appliances. In this section, we take a look at a few examples of each and provide pointers to where you can get further information. We begin with a look at software load balancers.

Software Load Balancers

The LVS solutions discussed in Chapter 16 are examples of software-based load-balancing solutions. These products are designed to run on top of a network operating system, such as Linux, Unix, or Windows NT. The advantage here is that you also can run other software on your load-balancing system if you desire. Some examples of software-based load-balancing solutions include

- Central Dispatch
- TurboLinux Cluster Server
- Zeus Load Balancer

Central Dispatch

Of these products, the most highly acclaimed is Central Dispatch from Resonate. This product is available for multiple platforms including Solaris, AIX, HP/UX, Linux, and Windows NT/2000. It is capable of supporting just about any TCP-based protocol, including HTTP, SSL, POP3, SMTP, and FTP, to name a few. One interesting feature of this product is the capability to set quality of service rules to affect the load-balancing decisions, in addition to standard load-balancing algorithms such as round robin, least connection, fastest, and CPU load. This means that you can base your load-balancing decisions on business rules. For example, you can specify that connections from specific addresses get priority treatment. Documentation of this product is available from the Resonate Web site at `http://www.resonate.com/`. On the down side, Central Dispatch is not capable of load balancing UDP traffic. This means that you cannot use Central Dispatch to load balance DNS traffic or some forms of streaming data.

TurboLinux Cluster Server

Yet another software-based load balancer is the TurboLinux Cluster Server product from TurboLinux. This software is based on LVS; however, the current version is not open source. TurboLinux decided that it would keep the most recent release of this product closed source to maintain competitive advantage and to release only older versions of the software with source code. With the release of projects such as Ultramonkey and Piranha, there are no compelling reasons to run TurboLinux Cluster Server unless you also choose to run TurboLinux as your network operating system. The feature set of TurboLinux Cluster Server is almost identical to Piranha. This product is licensed based on the number of real servers that you want to support. One advantage this product has over the competition is the price, which is very reasonable. In addition, with the newest releases, TurboLinux Cluster Server runs not only on TurboLinux, but also on Red Hat Linux systems. More details regarding this product can be found at `http://www.turbolinux.com/`.

Zeus Load Balancer

A lesser-known load balancer from the people who created the Zeus Web server, Zeus Technology, is the Zeus Load Balancer. This product is very similar to Central Dispatch in that it supports a variety of platforms, including Solaris (Sparc and Intel), Linux (Intel and Alpha), HP/UX, Compaq True 64 Unix, Irix, and FreeBSD, with more platforms promised soon. It supports TCP-based services and comes with an easy-to-use Web-based configuration tool. Like Central Dispatch, it lacks support for UDP-based protocols. The Zeus Load Balancer, like Piranha and Ultramonkey, includes support for running in a high-availability pair, and in fact, this is the recommended method. This product differs from the TurboLinux Cluster Server in that the pricing is not based on the number of back-end servers in the real server pool, but it is rather pricey, at $10,000 for the base license plus an additional $5,000 for the annual support contract. One nice thing about this product is that you can try before you buy by downloading a fully functional demo copy from the company's Web site at `http://www.zeus.com/`.

Load-Balancing Switches

The next category of products are load-balancing switches, which differ from appliances like the BigIP product line in that they are simply "smart" switches instead of special-purpose computers. These "smart" switches work like any other switch; however, their operating systems are enhanced to support load-balancing functions. One of the advantages of this approach is that these products often outperform appliances for the same reasons that dedicated routers usually outperform routing daemons. Examples of products that fall into this category include

- Foundry ServerIron
- Alteon ACEDirector
- Radware WebSite Director

One advantage of these products is that you are no longer required to have a separate system for load balancing, which can reduce cost. Many industry analysts believe that these are the products of the future and that appliances such as the BigIP product line will eventually be phased out in favor of these "smart" switches.

Load-Balancing Appliances

The final category of load-balancing tools is the load-balancing appliance. You have already seen two examples of this category in our discussion of the BigIP product line and the Cisco LocalDirector. These systems are basically special-purpose computers. The biggest advantage of these products is that they are usually the most advanced when it comes to configuration utilities and capabilities. As you saw with the BigIP product, the feature list includes many features that are the result of being built on top of a full network operating system. The trade-off is in performance. The load-balancing switches normally run circles around the appliances in benchmarks because of the lesser overhead of their embedded operating systems. In addition to the load-balancing appliances from F5 Networks and Cisco, another example of a product in this category includes the HydraWEB Mercury series, which is described at the company's Web site, `http://www.hydraweb.com/`.

Summary

In this chapter, we have taken a brief look at some of the commercial alternatives for load balancing that are available if you do not want to implement the open source load-balancing solutions described in Chapter 16. We have discussed in some detail two of the most popular load-balancing solutions currently available, BigIP and LocalDirector, and also have taken a brief look at some of the other alternatives that are available for scaling your Internet site.

Appendixes

IN THIS PART

A Sources of Further Interest 369

B Installation and Configuration of Linux 377

C Getting the Tools Covered in the Book 401

Sources of Further Interest

APPENDIX

A

IN THIS APPENDIX

- Linux-Related Sites 370
- Open Source Software Sites 371
- General News and Information Sites 372
- Other Sites 373
- Usenet and Mailing Lists 375

We have talked about a lot of software throughout this book. In this appendix, we cover many of the Internet sites where this software and further information about it can be found. We begin with sites related to the Linux kernel and operating system. We then take a look at some open source software repositories and finish up with a look at a few sites for specific pieces of software mentioned in the book.

Linux-Related Sites

Because the sites in this section are related to Linux, both the kernel proper and other aspects of the Linux operating system, let's start by looking at a site specifically related to the Linux kernel. Following that, we look at sites for Linux documentation and knowledge bases. Finally, we look at the sites of various Linux vendors mentioned in the text.

Kernel.org

The definitive source for the Linux kernel source code and information is Kernel.org and its series of regional mirror sites. You can find this site at `http://www.kernel.org/`, or if you prefer to access your regional site directly, you can access `http://www.XX.kernel.org/` (where XX is the two-letter country code for the country in which you are interested; for example, `http://www.us.kernel.org/` for the United States). Highlights of this site include pristine kernel source code, links to other Linux sites, and a listing of all the mirror sites located around the world where you can obtain the kernel source. You can access the source repository via HTTP using the addresses previously noted or via anonymous FTP using the address `ftp.kernel.org` or `ftp.XX.kernel.org`. Note that these sites are usually very busy around the time that new kernels are released, and if it is a major release, expect delays.

The Linux Documentation Project

One of the interesting things about Linux is that a wealth of documents are available about various aspects of the operating system and associated software. Many of these documents are referred to as HOWTOs because they give information about how to perform various tasks using Linux and the software that typically comes with a Linux distribution. In addition to these informal documents, several open source books have been written by various members of the Linux community. This documentation is collated and maintained as part of a community project called the Linux Documentation Project, or LDP. Some of the books written for the LDP are incomplete and are still being worked on by their authors. Others, such as the *Network Administrator's Guide*, by Olaf Kirsch and Terry Dawson, have been published by multiple publishers as standalone books and as part of documentation collections and can be purchased from many bookstores, both on and off the Web. If you are looking for information regarding some specific aspect of Linux, chances are that there is a HOWTO to address your needs, and the LDP Web site at `http://www.linuxdoc.org/` is an excellent place to start looking for it.

Linuxcare

In the tradition of open source and free software, one of the ways people are encouraged to make a living from software is to provide support. This is one of the missions of Linuxcare, which, among other things, provides a Web site at `http://www.linuxcare.com/`. Highlights of this site include the Linux knowledge base, which is a database of tips and tricks that visitors can search if in need of help. In addition, the Linuxcare Web site hosts a summary of the linux-kernel mailing list, which is an excellent resource if you want to follow kernel development as it happens. If you are interested in commercial support of Linux, you also can find information on how to purchase this support from Linuxcare at its Web site.

Red Hat Linux

One of the most popular Linux distributions is the one produced and supported by Red Hat Linux Systems. The Web site at `http://www.redhat.com/` allows you to purchase boxed sets of their products, read the online documentation, obtain support, and learn about their certification and training programs. This site is also where you should look for security announcements and updates to the operating system.

Caldera Systems

A popular distribution among VARs and ISVs is Caldera OpenLinux from Caldera Systems. Their Web site at `http://www.caldera.com/`, like the one provided by Red Hat, is the ultimate resource for information regarding this fine distribution.

The Debian Project

If you opt to go with a noncommercial distribution, Debian might be the choice for you. The Debian project is dedicated to producing a high-quality distribution that contains only software that meets the open source definition. Unlike other distributions that will bundle non-free software with their products, Debian is a volunteer project, and all software that comes with the Debian GNU/Linux distribution is totally free in the free-software sense. An excellent server OS with a robust package-management tool suite, Debian is worth a look if you are interested in a distribution without a lot of demos and other superfluous junk. You can find more information regarding the Debian GNU/Linux distribution at `http://www.debian.org/`.

Open Source Software Sites

The next class of sites we will look at are sites that serve as collection points for open source software that runs on Linux and other freely available operating systems. These sites provide a central clearing house for all types of software, from simple utilities to application suites.

Freshmeat

One of the first places you should look if you are trying to find software for a Linux system is Freshmeat at `http://freshmeat.net/`. As new software products are created and released to the Internet community, they often are announced here, and Freshmeat maintains a searchable database of these projects. The software is categorized according to function and interface, and it is not unusual for fifty or more updates or new projects to be announced at Freshmeat in a single day. Whether you are looking for a battery status monitor for your laptop or the latest version of an open source groupware suite, chances are that you can find it at Freshmeat. One thing to note about this site is that not all the software announced here is open source; however, the licenses of each piece of software are noted in the announcements, so you will know up front whether a license is required for use.

SourceForge.net

In the past two years, there has been an explosion of open source software projects. One of the key ingredients required for a successful open source project is collaboration between developers in a distributed environment. To help address the needs of these developers, SourceForge.net was established to serve as a place where open source projects could be hosted. Some of the services provided to project developers include mailing lists, Web pages, and source code repositories for their projects. This has turned out to be a popular answer to the needs of the open source development community, and at the time this book was written, more than 12,000 open source projects were hosted at the SourceForge.net Web site at `http://www.sourceforge.net/`. This site not only hosts these projects, but also maintains a searchable software map so that end users can find the work of all these developers.

General News and Information Sites

If you are interested in following developments in the Linux and Open Source communities, you can visit any number of sites. At these sites, you can get the latest news, rumors, and discussions regarding Linux, open source, and computing in general from the perspective of community insiders.

Slashdot

A site so popular that it has become a part of computer jargon, Slashdot, located at `http://www.slashdot.org`, is a site whose primary focus is discussion of all things related to computing, open source, and the Internet. The site maintainers, contributing authors, and registered users post links to interesting news articles or write editorials, and visitors to the site are invited to comment. The discussions can get pretty heated at times, and the site traffic is so high that if a particularly interesting link is posted, people clicking through to the linked site have been known to cause Web servers to buckle under the strain. This is sometimes referred to as the Slashdot Effect.

Linux Today

This site scans the Web for references to Linux and related news articles, editorials, and press releases and presents a synopsis to the visitors. If you want to follow what is happening around the Linux community, this is a good place to start. Located at `http://linuxtoday.com`, you can register at this site and customize the presentation of the headlines to suit your tastes. Registering also allows the site to keep track of which articles you have already seen, and then you can easily see when new articles have been posted. The news links on the main page lead to synopsis pages, and from there you can click through to the original article and comment using the user feedback tools.

Linux Weekly News

Another Linux news site is Linux Weekly News, located at `http://www.lwm.net`. This site contains much more original content than Linux Today because it is not a news collector, but rather an online magazine with regular columnists and writers on staff. The site is an excellent source for information on a wide range of topics, including the latest kernel developments, commentaries on various projects within the Linux community, and editorials.

NewsForge

The people who brought you SourceForge also bring you NewsForge. Located at `http://www.newsforge.net`, NewsForge is very much like Linux Today in that it is primarily a news-collection site, but like Linux Weekly News, it also includes a fair amount of original content as well.

Other Sites

In addition to the sites already mentioned, there are some sites that any person interested in Web development using Linux and open source should be aware of. These include sites devoted to Perl, the Apache Web server, the PHP language, and to the databases, MySQL, and PostgreSQL. In this section, we will note a few of these sites, starting with sites devoted to Perl.

Perl Resources

Perl is one of the most popular languages for Web development and is also an excellent general-purpose scripting language. It's C-like syntax and flexibility make it indispensable to developers and system administrators alike. To get the most out of Perl, you will want to become familiar with the Comprehensive Perl Archive Network, or CPAN. This site, which can be found at `http://www.cpan.org/`, and its many mirror sites contain a huge repository of modules that add functionality to the basic Perl language. These sites also serve as the definitive location for new releases of Perl. Modules are categorized and are searchable by function, author, and name. If you want to know if a module exists to perform a particular task in Perl or if a package you want to use for a Web site requires a specific module, CPAN is the place to start looking.

The Apache Web Server

At the time this book was written, the number one Web server package on the Internet was the Apache Web Server. This Web server powers more than half of all sites on the Internet, and the number of sites using it grows daily. To obtain the latest version of this software, the definitive source is located at `http://www.apache.org/`. At this site, you can get the latest stable and development versions of Apache as well as many of the various modules available for it. In addition, security announcements, patches, and general news about the Web server are available here. Another Web site for those interested in tracking developments and news in the Apache community is the one located at `http://www.apachetoday.com/`. From the same people who brought us LinuxToday, this Web site collects news and information about the Apache Web server to help you keep up-to-date with the latest news, both from the open source side of the house as well as press releases of new commercial software intended to work with it.

PHP Resources

As the popularity of the Web has grown, one of the quiet players on the scene has been the PHP server-side scripting language. This embedded scripting language is rapidly overtaking Perl as the development language of choice for Web applications. With a wealth of features that ease the use of database back ends and other functions once relegated to CGI programs, PHP has transformed the Web from a place consisting of largely static content to a dynamic application platform. An excellent source of information regarding this language can be found at the PHPBuilder Web site at `http://www.phpbuilder.org/`. If you want to do development using PHP, this should be one of your first stops after visiting the PHP home page at `http://www.php.net/`. Among other things, this site includes an online reference to the PHP language. Another excellent site is `http://www.zend.com/`, the home site for the Zend optimizing engine that was incorporated into PHP version 4.

MySQL and PostgreSQL

As the Web has evolved, the need for database back ends to create dynamic content has grown, and two primary database systems that have been developed to meet them are available in the open source community. These two database systems are MySQL and PostgreSQL. MySQL is a database that implements a subset of the SQL language and that was designed specifically with the needs of Web developers in mind. MySQL is now one of the most popular database systems used to back Web sites. Features of SQL and commercial RDBMS systems that are missing from MySQL have been purposely left out to make it better suited for use as a Web data store. You can find out more about MySQL at its home page at `http://www.mysql.org/`. If you require closer adherence to the SQL standard, you might want to look at PostgreSQL. A descendent of the Ingres project at Berkeley, PostgreSQL is actively maintained and is constantly being enhanced to make it one of the most robust database projects in the open source community. PostgreSQL can be found at `http://www.pgsql.com/`.

Usenet and Mailing Lists

In addition to visiting Web sites, you can find a wealth of information from developers as well as end users by using Usenet and mailing lists. Most major open source projects maintain a mailing list for developers and users to converse and to report bugs. In addition, numerous Usenet newsgroups are related to various software products. The nice thing about these newsgroups and mailing lists is that they are a good place to request help. Chances are good that if you are having difficulty with a particular aspect of some open source product, others have had problems as well, and you can often find answers to your implementation or operational problems by conversing with other users or the developers. A good place to access Usenet is through the searchable archives at `http://www.deja.com/usenet/`. Mailing list maintainers usually keep archives of their lists online, and these are often searchable, as well.

Installation and Configuration of Linux

APPENDIX

B

IN THIS APPENDIX

- Obtaining a Linux Distribution 378
- Installing Your Linux Distribution 379
- Basic Network Setup 381
- Protecting Your Linux System 383

Unlike Windows Me and Windows 2000, which are available only from a single vendor and have only a single method of installation, Linux is available from multiple commercial vendors as well as a large number of community-based projects, each with a slightly different focus and with multiple methods for installation. In this appendix, we will discuss some of the means of obtaining Linux, some basic configuration tips, and ways to protect your systems after they have been installed.

Obtaining a Linux Distribution

There are many ways that you can obtain Linux-based operating systems, including traditional methods—purchasing a CD from a Linux vendor such as Red Hat or SuSE, for example—or downloading it from the Internet.

Purchasing a CD

One method of obtaining Linux is to purchase it from a Linux vendor, such as Red Hat. These vendors package the Linux kernel with all the supporting software required to make a complete operating environment. The price of Linux on CD ranges from less than $5 to more than $1,000, depending on the vendor. Some vendors of Linux CDs are

- Red Hat Software at `http://www.redhat.com`
- Caldera Systems at `http://www.caldera.com`
- SuSE at `http://www.suse.com`
- Linuxmall at `http://www.linuxmall.com`
- Cheapbytes at `http://www.cheapbytes`

The big difference in price is usually because of the service and software that are bundled with the CD, as well as the documentation that comes with the boxed sets from the distribution producers. Although Linux is freely available, some of the software that you can run on it is not free, such as Oracle, and the cost of these packages or service for products, such as Red Hat's High Availability Server, is what accounts for the difference. If you are interested in trying out Linux simply as an experiment, you can opt for the next option, downloading from the Internet.

Downloading from the Internet

From the beginning, Linux and Linux distributions have been available for download from the Internet. In the early days of Linux, you might have been required to download hundreds of individual packages to make up a distribution. Today, however, the situation is much different. Many distribution vendors make available for download CD images, also known as ISO images, of the freely available portions of their distributions. You can download a single file that you burn to CD that contains all the files required to install Linux on your systems. A popular site for downloading such images is `http://www.linuxiso.org/`, which carries ISO images for many of the popular distributions of Linux, as well as other freely available operating systems, such as FreeBSD and NetBSD. If you have a high bandwidth connection and a CD burner, this might be a good option for you to get your hands on a Linux distribution.

Installing Your Linux Distribution

After you have obtained the Linux distribution of your choice, you must install it. Linux supports many installation methods, and each distribution has its own installation instructions. These instructions are included with the distributions either as printed manuals, if you purchased a boxed set of the distribution, or in electronic form on the distribution media. Instead of covering in detail any particular distribution, following are some basic steps that you will need to take for any installation:

- Conduct a hardware inventory.
- Decide on an installation method.
- Decide on a partitioning scheme to use.
- Decide on the packages to install.

Conducting a Hardware Inventory

Before you begin your Linux installation, it is a good idea to do an inventory of the PC on which you will be installing. The following checklist contains some information that you should gather prior to any installation that will make the process go more smoothly:

- Processor type and speed:
- Amount of RAM:
- Hard drive type (IDE, SCSI):
- Hard drive size:
- Mouse type and port (if a serial mouse):
- Video card make and model:
- Amount of video RAM:
- Monitor horizontal and vertical sync ranges:
- Network interface card type:

- Special-purpose hardware:
    - SCSI controllers (add-on cards and onboard):
    - RAID controllers:
    - Sound cards:
    - Other:

After you have gathered this information, which should be in your system documentation, keep it handy so that you can refer to it during the installation. You are ready to move on to the next step—deciding on the installation method to use.

Selecting an Installation Method

Linux distributions typically support multiple installation methods. Some of the most popular methods are

- Installation from a CD
- Installation over a network
- Installation from a hard drive

The choice of installation method is up to you, and each has advantages and disadvantages. By far, the most popular method of installation is from a local CD-ROM drive because this method does not require network access or lots of space on your hard drive. Normal installation from a CD is a matter of putting the CD containing the Linux distribution into the drive and rebooting the system. This assumes, of course, that your BIOS is configured to boot from CD-ROM and that your system supports it. If not, you will be required to use a boot floppy disk, which usually can be created by following instructions on the installation media.

From there, most of the current distributions guide you step-by-step through the configuration. This is where the system inventory you did previously will come in handy. If you do not have a CD-ROM drive, but do have a network interface card, you can opt to install over a network. Network installations are possible from NFS servers, HTTP servers, and FTP servers, depending on the distribution that you are installing. To install over a network, you must have a network card supported by Linux, a connection to a network, and a floppy disk. The basic steps are to create the network installation floppy disk from the distribution media, boot with the floppy disk and connect to the network, and then specify the installation server and protocol to use to retrieve the files. Finally, you also have the option to install from a hard drive. Using this installation method, you must have a partition with enough space to hold the distribution files in addition to the space that will be allocated to the Linux installation. For server installations, this method is not recommended; however, for dual boot systems, it is a viable option and it differs very little from the CD-ROM–based installation.

Selecting a Partitioning Scheme

Two basic schools of thought exist on how to partition the disk drive for use with Linux. The first is that you should create a lot of separate partitions, with partitions for /boot, /, /home, /usr, /var, /tmp, and optionally /usr/local and /opt. This is similar to the defaults of systems such as Solaris, which use separate slices for each of these filesystems. If you let the installation program for Red Hat choose your partitions for you, you will get a setup along these lines.

The other school of thought is that you should use fewer partitions and that the traditional separation between / and /usr is not needed. Under this school of thought, you would create partitions for /boot, /, /var, and /home, and /tmp should be a symbolic link to /var/tmp. The argument for this arrangement is that unlike older systems in which drives were much smaller than today's and you often had to spread the OS partitions (or slices) over multiple drives to have enough room to fit, today's systems, which typically come with hard drives of 9GB or greater, no longer require this separation. Having more partitions means longer boot times as you wait for consistency checks, and the like, during the boot sequence. This discussion ignores swap partitions because regardless of the strategy you employ, you will have to have at least one swap partition.

Selecting Packages for Installation

The final decision you will have to make during the installation is which packages you want to install. Linux distributions come with a variety of software packages from the basic utilities to compilers and scripting languages to multiple desktop interfaces such as GNOME or KDE. Some of the choices you have to make are the following:

- Will the system be a workstation or a server?
- Do you require development tools?
- Will the system be networked?

Most installation programs offer you several options ranging from a custom installation, in which you select every package individually, to several package groups, such as development workstation or network server. Using Red Hat, if you want to see what will be installed by one of these package groups, you can select one of them and also check the Select Individual Packages option, which will show you a listing of all the available packages with an indication of those that have been selected for that group. Other distribution installation packages have similar options.

Basic Network Setup

After you have installed the Linux distribution of your choice, you need to configure the network connection unless this was handled by the installation program. In this section, we take a brief look at the basics of setting up networking on your Linux systems. The examples given here are based on Red Hat Linux version 6.0 or greater. If you are using another distribution, you should refer to the documentation that comes with your distribution for guidance.

Assigning IP Addresses

At the most basic level, assigning an IP address to your Linux system is a simple matter of running the appropriate `ifconfig` command. In the early days of Linux distribution, to set up networking, you figured out what this command was and added it to one of the run control or rc scripts that is run by the init program at boot. For example, if you wanted to assign the IP address 192.168.50.101 to your Linux host, you would run the following command:

```
[root@server1 etc]# ifconfig eth0 192.168.50.101 netmask 255.255.255.0
```

That would result in device /dev/eth0 being assigned the IP address indicated with the specified netmask. Today, the distributions have made things easier by providing tools, such as Linuxconf for Red Hat or Yast for SuSE, to configure the network interfaces. To use these tools, you first should refer to the documentation provided by the distribution vendor. After you have done so, these menu-driven applications will prompt you for the various pieces of information required to get your Linux system talking on a network. Regardless of the distribution you use, you should obtain the information in the following checklist before you begin:

- IP address allocation method (Dynamic (DHCP or BOOTP) or Static):
- Network mask:
- Broadcast address:
- Hostname:
- Domain name:
- Gateway:
- Name server(s):

With this information in hand, you should be able to easily use the system administration tools for your distribution to enter it and get your Linux system onto the network.

Network Hardware Issues

The other aspect of getting your Linux system configured to work on a network is related to loading the appropriate device drivers for your network hardware. Network devices differ from other devices on Linux systems in that the device names are assigned as they are detected by the kernel. This can lead to some confusion if you have multiple network cards in your system, especially if they are the same type of network cards. For example, if you have two Intel EtherExpress 10/100 network interface cards in your system, which one is eth0? Unfortunately, this depends somewhat on PCI scan order. Alternatively, if you have a dual ethernet card, which port will be referred to as eth0? Usually, finding out requires some trial and error. Fortunately, after you figure it out and get your system configured with the appropriate IP addresses, you should not have to worry about it again unless you need to change IP addresses. Another option is to use different types of network cards, which brings up the next point—loading device drivers.

The common scenario used when building Linux systems is to build all the available network drivers with your Linux kernel as modules, and then load the appropriate one at boot. In this case, you can influence the order in which names are assigned to network devices through entries in the `/etc/modules.conf` file. This file also might be called the `/etc/conf.modules` file, depending on the distribution. To make sense of this, let's consider an example.

Suppose that you are building a server in which you will have two network interfaces. One is a 3C509 card from 3Com, which you will use as an internal interface for maintenance. The other is a 3C905B card, also from 3Com, which will connect your system to the outside-facing network. You want the outside network interface to be known as eth0, and the maintenance network interface to be known as eth1. To accomplish this, you would add the following lines, shown in Listing B.1, to `/etc/modules.conf`.

LISTING B.1 Specifying Network Drivers in `/etc/modules.conf`

```
alias eth0 3c59x
alias eth1 3c509
```

The first line in the preceding code specifies that the device eth0 refers to hardware that is supported by the 3c59x driver module. The second line specifies that the device eth1 refers to hardware supported by the 3c509 module. During system boot, when the network configuration starts and references device eth0, the kernel will load the appropriate modules. Naturally, if these two devices were the same, the alias lines would both reference the same module.

Protecting Your Linux System

Like many other operating systems, most Linux distributions do little out of the box to secure the system from intruders, leaving that task to the system administrator. In this section, we take a look at some of the things that you, as a system administrator, should do to reduce the risks to your systems. These things can be broken down into two broad categories:

- Managing services running on the system
- Monitoring access to the systems and the services running on them

We will examine both of these areas and look at some of the tools that you can use to improve the security of your systems.

Managing Services Running on the System

One of the most common mistakes made by administrators of Linux systems is not keeping track of the services that run on their systems. Often, the system administrators simply do not know that their systems are vulnerable, because they are not aware that a service that can be exploited is running. To see the truth of this statement, let's take a look at a file that is often ignored by administrators, the `/etc/inetd.conf` file.

The inetd.conf file is the configuration file of the inetd super server. It defines which services are available through the inetd daemon. Listing B.2 is the `/etc/inetd.conf` file from a recently installed Red Hat 6.2 system. It has not been modified, but reflects the default installed with the system.

LISTING B.2 `/etc/inetd.conf`

```
#
# inetd.conf      This file describes the services that will be available
#         through the INETD TCP/IP super server.  To re-configure
#         the running INETD process, edit this file, then send the
#         INETD process a SIGHUP signal.
#
# Version:        @(#)/etc/inetd.conf     3.10    05/27/93
#
# Authors:        Original taken from BSD UNIX 4.3/TAHOE.
#         Fred N. van Kempen, <waltje@uwalt.nl.mugnet.org>
#
# Modified for Debian Linux by Ian A. Murdock <imurdock@shell.portal.com>
#
# Modified for RHS Linux by Marc Ewing <marc@redhat.com>
#
# <service_name> <sock_type> <proto> <flags> <user> <server_path> <args>
#
# Echo, discard, daytime, and chargen are used primarily for testing.
#
# To re-read this file after changes, just do a 'killall -HUP inetd'
#
#echo     stream  tcp     nowait  root    internal
#echo     dgram   udp     wait    root    internal
#discard  stream  tcp     nowait  root    internal
#discard  dgram   udp     wait    root    internal
#daytime  stream  tcp     nowait  root    internal
#daytime  dgram   udp     wait    root    internal
#chargen  stream  tcp     nowait  root    internal
#chargen  dgram   udp     wait    root    internal
#time     stream  tcp     nowait  root    internal
```

LISTING B.2 Continued

```
#time      dgram   udp     wait    root    internal
#
# These are standard services.
#
ftp        stream  tcp     nowait  root    /usr/sbin/tcpd  in.ftpd -l -a
telnet     stream  tcp     nowait  root    /usr/sbin/tcpd  in.telnetd
#
# Shell, login, exec, comsat and talk are BSD protocols.
#
shell      stream  tcp     nowait  root    /usr/sbin/tcpd  in.rshd
login      stream  tcp     nowait  root    /usr/sbin/tcpd  in.rlogind
#exec      stream  tcp     nowait  root    /usr/sbin/tcpd  in.rexecd
#comsat    dgram   udp     wait    root    /usr/sbin/tcpd  in.comsat
talk       dgram   udp     wait    nobody.tty      /usr/sbin/tcpd  in.talkd
ntalk      dgram   udp     wait    nobody.tty      /usr/sbin/tcpd  in.ntalkd
#dtalk     stream  tcp     wait    nobody.tty      /usr/sbin/tcpd  in.dtalkd
#
# Pop and imap mail services et al
#
#pop-2   stream  tcp     nowait  root    /usr/sbin/tcpd   ipop2d
#pop-3   stream  tcp     nowait  root    /usr/sbin/tcpd   ipop3d
#imap    stream  tcp     nowait  root    /usr/sbin/tcpd   imapd
#
# The Internet UUCP service.
#
#uucp      stream  tcp     nowait  uucp  /usr/sbin/tcpd /usr/lib/uucp/uucico -l
#
# Tftp service is provided primarily for booting.  Most sites
# run this only on machines acting as "boot servers." Do not uncomment
# this unless you *need* it.
#
#tftp      dgram   udp     wait    root    /usr/sbin/tcpd  in.tftpd
#bootps    dgram   udp     wait    root    /usr/sbin/tcpd  bootpd
#
# Finger, systat and netstat give out user information which may be
# valuable to potential "system crackers."  Many sites choose to disable
# some or all of these services to improve security.
#
finger     stream  tcp     nowait  nobody  /usr/sbin/tcpd  in.fingerd
#cfinger stream    tcp     nowait  root    /usr/sbin/tcpd  in.cfingerd
#systat    stream  tcp     nowait  guest   /usr/sbin/tcpd  /bin/ps -auwwx
#netstat   stream  tcp     nowait  guest   /usr/sbin/tcpd /bin/netstat -f inet
#
# Authentication
```

LISTING B.2 Continued

```
#
# identd is run standalone now
#
#auth     stream  tcp     wait    root    /usr/sbin/in.identd in.identd -e -o
#

linuxconf stream tcp wait root /bin/linuxconf linuxconf --http
#swat      stream  tcp     nowait.400      root /usr/sbin/swat swat
```

Lines beginning with a # character are commented out, and as you can see, this system will listen to a number of services. Some of these include ftp, telnet, finger, shell, and login. This is less than desirable because if this system had been deployed as a Web server in a production environment, these services would have been available, even though the system administrator might not want them to be. Given the known vulnerabilities of services such as telnet and the r-commands (rlogin, rsh, and so on), it is probably a good idea to turn these services off. So the first step that administrators of Linux systems should take to improve the security of their systems, is to audit the `/etc/inetd.conf` file and turn off any services that they will not be needing.

A Practical Example

Suppose that you are building a Web server. This system should offer only Web services and should be remotely accessible to the system administration staff, but in a secure fashion. To accomplish this, start by auditing the inetd.conf file. First, comment out the FTP and Telnet service stanzas because this system will not be serving in either of these roles. In addition, comment out linuxconf (the Web interface to the system configuration utility), talk, ntalk, and finger services. You are then left with the r-commands (rlogin and rsh). Because these services are not very secure, we opt to install openssh as a replacement, which is available at `http://www.openssh.org/`.

As you can see, you have now turned off all services controlled by the inetd daemon, which means that you can now turn it off by issuing the following command:

```
[root@server root]# chkconfig --level 12345 inetd off
```

You now have a system that is accessible for remote administration and that can answer HTTP requests (assuming that the httpd is running), which was our stated goal.

Further Steps to Take

Now that we have taken care of the inetd daemon and the services associated with it, let's take a look at the services started at boot. To accomplish this, we will use the `chkconfig` utility and issue the following command:

```
[root@server root]# chkconfig --list
```

The command gives output similar to the following:

```
keytable        0:off   1:off   2:on    3:on    4:on    5:on    6:off
crond           0:off   1:off   2:on    3:on    4:on    5:on    6:off
syslog          0:off   1:off   2:on    3:on    4:on    5:on    6:off
netfs           0:off   1:off   2:off   3:on    4:on    5:on    6:off
network         0:off   1:off   2:on    3:on    4:on    5:on    6:off
random          0:off   1:on    2:on    3:on    4:on    5:on    6:off
xfs             0:off   1:off   2:on    3:on    4:on    5:on    6:off
portmap         0:off   1:off   2:off   3:on    4:on    5:on    6:off
nfs             0:off   1:off   2:off   3:off   4:off   5:off   6:off
nfslock         0:off   1:off   2:off   3:on    4:on    5:on    6:off
linuxconf       0:off   1:off   2:on    3:on    4:on    5:on    6:off
sshd            0:off   1:off   2:on    3:on    4:on    5:on    6:off
amd             0:off   1:off   2:off   3:off   4:off   5:off   6:off
anacron         0:off   1:off   2:off   3:off   4:off   5:off   6:off
httpd           0:off   1:off   2:off   3:on    4:on    5:on    6:off
apmd            0:off   1:off   2:on    3:on    4:on    5:on    6:off
arpwatch        0:off   1:off   2:off   3:off   4:off   5:off   6:off
atd             0:off   1:off   2:off   3:on    4:on    5:on    6:off
autofs          0:off   1:off   2:off   3:on    4:on    5:on    6:off
named           0:off   1:off   2:off   3:off   4:off   5:off   6:off
bootparamd      0:off   1:off   2:off   3:off   4:off   5:off   6:off
dhcpd           0:off   1:off   2:off   3:off   4:off   5:off   6:off
gated           0:off   1:off   2:off   3:off   4:off   5:off   6:off
genpowerd       0:off   1:off   2:off   3:off   4:off   5:off   6:off
inet            0:off   1:off   2:off   3:on    4:on    5:on    6:off
ipchains        0:off   1:off   2:off   3:off   4:off   5:off   6:off
irda            0:off   1:off   2:off   3:off   4:off   5:off   6:off
pcmcia          0:off   1:off   2:off   3:off   4:off   5:off   6:off
kdcrotate       0:off   1:off   2:off   3:off   4:off   5:off   6:off
kudzu           0:off   1:off   2:off   3:on    4:on    5:on    6:off
lpd             0:off   1:off   2:on    3:on    4:on    5:on    6:off
mars-nwe        0:off   1:off   2:off   3:off   4:off   5:off   6:off
mcserv          0:off   1:off   2:off   3:off   4:off   5:off   6:off
nscd            0:off   1:off   2:off   3:off   4:off   5:off   6:off
ntop            0:off   1:off   2:on    3:on    4:on    5:on    6:off
ldap            0:off   1:off   2:off   3:off   4:off   5:off   6:off
phhttpd         0:off   1:off   2:off   3:off   4:off   5:off   6:off
identd          0:off   1:off   2:off   3:on    4:on    5:on    6:off
pulse           0:off   1:off   2:off   3:off   4:off   5:off   6:off
postgresql      0:off   1:off   2:off   3:off   4:off   5:off   6:off
pxe             0:off   1:off   2:off   3:off   4:off   5:off   6:off
routed          0:off   1:off   2:off   3:off   4:off   5:off   6:off
rstatd          0:off   1:off   2:off   3:off   4:off   5:off   6:off
```

```
rusersd         0:off   1:off   2:off   3:off   4:off   5:off   6:off
rwalld          0:off   1:off   2:off   3:off   4:off   5:off   6:off
rwhod           0:off   1:off   2:off   3:off   4:off   5:off   6:off
smb             0:off   1:off   2:off   3:off   4:off   5:off   6:off
sendmail        0:off   1:off   2:on    3:on    4:on    5:on    6:off
squid           0:off   1:off   2:off   3:off   4:off   5:off   6:off
snmpd           0:off   1:off   2:off   3:off   4:off   5:off   6:off
xntpd           0:off   1:off   2:off   3:off   4:off   5:off   6:off
ypbind          0:off   1:off   2:off   3:off   4:off   5:off   6:off
gpm             0:off   1:off   2:off   3:off   4:off   5:off   6:off
vmware          0:off   1:off   2:off   3:off   4:off   5:on    6:off
```

Each line here represents a service that potentially can be started by the init process. The columns represent runlevels and whether a service is on or off at that particular runlevel.

Just as with `/etc/inetd.conf`, we should audit this output, determine which services are not required for the system in question, and turn those services off. You can do this, again with the chkconfig command. Suppose, for example, I wanted to turn off sendmail on the system used to create the preceding output. I can see by examining the sendmail line in the output that sendmail runs at runlevels 2, 3, 4, and 5. Therefore, to shut off the sendmail service, I would issue the following command:

```
[root@server1 root]# chkconfig --level 2345 sendmail off
```

After we have completed our audit of those services managed by `chkconfig`, we have to look only at those services that we might have added to the system using the rc.local file or that `chkconfig` is not aware of.

NOTE

If you add a service to the init.d directory, you can add it to the list of chkconfig managed services very simply. The following is an example that illustrates how to do this. Suppose you have a service, foo, and you create a System V style init script called foo. You place your script, `foo`, into the `/etc/rc.d/init.d` directory. If you want chkconfig to know about it, you simply add a line as follows to the top of your script:

```
# chkconfig: 345 85 28
```

This line is a shell script comment line and is interpreted as follows:

- The number 345 indicates the runlevels that this service should run at—in this case, runlevels 3, 4, and 5.

- The number 85 is used to construct the symbolic link for starting the service. In this example, in the `/etc/rc.d/rc3.d` directory, a symbolic link S85foo pointed to `/etc/rc.d/init.d/foo`. As you are aware, the number is used to determine the order in which services are started.
- The final number on the line, 28, is used to construct the symbolic link for shutting down the service. In this case, the symbolic link to ensure that `foo` is not running at runlevel 2 is `/etc/rc.d/rc2.d/K28foo`.

Having audited the services running on our system and removing those that are not needed, we now can move on to take a look at the next area of concern: monitoring access to our systems and the services running on them.

Monitoring Systems and Services

As you are no doubt aware, one of the tasks required of all system administrators, is the monitoring of systems. This is one of the reasons why log files are maintained. In this section, we take a look at some of the tools that you can use to monitor the security of your systems.

The Simple Watcher (swatch)

The first tool we will look at is called swatch. This utility is a Perl script that watches log files, looking for user-defined regular expressions, and performing a user-defined action when it finds one. For example, suppose that you have sudo installed, and you want to watch for users attempting to use it who are not in the sudoers file. You could tell swatch to watch for the string: user NOT in sudoers in the `/var/log/secure` log file and to send an e-mail to the system administrator. As you might have deduced, this is useful not only for security monitoring, but for general monitoring as well. The swatch utility is available at `http://www.engr.ucsb.edu/~eta/swatch/`.

The sudo Utility

Another tool that you should consider for your systems is sudo. This utility gives you the capability to grant limited access to privileged commands without giving full root access. Some of the nice features of the sudo utility include

- Extensive logging
- The capability to limit access by host
- The capability to group users using aliases and to grant access to all members of the group with a single line
- The capability to give access to only specific commands

The sudo utility is available from `http://www.courtesan.com/sudo/index.html`.

Tripwire

A very useful tool that is available for Linux systems is Tripwire. The Tripwire tool is a filesystem watcher that detects when changes are made to the set of files that it monitors. This tool is very useful in making sure that Trojan horses and other malicious software are not installed on your system. Tripwire works by collecting various data about the files it is configured to watch, such as file sizes, checksums, and permissions, and by notifying the system administrator when a watched file changes. For more information about Tripwire, you can visit the Tripwire home page at `http://www.tripwire.org/`.

Packet Filtering with the ipchains Utility

Another utility that you can use to help secure your systems is the ipchains utility that comes with Linux. This software is a packet filter that enables you to construct firewalls to limit traffic passing through your systems. To use ipchains, your Linux kernel must have been compiled with packet filter support. Let's take a look at how you can use ipchains to restrict access to your system to only the traffic that you want to allow. If you are using a system based on the 2.4.x Linux kernel, you can implement a packet filter using the netfilter facility that includes backward compatibility with ipchains. Refer to `http://netfilter.samba.org/` for more information about this new packet-filtering package.

Some ipchains Scripts

In this section, we take a look at some firewall scripts that could be used to build a packet filtering system using ipchains. First, we have a script that would go into `/etc/rc.d/init.d` to start our firewall at boot. This script is shown in Listing B.3.

LISTING B.3 Firewall Script

```
#!/bin/sh
# firewall
# description: Control script for firewall
#
# chkconfig: 345 5 95
#

CONFIG_DIR=/etc/sysconfig/firewall

# Source function library.
. /etc/rc.d/init.d/functions


## Read Configuration File
. $CONFIG_DIR/firewall.conf
```

LISTING B.3 Continued

```
case "$1" in

  #####START FIREWALL#####
  start)
     echo -n "Starting Firewall:"
     ## Flush rule sets, start from scratch
     $IPCHAINS -F input
     $IPCHAINS -F output
     $IPCHAINS -F forward
     $IPCHAINS -F icmp-in
     $IPCHAINS -F icmp-out

     ## Read firewall rules
     . $CONFIG_DIR/firewall.rules

     ## Read the masquerading rules
     . $CONFIG_DIR/firewall.rules.masq

     ## Set default policy
     $IPCHAINS -A output -j ACCEPT
     $IPCHAINS -A input -i ! eth0:0 -j DENY -l
     echo "               Done!"
     echo ""
     echo "Internal: $INTERNALIF  $INTERNALNET"
     echo "External: $OUTERIF     $OUTERNET"
     echo "" ;;

  #####STOP FIREWALL####
  stop)
     echo ""
     echo -n "Shutting down Firewall:"
     $IPCHAINS -F input
     $IPCHAINS -F output
     $IPCHAINS -F forward
     $IPCHAINS -F icmp-in
     $IPCHAINS -F icmp-out
     $IPCHAINS -P forward DENY
     echo "               Done!"
     echo "" ;;

  restart)
        $0 stop
        $0 start
        ;;
```

LISTING B.3 Continued

```
  *)
      echo ""
      echo "Usage: firewall {start|stop|restart}"
      echo ""
      echo "start   Turn on Firewall and IP Masquerading"
      echo "stop    Turn off Firewall and IP Masquerading"
      echo "restart         Restart Firewall and IP Masquerading"
      echo ""
      exit 1 ;;

esac
exit 0
```

As you can see, this is a fairly standard System V style init script that takes arguments to start, stop, and restart the packet filtering software. At the top, you can see that I have added the line to allow chkconfig to manage this service. In addition, take note of the definition of CONFIG_DIR. This directory contains the actual rules that will be implemented for this packet filter. Let's take a look at each file here in turn. The first thing that the preceding script does is to source the `firewall.conf` file in the CONFIG_DIR. This file is shown in Listing B.4.

LISTING B.4 `firewall.conf`

```
#!/bin/sh
# firewall.conf - used by firewall package
IPCHAINS=/sbin/ipchains
ATBOOT=1
CONFIG_DIR=/etc/sysconfig/firewall

OUTERIF=eth0
if [ -f /etc/sysconfig/network-scripts/ifcfg-${OUTERIF} ]; then
    source /etc/sysconfig/network-scripts/ifcfg-${OUTERIF}
    OUTERIP=$IPADDR
    OUTERMASK=$NETMASK
    OUTERNET=$OUTERIP/$OUTERMASK
else
    OUTERIP=`ifconfig $OUTERIF | grep inet | cut -d : -f 2 | cut -d \  -f 1`
    OUTERMASK=`ifconfig $OUTERIF | grep Mask | cut -d : -f 4`
    OUTERNET=$OUTERIP/$OUTERMASK
fi

INTERNALIF=eth1
if [ -f /etc/sysconfig/network-scripts/ifcfg-${INTERNALIF} ]; then
    source /etc/sysconfig/network-scripts/ifcfg-${INTERNALIF}
```

LISTING B.4 Continued

```
    INTERNALIP=$IPADDR
    INTERNALMASK=$NETMASK
    INTERNALNET=$INTERNALIP/$INTERNALMASK
else
    INTERNALIP=`ifconfig $INTERNALIF | grep inet | cut -d : -f 2 | cut -d \  -f 1`
    INTERNALMASK=`ifconfig $INTERNALIF | grep Mask | cut -d : -f 4`
    INTERNALNET=$INTERNALIP/$INTERNALMASK
fi

REMOTENET=0/0
```

This file sets up a number of variables that will be used by other parts of the system later. Now let's take a look at the next file called by our firewall init script, called `firewall.rules`, shown in Listing B.5.

LISTING B.5 `firewall.rules`

```
#!/bin/sh
# firewall.rules used by firewall package
#
#### Start Firewall ####

# Define config dir
CONFIGDIR="/etc/sysconfig/firewall"

## Allow loopback interface
$IPCHAINS -A input -i lo -s 0/0 -d 0/0 -j ACCEPT
$IPCHAINS -A output -i lo -s 0/0 -d 0/0 -j ACCEPT

# Block incoming IP Spoofing
#
# Turn on Source Address Verification and get
# spoof protection on all interfaces.
if [ -e /proc/sys/net/ipv4/conf/all/rp_filter ]
  then
    for f in /proc/sys/net/ipv4/conf/*/rp_filter
      do
        echo 1 > $f
      done
  else
    echo "PRIMARY SPOOFING PROTECTION FAILED"
    echo "INSERTING BACKUP SPOOFING PROTECTION"
```

LISTING B.5 Continued

```
    $IPCHAINS -A input -j DENY -s 10.0.0.0/8 -d $OUTERNET
    $IPCHAINS -A input -j DENY -s 127.0.0.0/8 -d $OUTERNET
    $IPCHAINS -A input -j DENY -s 172.16.0.0/12 -d $OUTERNET
    $IPCHAINS -A input -j DENY -s 192.168.0.0/16 -d $OUTERNET
fi

# - Specific port blocks on the external interface -
# This section blocks off ports/services to the outside that have
# vulnerabilities. This will not affect the ability to use these services
# within your network.
#
# Those with the -l are logged to /var/log/messages

# We look for a local rules set in firewall.rules.local and if it exists
# source it
if [ -f $CONFIGDIR/firewall.rules.local ]; then
    . $CONFIGDIR/firewall.rules.local
fi

# At this point we look for a services specific rule set in firewall.rules.svcs
# and if it exists, put these rules in first for efficiency
if [ -f $CONFIGDIR/firewall.rules.svcs ]; then
    . $CONFIGDIR/firewall.rules.svcs
fi

# Back Orifice
$IPCHAINS -A input -p tcp -i $OUTERIF -s $REMOTENET -d $OUTERNET 31337 \
  -j DENY -l
$IPCHAINS -A input -p udp -i $OUTERIF -s $REMOTENET -d $OUTERNET 31337 \
  -j DENY -l

# NetBus
$IPCHAINS -A input -p tcp -i $OUTERIF -s $REMOTENET -d $OUTERNET 12345:12346 \
  -j DENY -l
$IPCHAINS -A input -p udp -i $OUTERIF -s $REMOTENET -d $OUTERNET 12345:12346 \
  -j DENY -l

## DENY without logging (too many entries are generated) ##

# BOOTP
$IPCHAINS -A input -p tcp -i $OUTERIF -s $REMOTENET -d $OUTERNET 67:68 -j DENY
$IPCHAINS -A input -p udp -i $OUTERIF -s $REMOTENET -d $OUTERNET 67:68 -j DENY

# NetBIOS
```

LISTING B.5 Continued

```
$IPCHAINS -A input -p tcp -i $OUTERIF -s $REMOTENET -d $OUTERNET 137:139 \
  -j DENY -l
$IPCHAINS -A input -p udp -i $OUTERIF -s $REMOTENET -d $OUTERNET 137:139 \
  -j DENY -l

# NFS
$IPCHAINS -A input -p tcp -s $REMOTENET 2049 -i $OUTERIF -j DENY
$IPCHAINS -A input -p udp -s $REMOTENET 2049 -i $OUTERIF -j DENY

# Multicast
$IPCHAINS -A input -i $OUTERIF -s 224.0.0.0/8 -d $REMOTENET -j DENY
$IPCHAINS -A input -i $OUTERIF -s $REMOTENET -d 224.0.0.0/8 -j DENY


# These are open to sockets created by connections allowed by ipchains
$IPCHAINS -A input -p tcp -s $REMOTENET -d $OUTERNET 1023:65535 -j ACCEPT
$IPCHAINS -A input -p udp -s $REMOTENET -d $OUTERNET 1023:65535 -j ACCEPT

# Allow packets with ack bit set, they are from an established connection.
$IPCHAINS -A input ! -y -p tcp -s $REMOTENET -d $OUTERNET -j ACCEPT

# Setup a chain for all of the icmp rules
$IPCHAINS -N icmp-in
$IPCHAINS -N icmp-out

# Allow incoming ICMP for types 0,3,4,8, and 11
$IPCHAINS -A icmp-in -p icmp -i $OUTERIF -s $REMOTENET \
  echo-reply -d $OUTERIP -j ACCEPT
$IPCHAINS -A icmp-in -p icmp -i $OUTERIF -s $REMOTENET \
  destination-unreachable -d $OUTERIP -j ACCEPT
$IPCHAINS -A icmp-in -p icmp -i $OUTERIF -s $REMOTENET \
  source-quench -d $OUTERIP -j ACCEPT
$IPCHAINS -A icmp-in -p icmp -i $OUTERIF -s $REMOTENET \
  time-exceeded -d $OUTERIP -j ACCEPT
$IPCHAINS -A icmp-in -p icmp -i $OUTERIF -s $REMOTENET \
  parameter-problem -d $OUTERIP -j ACCEPT

# Disallow pings from the outside and log any other weird ICMP requests
$IPCHAINS -A icmp-in -p icmp -i $OUTERIF -s $REMOTENET \
  echo-request -d $OUTERIP -j DENY
$IPCHAINS -A icmp-in -p icmp -i $OUTERIF -s $REMOTENET -d $OUTERIP -j DENY -l

# Allow outgoing ICMP for types 0,3,4,8,11, and 12
$IPCHAINS -A icmp-out -p icmp -i $OUTERIF -s $OUTERNET \
  destination-unreachable -d $REMOTENET -j ACCEPT
```

LISTING B.5 Continued

```
$IPCHAINS -A icmp-out -p icmp -i $OUTERIF -s $OUTERNET \
  source-quench -d $REMOTENET -j ACCEPT
$IPCHAINS -A icmp-out -p icmp -i $OUTERIF -s $OUTERNET \
  echo-request -d $REMOTENET -j ACCEPT
$IPCHAINS -A icmp-out -p icmp -i $OUTERIF -s $OUTERNET \
  time-exceeded -d $REMOTENET -j ACCEPT
$IPCHAINS -A icmp-out -p icmp -i $OUTERIF -s $OUTERNET \
  parameter-problem -d $REMOTENET -j ACCEPT

# Deny and log weird ICMP requests from us
$IPCHAINS -A icmp-out -p icmp -i $OUTERIF -s $OUTERNET -d $REMOTENET -j DENY -l

# Provide jumps to the icmp rules chains
$IPCHAINS -A input -p icmp -j icmp-in
$IPCHAINS -A output -p icmp -j icmp-out
```

This first file sets up some basic rules and then sources two additional files: the `firewall.rules.local` and the `firewall.rules.svcs`. Let's take a look at an example of the `firewall.rules.svcs`, shown in Listing B.6, which allows specific services to pass through the packet filter.

LISTING B.6 `firewall.rules.svcs`

```
#!/bin/sh
# firewall.rules.svcs - used by firewall package
#

# Rules to allow FTP
#$IPCHAINS -A input -p tcp -i $OUTERIF -s $REMOTENET -d $OUTERNET 20 -j ACCEPT
#$IPCHAINS -A input -p tcp -i $OUTERIF -s $REMOTENET -d $OUTERNET 21 -j ACCEPT

# Rule to allow SSH
$IPCHAINS -A input -p tcp -i $OUTERIF -s $REMOTENET -d $OUTERNET 22 -j ACCEPT

# Rule to allow telnet
#$IPCHAINS -A input -p tcp -i $OUTERIF -s $REMOTENET -d $OUTERNET 23 -j ACCEPT

# Rule to allow SMTP
#$IPCHAINS -A input -p tcp -i $OUTERIF -s $REMOTENET -d $OUTERNET 25 -j ACCEPT

# Rules to allow DNS
$IPCHAINS -A input -p tcp -i $OUTERIF -s $REMOTENET -d $OUTERNET 53 -j ACCEPT
$IPCHAINS -A input -p udp -i $OUTERIF -s $REMOTENET -d $OUTERNET 53 -j ACCEPT
```

LISTING B.6 Continued

```
# Rule to allow HTTP
#$IPCHAINS -A input -p tcp -i $OUTERIF -s $REMOTENET -d $OUTERNET 80 -j ACCEPT

# Rule to allow POP3
#$IPCHAINS -A input -p tcp -i $OUTERIF -s $REMOTENET -d $OUTERNET 110 -j ACCEPT

# Rule to allow identd
$IPCHAINS -A input -p tcp -i $OUTERIF -s $REMOTENET -d $OUTERNET 113 -j ACCEPT

# Rule to allow NNTP
#$IPCHAINS -A input -p tcp -i $OUTERIF -s $REMOTENET -d $OUTERNET 119 -j ACCEPT

# Rules to allow NTP
$IPCHAINS -A input -p tcp -i $OUTERIF -s $REMOTENET -d $OUTERNET 123 -j ACCEPT
$IPCHAINS -A input -p udp -i $OUTERIF -s $REMOTENET -d $OUTERNET 123 -j ACCEPT

# Rule to allow IMAP
#$IPCHAINS -A input -p tcp -i $OUTERIF -s $REMOTENET -d $OUTERNET 143 -j ACCEPT

# Rule to allow SHTTP
#$IPCHAINS -A input -p tcp -i $OUTERIF -s $REMOTENET -d $OUTERNET 443 -j ACCEPT
```

This file is heavily commented; to allow a particular service, you have to uncomment the appropriate lines in this file. The next file is the `firewall.rules.local` shown in Listing B.7. This file is intended to be similar in function to a rc.local file in that you can use it to declare rules for nonstandard services or to enforce local security policy rules.

LISTING B.7 `firewall.rules.local`

```
#!/bin/sh
# firewall.rules.local
#
# This file is where custom rules should be added.


### ALLOWED NETWORKS
# Add in any rules to specifically allow connections from hosts/nets that
# would otherwise be blocked.
$IPCHAINS -A input -s 207.8.63.77/30 -d $OUTERNET -j ACCEPT
$IPCHAINS -A input -i vmnet1 -s 172.16.156.0/12 -j ACCEPT

# Allow netbios from my VMWare virtual machine
$IPCHAINS -A input -p tcp -s 172.16.156.0/12 -d $INTERNALNET 137:139 -j ACCEPT
```

LISTING B.7 Continued

```
$IPCHAINS -A input -p udp -s 172.16.156.0/12 -d $INTERNALNET 137:139 -j ACCEPT
$IPCHAINS -A input -p tcp -s 172.16.156.0/12 -d 172.16.156.1 137:139 -j ACCEPT
$IPCHAINS -A input -p udp -s 172.16.156.0/12 -d 172.16.156.1 137:139 -j ACCEPT

### BLOCKED NETWORKS
# Add in any rules to specifically block connections from hosts/nets that
# have been known to cause problems. These packets are logged.
#$IPCHAINS -A input -s [banned host/net] -d $OUTERNET <ports> -j DENY -l

# This one blocks ICMP attacks
#$IPCHAINS -A input -b -i $OUTERIF -p icmp -s [host/net] -d $OUTERNET -j DENY -l
```

The final file of interest is a file that establishes masquerading rules. In addition to packet filtering, the ipchains utility allows a Linux host to act as a masquerader for a private network. This file, shown in Listing B.8, defines the rules for masquerading.

LISTING B.8 `firewall.rules.masq`

```
#!/bin/sh
# firewall.rules.masq - used by firewall package
#

## Masquerading

## Modules to help certain services

# TODO (Do modules really exist?)
/sbin/depmod -a
/sbin/modprobe ip_masq_ftp
/sbin/modprobe ip_masq_raudio
/sbin/modprobe ip_masq_irc
/sbin/modprobe ip_masq_quake
/sbin/modprobe ip_masq_user
/sbin/modprobe ip_masq_vdolive

## Masquerading firewall timeouts:
# tcp conns 8hrs, tcp after fin pkt 60s, udp 10min
$IPCHAINS -M -S 14400 60 600

## Set up kernel to enable IP masquerading
echo 1 > /proc/sys/net/ipv4/ip_forward
```

LISTING B.8 Continued

```
## Set up kernel to handle dynamic IP masquerading
echo 1 > /proc/sys/net/ipv4/ip_dynaddr

## Don't Masquerade internal-internal traffic
$IPCHAINS -A forward -s $INTERNALNET -d $INTERNALNET -j ACCEPT

## Don't Masquerade external interface direct
$IPCHAINS -A forward -s $OUTERNET -d $REMOTENET -j ACCEPT

## Masquerade all internal IP's going outside
$IPCHAINS -A forward -s $INTERNALNET -d $REMOTENET -j MASQ

## Set Default rule on MASQ chain to Deny
$IPCHAINS -P forward DENY

## Allow all connections from the network to the outside
$IPCHAINS -A input -s $INTERNALNET -d $REMOTENET -j ACCEPT
$IPCHAINS -A output -s $INTERNALNET -d $REMOTENET -j ACCEPT

# This section manipulates the Type Of Service (TOS) bits of the
# packet. For this to work, you must have CONFIG_IP_ROUTE_TOS enabled
# in your kernel

# Set telnet, www, smtp, pop3 and FTP for minimum delay
$IPCHAINS -A output -p tcp -d 0/0 80 -t 0x01 0x10
$IPCHAINS -A output -p tcp -d 0/0 22 -t 0x01 0x10
$IPCHAINS -A output -p tcp -d 0/0 23 -t 0x01 0x10
$IPCHAINS -A output -p tcp -d 0/0 21 -t 0x01 0x10
$IPCHAINS -A output -p tcp -d 0/0 110 -t 0x01 0x10
$IPCHAINS -A output -p tcp -d 0/0 25 -t 0x01 0x10

# Set ftp-data for maximum throughput
$IPCHAINS -A output -p tcp -d 0/0 20 -t 0x01 0x08

# Allow outgoing ICMP
$IPCHAINS -A output -p icmp -s $INTERNALNET -d $REMOTENET -j ACCEPT
```

If you are interested in downloading these scripts, you can obtain them from `http://www.techdog.org/downloads/ipchains-scripts.tgz`. A detailed description of all the options to ipchains can be found in the manual page and in the ipchains HOWTO, which is installed with the ipchains software in `/usr/doc/ipchains-x.x.x`, in which `x.x.x` is the version number of the ipchains package.

Debugging ipchains Rules

One of the most useful features of the ipchains software is the extensive logging that is available. When building rules, it is very useful to use the `-L` option on any DENY rules so that attempts to get through the packet filter are logged. If you do this and then find that a required service is being blocked, you can refer to the system log files and see which ports need to be opened to accommodate that service. In addition, if you have sufficient space on the filesystem containing the logs, you can leave logging on all the time to see who is attempting to access your machines. This is very useful in detecting port scans and other attempts to bypass the security of your systems.

Other Sources of Information

A wealth of other security tools is available for Linux systems. Here are some sites that you can visit to find out more:

- `http://ciac.llnl.gov/ciac/SecurityTools.html`
- `http://cs-www.ncsl.nist.gov/tools/tools.htm`
- `http://www.rootshell.org/`

The first two of these sites are repositories of security tools, many of which are usable on Linux systems, and the final one is a site that lists many of the exploits currently known and describes how to prevent them.

Getting the Tools Covered in the Book

APPENDIX

C

IN THIS APPENDIX

- Web and FTP Sites 402
- Building Software from Source Code 403

Throughout this book, we have discussed various open source tools that can be used to build Internet sites. In this appendix, we cover some of the sites that were used to find these tools and then discuss how to build software from source code after you have downloaded it.

Web and FTP Sites

In this section, we take a look at a few of the sites I relied on to find the tools described in this book. Literally hundreds of sites are out there that have open source software on them; however, I will focus here on just three. These three are the ones that I most heavily rely on when looking for software for my Linux- and FreeBSD-based systems.

Freshmeat

One of the first places I always look to find software is Freshmeat, located at `http://www.freshmeat.net/`. Each day, dozens of software packages are released or updated, and if the software creator wants to get the word out to the Internet community, Freshmeat is one place where these releases and updates are announced. In addition, the Freshmeat site also maintains a database of software projects that includes links to the product home page, download sites, sources of RPMs (Red Hat Package Manager packages), and in some cases, screen shots of the software in action. They also include descriptions of the software and provide a mechanism to search the database. In addition to maintaining this database, visitors to the Freshmeat site have the option to register with the site; after you do so, you can choose to receive e-mail notification of software releases or updates. You also can subscribe to a project, which means that whenever a new version of the software is released, you receive a notification via e-mail.

SourceForge

Another excellent resource that you can use to find tools for building Internet sites is SourceForge, located at `http://www.sourceforge.net/`. This site was created for the sole purpose of hosting open source projects, and it currently hosts more than 12,000 projects. Much of the software announced on Freshmeat is hosted at SourceForge. SourceForge provides project developers with a variety of tools designed to help make their projects successful, including source code revision and control using CVS, mailing list management, bug tracking, Web space for a project home page, FTP space for file and package distribution, and a document management system. In addition, SourceForge projects are searchable based on the language the source code is written in, developer names, software development stage (such as alpha or beta), and by developer-defined software category. Like Freshmeat, registration at SourceForge enables you to subscribe to a project so that you can track the development and be notified of updates.

RPMfind.net

If you are using a Linux distribution that uses the Red Hat Package Manager (RPM) system, an excellent resource for finding source code and binary RPMs is `http://www.rpmfind.net/`. This is actually a group of sites that maintains a searchable database of RPMs. The RPMs are indexed by distribution, name, and other methods to make finding a particular package easier. The other nice thing about this site is that if you do not want to build the software from source code, you can just download a prebuilt binary for your particular distribution and install it. If you do not want to wade through the indices looking for a particular package, you can use the search capabilities of the site to locate the files you are looking for. When you select a package, you can view the contents of the package online prior to downloading it to your system and determine the dependencies, the list of files in the package, and a description of what the package consists of. This site provides links to download the packages from the distributor's sites and, in many cases, provides a local mirror of the packages, as well.

Building Software from Source Code

After you have located the source code to a particular piece of software, you must convert that source code into an executable binary. In this section, we discuss why it might be desirable to build from source code instead of downloading binary packages; we also give some tips on setting up a build environment, talk a little about building from a raw source package, and touch on building using source RPMs or SRPMs.

Why Build from Source Code?

If you can download a binary package from the Internet, why would you want to build a package from source code? Several reasons why you might want to do this are

- You want to build the package with a specific set of configuration options.
- You need to apply a patch to the source code you have downloaded.
- You do not know or trust the person or group that built the binary package.
- You want to ensure that any library or other dependencies are resolved.

Let's consider each of these reasons for a moment, and then you can make your own decision.

Building with Specific Configuration Options

Many open source packages enable you, as the user, to decide whether a particular feature is built into the software at compile time. These are called compile-time options. For example, suppose that you want to build the most recent version of PHP that you have downloaded from the PHP home page. Some of the options that you could select at compile time include support for various databases, such as MySQL and PostgresSQL. By building the source code yourself, you get to control the features that go into the PHP executable, and you can turn on only those features that suit your particular needs.

Applying Patches

Another reason for building software from source code is that you need to apply a patch to the source code. Consider the following example. You are using Apache as your Web-serving software and you have the latest released version. A security announcement comes out about Apache that includes a patch to correct a deficiency. You can wait for the next release of Apache to come out and hope that they have corrected the security flaw, or you can apply the patch yourself and rebuild the software, thus eliminating the delay between the discovery of a defect and the application of a fix. This is one of the nice things about open source software. Access to the source code means that you do not have to wait for the software developers to fix problems for you. You can simply recompile the software with the fix.

Trusting the Builder

One reason why open source is popular is that unlike proprietary software, which requires that you trust the software vendor for binaries, you do not have to trust the developers of open source. Access to the source code means that you can determine what the software does by direct examination. You no longer have to trust that there are no security flaws, either accidental or intentional, in the package. You can know with certainty that these flaws do not exist.

Resolving Dependencies

Yet another reason for building the software yourself is so that you can be certain it will run in your environment. Because Linux uses shared libraries, in order to run a piece of software on your system, you require not only the binary, but any shared libraries that the binary was built against. By compiling the source code yourself, you learn before installing the binary whether unresolved library or other dependencies exist. To see the value in this, consider the following example. You decide to upgrade to a new version of PHP on your system. You download a binary package of the latest version and install it. Suddenly, your Web site stops working. You determine that this is because of a new dependency that did not exist in the previous version of PHP. You have just caused unnecessary downtime that could have been avoided if you had built the software yourself—because you would have discovered the dependency at build time.

There are other reasons why you might want to build from source code, but no matter what reason you use, the beauty of open source is that the choice is yours.

Setting Up a Build Environment

After you have decided that you want to build source packages, you must set up a build environment. This means installing compilers, build tools such as make, header files, development libraries, as well as debuggers and other tools. The key thing to keep in mind when setting up your build environment is that changes to your build system means that you must change your production systems as well. If you are managing a large Web site for a company that does in-house development, this might be harder than it sounds. Some of the items you need to consider are

- Binary compatibility between built software and production systems
- Library version dependencies
- Support software dependencies

Let's take a look at these areas and discuss ways to manage this problem.

Binary Compatibility

Although not a common occurrence, occasionally circumstances occur in which you must concern yourself with binary compatibility between different versions of a distribution, or between different distributions. For example, when Red Hat first introduced the GNU C library into its distribution, it broke binary compatibility between the current version and older versions of the distribution, which used the older Linux C library. As a result, binaries built for the current (at that time) version of Red Hat distribution would not run properly on older versions or on distributions from other vendors. This issue arose again with the introduction of Red Hat 7.0, which included a compiler that produced binaries that were incompatible with older versions of Red Hat. It is therefore important that you ensure that your build systems are compatible with your production systems. The easiest way to ensure this is to designate a build server that contains all the software found on the production server plus only the development tools. This means that your build server should not be used for any purpose other than building software. As such, it should not contain any software not found on the production servers other than the tools required for building software. Software that is going into production must be built on this build server and then be submitted for quality assurance. Only when it has passed this testing can it be installed on production systems. This build server must be controlled by the quality assurance person or team, and developers should not be permitted to install software onto this system. Granting developers access to your build servers is the quickest way to ensure that your build server and production servers will become out of sync.

Library Version Dependencies

Another area where you need to keep a close eye on your systems is library versions. It is an unfortunate fact that many developers like to work with the latest bleeding edge libraries. This is fine for projects that they will run only on their workstations; however, if they build software on their workstations for installation in production, you must make sure that there are no library version issues.

When I was a system administrator at DejaNews, for example, we used the Berkeley database library for a number of projects. The official version that we were using was version 1.74, which had been through our QA cycle and was available on every production system. A new developer was hired to create a new software package, and one of the things he did was to install the then-new version 2 of the Berkeley database library on his workstation. He went through the entire development cycle for the project he was working on and it was not until the software was to be installed on a beta system for live testing that a problem was discovered. Software built against version 2 of the Berkeley database library would not run on our production systems because of the library version problem. To add insult to injury, it also was found that we could not simply upgrade the Berkeley database library on the production systems to version 2, because it was not binary compatible with software built for version 1.74 of the library. This required that we use a workaround that allowed both libraries to coexist on the system. The workaround was to install the version 2 library in a private library path and to use the LD_LIBRARY_PATH environment variable to tell the application where to look for it. This problem could have been avoided altogether if the developer had done his homework regarding what was involved in upgrading the library and tested to see if any library version issues existed.

Supporting Software Dependencies

One other area where it is important to be vigilant is the area of supporting software. When developing software for the Web, it is not uncommon to call on external programs from your software. You might need to invoke a shell or call a utility to do some processing and then pass control back to the calling program. This creates dependencies between the software you develop and the external programs that you call on to do work. This can lead to problems where different versions of the same program work differently, and what works with one version of the program might not work with another version of the software. An example of this is the Bourne Again Shell, or Bash. This is one of the most popular command interpreters on Linux systems and is used by many shell scripts. When Bash version 2.0 was released, it behaved differently than the previously released version 1.14.7 and broke many shell scripts. If a program relied on a shell script to perform some function, and the version of Bash did not match between development and production systems, you could run into trouble.

Building from Raw Source Code

So we now have decided to build from source code and have set up a tightly controlled build environment on which to compile the software packages we want. So how do we actually build the software? For the purposes of example, we will demonstrate building two packages. These packages are

- `sudo`
- C-Kermit

These two packages were selected because they demonstrate two common methodologies employed in the open source community for building software on multiple platforms. We will start with a look at sudo.

Building sudo

The sudo command is designed to allow system administrators to delegate specific rights to run privileged software on a system without giving a user full access to the system. You can find the most recent version of sudo at their homepage, http://www.courtesan.com/sudo/. Visit this page and download the source code to /tmp. This should result in a file in /tmp named sudo-<VERSION>.tar.gz, in which <VERSION> is the current version number of the software. After you have downloaded the source code, become the root user and issue the following commands:

```
[root@bserver1 root]# cd /usr/local/src
[root@bserver1 src]# tar xzf /tmp/sudo-1.6.3p7.tar.gz
[root@bserver1 src]# cd sudo-1.6.3p7
[root@bserver1 sudo-1.6.3p7]#
```

The sudo package is relatively easy to build, but it does have a fairly large number of compile-time options, which can be selected through the use of the GNU autoconf system. The GNU autoconf system was designed to make it easier for developers to support multiple platforms, such as the many flavors of Unix with a single source package. Software built using this system typically comes with a script called configure that the software builder must run to set compile-time options. The configure script, in addition to setting compile-time options, does various checks to determine which operating system it is being built on, and to set various options accordingly. To determine the available compile-time options, this script includes a Help option. The following command-line session shows how to use the configure script to determine the available compile-time options.

```
 [root@bserver1 sudo-1.6.3p7]# ./configure -help
Usage: configure [options] [host]
Options: [defaults in brackets after descriptions]
Configuration:
  --cache-file=FILE       cache test results in FILE
  --help                  print this message
  --no-create             do not create output files
  --quiet, --silent       do not print `checking...' messages
  --version               print the version of autoconf that created configure
Directory and file names:
  --prefix=PREFIX         install architecture-independent files in PREFIX
                          [/usr/local]
```

```
    --exec-prefix=EPREFIX   install architecture-dependent files in EPREFIX
                            [same as prefix]
    --bindir=DIR            user executables in DIR [EPREFIX/bin]
    --sbindir=DIR           system admin executables in DIR [EPREFIX/sbin]
    --libexecdir=DIR        program executables in DIR [EPREFIX/libexec]
    --datadir=DIR           read-only architecture-independent data in DIR
                            [PREFIX/share]
    --sysconfdir=DIR        read-only single-machine data in DIR [/etc]
    --sharedstatedir=DIR    modifiable architecture-independent data in DIR
                            [PREFIX/com]
    --localstatedir=DIR     modifiable single-machine data in DIR [PREFIX/var]
    --libdir=DIR            object code libraries in DIR [EPREFIX/lib]
    --includedir=DIR        C header files in DIR [PREFIX/include]
    --oldincludedir=DIR     C header files for non-gcc in DIR [/usr/include]
    --infodir=DIR           info documentation in DIR [PREFIX/info]
    --mandir=DIR            man documentation in DIR [PREFIX/man]
    --srcdir=DIR            find the sources in DIR [configure dir or ..]
    --program-prefix=PREFIX prepend PREFIX to installed program names
  --program-suffix=SUFFIX append SUFFIX to installed program names
  --program-transform-name=PROGRAM
                          run sed PROGRAM on installed program names
Host type:
  --build=BUILD           configure for building on BUILD [BUILD=HOST]
  --host=HOST             configure for HOST [guessed]
  --target=TARGET         configure for TARGET [TARGET=HOST]
Features and packages:
  --disable-FEATURE       do not include FEATURE (same as --enable-FEATURE=no)
  --enable-FEATURE[=ARG]  include FEATURE [ARG=yes]
  --with-PACKAGE[=ARG]    use PACKAGE [ARG=yes]
  --without-PACKAGE       do not use PACKAGE (same as --with-PACKAGE=no)
  --x-includes=DIR        X include files are in DIR
  --x-libraries=DIR       X library files are in DIR
--enable and --with options recognized:
  --with-otp-only         deprecated
  --with-alertmail        deprecated
  --with-CC               C compiler to use
  --with-incpath          additional places to look for include files
  --with-libpath          additional places to look for libraries
  --with-libraries        additional libraries to link with
  --with-devel            add developement options
  --with-csops            add CSOps standard options
  --without-passwd        don't use passwd/shadow file for authentication
  --with-skey             enable S/Key support
  --with-opie             enable OPIE support
  --with-long-otp-prompt  use a two line OTP (skey/opie) prompt
  --with-SecurID          enable SecurID support
```

```
--with-fwtk               enable FWTK AuthSRV support
--with-kerb4              enable kerberos v4 support
--with-kerb5              enable kerberos v5 support
--with-authenticate       enable AIX general authentication support
--with-pam                enable PAM support
--with-AFS                enable AFS support
--with-DCE                enable DCE support
--with-logincap           enable login class support
--without-lecture         don't print lecture for first-time sudoer
--with-logging            log via syslog, file, or both
--with-logfac             syslog facility to log with (default is local2)
--with-goodpri            syslog priority for commands (def is notice)
--with-badpri             syslog priority for failures (def is LOG_ALERT)
--with-logpath            path to the sudo log file
--with-loglen             maximum length of a log file line (default is 80)
--with-ignore-dot         ignore '.' in the PATH
--with-mailto             who should get sudo mail (default is root)
--with-mailsubject        subject of sudo mail
--without-mail-if-no-user do not send mail if user not in sudoers
--with-mail-if-no-host    send mail if user in sudoers but not for this host
--with-mail-if-noperms    send mail if user not allowed to run command
--with-passprompt         default password prompt
--with-badpass-message    message the user sees when the password is wrong
--with-fqdn               expect fully qualified hosts in sudoers
--with-timedir            path to the sudo timestamp dir
--with-sendmail=path      set path to sendmail
--without-sendmail        do not send mail at all
--with-sudoers-mode       mode of sudoers file (defaults to 0440)
--with-sudoers-uid        uid that owns sudoers file (defaults to 0)
--with-sudoers-gid        gid that owns sudoers file (defaults to 0)
--with-umask              umask with which the prog should run (default is 0022)
--without-umask           Preserves the umask of the user invoking sudo.
--with-runas-default      User to run commands as (default is root
--with-exempt=group       no passwd needed for users in this group
--with-editor=path        Default editor for visudo (defaults to vi)
--with-env-editor         Use the environment variable EDITOR for visudo
--with-passwd-tries       number of tries to enter password (default is 3)
--with-timeout            minutes before sudo asks for passwd again (def is 5)
--with-password-timeout passwd prompt timeout in minutes (default is 5)
--with-execv              use execv() instead of execvp()
--with-tty-tickets        use a different ticket file for each tty
--with-insults            insult the user for entering an incorrect password
--with-all-insults        include all the sudo insult sets
--with-classic-insults    include the insults from the classic sudo
--with-csops-insults      include CSOps insults
--with-hal-insults        include 2001-like insults
```

```
  --with-goons-insults    include the insults from the "Goon Show"
  --with-secure-path      override the user's path with a builtin one
  --without-interfaces    don't try to read the ip addr of ether interfaces
  --disable-authentication
                          Do not require authentication by default
  --disable-shadow        Never use shadow passwords
  --disable-root-sudo     don't allow root to run sudo
  --enable-log-host       Log the hostname in the log file
  --enable-noargs-shell   If sudo is given no arguments run a shell
  --enable-shell-sets-home
                          set $HOME to target user in shell mode
  --disable-path-info     Print 'command not allowed' not 'command not found'
  --disable-sia           Never use SIA on Digital UNIX
[root@bserver1 sudo-1.6.3p7]#
```

As you can see, a large number of options are available. For demonstration purposes, we will select a few that I commonly select when building sudo. To do this, I would invoke the configure script as follows:

```
[root@bserver1 sudo-1.6.3p7]# ./configure --with-passwd-tries=2
--with-tty-tickets --with-insults --with-all-insults --with-secure-path
--disable-root-sudo
```

With this command, I am telling the configure script that I want sudo to be built in such a way that

- It will prompt the user two times for a password before issuing a warning and exiting.
- Each shell will keep track of the last time sudo was invoked independently.
- sudo should insult the user if the user enters the wrong password.
- All available insult strings should be built in to the binary.
- The users' path should be replaced with a secure built-in path.
- The root user should not be allowed to use the sudo command.

After I have entered the preceding command, the configure script will begin checking my system to ensure that I have all the required libraries, ensure that any required supporting software is present, and then set the compile time options I selected. When this has completed without errors, I am ready to issue the next command, which will invoke the compiler and turn the source code into a binary (assuming that no errors are in the build). This command is

```
[root@bserver1 sudo-1.6.3p7]# make
```

The make utility looks for a file called Makefile in the current directory, which was created by the configure script. Using the rules defined in the Makefile, make will invoke the commands required to compile and link the source code to create the sudo executable and any other executables that are part of the sudo package. This generates a lot of output, but at the end, again assuming that no errors occurred, you should have a working executable of the sudo command. You then can usually issue the following command:

```
[root@bserver1 sudo-1.6.3p7]# make install
```

The software will be installed on your system. This does not always work, because the developers of the software might require that you copy the files to the appropriate locations manually, but in this case, it would install the sudo command on your system. You should now be able to use the sudo command, assuming, of course, that it was installed in your path.

Building C-Kermit

Another strategy that is sometimes used by software developers is to use makefile targets to set various options. C-Kermit is one such package. C-Kermit is a terminal emulator and file transfer protocol that supports literally hundreds of computing platforms, including just about every known flavor of Unix. Unlike the sudo package, the way that C-Kermit manages this is via make targets. To build the C-Kermit package, visit the Kermit project home page at http://kermit.columbia.edu/. From there, you can follow the links to the C-Kermit page and download the source code to /tmp. This should result in a file named something like ckuXXX.tar.gz, in which XXX is a version number. Now you are ready to start building the C-Kermit package. To do this, issue the following commands:

```
[root@bserver1 root]# cd /usr/local/src
[root@bserver1 src]# mkdir ckermit
[root@bserver1 src]# cd ckermit
[root@bserver1 ckermit]# tar xzf /tmp/cku197.tar.gz
[root@bserver1 ckermit]#
```

You will notice that there is no configure script in this directory—just a bunch of source code and text files. One of these files is called makefile. If you examine this file with a text editor, you will see that it is quite long; more than 6,000 lines, in fact. This is because it contains a stanza for each supported operating system that is used to build the software for that platform. To build this package for Linux, you should follow the directions at the top of the makefile and issue the following command:

```
[root@bserver1 src]# make linux
```

This results in a binary called wermit. To install this on your system, you now have two options. The first is to edit the makefile and modify the install target to do the right thing for your system. This assumes, of course, that you are familiar with makefile syntax. Your other option is to copy the wermit binary to a directory in your path and rename it as kermit. Fortunately, detailed instructions come with the source code on how to install the software in a file called ckuins.txt. Follow those directions, and you should have a working, installed Kermit binary with support files and a manual page.

NOTE

When building open source software from the source code, it is a good idea to read all the text files that come with the package. You often will find files such as README or INSTALL, which contain instructions on building and installing the software. Another good place to look is in any subdirectories of the source tree named doc, docs, or documentation (or variations on this theme).

Building Using Source RPMs

If you are using a Red–Hat-like distribution of Linux that uses RPM as the package manager, you have still another option for building source code into binary packages. This option is to download the source RPM. Source RPMs, SRPMs for short, are RPM packages that contain source code instead of executables, and contain some other files required to turn that source code into a binary RPM. The naming convention for SRPMs is `<package-name>-<version>.src.rpm`, in which `<package-name>` is the name of the software package, and `<version>` is a version number. When you install an SRPM, it installs the source code and a specification, or spec, file into a special build directory on your system. On Red Hat systems, this directory is /usr/src/redhat, which contains subdirectories BUILD, SOURCE, RPMS, SRPMS, and SPECS. Let's take a look at an example so that you can see how this system works. This is a fairly basic example. If you are interested in details of using RPM, you should visit the RPM homepage at `http://www.rpm.org/`. If you are using a distribution that supports the RPM standard, I highly recommend that you use it when building packages, because it will make upgrades to packages more manageable.

Building gnupg from an SRPM

For our example, we will build gnupg, an encryption package, from an SRPM. To locate the SRPM, we will visit `http://www.rpmfind.net/`. Using their search tool, we locate the file gnupg-1.0.6-0.6.x.src.rpm, which we download to /tmp. You now have two options. If you are interested only in compiling the SRPM, and have no interest in peeking inside or changing options, you can issue the following command:

```
[root@bserver1 root]# rpm --rebuild /tmp/gnupg-1.0.6-0.6.x.src.rpm
```

The SRPM will be unpacked, configured, and compiled for you with the resulting binary packages being deposited into the /usr/src/redhat/RPMS/i386 directory. You then can install the resulting binary packages using the following command:

```
[root@bserver1 root]# rpm -ivh /usr/src/redhat/RPMS/i386/gnupg*.rpm
```

The command installs the binary packages onto your system and updates the RPM database to reflect this fact. However, if you want to examine the options used by the RPM packager, look at any patches that were applied, or just want to try an alternative method, you could instead do the following:

```
[root@bserver1 root]# rpm -ivh /tmp/gnupg-1.0.6-0.6.x.src.rpm
[root@bserver1 SPECS]# cd /usr/src/redhat/SPECS
[root@bserver1 SPECS]# vi gnupg.spec
```

The specification file, gnupg.spec, contains various information about who built the package, the options passed to the configure script, where the files will be installed, as well as a description of the software. It also contains a list of the patches applied to the source code to build the package. The actual source code and any patches that need to be applied are located in /usr/src/redhat/SOURCES. After you have finished making any modifications to the spec file, you are ready to build the software. This is accomplished by issuing the following command:

```
[root@bserver1 SPECS]# rpm -ba gnupg.spec
```

As you will notice by looking at the output on the screen, this unpackages the source code, applies any patches required, configures the software, runs the make command, packages the resulting binaries into a binary RPM, and puts it in /usr/src/redhat/RPMS/i386. You then can install the binary RPMs using the same command that you used previously:

```
[root@bserver1 root]# rpm -ivh /usr/src/redhat/RPMS/i386/gnupg*.rpm
```

As you can see, the process of building from source code can be quite easy. Of course, if you run into problems, you should consult with a developer or the maintainer of the software you are trying to compile.

Summary

This appendix discussed some of the popular sites for obtaining the software described in this book. It also covered very briefly the basic steps to compiling the source code into a working executable. It is not highly detailed, because open source projects have a tendency to move around on occasion and the build instructions change over time. Keep in mind that the basic rules to follow when obtaining and building open source software are the following:

- Obtain the software from the software home page, if possible. If not, the RPMfind network is a good place to start.
- Unpack the source code and read every text file that accompanies the package. You usually will find all the instructions you require there.
- Maintain a clean build environment that closely matches your production environment to avoid dependency issues and binary compatibility problems.
- If all else fails, contact the software developers and ask for their help.

INDEX

SYMBOLS AND NUMBERS

 # (pound sign), 386
+ (plus sign), 146
- (minus sign), 146
3C509 card, 383
3C905B card, 383
3Com, 383

A

-A option, 209, 327
A&M University, 16
Accelerated Server Load Balancing, 363
accessing
  developers, open source software (OSS) projects, 36-37
  disks, improving performance of, 266-267
  Internet content, 353-354, 356
  Piranha Web-based interface, 348
  root directories, Web sites, 235
adding
  back-end servers, virtual services, 328
  features to Web sites, limitations of support by Internet Service Providers (ISPs), 48
  missing features, open source software (OSS), 34
  products to shopping carts, 166
  virtual services, 328, 351
addresses
  Internet Protocol (IP), 215, 382
  virtual IP (VIP), 321-322, 333-338
administrative costs
  Linux administrators, 26
  self-hosting Web sites, 302-303
Agents, mail transport (MTA), 66
AIM instant messaging, 230
AIX, 20-21
algorithms, load-balancing, 323-325
alias files, Majordomo, 96
America Online (AOL), 230

analyzing server logs, Web sites, 217-227
Angel, 214
answers to questions, finding on community sites, 108
AOL (America Online), 230
Apache, 75-76, 132-133, 169, 268
Apache Jmeter, 291
Apache servers, redirecting Uniform Resource Locators (URLs), global load balancing, 355-356
Apache Tomcat, 310
Apache Web server, 38-39, 374
Apache-SSL, 180, 196
ApacheToday, 39
appliances, load-balancing, 366
applications
- building from source code, 403-408, 410-413
- calendars, 109-110
- chat, 111-113
- content management, Web sites, 235-242
- issue-tracking, Web sites, 227-231
- licensing costs
  - *Linux, 24-25*
  - *Windows, 24*
- load balancers, 364-365
- mailing list, notice boards and, 108-109
- managing documents, 63-64
- managing searches, 68-69
- managing user feedback, 65-67
- monitoring, self-hosting Web sites, 303
- notice boards, 110-111
- open source (OSS), 179
  - *advantages and disadvantages of, 33-38*
  - *Apache Web server, 38-39*
  - *consultants' experience with, 52*
  - *MySQL, 39-40*
  - *PHP server-side scripting module, 40*
  - *support for, 38, 40-42*
  - *vs. proprietary software, 30, 32-33*
  - *Web resources, 371-372*
- peer to peer (P2P) computing, 307
- piracy of, 30
- proprietary vs. open source software, 30, 32-33
- reliability of, 245, 295-297
  - *benchmarks, 292-293*
  - *determining reliability of, 290-291*
  - *factors affecting, 293, 295*
  - *stress testing, 291-292*
- remote-sensing, 304-305
- replacement costs, 247
- security monitoring, 206-209
- server monitoring, 209-214
- stress testing Web servers, 216
- synchronizing hot-swap systems, 257-258
- system imaging, synchronizing hot-swap systems, 259-260
- test, creating, 265
- tracking site statistics, 221-227

applying patches to source code, 404
architecture
- high availability
  - *failover systems, 260-261, 264*
  - *hot-swap systems, 256, 258, 260-261, 264*
- NetSaint, 213

archives, content and media sites, 59
ARSC, 136-139, 141-145, 147
ARSC Really Simple Chat, 112
ArsDigita, 236
Artistic License, 33
attacks, detecting on Web servers, 206
authentication, node responses during failovers, 336-337
authkeys file, 336-337
availability
- high
  - *backup power, 245*
  - *calculating, 245-246*
  - *costs of, 246-247*
  - *failover systems, 260-261, 264*
  - *hot-swap systems, 256, 258, 260-261, 264*
  - *network designs, 316-318*
  - *redundant hardware, 244*
  - *software reliability, 245*
- load balancing
  - *Linux Virtual Server (LVS), 318-319, 321-322, 324-325, 327-331*
  - *Piranha, 341-348, 351, 353*
  - *Super Sparrow, 353-354, 356-357*
  - *Ultramonkey, 332, 334-341*

AWStats, 219, 225-226

B

B2B (business-to-business) computing, 305
back-end servers, virtual services, 327-328
backbones, colocation sites, 310-311
backup nodes, failures of, 336-337, 343
backup servers, enabling, 351
backups, power, 245
balancing loads
- custom-rules method, 252
- geographic, 353-354, 356-357
- global load balancing, 353-354, 356
- least-connection method, 251
- least-loaded method, 251
- Linux Virtual Server (LVS), 318-319, 321-322, 324-325, 327-331
- Piranha, 341-348, 351, 353
- response-time method, 251
- round-robin method, 250

service level agreement method, 251-252
Super Sparrow, 353-354, 356-357
Ultramonkey, 332, 334-341
weight round-robin method, 250
weighted least-connection method, 251
bandwidth, routers, 281-282
Barrett, Bradford, 221
Bash (Bourne Again Shell), 406
batteries as backup power, 245
BB (Big Brother), 210-211
Bell Canada, 210
benchmarks, 265-266, 268, 292-293
beta testing, Web sites, 265
BGP (border gateway protocol), 354
Big Brother (BB), 210-211
BigIP, 360-362
Binaries, wermit, 411
binary compatibility, build environments, 405
binary support, FreeBSD vs. Linux, 23
Blaze Board, 67
boards
bulletin, 108-109
notice, 106-107, 110-111
Boeing, 177
border gateway protocol (BGP), 354
bots, 230-231
Bourne Again Shell (Bash), 406
browsers
reloading Web pages, 167
used when visiting Web sites, tracking, 220
BSD License, 33
BSD Unix, 16
BSDI, BigIP, 360
bugs
fixing, open source software, 35
FOOF, 20, 35
software, 290
system components, 294
build environments, setting up, 404-406
building
applications from source code, 403-408, 410-413
sites
in-house development vs. outsourcing, 50-53
maintaining, 46-50
reasons for, 44-46
test software, 265
building security, colocation sites, 311
bulletin boards, 108-109
business expansion, building Web sites for, 45-46
business models, Mia Casa, 186
business requirements
analyzing server logs, 217-219
content management, 236-237
issue-tracking software, 227-228
selecting colocation providers, 309-310
updating Web sites, 233
Web site performance, 203, 205
business-to-business (B2B) computing, 305
button menus, Telecommuter's Journal, The Web site, 78-81
buttons, Reload, 167

C

-C option, 329
C-Kermit package, 411-412
Cable News Network (CNN), 58
cables, null modem, 332
calculating high availability, 245-246
Caldera Systems, 17, 210, 371, 378
calendars, community sites, 105-106, 109-110
camserv Webcam application, 304
Canadian Broadcasting Corporation (CBC), 305
CANet, 214
capacity, Web servers, 204-205
cards, 3C509 and 3C905B, 383
carts, shopping, 165-167, 170, 172-173
case studies
Firebreath.com, 190-193, 195
Mia Casa, 183-190
catalogs
Mia Casa, 186-187
online, 164-165, 169-170, 172
placement of products in, 178
Cathedral and the Bazaar, The, 31
cathedral model, 31
CBC (Canadian Broadcasting Corporation), 305
CDs (compact discs), installing Linux from, 380
Central Dispatch, 365
CERT, 206
changing
docman.conf, 75
passwords, Piranha, 349
channels
COBRA, 304
Communication, Del Valle Junior High School Parent/Teacher/Student Organization (PTSO) Web site, 117
charters
Del Valle Junior High School Parent/Teacher/Student Organization (PTSO), 116-117
Telecommuter's Journal, The, 72-73
chat, ARSC software, 136-139, 141-145, 147
chat systems, 107-108, 111-113
chatterbots, 230-231

Cheapbytes, 378
checkinterval variable, 340
checktimeout variable, 340
chips, Pentium, 20, 35
chkconfig utility, 386-389
choosing
colocation providers, 309-313
companies for outsourcing Web site development, 51-53
hardware vendors, 275, 277, 283-286
installation methods, Linux, 380
network drivers in /etc/modules.conf, 383
packages to install Linux, 381
partitioning schemes, Linux, 381
services, 349
software vendors, 295-297
Cisco
Global Director, 353
LoadDirector, 362-364
Cisco IOS, 356
classes, CP Application Construction, 183
classifieds.cgi, 151-153
classifieds.sql, 149-150
Clatter, 112
clearing
kernels from Linux Virtual Server (LVS) tables, 329
ClearingPoint Commerce. *See* CP Commerce, 179
closets, wiring, 301
Cluster Server, 365
CNN (Cable News Network), 58
Cnnfn.com, 189
COBRA channels, 304
code listings
/etc/inetd.conf, 384-386
authkeys file, 336-337
button menu frame source, Telecommuter's Journal, The Web site, 78-81
classifieds.cgi, 151-153
classifieds.sql, 149-150
config.inc, 155
config.inc.php, 137
configuration variables, Phorums, 157
contact frame source, Telecommuter's Journal, The Web site, 84-87
contacts page source, Del Valle Junior High School Parent/Teacher/Student Organization (PTSO) Web site, 128-129
customizations to ARSC, 141-146
firewall scripts, ipchains utility, 390-399
frameset creation source, Telecommuter's Journal, The Web site, 77
ha.cf files, 333-336
haresources files, 337-338
help message, lvs daemon, 343-344
httpd.conf, 132-133
index, Del Valle Junior High School Parent/Teacher/Student Organization (PTSO) Web site, 119
install.php, 137-138
ldirectord.cf, 339-340
lvs.cf files, 344-347
lvs_setup script, 331
main content frame source, Del Valle Junior High School Parent/Teacher/Student Organization (PTSO) Web site, 123-127
main frame source, Telecommuter's Journal, The Web site, 82-84
Majordomo aliases file, 96
Majordomo configuration file, 97-99
navigation frame source, Del Valle Junior High School Parent/Teacher/Student Organization (PTSO) Web site, 120-123
newsletter page source, Del Valle Junior High School Parent/Teacher/Student Organization (PTSO) Web site, 129, 131
page footer frame source, Telecommuter's Journal, The Web site, 81-82
README file, piranha-docs package, 348
specifying network drivers in /etc/modules.conf, 383
SQL commands, chat user creation, 136-137
SQL commands, creating calendars, 154-155
SQL commands, creating forum users, 157
SQL commands, creating notice boards, 148-149
synchronization with Content Master and rsync, 258
templates for *Telecommuter's Journal, The* Web site
columns, 91-94
feature articles, 87-90
title frame source, Del Valle Junior High School Parent/Teacher/Student Organization (PTSO) Web site, 119-120
title frame source, Telecommuter's Journal, The Web site, 78
collaboration features, community sites, 104
colocation
selecting providers for, 309-313
tunneling and, 323
vertical vs. horizontal scalability, 252
vs. self hosting, Web sites, 300-309
Colocation Directory, 310
colocation providers, 49-50
Colosource, 313
Colosource Colocation Facilities map, 311

commands
chkconfig, 386-389
configure, 216, 330
fos, 341
Gated, 356
gnupg, 412-413
gnuplot, 209
httpdMonitor, 330
ifconfig, 382
ipchains, packet filtering, 390-400
ipvsadm, 325, 327-329, 342
ldirectord, 329, 339-341
ln, 75
lvs, 341, 343-346
make, 216, 410
mon, 330
nanny, 341, 347
netsaint stop, 213
piranha-passwd, 349
pulse, 343, 349
rdist, 239-240
rsync, 240-242
sa2, 209
sadc, 209
sal interval count, 209
sar, 209
send_arp, 347-348
SQL, chat user creation, 136-137
SQL, creating calendars, 154-155
SQL, creating forum users, 157
SQL, creating notice boards, 148-149
sudo, 389, 407-408, 410-411
swatch, 389
Zebra, 356
communication channels, Del Valle Junior High School Parent/Teacher/Student Organization (PTSO) Web site, 117
communication costs, self-hosting Web sites, 49
community sites
calendars, 105-106, 109-110
characteristics of, 104-105
chat systems, 107-108, 111-113
mailing lists and bulletin boards, 108-109
notice boards, 106-107, 110-111
compact discs (CDs), installing Linux from, 380
compatibility
binary, build environments, 405
Microsoft Word with Concurrent Versioning System (CVS), 63
StarOffice with Concurrent Versioning System (CVS), 63
compile-time options, building applications with, 403-404
compiling Linux kernels, 318
components, hot-swappable, 279-280
Comprehensive Perl Archive Network (CPAN), 374
Concurrent Versioning System (CVS), 63-64, 237-239
config.inc, 155
config.inc.php, 137
configuration files, Majordomo, 97-99
configuration options, building applications with, 403-404
configuration variables, Phorums, 157
configure command, 216
configure script, 330, 407-408, 410
configuring
Apache, 75-76
File Transfer Protocol (FTP) servers, 327-329
fos daemon to implement mail servers, 346-347
heartbeat utility, 333-338
Linux
assigning Internet Protocol (IP) addresses to networks, 382
choosing installation methods, 380
choosing packages, 381
choosing partitioning schemes, 381
finding distribution of, 378-379
hardware inventories, 379-380
hardware issues, 382-383
security, 383-399
Linux kernels, 318
load balancers, Linux Virtual Server (LVS), 330-331
load-balancing hosts, 327-329
passwords, Piranha, 348
virtual IP addresses, heartbeat utility, 333-338
virtual services, 327-328
Web servers, 327-329
connections
backbones, colocation sites, 310-311
virtual IP addresses (VIPs), 321
consultants
choosing for Web site development, 51-53
tips for working with on e-commerce sites, 178
contact pages
Telecommuter's Journal, The Web site, 84-87
Del Valle Junior High School Parent/Teacher/Student Organization (PTSO) Web site, 128-129
content
accessing on the Internet, 353-354, 356
e-commerce sites, 162-163
managing, Web sites, 231-242
static, content and media sites, 58
storage for optimal synchronization, 258-259
Telecommuter's Journal, The Web site, 101
content and media sites
characteristics of, 58-59

- document management systems, 59-61, 63-64
- search capabilities, 62-63, 68-69
- user feedback, 61-62, 65-67

content-user-driven, community sites, 105
contractors, choosing for Web site development, 51-53
contracts, vendor support, 284
Control/Monitoring screen
- Piranha Web-based interface, 349

controls, environmental
conversations by groups, chat systems, 108
copy left, 32
costs
- BigIP, 362
- colocation provider services, 308, 310
- high availability, 246-247
- Linux operating system, 23, 26-27
- LoadDirector, 364
- replacement, hardware and software, 247
- scability, 252
- self-hosting Web sites, 48-49
  - *hardware, 301-302*
  - *operations and maintenance, 302-303*
- spare systems and components, 275
- Web sites, 44

Cox, Alan, 36
CP Application Adapters, 183
CP Application Construction Classes, 183
CP Commerce, 182-183, 188, 191-192
CP Exporter, 183
CP Foundation Server, 183
CP Messaging Server, 183
CP Reporting tools, 183
CP XML Translation Filters, 183, 189
CPAN, 169, 224, 374
creating
- notice boards, 148-149
- test software, 265
- virtual IP addresses, heartbeat utility, 333-338
- virtual services, 351
- Web sites
  - *in-house development vs. outsourcing, 50-53*
  - *maintaining, 46-50*
  - *reasons for, 44-46*

credit card verification suite, 168
credit cards, processing, 167-168, 171, 173
CRM (Customer Relations Management), 228
custom-rules load balancing, 252
customer convenience, building Web sites for, 45
Customer Relations Management (CRM), 228
customer support, Web sites, 228
customers
- attracting to Telecommuter's Journal, The Web site, 101
- loss of, 246-247
- Mia Casa, 185
- receiving feedback from, e-commerce sites, 168
- referrals for colocation providers, 313
- replies to requests from, 179

customizing
- ARSC, 141-146
- open source software (OSS), 35-36

CVS (Concurrent Versioning System), 237-239
CVS. *See* Current Versioning System, 63
CyberCalendar, 110
CyberCash, 172
CyberWeavers, 110
Cyclic Software, Concurrent Versioning System (CVS), 237-239

D

daemons
- fos, 341
- Gated, 356
- inetd, 386
- ldirectord, 329, 339-341
- lvs, 341, 343-346
- pulse, 343, 349
- Zebra, 356

databases
- e-commerce sites, 162-163
- e-commerce systems, 180
- mSQL, 39
- population tools, e-commerce sites, 164-165
- schema management tools, e-commerce sites, 164
- storing content in, 58
- testing, 292
- updating, 178

Dawson, Terry, 370
DBM files, 172
deadcat.net, 210
Debian Project, 15, 17, 371
Debugging, systems and services, ipchains utility, 400
dedicated servers, colocation providers, 308
Deja.com, 59
Del Valle Junior High School Parent/Teacher/Student Organization (PTSO)
- challenges in making site successful, 158-160
- features of, 117, 119-122, 124-129, 131-139, 141-145, 147, 149-153, 155-157
- site charter and design, 116-117

Dents Domain Name System (DNS) server, 356-357
DENY rules, 400
dependencies
- library, resolving when building applications, 404-406

software
resolving when building applications, 404
supporting, 406
design
Del Valle Junior High School Parent/Teacher/Student Organization (PTSO), 116-122, 124-129, 131
Telecommuter's Journal, The, 72-73
Web sites, 218
detecting attacks, Web servers, 206
developers, access to for open source software (OSS) projects, 36-37
development models, cathedral, 31
dialog boxes, Networking Options, kernel configurator, 318
direct routing, Linux Virtual Server (LVS), 321-322
Directed mode, LoadDirector support of, 363
directories
/proc, 208
/var/log, 207
root, accessing in Web sites, 235
disaster plans, colocation sites, 312
discussions by groups, chat systems, 108
disks, accessing, 266-267
Dispatched mode, LoadDirector support of, 363
displaying
shopping carts, 166
tables maintained by kernels, ipvsadm utility, 328
distributed processing, Web server reports, 218
DNS servers. *See* Domain Name System servers, 354
docman.conf, editing, 75
document management systems
content and media sites, 59-61, 63-64
Telecommuter's Journal, The Web site, 74-76
Document Manager, 64, 74-75
Domain Name System (DNS) servers, global load balancing, 354-355
downloading Linux from the Internet, 378-379
drivers, network, 383
drives
hard, installing Linux from, 380
IDE, advantages and disadvantages of, 266
SCSI, advantages and disadvantages of, 266-267
dynamic pages, e-commerce sites, 163

E

e-commerce
Apache-SSL, 180
CP Commerce, 182-183, 188
databases, 180
Firebreath.com case study, 190-193, 195
history of, 176-177
hosting sites, 196
Mia Casa case study, 183-190
open source applications, 179
Perl, 181-182
preparing businesses for, 196
tips for success in, 178-179
Web servers, 180
e-commerce sites
characteristics of, 162-163
credit card processing, 167-168
online catalogs, 164-165
receiving customer feedback, 168
shopping carts, 165-167
tools for creating, 168-173
e-mail
from customers, replies to, 179
tracking Web site issues by, 229
editing
docman.conf, 75
passwords, Piranha, 349
electricity
fluctuations in power, 273
loss of, backup power, 245
emulators, C-Kermit package, 411-412
enabling backup servers, 351
encapsulation, IP. *See* tunneling, 322
encryption packages, gnupg, 412-413
engineers, Microsoft Certified Systems (MCSE), 26
engines, search, 99-100
enterprise features, FreeBSD vs. Linux, 23
environmental controls, colocation sites, 311
environments, build, 404-406
equipment maintenance, self-hosting Web sites, 49-50
/etc/inetd.conf, 384-386
/etc/modules.conf, specifying network drivers in, 383
events, 106, 117
Exim, 66
Exmlm, 66
expanding businesses, building Web sites for, 45-46
Extranet, 305

F

-f option, 328
F5 Networks, BigIP, 360-362
failover hardware, 272
failover systems, 260-261, 264
implementing, Ultramonkey, 332, 334-341
Piranha, 341-348, 351, 353

Failover tab, Piranha Web-based interface, 351
failure, single points of, 252
backup nodes, 336-337, 343
mean time between (MTBF), 246
mean time between (MTTR), 246
primary nodes, 336-337, 343
rates of, 272
servers, maintaining spare systems and components, 274-275
FCC (Federal Communications Commission), 286-287
feedback
content and media sites, 61-62, 65-67
receiving from users, Telecommuter's Journal, The Web site, 94-95, 97-99
fees
colocation provider services, 308, 310
self-hosting Web sites
hardware, 301-302
operations and maintenance, 302-303
File Transfer Protocol (FTP), 319
File Transfer Protocol (FTP) servers, configuring, 327-329
files
/etc/inetd.conf, 384-386
/etc/modules.conf, specifying network drivers in, 383
alias, Majordomo, 96
authkeys, 336-337
classifieds.cgi, 151-153
classifieds.sql, 149-150
config.inc, 155
config.inc.php, 137
configuration, Majordomo, 97-99
customizations to ARSC, 141-146
DBM, 172
docman.conf, editing, 75
flat, storing content in, 58
ha.cf, 333-336
haresources, 337-338
httpd.conf, 132-133
install.php, 137-138
journaling file systems, FreeBSD vs. Linux, 23
ldirectord.cf, 339-340
lvs.cf, 344-347
README, piranha-docs package, 348
spreading across SCSI drives, 267
Filesystem Hierarchy Standard (FHS), 22
filtering packets, ipchains utility, 390-400
filters, CP XML Translation, 183, 189
finding help on community sites, 108
fire systems, colocation sites, 312
Firebreath.com case study, 190-193, 195
firewall mark service definition method, 320
firewall scripts, ipchains utility, 390-399
firewalls
role of in self-hosting Web sites, 301
security of, self-hosting Web sites, 303-304
flat files, storing content in, 58
flexibility, open source software (OSS), 34-36
fluctuations in power, 273
FOOF bug, 20, 35
footers, Telecommuter's Journal, The Web site, 81-82
forms, tracking Web site issues by, 229
forums, software for managing, 67
forward tag, JavaServer Pages (JSPs), 220
fos daemon, 341
frameworks
Del Valle Junior High School Parent/Teacher/Student Organization (PTSO), 118-122, 124-129, 131
Telecommuter's Journal, The Web site, 76, 78-79, 81-87
Free Software Foundation, 17
FreeBSD operating system vs. Linux, 22-23
Freelancers, choosing for Web site development, 51-53
Freshmeat, 39-40, 168, 236, 372, 402
Freshmeat.net, 179
fsck issue-tracking kit, 229
FTP servers. *See* File Transfer Protocol servers, 327
FTP. *See* File Transfer Protocol, 319

G

GAIM, 230
Galstad, Ethan, 212
Gartner Group, 285
Gated daemon, 356
general purpose distributions, Linux operating system, 17
generators, as backup power, 245
geographic load balancing, 353-354, 356-357
geographic usage, Web sites, 217
GET method, 216
Giles, Steve, 211
Gimp, The, 78
Global Director, 353
global load balancing, 353-354, 356
Global Settings tab, Piranha Web-based interface, 349
GNU autoconf system, 407
GNU C library, 405

GNU General Pubic License, 17
GNU General Public License (GPL), 32
GNU Lesser General Public License (LGPL), 32-33
GNU Manifesto, The, 32
GNU project, 17
GNU Web site, 30
gnupg package, 412-413
gnuplot command, 209
Godard, Sebastien, 208
Google, 221
GPL. *See* GNU General Public License, 32
graphics, synchronizing hot-swap systems with, 259-260
Groundhog Day, 204
group discussions, chat systems, 108

H

-h option, 325
ha.cf files, 333-336
hacking Web sites live, 234-235
hard drives, installing Linux from, 380
hardware
- costs of, self-hosting Web sites, 301-302
- inventories of, 379-380
- issues in Linux networks, 382-383
- rackmount, role of in self-hosting Web sites, 301
- redundancy, 244
- reliability of
  - *choosing hardware vendors, 275, 277, 283-286*
  - *failover hardware, 272*
  - *failure rates, 272*
  - *Federal Communications Commission (FCC) and Underwriters Laboratories (UL) ratings, 286-287*
  - *hot-swappable components, 279-280*
  - *infrastructure requirements, 280-283*
  - *maintaining spare systems and components, 274-275*
  - *mean time between failures (MTBF), 272-274*
  - *technologies used for achieving, 277-279*
- replacement costs, 247
- scability of, 294
- vendor partnerships, colocation providers, 310

hardware requirements
- Linux, 25-26
- Solaris Unix vs. Linux, 21
- Windows NT, 25
- Windows vs. Linux, 20

haresources files, 337-338
heartbeat utility, 332, 334-338
help, finding on community sites, 108
help messages, lvs daemon, 343-344
help option, 343
Hewlett-Packard, 177, 211
high availability
- backup power, 245
- calculating, 245-246
- costs of, 246-247
- failover systems, 260-261, 264
- hot-swap systems, 256, 258, 260-261, 264
- load balancing
  - *Linux Virtual Server (LVS), 318-319, 321-322, 324-325, 327-331*
  - *Piranha, 341-348, 351, 353*
  - *Super Sparrow, 353-354, 356-357*
  - *Ultramonkey, 332, 334-341*
- network designs, 316-318
- redundant hardware, 244
- software reliability, 245

High Availability Server, 378
High Availability Server product, Red Hat, 341
hits, Web sites, 219
horizontal scalability, 249-253
Hormans, Simon, 357
hosting Web sites, self-hosting vs. colocation, 300-309
hosting services
- maintaining Web sites through, 46-48
- maintaining your own servers, 48-50

hosts
- load-balancing, configuring, 327-329
- shared virtual, colocation providers, 309

hot-swap systems, 256, 258, 260-261, 264
hot-swappable components, 279-280
hot-swappable server components, role of in self-hosting Web sites, 302
HP/UX, 21
ht://Dig, 68
HTTP. *See* Hypertext Transfer Protocol, 319
httpd.conf, 132-133
httpdMonitor script, 330
hubs, requirements for, 280-281
HydraWEB Mercury, 366
Hypertext Transfer Protocol (HTTP), 319

I

Ibiblio Linux system status archive, 209
IBM, 15
ICat, 177
ICQ, tracking Web site issues by, 229-230
IDE, as hot-swappable component, 279
IDE drives, advantages and disadvantages of, 266
ifconfig command, 382
images, synchronizing hot-swap systems with, 259-260

in-house Web site development, 50-53
indexes, Del Valle Junior High School Parent/Teacher/Student Organization (PTSO) Web site, 119
inetd daemon, 386
inetd.conf, 384-386
infrastructures
- requirements for, 280-283

Ingres project, 375
Inktomi, 189
install.php, 137-138
installing
- ARSC, 136
- AWStats, 225
- Big Brother (BB), 211
- Document Manager, 74-75
- Linux
  - *assigning Internet Protocol (IP) addresses to networks, 382*
  - *choosing installation methods, 380*
  - *choosing packages, 381*
  - *choosing partitioning schemes, 381*
  - *finding distribution of, 378-379*
  - *hardware inventories, 379-380*
  - *hardware issues, 382-383*
  - *security, 383-399*
- Linux kernels, 318
- NetSaint, 213
- OpenNMS, 212
- OpenStats, 226
- Perl Webstats, 224
- rsync utility, 240-242
- Siege, 216
- site monitors, 215
- Webalizer, 222-223

Intel Corporation
- purchase of ICat by, 177

Interchange, 172-173, 179
interfaces
- Piranha, 348, 351, 353

Internet
- accessing content on, 353-354, 356
- building sites
  - *in-house development vs. outsourcing, 50-53*
  - *maintaining, 46-50*
  - *reasons for, 44-46*
- downloading Linux from, 378-379
- simulating traffic on, 215

Internet Protocol (IP) addresses
- assigning to Linux networks, 382
- excluding from site log analysis reports, 215

Internet Relay Chat (IRC), 112, 230
Internet Seer, 215
Internet Service Providers (ISPs), maintaining Web sites through, 46-48
inventory tracking, e-commerce sites, 165
IP addresses. *See* Internet Protocol addresses, 215, 382
IP encapsulation. *See* tunneling, 322
IP:ip fwmark Masq-Forwarding Support option, 319
IP:Masquerading Virtual Server Support option, 318
ipchains utility, packet filtering, 390-400
ipvsadm utility, 325, 327-329, 342
IRC (Internet Relay Chat), 112, 230
Irix, 21
ISP-Planet, 313
ISPs (Internet Service Providers), maintaining Web sites through, 46-48
issue-tracking software, Web sites, 227-231
Iwon.com, 189

J

Jabber instant messaging, 230
JBOD (Just a Bunch Of Disks), 278
Jmeter, 291
journaling filesystem support, FreeBSD vs. Linux, 23
Just a Bunch of Disks (JBOD), 278

K

kernel configurator, Networking Options dialog box, 318
Kernel.org, 370
kernels
- clearing from Linux Virtual Server (LVS) tables, 329
- configuring, compiling, and installing, 318
- Linux operating system, 14-16
- tables maintained by, viewing with ipvsadm utility, 328

Keyboard/Mouse/Video (KVM) switches, 283
Kirsch, Olaf, 370
KVM (Keyboard/Mouse/Video) switches, 283

L

-l option, 329, 400
ldirectord daemon, 329, 339-341
ldirectord.cf, 339-340
leaks, memory, 293-294
least-connection load balancing, 251
least-connection scheduling algorithm, 324
least-loaded load balancing, 251
LGPL. *See* GNU Lesser General Public License, 32

libraries
GNU C, 405
Linux C, 405
Support, Super Sparrow, 356
library version dependencies, resolving when building applications, 404-406
libsupersparrow support library, 356
licenses
Big Brother (BB), 211
open source software (OSS) (OSS)
Artistic License, 33
BSD, 33
GNU General Public (GPL), 32
GNU Lesser General Public (LGPL), 32-33
software costs, 24-25
LICQ, 230
linking Web sites to Document Manager, 75
Linux
/proc directory, 208
/var/log directory, 207
Concurrent Versioning System (CVS), 237-239
Ibiblio Linux system status archive, 209
installing and configuring
assigning Internet Protocol (IP) addresses to networks, 382
choosing installation methods, 380
choosing packages, 381
choosing partitioning schemes, 381
finding distribution of, 378-379
hardware inventories, 379-380
hardware issues, 382-383
security, 383-399
Mindcraft study, 293
Redundant Array of Inexpensive Disks (RAID) support, 278
support from vendors, 295-296
System Activity Reporting (SAR), 208
Web resources, 370-371
worm attacks, 206
Linux C library, 405
Linux Documentation Project, 370
Linux operating system
costs of, 23, 26-27
described, 14-16, 18-19
distributions of, 16, 18-19
performance tuning and, 266
spreading files across SCSI drives, 267
swap space, 268
technical support, 18
vs. BSD, 22-23
vs. Unix, 14, 20-21
vs. Windows, 19-20
Web site of, 268
Linux Standard Base (LSB), 22
Linux Today, 61, 373
Linux Virtual Server (LVS)
configure script, 330
defining virtual services, 319-320
described, 318-319
httpdMonitor script, 330
ipvsadm utility, 325, 327-329, 342
ldirectord daemon, 329
load-balancing algorithms, 323-325, 328
Piranha, 341-348, 351, 353
routing methods, 320-323
sample network designs, 316-317, 330-331
Ultramonkey, 332, 334-341
vs. BigIP, 361
Linux Weekly News, 373
Linuxcare, 371
Linuxmall, 378
linuxperf.org, 268
listings
/etc/inetd.conf, 384-386
authkeys file, 336-337
button menu frame source, *Telecommuter's Journal, The* Web site, 78-81
classifieds.cgi, 151-153
classifieds.sql, 149-150
config.inc, 155
config.inc.php, 137
configuration variables, Phorums, 157
contact frame source, *Telecommuter's Journal, The* Web site, 84-87
contacts page source, Del Valle Junior High School Parent/Teacher/Student Organization (PTSO) Web site, 128-129
customizations to ARSC, 141-146
firewall scripts, ipchains utility, 390-399
frameset creation source, *Telecommuter's Journal, The* Web site, 77
ha.cf files, 333-336
haresources files, 337-338
help message, lvs daemon, 343-344
httpd.conf, 132-133
index, Del Valle Junior High School Parent/Teacher/Student Organization (PTSO) Web site, 119
install.php, 137-138
ldirectord.cf, 339-340
lvs.cf files, 344-347
lvs_setup script, 331
main content frame source, Del Valle Junior High School Parent/Teacher/Student Organization (PTSO) Web site, 123-127
main frame source, Telecommuter's Journal, The Web site, 82-84
Majordomo aliases file, 96
Majordomo configuration file, 97-99

navigation frame source, Del Valle Junior High School Parent/Teacher/Student Organization (PTSO) Web site, 120-123
newsletter page source, Del Valle Junior High School Parent/Teacher/Student Organization (PTSO) Web site, 129, 131
page footer frame source, Telecommuter's Journal, The Web site, 81-82
README file, piranha-docs package, 348
specifying network drivers in /etc/modules.conf, 383
SQL commands, chat user creation, 136-137
SQL commands, creating calendars, 154-155
SQL commands, creating forum users, 157
SQL commands, creating notice boards, 148-149
synchronization with Content Master and rsync, 258
templates for Telecommuter's Journal, The Web site
columns, 91-94
feature articles, 87-90
title frame source, Del Valle Junior High School Parent/Teacher/Student Organization (PTSO) Web site, 119-120
title frame source, Telecommuter's Journal, The Web site, 78

live hacking, Web sites, 234-235
live operators, tracking Web site issues by, 229-231
-ln option, 329
ln command, 75
load, Web servers, 204-205
load balancing
appliances, 366
BigIP, 360-362
custom-rules method, 252
geographic, 353-354, 356-357
global, 353-354, 356
least-connection method, 251
least-loaded method, 251
Linux Virtual Server (LVS), 318-319, 321-322, 324-325, 327-331
LoadDirector, 362-363
Piranha, 341-348, 351, 353
response-time method, 251
round-robin method, 250
service level agreement method, 251-252
software load balancers, 364-365
Super Sparrow, 353-354, 3 56-357
switches, 366
Ultramonkey, 332, 334-341
weight round-robin method, 250
weighted least-connection method, 251
Zeus Load Balancer, 365

load-balancing algorithms, Linux Virtual Server (LVS), 323-325
load-balancing hosts, configuring, 327-329
load-balancing switches, 366
LoadDirector, 362-364
locality-based least-connection scheduling algorithm, 325
locality-based least-connection with replication scheduling algorithm, 325
logging systems and services, ipchains utility, 400
logs
site log analysis reports, excluding Internet Protocol (IP) addresses, 215
system, security of, 207
Web servers, analyzing, 217-227

LPRng, 206
LSB. *See* Linux Standard Base, 22
lvs daemon, 341, 343-346
LVS. *See* Linux Virtual Server
lvs.cf files, 344-347
lvs_setup script, 331

M

-m option, 327
magazines, *Telecommuter's Journal, The Web site*, 72
mail servers, configuring fos deamon to implement, 346-347
mail transport agents (MTAs), 66
mailing list software, bulletin boards, 108-109
mailing lists, 65-66, 375
MailMan, 66
main content frame source, Del Valle Junior High School Parent/Teacher/Student Organization (PTSO) Web site, 123-127
maintenance
community calendars, 106
costs of
Linux, 26
self-hosting Web sites, 302-303
equipment for self-hosting Web sites, 49-50
Web sites, 46-50, 202-203
analyzing server logs, 217-227
business requirements, performance, 203, 205
issue-tracking software, 227-231
live hacking, 234-235
managing content, 231-242
monitoring servers, 205, 207-216
personnel, hardware and software, 247

maintenance costs, self-hosting Web sites, 48
Majorcool, 66

Majordomo, 66, 96-99, 171
make command, 216
make utility, 410
managing
content, Web sites, 231-242
documents
content and media sites, 59-61, 63-64
software for, 63-64
searches, software for, 68-69
user feedback, software for, 65-67
Web sites, self-hosting vs. colocation, 300-309
Manchester Computing Center, 16
Mandrake, 17
Marketing, building Web sites for, 44-45
masquerading, 317
Mayville, Paul, 190-193, 195
MCC Linux distribution, 16
MCSE (Microsoft Certified Systems Engineers), 26
mean time between failures (MTBF), 246, 272-274
mean time to repair (MTTR), 246
memory, improving performance, 267-268
memory leaks, 293-294
menus, *Telecommuter's Journal, The* Web site, 78-81
MeritGated Consortium, 356
messages, help, 343-344
methods
GET, 216
POST, 216
sendRedirect(), 220
Mia Casa case study, 183-190
microchips, Pentium, 20, 35
Microsoft, 24
Microsoft Certified Systems Engineers (MCSE), 26
Microsoft Word, compatibility with Concurrent Versioning System (CVS), 63
Mindcraft study, Linux performance, 293
Mini-Vend, 172
MiniSearch, 69
Minix operating system, 15
minus (-) sign, 146
mirror sites, 353
mnoGoSearch, 68
mnuGoSearch, 99
models, development, 31
modem cables, null, 332
modes, LoadDirector support of, 363
modified Domain Name System (DNS) servers, global load balancing, 354-355
modifying
docman.conf, 75
passwords, Piranha, 349
modular updates, Web sites, 234
modules
CP Commerce, 183
mod_rewrite, 355-356
mod_supersparrow, 356-357
modules.conf, specifying network drivers in, 383
mod_rewrite module, 355-356
mod_supersparrow module, 356-357
MON, 214
mon utility, 330
monitoring
real server pools, 330
systems and services on Linux networks, 389-390
Web sites, 205, 207-216
monitoring software, self-hosting Web sites, 303
monitors
networks, 209-214
security, 205, 207-209
servers, 205, 209-216
moreover.com, 206
Mozilla, 219
mSQL database, 39
MTA. *See* mail transport agents, 66
MTBF (mean time between failures), 272-274
MTBF. *See* mean time between failures, 246
MTTR. *See* mean time to repair, 246
multiprocessor support, FreeBSD vs. Linux, 23
My Classifieds, 111, 147, 149-153
MySQL, 134, 196
described, 39-40
downloading, 169
Interchange support, 172
Web resources, 374-375

N

-n option, 329
Nagano Olympics, 204
nanny utility, 341, 347
Napster, 307
NAS. *See* network attached storage, 258
NAT. *See* network address translation
National Center for Supercomputer Applications (NCSA), 38
National Laboratory for Parallel and Distributed Processing, 318
navigation frame source, Del Valle Junior High School Parent/Teacher/Student Organization (PTSO) Web site, 120-123
NcFTP, 33
NCSA. *See* National Center for Supercomputer Applications, 38
NetBSD operating system vs. Linux, 22-23
NetSaint, 212-214
netsaint stop command, 213
network address translation (NAT)
BigIP support of, 361
described, 316
Linux Virtual Server (LVS), 320-321
***Network Administrator's Guide*, 370**

network attached storage (NAS), synchronizing hot-swap systems, 258-259
network drivers, specifying in /etc/modules.conf, 383
network monitors, 209-214
Networking Options dialog box, kernel configurator, 318
networks
assigning Internet Protocol (IP) addresses to, 382
designs for high availability and scalability, 316-318
hardware issues, Linux, 382-383
infrastructures requirements, 280-283
installing Linux over, 380
monitoring systems and services on, 389-390
packet filtering, ipchains utility, 390-400
Storage Area (SAN), 274
tracking services on, 384-389
Netzbrett, 67, 95
***New York Times*, 58**
news sites, 372-373
NewsForge, 373
newsgroups, 62. 231, 375
newsletters, Del Valle Junior High School Parent/Teacher/Student Organization (PTSO) Web site, 117, 129, 131
nodes, failures of, 336-337, 343
—nofork option, 345-346
notice boards, 106-107, 110-111, 148-149
nPath, BigIP support of, 361
null modem cables, 332

O

O'Donnell, Shane, 211
offsite monitoring, Web servers, 214-215
Olavarria, Alexandra, 178, 186, 189
Olympics, 204
online catalogs, 164-165, 169-170, 172, 178
online magazines, *Telecommuter's Journal, The Web site*, 72
online newsletters, Del Valle Junior High School Parent/Teacher/Student Organization (PTSO) Web site, 117, 129, 131
Ontario Science Center Information Highway Internet café exhibit, 217
Open CMS, 235
Open Group, The, 14
open source applications, 179
open source community, consultants' relationships with, 52-53
open source software (OSS)
advantages and disadvantages of, 33-38
Apache Web server, 38-39
consultants' experience with, 52
MySQL, 39-40
PHP server-side scripting module, 40
support for, 38, 40-42
vs. proprietary software, 30, 32-33
Web resources, 371-372
OpenBSD operating system vs. Linux, 22-23
OpenCola, 307
OpenNMS, 211-212
OpenServer Suite, 210
openssl package, 216
OpenStats, 226-227
OpenView, 211
operating systems (OS)
FreeBSD vs. Linux, 22-23
Internet Service Provider (ISP) support, limitations of, 47
Linux
described, 14-16, 18-19
distributions of, 16, 18-19
technical support, 18
vs. BSD, 22-23
vs. Unix, 14, 20-21
vs. Windows, 19-20
Web resources, 370-371
Minix, 15
NetBSD vs. Linux, 22-23
OpenBSD vs. Linux, 22-23
Unix vs. Linux, 14, 20-21
used when visiting Web sites, tracking, 220
Windows vs. Linux, 19-20
operations costs, self-hosting Web sites, 302-303
operators, tracking Web site issues by, 229-231
optimizing servers, 268
options
-A, 209
configuration, building applications with, 403-404
IP:ip fwmark Masq-Forwarding Support, 319
IP:Masquerading Virtual Server Support, 318
Oracle, 18, 172
OS. *See* operating systems
OSS. *See* open source software
outsourced monitoring, Web servers, 214-215
outsourcing Web site development, 50-53

P

-p option, 328
P2P (peer to peer) computing, 307
packages
C-Kermit, 411-412
choosing for installation, Linux, 381
gnupg, 412-413
sudo, 407-408, 410-411
packet filtering, ipchains utility, 390-400

packets, routing with Linux Virtual Server (LVS), 320-323
page counts, Web sites, 217
pages
- contact, *Telecommuter's Journal, The* Web site, 84-87
- contacts, Del Valle Junior High School Parent/Teacher/Student Organization (PTSO) Web site, 128-129
- dynamic, e-commerce sites, 163
- footers, Telecommuter's Journal, The Web site, 81-82
- newsletter, Del Valle Junior High School Parent/Teacher/Student Organization (PTSO) Web site, 129, 131
- refreshing, 167
- static, community sites, 104-105
- tracking pages viewed, Web sites, 219-220

Paginators, 188, 193
partitioning Linux, 381
passwords, 348-349
- changing

patches
- applying to source code, 404
- availability of, Linux vs. Windows, 20
- System Activity Reporting (SAR), 209

PCI, as hot-swappable component, 279
peer to peer (P2P) computing, 307
Penguin Computing, 51
Pentium processors, FOOF bug, 20, 35
performance
- accessing disks, improving, 266-267
- memory, improving, 267-268
- servers, improving response time, 268
- swap partitions, improving, 267-268
- Web servers, 204-205
- Web sites, business requirements, 203, 205

performance tuning, 266-268
Perl, 135, 181-182
- configure script, 330
- downloading, 169
- Web resources, 373-374

Perl scripts, Del Valle Junior High School Parent/Teacher/Student Organization (PTSO) Web site newsletter page, 130-131
Perl scripting language, Artistic License, 33
Perl Template Toolkit, 224
Perl Webstats, 223-224
Personal Web Server (PWS), 19
personnel costs
- Linux maintenance, 26
- maintaining Web sites, 247

Phorum, 67
Phorums, 156-157
PHP, 133-134, 374
PHP Builder, 40, 374
PHP server-side scripting module, 40
phpMyAdmin, 134
phpMyBoard, 111
phpMyChat, 113
piracy, 30
Piranha
- advantages and disadvantages of, 341
- described, 341-342
- fos daemon, 341
- lvs daemon, 341, 343-346
- nanny utility, 341, 347
- pulse daemon, 343, 349
- send_arp utility, 347-348

piranha RPM package, 342
piranha-docs package, README file, 348
piranha-docs RPM package, 342
piranha-gui RPM package, 342
piranha-passwd command, 349
platforms, support by *Telecommuter's Journal, The* Web site, 74
plus sign (+), 146
PML (Product Mark-up Language), 189
pools, real server, 329-330, 340-341
Popular Power, 307
population tools, e-commerce site databases, 164-165
POSIX specification, Linux operating system, 14
POST method, 216
Postfix, 66
PostgreSQL, 33, 40, 196
- Interchange support, 172
- Web resources, 374-375

posting events, community sites, 106
pound sign (#), 386
power, backups, 245
power fluctuations, 273
power supplies
- as hot-swappable component, 280
- Uninterruptible Power Supply (UPS), 273, 282-283

prices
- BigIP, 362
- colocation provider services, 308, 310
- high availability, 246-247
- Linux operating system, 23, 26-27
- LoadDirector, 364
- scability, 252
- self-hosting Web sites, 48-49
  - *hardware, 301-302*
  - *operations and maintenance, 302-303*
- spare systems and components, 275
- Web sites, 44

primary nodes, failures of, 336-337, 343
/proc directory, 208
processing
- credit cards, 167-168, 171, 173
- distributed, Web server reports, 218

processors, Pentium, 20, 35
Product Mark-up Language (PML), 189
production servers
moving Web site updates to, 233-234
publishing content, Concurrent Versioning System (CVS), 238-239
products
adding to shopping carts, 166
focusing on, e-commerce sites, 178
Mia Casa, 184
programs
building from source code, 403-408, 410-413
calendars, 109-110
chat, 111-113
content management, Web sites, 235-242
issue-tracking, Web sites, 227-231
licensing costs
Linux, 24-25
Windows, 24
load balancers, 364-365
mailing list, notice boards and, 108-109
managing documents, 63-64
managing searches, 68-69
managing user feedback, 65-67
monitoring, self-hosting Web sites, 303
notice boards, 110-111
open source (OSS), 179
advantages and disadvantages of, 33-38
Apache Web server, 38-39
consultants' experience with, 52
MySQL, 39-40
PHP server-side scripting module, 40
support for, 38, 40-42
vs. proprietary software, 30, 32-33
Web resources, 371-372
peer to peer (P2P) computing, 307
piracy of, 30
proprietary vs. open source software, 30, 32-33
reliability of, 245, 295-297
benchmarks, 292-293
determining reliability of, 290-291
factors affecting, 293, 295
stress testing, 291-292
remote-sensing, 304-305
replacement costs, 247
security monitoring, 206-209
server monitoring, 209-214
stress testing Web servers, 216
system imaging, synchronizing hot-swap systems, 257-260
test, creating, 265
tracking site statistics, 221-227
promotions, building Web sites for, 44-45
proprietary software vs. open source software, 30, 32-33
protocol, port, IP address service definition method, 319, 327-329
protocols
border gateway (BGP), 354
File Transfer (FTP), 319
Hypertext Transfer (HTTP), 319
routing, 354
Transmission Control (TCP), 319
Transmission Control Protocol/Internet (TCP/IP) support, Windows and Linux, 19
User Datagram (UDP), 319
PTSO. *See* Del Valle Junior High School Parent/Teacher/Student Organization, 116
publicity
Del Valle Junior High School Parent/Teacher/Student Organization (PTSO) Web site, 158-159
purpose of Del Valle Junior High School Parent/Teacher/Student Organization (PTSO), 116-117
pulse daemon, 343, 349
Purdue University COAST Security Archive, 207
PWS. *See* Personal Web Server, 19
Python scripting language, 66

Q-R

Qmail, 66
questions, finding answers on community sites, 108

rackmount hardware, role of in self-hosting Web sites, 301
RAID. *See* redundant array of inexpensive disks
rapid response, Web sites, 204
RATEaSERVER.com, 313
raw source code, building applications from, 406-408, 410-411
Raymond, Eric, 31
rdist, 257-258
rdist utility, 239-240
readers, attracting to *Telecommuter's Journal, The* Web site, 101
reading server logs, Web sites, 219-227
README file, piranha-docs package, 348
real server pools
managing, 329, 340-341
monitoring, 330
Red Hat, 51, 378
Interchange, 179
introduction of GNU C library, 405

Linux distribution from, 15, 17
LPRng, 206
Oracle support, 18
Piranha, 341
training offered by, 27
Red Hat Linux, 371
Red Hat Professional Server, 24
redundancy
hardware, 244
server components, role of in self-hosting Web sites, 302
Redundancy tab, Piranha Web-based interface, 351
Redundant Array of Inexpensive Disks (RAID), 274, 267, 277-279
referrers to Web sites, tracking, 221
refreshing Web pages, 167
reliability
hardware
choosing hardware vendors, 275, 277, 283-286
failover hardware, 272
failure rates, 272
Federal Communications Commission (FCC) and Underwriters Laboratories (UL) ratings, 286-287
hot-swappable components, 279-280
infrastructure requirements, 280-283
maintaining spare systems and components, 274-275
mean time between failures (MTBF), 272-274
technologies used for achieving, 277-279
software, 245
benchmarks, 292-293
choosing software vendors, 295-297
determining reliability of, 290-291
factors affecting, 293, 295
stress testing, 291-292
Reload button, Web browsers, 167
Remote Method Invocation (RMI), 304
remote-sensing applications, 304-305
replacement costs, hardware and software, 247
replies to customers, 179
reports, site log analysis, 215
resolving dependencies when building applications, 404-406
Resonate, Central Dispatch, 365
response time
Web sites, 204
servers, improving, 268
response-time load balancing, 251
retail space, treating e-commerce sites as, 179
revisions to documents, tracking, 60-61
RMI (Remote Method Invocation), 304
root directories, accessing on Web sites, 235
round-robin load balancing, 250
round-robin scheduling algorithm, 324, 328
route servers, Super Sparrow, 356
router query tools, Super Sparrow, 356-357
routers
requirements for, 280-281
role of in self-hosting Web sites, 301
routing packets, Linux Virtual Server (LVS), 320-323
routing protocols, 354
RPMfind.net, 403
rsync utility, 240-242, 257-258
rules
DENY, 400
firewalls, 393-399
runlevels, 388

S

-s option, 327
sa2 command, 209
sadc command, 209
sal interval count command, 209
sales, loss of, 246-247
Samba, 17, 37
Samhain, 206-207
SAN (Storage Area Network), 274
sar command, 209
SAR (System Activity Reporting), 208-209
Satan, 206
scalability
benchmarks, 265-266, 268
described, 247
hardware, 294
horizontal, 249-253
network designs, 316-318
performance tuning, 266-268
planning for, 268
vertical, 248-249, 252-253
scheduling algorithms
least-connection, 324
locality-based least-connection, 325
locality-based least-connection with replication, 325
round-robin, 324, 328
weighted least-connection, 324
weighted round-robin, 324
schema, e-commerce site management tools, 164
screens, Piranha Web-based interface, 349, 351
scripts
configure, 330, 407-408, 410
httpdMonitor, 330
ipchains utility, 390-396, 398-399
lvs_setup, 331
Perl, Del Valle Junior High School Parent/Teacher/Student Organization (PTSO) newsletter page, 130-131

SCSI drives, advantages and disadvantages of, 266-267
search engines, *Telecommuter's Journal, The* Web site, 99-100
searches, content and media sites, 62-63, 68-69
Secure Sockets Layer (SSL), 196
security
- colocation sites, 311-312
- Linux networks, 383-399
- self-hosting Web sites, 303-304
- tools for, Linux systems, 400
- Web sites, 204
- Windows vs. Linux, 19

security monitors, 205, 207-209
selecting
- colocation providers, 309-313
- companies for outsourcing Web site development, 51-53
- hardware vendors, 275, 277, 283-286
- installation methods, Linux, 380
- network drivers in /etc/modules.conf, 383
- packages to install, Linux, 381
- partitioning schemes, Linux, 381
- services, 349
- software vendors, 295-297

self-hosting Web sites vs. colocation, 300-309
Sendmail, 66
sendRedirect() method, 220
send_arp utility, 347-348
server monitors, 205, 209-216
servers
- Apache, redirecting Uniform Resource Locators (URLs), global load balancing, 355-356
- back-end
  - *adding for virtual services, 328*
  - *defining for virtual services, 327*
- backup, enabling, 351
- CP Foundation, 183
- CP Messaging, 183
- dedicated, colocation providers, 308
- Dents Domain Name System (DNS), 356-357
- failures in, maintaining spare systems and components, 274-275
- File Transfer Protocol (FTP), configuring, 327-329
- High Availability product, Red Hat, 341
- hot-swappable and redundant components, role of in self-hosting Web sites, 302
- improving response time, 268
- Linux Virtual (LVS)
  - *configure script, 330*
  - *defining virtual services, 319-320*
  - *described, 318-319*
  - *httpdMonitor script, 330*
  - *ipvsadm utility, 325, 327-329, 342*
  - *ldirectord daemon, 329*
  - *load-balancing algorithms, 323-325, 328*
  - *Piranha, 333-338, 341-348, 351, 353*
  - *routing methods, 320-323*
  - *sample network designs, 316-317, 330-331*
  - *Ultramonkey, 332, 334-341*
  - *vs. BigIP, 361*
- mail, configuring fos daemon to implement, 346-347
- modified Domain Name System (DNS), global load balancing, 354-355
- Personal Web (PWS), 19
- production
  - *moving Web site updates to, 233-234*
  - *publishing content, Concurrent Versioning System (CVS), 238-239*
- real server pools
  - *managing, 329, 340-341*
  - *monitoring, 330*
- root, Super Sparrow, 356
- self-hosting Web sites, 48-50
- shared, Web sites hosted through Internet Service Providers (ISPs), 47
- shared virtual, colocation providers, 308-309
- Web
  - *configuring, 327-329*
  - *e-commerce systems, 180*
  - *staging, 233-234*
  - *Unix, 20*
- Web sites
  - *analyzing server logs, 217-227*
  - *monitoring, 205, 207-216*
  - *performance, 204-205*

service level agreement load balancing, 251-252
services
- fees, colocation providers, 308, 310
- focusing on, e-commerce sites, 178
- hosting
  - *maintaining Web sites through, 46-48*
  - *maintaining your own servers, 48-50*
- monitoring on Linux networks, 389-390
- packet filtering, ipchains utility, 390-400
- selecting, 349
- site monitor, 216
- tracking on Linux networks, 384-389
- transferring from primary to secondary systems during failovers, 337-338
- virtual
  - *adding, 351*
  - *defining, Linux Virtual Server (LVS), 319-320, 327-329*

sessions, maintaining shopping carts across, 166-167
setting passwords, Piranha, 348

SGI, 15
shared servers, Web sites hosted through Internet Service Providers (ISPs), 47
shared virtual hosts, colocation providers, 309
shared virtual servers, colocation providers, 308-309
shells, Bourne Again, 406
shopping carts, 165-167, 170, 172-173
Siege, 216
simulating Web traffic, 215
single points of failure, horizontal vs. vertical scability, 252
site log analysis reports, excluding Internet Protocol (IP) addresses, 215
site monitor services, 216
sites
- Cathedral and the Bazaar, The essay, 31
- GNU Manifesto, The, 32
- accessing Piranha Web-based interface, 348
- Angel, 214
- Apache, 132, 268
- Apache Jmeter, 291
- Apache Web server, 39
- Apache Web Server information, 374
- ApacheToday, 39
- ARSC, 136
- ARSC Really Simple Chat, 112
- ArsDigita, 236
- beta testing, 265
- Big Brother (BB) plug-ins, 210
- Blaze Board, 67
- BSD License, 33
- building
  - *in-house development vs. outsourcing, 50-53*
  - *maintaining, 46-50*
  - *reasons for, 44-46*
- building C-Kermit package, 411
- Cable News Network (CNN), 58
- Caldera Systems, 371, 378
- camserv Webcam application, 304
- Canadian Broadcasting Corporation (CBC), 305
- CERT, 206
- Cheapbytes, 378
- Cisco, 364
- Clatter, 112
- Cnnfn.com, 189
- Colocation Directory, 310
- Colosource, 313
- Colosource Colocation Facilities map, 311
- community
  - *calendars, 105-106, 109-110*
  - *characteristics of, 104-105*
  - *chat systems, 107-108, 111-113*
  - *mailing lists and bulletin boards, 108-109*
  - *notice boards, 106-107, 110-111*
- content and media
  - *characteristics of, 58-59*
  - *document management systems, 59-61, 63-64*
  - *search capabilities, 62-63, 68-69*
  - *user feedback, 61-62, 65-67*
- CP Commerce, 183
- CPAN, 169, 224
- CyberWeavers, 110
- deadcat.net, 210
- Debian Project, 371
- Deja.com, 59
- Del Valle Junior High School Parent/Teacher/Student Organization (PTSO)
  - *challenges in making site successful, 158-160*
  - *features of, 117, 119-122, 124-129, 131-139, 141-145, 147, 149-153, 155-157*
  - *site charter and design, 116-117*
- Document Manager, 64, 74
- e-commerce
  - *characteristics of, 162-163*
  - *credit card processing, 167-168*
  - *focusing on products and services, 178*
  - *hosting, 196*
  - *online catalogs, 164-165*
  - *receiving customer feedback, 168*
  - *shopping carts, 165-167*
  - *tools for creating, 168-173*
  - *traffic reports, 178*
  - *treating as additional retail space, 179*
- F5 Networks, 360
- Freshmeat, 168, 179, 236, 372
- fsck issue-tracking kit, 229
- GNU, 30
- GNU General Public License (GPL), 32
- GNU Lesser General Public License (LGPL), 33
- GNU project, 17
- Google, 221
- ht://Dig, 68
- HydraWEB Mercury, 366
- Ibiblio Linux system status archive, 209
- Interchange, 173
- Internet Seer, 215
- ISP-Planet, 313
- Iwon.com, 189
- Kernel.org, 370
- libsupersparrow support library, 356
- linking to Document Manager, 75
- Linux, 268
- Linux as development platform for, 18
- Linux custom kernel configuration, compilation, and installation, 318
- Linux Documentation Project, 370
- Linux Today, 61, 373
- Linux Virtual Server (LVS) project goals, 318

Linux Weekly News, 373
Linuxcare, 371
Linuxmall, 378
linuxperf.org, 268
LogCheck, where and why to apply, 208
MailMan, 66
maintaining, 202-203
analyzing server logs, 217-227
business requirements, performance, 203, 205
issue-tracking software, 227-231
live hacking, 234-235
managing content, 231-242
monitoring servers, 205, 207-216
personnel costs, 247
Majordomo, 66, 96
Microsoft, 24
Mini-Vend, 172
MiniSearch, 69
mirror, 353
mnoGoSearch, 68
mnuGoSearch, 99
MON, 214
moreover.com, 206
My Classifieds, 111
MySQL, 39, 134
MySQL information, 374-375
NetSaint, 214
NetSaint plug-ins, 213
Netzbrett, 67, 95
New York Times, 58
news and information, 372-373
NewsForge, 373
Open CMS, 235
open source e-commerce applications, 179
open source software, 371-372
OpenCola, 307
openssl package, 216
Perl, 135, 181
Perl information, 373-374
Perl Template Toolkit, 224
Phorum, 67, 156
PHP, 133
PHP Builder, 374
PHP information, 374
PHPBuilder, 40
phpMyAdmin, 134
phpMyBoard, 111
phpMyChat, 113
Popular Power, 307
PostgreSQL information, 374-375
preventing stagnation in, 159
Purdue University COAST Security Archive, 207
RATEaSERVER.com, 313
ratings of colocation providers, 313
Red Hat, 27, 378
Red Hat Linux, 371
Resonate, 365
RPM, 412
search services, 68
security tools, Linux systems, 400
self-hosting vs. colocation, 300-309
Slashdot, 61, 232, 372
Snort, 207
Software RAID HOWTO, 279
Solaris Systems Administration Guide, 209
SoundForge.net, 372
Source RPMs (SPRMs), 412
SourceForge, 40
sudo package, 407
sudo utility, 389
Super Sparrow project, 353
SuSE, 378
swatch utility, 389
Symphero, 169
Sysmon, 214
System Activity Reporting (SAR) download, 208-209
System Imager, 259
Talk the Web, 67
Tallyman, 172
Telecommuter's Journal, The
challenges for making site successful, 100-101
features of, 73-76, 78-79, 81-91, 93-95, 97-100
site charter and design, 72-73
TripWire, 207, 390
TurboLinux, 365
Typo3, 235
Ultramonkey project, 332
unruly visitors, 160
VAnessa, 356
Web Hosting Directories, 313
WebCalendar, 110
whatuseek.com, 68
Wiarton Willie, 204
xmysqladmin, 134
ZDNet, 61
Zend optimizing engine, 374
Zend Technology, 40
Zeus Technology, 365
Slackware, 17
Slashdot, 39-40, 61, 232, 372
SlashDotted, 215
SLS Linux distribution, 16
Snort, 207
Softlanding systems, 16
software
building from source code, 403-408, 410-413
calendars, 109-110
chat, 111-113
content management, Web sites, 235-242
issue-tracking, Web sites, 227-231
licensing costs
Linux, 24-25
Windows, 24
load balancers, 364-365
mailing list, notice boards and, 108-109
managing documents, 63-64
managing searches, 68-69
managing user feedback, 65-67
monitoring, self-hosting Web sites, 303
notice boards, 110-111
open source (OSS), 179
advantages and disadvantages of, 33-38
Apache Web server, 38-39
consultants' experience with, 52
MySQL, 39-40

PHP server-side scripting module, 40
support for, 38, 40-42
vs. proprietary software, 30, 32-33
Web resources, 371-372
peer to peer (P2P) computing, 307
piracy of, 30
proprietary vs. open source software, 30, 32-33
reliability of, 245, 295-297
benchmarks, 292-293
determining reliability of, 290-291
factors affecting, 293, 295
stress testing, 291-292
remote-sensing, 304-305
replacement costs, 247
security monitoring, 206-209
server monitoring, 209-214
stress testing Web servers, 216
synchronizing hot-swap systems, 257-258
system imaging, synchronizing hot-swap systems, 259-260
test, creating, 265
tracking site statistics, 221-227
software dependencies
resolving when building applications, 404
supporting, 406
Solaris, 20-21
Solaris Systems Administration Guide, 209
SoundForge.net, 372, 402
source code
building applications from, 403-408, 410-413
Linux operating system, 16
Source RPMs (SPRMs), building applications from, 412-413
source-code revision-control systems, 63
SourceForge, 40
NetSaint plug-ins, 213
WebCalendar, 110
space limitations, Web sites hosted through Internet Service Providers (ISPs), 47
Specials tool, Symphero, 171
SpecWeb, 265, 268
speed
accessing disks, improving, 266-267
memory, improving, 267-268
servers, improving response time, 268
swap partitions, improving, 267-268
Web servers, 204-205
Web sites, business requirements, 203, 205
SPRMs (Source RPMs), building applications from, 412-413
SQL, Web resources, 374-375
SQL commands, chat user creation, 136-137
SQL commands, creating calendars, 154-155
SQL commands, creating forum users, 157
SQL commands, creating notice boards, 148-149
SSL (Secure Sockets Layer), 196
SSLeay/OpenSSL, 180
staging Web servers, 233-234
stagnation, preventing in Web sites, 159
Stallman, Richard, 32
StarOffice, compatibility with Concurrent Versioning System (CVS), 63
state, maintaining for transactions, e-commerce sites, 163
static content, content and media sites, 58
static pages, community sites, 104-105
statistics, Web servers, 208-209
status, pulse daemon, 349
storage
backup, servers, 274
content
databases, 58
flat files, 58
Storage Area Network (SAN), 274
stress testing, 215-216, 291-292
sudo command, 407-408, 410-411
sudo utility, 389
Super Sparrow
described, 353
global load balancing, 353-354, 356
route servers, 356
router query tools, 356-357
support libraries, 356
support
customers, Web sites, 228
FreeBSD vs. Linux, 23
Linux operating system, 18
open source software (OSS), 38, 40-42
software dependencies, 406
Transmission Control Protocol/Internet Protocol (TCP/IP), Windows and Linux, 19
support libraries, Super Sparrow, 356
support personnel, costs for, 26
support platforms, *Telecommuter's Journal, The* Web site, 74
support tools, Del Valle Junior High School Parent/Teacher/Student Organization (PTSO), 131-139, 141-145, 147, 149-153, 155-157
SuSE, 17, 378
swap partitions, improving performance, 267-268
Swarmcast, 307
swatch utility, 389

switches
Keyboard/Mouse/Video (KVM), 283
load-balancing, 366
requirements for, 280-281
role of in self-hosting Web sites, 301
Symphero, 168-172, 179
synchronization, hot-swap systems, 256, 258, 260
Sysmon, 214
System Activity Reporting (SAR), 208-209
system administrators, costs for, 26
System Imager, 259
system imaging software, synchronizing hot-swap systems, 259-260
system logs, security of, 207
systems, upgrading for self-hosting Web sites, 303

T

-t option, 327-328
tables, 328-329
tabs, Piranha Web-based interface, 349, 351
Talk the Web site, 67
Tallyman, 172
TAMU Linux distribution, 16
Tarantella, 306
target audiences, Web server reports, 218
TCP. *See* Transmission Control Protocol, 319
TCP/IP. *See* Transmission Control Protocol/Internet Protocol, 19
TCX DataKonsult AB, 39
technical support
Linux operating system, 18
open source software (OSS), 38, 40-42
Telecommuter's Journal, The
challenges for making site successful, 100-101
features of, 73-76, 78-79, 81-91, 93-95, 97-100
site charter and design, 72-73
templates, *Telecommuter's Journal, The* Web site, 87-91, 93-94
terminal emulators, C-Kermit package, 411-412
test software, 265
testing
beta, Web sites, 265
databases, 292
stress, 215-216, 291-292
Web applications, 228
Web site updates, staging servers, 233-234
Texas A&M University, 16
time, improving response time for servers, 268
title frame source
Del Valle Junior High School Parent/Teacher/Student Organization (PTSO) Web site, 119-120
Telecommuter's Journal, The Web site, 78
Tomcat, 310
tools
chkconfig, 386-389
CP Reporting, 183
creating e-commerce sites, 168-173
heartbeat, 332, 334-338
Internet Service Provider (ISP) support, limitations of, 47
ipchains, packet filtering, 390-400
ipvsadm, 325, 327-329, 342
make, 410
mon, 330
nanny, 341, 347
population, e-commerce site databases, 164-165
router query, Super Sparrow, 356-357
schema management, e-commerce sites, 164
security, Linux systems, 400
send_arp, 347-348
Specials, Symphero, 171
sudo, 389
support, Del Valle Junior High School Parent/Teacher/Student Organization (PTSO), 131-139, 141-145, 147, 149-153, 155-157
swatch, 389
Tripwire, 390
Torvalds, Linus, 15, 31
Tracking document revisions, 60-61
tracking inventories, e-commerce sites, 165
traffic, simulating on Internet, 215
traffic reports, e-commerce sites, 178
training for Linux, costs for, 26-27
transactions, maintaining state of for e-commerce sites, 163
transferring services from primary to secondary systems during failovers, 337-338
translation, network address (NAT), 316, 320-321, 361
Transmeta, MON, 214
Transmission Control Protocol (TCP), 319
Transmission Control Protocol/Internet Protocol (TCP/IP), 19
Travis, Jon, 304
Tridgell, Andrew, 37
TripWire utility, 207, 390
troubleshooting bugs, open source software, 35
True-64, 21
trust in source code builders, 404
tuning performance, 266-268
tunneling Linux Virtual Server (LVS), 322-323
TurboLinux, Cluster Server, 365

turning on backup servers, 351
Tweedie, Stephen, 209
Typo3, 235

U

UDMSearch, 68
UDP. *See* User Datagram Protocol, 319
UL (Underwriters Laboratories), 286-287
Ultramonkey
- described, 332
- heartbeat utility, 332, 334-338
- ldirectord daemon, 339-341

Underwriters Laboratories (UL), 286-287
Uniform Resource Locators (URLs), 221, 355-356
Uninterruptible Power Supply (UPS), 273, 282-283, 302
Universal Serial Bus (USB), as hot-swappable component, 279
Unix operating system
- rdist, 257-258
- rsync, 257-258
- swap space, 268
- System Activity Reporting (SAR), 208-209
- vs. Linux, 14, 20-21

Unixware, 21
updating
- content and media sites, 58-59
- Web sites, managing, 232-234

upgrades, Linux vs. Windows, 25
upgrading systems, self-hosting Web sites, 303
UPS (Uninterruptible Power Supply), 273, 282-283, 302
uptime
- disclosure by colocation providers, 311
- Web sites, 203-204

URL (Uniform Resource Locators), 221, 355-356
USB (Universal Serial Bus), as hot-swappable component, 279
Usenet, 62, 375
User Datagram Protocol (UDP), 319
user feedback, content and media sites, 61-62, 65-67
user-driven content, community sites, 105
users, attracting to *Telecommuter's Journal, The* Web site, 101
utilities
- chkconfig, 386-389
- CP Reporting, 183
- creating e-commerce sites, 168-173
- heartbeat, 332, 334-338
- Internet Service Provider (ISP) support, limitations of, 47
- ipchains, packet filtering, 390-400
- ipvsadm, 325, 327-329, 342
- make, 410
- mon, 330
- nanny, 341, 347
- population, e-commerce site databases, 164-165
- router query, Super Sparrow, 356-357
- schema management, e-commerce sites, 164
- security, Linux systems, 400
- send_arp, 347-348
- Specials, Symphero, 171
- sudo, 389
- support, Del Valle Junior High School Parent/Teacher/Student Organization (PTSO), 131-139, 141-145, 147, 149-153, 155-157
- swatch, 389
- Tripwire, 390

UUNet, 214

V

VA Linux, 51, 353, 356
value-added resellers (VARs), 52
VAnessa support libraries, 356
variables
- checkinterval, 340
- checktimeout, 340
- configuration, Phorums, 157

VARs (value-added resellers), 52
vendor partnerships, colocation providers, 310
vendors
- hardware, choosing, 275, 277, 283-286
- software, choosing, 295-297

vertical scalability, 248-249, 252-253
viewing
- shopping carts, 166
- tables maintained by kernels, ipvsadm utility, 328

Vincent, Jesse, 229
VIP. *See* virtual IP address
virtual hosts, colocation providers, 309
virtual IP address (VIP)
- creating, heartbeat utility, 333-338
- direct routing, 321-322
- network address translation (NAT), 321

virtual servers, colocation providers, 308-309
Virtual Servers tab, Piranha Web-based interface, 351
virtual services
- adding, 351
- defining, Linux Virtual Server (LVS), 319-320, 327-329

visitors to Web sites, unruly, 160
visits, Web sites, 220
VLAN, BigIP support of, 361

W

Wardley, Andy, 224
Warren, Trevor, 207-208
Web Hosting Directories, 313
Web pages
contact
Del Valle Junior High School Parent/Teacher/Student Organization (PTSO) Web site, 128-129
Telecommuter's Journal, The Web site, 84-87
dynamic, e-commerce sites, 163
footers, *Telecommuter's Journal, The* Web site, 81-82
newsletter, Del Valle Junior High School Parent/Teacher/Student Organization (PTSO) Web site, 129, 131
refreshing, 167
Web servers
configuring, 327-329
e-commerce systems, 180
Unix, 20
Web sites
Cathedral and the Bazaar, The essay, 31
GNU Manifesto, The, 32
accessing Piranha Web-based interface, 348
Angel, 214
Apache, 132, 268
Apache Jmeter, 291
Apache Web Server information, 34, 374
ApacheToday, 39
ARSC, 136
ARSC Really Simple Chat, 112
ArsDigita, 236
beta testing, 265
Big Brother (BB) plug-ins, 210
Blaze Board, 67
BSD License, 33
building
in-house development vs. outsourcing, 50-53
maintaining, 46-50
reasons for, 44-46
building C-Kermit package, 411
Cable News Network (CNN), 58
Caldera Systems, 371, 378
camserv Webcam application, 304
Canadian Broadcasting Corporation (CBC), 305
CERT, 206
Cheapbytes, 378
Cisco, 364
Clatter, 112
Cnnfn.com, 189
Colocation Directory, 310
Colosource, 313
Colosource Colocation Facilities map, 311
community
calendars, 105-106, 109-110
characteristics of, 104-105
chat systems, 107-108, 111-113
mailing lists and bulletin boards, 108-109
notice boards, 106-107, 110-111
content and media
characteristics of, 58-59
document management systems, 59-61, 63-64
search capabilities, 62-63, 68-69
user feedback, 61-62, 65-67
CP Commerce, 183
CPAN, 169, 224
CyberWeavers, 110
deadcat.net, 210
Debian Project, 371
Deja.com, 59
Del Valle Junior High School Parent/Teacher/Student Organization (PTSO)
challenges in making site successful, 158-160
features of, 117, 119-122, 124-129, 131-139, 141-145, 147, 149-153, 155-157
site charter and design, 116-117
Document Manager, 64, 74
e-commerce
characteristics of, 162-163
credit card processing, 167-168
focusing on products and services, 178
hosting, 196
online catalogs, 164-165
receiving customer feedback, 168
shopping carts, 165-167
tools for creating, 168-173
traffic reports, 178
treating as additional retail space, 179
F5 Networks, 360
Freshmeat, 168, 174, 236, 372, 402
fsck issue-tracking kit, 229
GNU, 30
GNU General Public License (GPL), 32
GNU Lesser General Public License (LGPL), 33
GNU project, 17
Google, 221
ht://Dig, 68
HydraWEB Mercury, 366
Ibiblio Linux system status archive, 209
Interchange, 173
Internet Seer, 215
ISP-Planet, 313
Iwon.com, 189
Kernel.org, 370
libsupersparrow support library, 356

linking to Document Manager, 75
Linux, 268
Linux as development platform for, 18
Linux custom kernel configuration, compilation, and installation, 318
Linux Documentation Project, 370
Linux Today, 61, 373
Linux Virtual Server (LVS) project goals, 318
Linux Weekly News, 373
Linuxcare, 371
Linuxmall, 378
linuxperf.org, 268
LogCheck, where and why to apply, 208
MailMan, 66
maintaining, 202-203
analyzing server logs, 217-227
business requirements, performance, 203, 205
issue-tracking software, 227-231
live hacking, 234-235
managing content, 231-242
monitoring servers, 205, 207-216
personnel costs, 247
Majordomo, 66, 96
Microsoft, 24
Mini-Vend, 172
MiniSearch, 69
mnoGoSearch, 68
mnuGoSearch, 99
MON, 214
moreover.com, 206
My Classifieds, 111
MySQL, 39, 134
MySQL information, 374-375
NetSaint, 214
NetSaint plug-ins, 213
Netzbrett, 67, 95
New York Times, 58
news and information, 372-373
NewsForge, 373
Open CMS, 235
open source e-commerce applications, 179
open source software, 371-372
OpenCola, 307
openssl package, 216
Perl, 135, 181, 373-374
Perl Template Toolkit, 224
Phorum, 67
Phorums, 156
PHP, 133
PHP Builder, 40, 374
PHP information, 374
phpMyAdmin, 134
phpMyBoard, 111
phpMyChat, 113
Popular Power, 307
PostgreSQL information, 374-375
preventing stagnation in, 159
Purdue University COAST Security Archive, 207
RATEaSERVER.com, 313
ratings of colocation providers, 313
Red Hat, 27, 378
Red Hat Linux, 371
Resonate, 365
RPM, 412
RPMfind.net, 403
search services, 68
security tools, Linux systems, 400
self-hosting vs. colocation, 300-309
Slashdot, 61, 232, 372
Snort, 207
Software RAID HOWTO, 279
Solaris Systems Administration Guide, 209
SoundForge.net, 372, 402
Source RPMs (SPRMs), 412
SourceForge, 40
sudo package, 407
sudo utility, 389
Super Sparrow project, 353
SuSE, 378
swatch utility, 389
Symphero, 169
Sysmon, 214
System Activity Reporting (SAR) download, 208-209
System Imager, 259
Talk the Web, 67
Tallyman, 172
Telecommuter's Journal, The
challenges for making site successful, 100-101
features of, 73-76, 78-79, 81-91, 93-95, 97-100
site charter and design, 72-73
TripWire, 207, 390
TurboLinux, 365
Typo3, 235
Ultramonkey project, 332
unruly visitors, 160
VAnessa, 356
Web Hosting Directories, 313
WebCalendar, 110
whatuseek.com, 68
Wiarton Willie, 204
xmysqladmin, 134
ZDNet, 61
Zend optimizing engine, 374
Zend Technology, 40
Zeus Technology, 365
Webalizer, 221-223
WebCalendar, 110, 153, 155-156
weight round-robin load balancing, 250
weighted least-connection load balancing, 251
weighted least-connection scheduling algorithm, 324
weighted round-robin scheduling algorithm, 324
wermit binary, 411
whatuseek.com, 68
Wiarton Willie, 204
Windows operating system
software licensing costs, 24
vs. Linux, 19-20
Windows operating systems
hardware upgrades, 25
wiring closets, role of in self-hosting Web sites, 301
Word, compatibility with Concurrent Versioning System (CVS), 63

World Wide Web
accessing content on, 353-354, 356
building sites
in-house development vs. outsourcing, 50-53
maintaining, 46-50
reasons for, 44-46
simulating traffic on, 215
worm attacks, 206
writing test software, 265

X-Y-Z

Xao, 183, 187-189, 191-192
xmysqladmin, 134

Young, Eric, 180

ZDNet, 61
Zebra daemon, 356
Zend optimizing engine, 374
Zend Technology, 40
Zeus Load Balancer, 365
Zhang, Wensong, 318